RAISING OUR CHILDREN ON BOURBON

A French Quarter Love Affair

BOB CARR

Cover and illustrations by Rolland Golden

Arthur Hardy Enterprises INC

To my wife, Jan, our children: Timothy, Tammy, Tom, Tiffany, and the multitude
of relatives and friends who lived and loved us enough through the years, to make
this episode in our lives come to life in this book. I offer my special thanks to my good
friend, Bob Carrow, for his generous assistance with this work. And to our beloved
chosen city of New Orleans, which enriched our lives beyond measure.

Carr, Robert Jacques (Bob) 1927
Raising Our Children On Bourbon — A French Quarter Love Affair
By Bob Carr

ISBN 978-0-930892-30-2

Printed in China
First Edition 2010

Published by:
Arthur Hardy Enterprises, Inc.
230 Devon Drive
Mandeville, LA 70448
arthurhardypublishing.com

CONTENTS

PROLOGUE

My great-grandparents, Antoinette Henriette La Roche, age 17, and Pierre Robért Aupagnier, 18, had been married at St. Louis Cathedral in Nouvelle Orléans only two years before the daily *Picayune* published in full page headlines:

!THE UNION IS DISSOLVED!

This ordinance, passed unanimously at 1:15 PM, December 20th, 1860, in Charleston, South Carolina, had an everlasting impact on the entire population of the United States of America. War was declared between the United States and the newly formed Confederate States of America, of which Louisiana and consequently New Orleans, soon became a part.

Faced with destruction and annihilation from the guns of Admiral Farragut's fleet on the Mississippi River, the City of New Orleans and its citizens chose to capitulate.

Before the surrender took place, many of the city's young men stole away in the dark of night to join the Louisiana militia as volunteers to serve in the Confederate Army. Pierre was determined to fight for his belle Nouvelle Orléans and the Southern way of life. Before departing, he embraced a tradition of the times by moving his cherished Antoinette into his parents home on Esplanade Avenue, adjacent to the Vieux Carré. Pierre was away from his beloved wife and family for nearly four years. Returning home from battle, weary and despondent, he found the joyous and confident city he remembered now melancholy, debt-ridden and heavily occupied by Federal troops.

Antoinette's father had been lost at sea while returning to France in search of money to help the Confederate cause. Her mother, always frail, had succumbed to tuberculosis; Antoinette's only sibling, Rochelle, lived with her husband, Jacques, and his family upriver in the country near St. Francisville.

Pierre's family had been severely disrupted during those frightful years of war and occupation. His two older brothers were still missing in action in the Carolinas and his oldest sister died during child birth. His fifteen year old sister, Felicia, shared the home on Esplanade with Antoinette and Pierre's parents.

Union commander Major-General Butler's rule over New Orleans had been harsh. Although not struck by artillery, the city had been ravaged and disheartened by four years of Yankee occupation. Bivouac tents still populated the garden pathway along the esplanade in front of the family home. The gaiety of the Créoles, loved by Pierre and Antoinette before the war, seemed to be lost forever. Even the lush green of the banana and camphor trees, as well as the honeysuckle vines, appeared pale; and there was the matter of money.

Pierre's father, a mainstay of the Roman Catholic Church, had loaned the parish a considerable amount of cash to see it through the years of hostility and blockade. With the Southern economy in shambles, the church was now in no position to repay the debt. The family was nearly destitute. Monsieur Apagnier could scarcely eke out a living as a cotton factor in association with Antoinette's brother-in-law, Jacques, in St. Francisville. Post war times in Louisiana were hellacious.

In the environment of these times, Pierre and Antoinette chose to lessen the burden on their families by migrating north to settle on free land offered near Grand Rapids, Michigan. The journey was long; fear and trepidation beset them. But it came to pass that they prospered greatly in their new life and multiplied. So, both reality and lore have been handed down as family history. One fact is certain, my great-grandmother, Antoinette Aupagnier, never let her children, grandchildren and beyond, forget their Nouvelle Orléans Créole lineage!

— Bob Carr

Pierre Robért Aupengier   Antoinette Henriette LaRoche

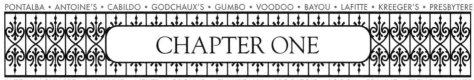

CHAPTER ONE

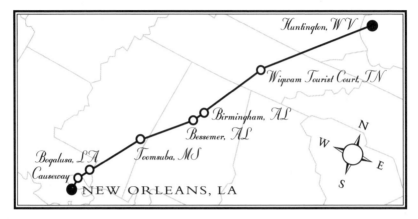

"Le Vieux Carré du Nouvelle Orléans, here we come!"

One hundred years after my great-grandparents had moved north, I found myself moving south, driving my wife, Jan, and two children toward a new life. Would we prosper and multiply? That was our dream. Whatever happened, our lives were about to change drastically.

Checking the map together, Jan and I decided to leave the main highway and enter New Orleans via the 24-mile-long Lake Pontchartrain Causeway, the longest bridge of its kind in the world. I wanted to show it to the children. We had heard it had been built because some Louisiana politicians wanted to have a short cut from New Orleans to their property on the north shore of the lake. It must have been a nice contract for someone's prestressed-concrete cement business, since the bridge crosses the lake at the widest point.

It was well into the afternoon as we left the Magnolia State of Mississippi and crossed over the Pearl River into our new homeland, Louisiana. A road marker indicated "Bogalusa 5 miles," "Pontchartrain Causeway 26 miles."

"Hey, kids, we're here!" I cheered, jarring their back seat slumber as I pumped the breaks of our 1959 Ford Fairlane station wagon.

"You mean this is Noo Orleens?" four-and-a-half-year-old Timmy asked. His tone denoted he was less than enthusiastic about the wilderness terrain along the meandering two-lane highway.

Tammy, who would soon make her third birthday, lifted her weary head just high enough to see over the windowsill of the car door. After glancing around she remarked, "*Yuk.*" Sliding back down into her pillow, she resumed sucking her left thumb. The rest of her hand was covered as usual by her "banket," a tattered piece of quilt, which through constant dragging had taken on the appearance of a dirty gunnysack. This sacred scrap of blanket was her tangible tie with constancy—though it always looked like "*yuk*" to me.

"Daddy, you really mean this is Noo Orleens?" Timmy questioned again.

"No, this isn't Noo Orleens. This is Loozeeana, the state. New Orleans is the city. Can you both say Loozeeana?"

"I don't know. Is that the same as Louisiana?"

"Yep, 'cept down here they say Loozeeana."

"I guess I can say that."

"Okay, say it."

"Loo-zana...I mean Loozee-ana."

"By Jove, you've got it!"

Peering into the backseat, Jan asked Tammy, "Can you say it?"

She shook her head to indicate a negative response but Jan encouraged her to try.

Timmy instructed, "Take your thumb out of your mouth to say a big word like that."

"If I'm gonna thay it, I want daddy to watch, too," she mumbled through her blanket.

Trying to keep my eyes on the narrow, ill-marked road, I agreed.

Jan, Timmy and I all focused on Tammy; her big brown eyes flashed as she pulled the shriveled thumb from her mouth and the blanket away from her face.

She blurted out "Loo-zee-ana" so perfectly that Jan complimented her—and the thumb descended immediately back into her mouth.

Timmy bragged, "I can say Noo Orleens, Loozeeana, too."

"Well, Timmy, that's good, though not perfect. Up north we say Noo Orleens, but in Noo Orleens they say, New Awlins."

"That's dumb, why don't they say it the way everybody else does?"

"I don't know, I guess everybody else is wrong."

"New Awlins, New Awlins, New Awlins, Loozeeana, New Awlins, Loozeeana, New Aw..."

"That's enough for now, Timmy," Jan instructed. "You don't want to make daddy nervous while he's driving, honey."

We continued on our way.

Suddenly, Tammy blurted out, "What *that!*"

"What's what?" Jan and I asked simultaneously.

"That thtink!" Tammy exclaimed, covering her nose with her dingy blanket.

"It wasn't *me!*" Timmy was quick to reply.

Jan sighed. "I hope it's not the car."

"I hope it's not Noo Awlins!" Timmy gasped.

Releasing her wizened thumb momentarily from her mouth, Tammy muttered, "That weely thtinks!"

"It smells like a factory to me," I told them.

A large sign loomed at the curve of the road announcing, "Crown Zellerback Paper Company Welcomes You To Bogalusa."

"I was right, it is a factory, a paper mill."

"Well, thank the Lord it wasn't our station wagon," Jan murmured in relief.

Crossing the Bogalusa Creek Bridge, we were plunged immediately into the flurry of Bogalusa main street traffic. A small sign indicated the Causeway 21-miles ahead. The commotion along the late-Victorian façaded thoroughfare seemed unusual for early evening.

"Look children, I think it's a parade," Jan exclaimed, pointing toward the left lane, where two motorcycle policemen approached, their red lights flashing.

As we proceeded along the right lane of traffic, people began pouring out of stores to line the street, as if waiting for a funeral cortege of one of the town's esteemed elders. Tammy lifted her head once again just high enough to peer over the window ledge. Timmy cranked down his window. The complete lack of any sound save for the roar of the motorcycle engines was eerie.

Jan commented, "If this is a parade, it's strangely quiet!"

"I don't hear any bands," remarked Timmy, who had been raised on the statewide band festival held yearly in Huntington, West Virginia. "It looks like mostly black people on this side of the street and all the white people are over there!"

The traffic in our lane had slowed to a crawl.

"Still think it's a funeral."

I was interrupted by Jan, "Look, look at that—in the convertible!"

"What's that anyway?" Timmy asked. "It looks like a ghostie to me!"

"Timmy, put up the window! I don't want any ghosth in here," Tammy exclaimed. "I'm thcared!"

"That's not a ghost, Tammy, it's just a man in a costume," I began to explain. "I think they call him a wizard. In fact, I think they call him a Grand Wizard, though I don't know for sure."

"I don't care, I'm thcared! He looks like a ghosth to me. Put up your window, right now!"

"Oh, Tammy, it's just a wizard like the *Wizard of Oz*," consoled Timmy.

"It dun't look like the *Wizard of Oz* to me. It thtill looks like a white ghosth with big black eyes and a pointed head!"

I rolled down my window as the convertible carrying the Wizard approached. It passed slowly, within a couple of yards, followed by a deafeningly silent parade of white robed marchers with conspicuously pointed hoods. The flutter of fabric in the winter breeze, together with the shuffle of shoe leather against the asphalt street, created the only sound. The sound and silence seemed solemnly sinister.

With the automobile traffic completely halted, the four of us were transfixed. The only movement came from our suspicious eyes flashing back and forth, like blinking lights on a cheap electric sign, as we scanned the rows of passing ghosties, one after the other. Suddenly, the parade was over. No fanfare, no applause, no shouting; just more quiet as people began to return obediently to the shops or go about their business.

"My God, Jan, that was the Ku Klux Klan!"

"I can't believe it!"

"What's the Klux Klan, daddy?"

"They're ghosth, Timmy!" Tammy insisted.

"No, children, they're just men dressed up to look like ghosties 'cause they like to scare people."

"It's not even Halloween!" Timmy pointed out.

"I know, but..."

My further explanation was interrupted by a shout from someone in the pickup truck behind us, ominously revving its engine.

"Hope you damn Yankees lahked owah parade!"

"How do they know we're Yankees?" Jan whispered, in a nervous tone.

"I don't know—must be our license plate."

Civil War sentiment runs deep in some parts of the country. We were learning our first lesson about being transplanted Yankees. Although most of "West-by-God-Virginia" is well below the Mason-Dixon Line, West Virginians were still considered by many to be "despicable breakaway Southerners."

The driver of the pickup tapped his rickety bumper against our back bumper with just enough force to further frighten us all. Then he backed up and sped around us, peeling rubber and laughing raucously. His final sound was a terrifying primal howl, like a Rebel yell in an MGM movie. I drove earnestly and cautiously through the rest of the town without speaking a word. Bogalusa seemed like a frightening illusion, the name becoming a synonym for boogieman in the children's vocabulary. My great-grandparents' trek north in the late 1860s must have been very difficult; I was beginning to question the wisdom of moving my family south.

Once out of town, we looked for road signs directing us to the Lake Pontchartrain Causeway. The parade experience had made us so anxious we rolled up the windows. I concentrated on driving, Jan studied the map, Timmy kept his eyes peeled for road signs and Tammy eased her withered thumb back into her mouth, settling once again into her pillow. We were back in the countryside on Louisiana State Highway 24, heading toward the town of Covington. *A million miles away from Covington, Kentucky,* I thought.

All of a sudden Tammy exclaimed, "Yuk, what's *that* thtink, another paper factory?"

Timmy giggled, "This time it was *me!* That parade almost scared my insides out!"

"Yuk," Tammy grumbled, as she cranked the window down a sliver.

We all began to laugh.

I accelerated to 65 miles per hour, feeling that the quicker I put space between us and that parade, the more comfortable we would all feel. A 45 miles per hour road sign appeared on the horizon. I immediately slowed to the speed limit.

"Something wrong, honey?"

"No, I just slowed to the speed limit. We certainly don't want to get taken back to Bogalusa by a cop!"

"Look, that sign says St. Tammany Parish."

"What does that mean, mommy?" Timmy asked. "Does that mean Tammy is named after a saint?"

"Well, not exactly—you see, this is Tammany, not Tammy. Tammany wasn't a saint, an Indian Chief, I think."

"What's a parish?" Timmy persisted.

"A parish is the same as a county. In Ohio and West Virginia, we had counties. We lived in the city of Huntington, in Cabel County."

Timmy jumped in. "In the state of West Virginia, in the country of America. I mean the United States of America, in the North...sa...sa...severe of the world."

"That's Northern Hemisphere, not severe," I corrected. "Now, why don't you sit back and rest until we get to the Causeway bridge?"

Timmy almost never slept in the automobile. Rather, he would stand behind the front seat with one foot on either side of the drive shaft hump, his arms folded on the back of the seat, and speak loudly into our ears, a habit that was most annoying on a long trip.

"Look! There's a Gulf station sign," Jan pointed out. "It might be a good idea to fill up one last time before we get into the city."

"Good idea, honey."

The rural filling station appeared at a crossroad. I swung off the highway and pulled up to the gas pumps. We all stayed in the car while the dumpy, grease-covered, redneck proprietor filled our tank and ordered a scrawny old man to clean the windshield.

"Yasir, yasir, ah *be* doin' it!"

With little commotion, and great relief, we were on our way.

How had this life-changing journey begun? I thought back to that evening several months ago as I drove the bleak 30 miles home to Huntington from the job I hated at the glass company. My mind was filled with a million thoughts, yet nothing remained focused for more than a few moments: *Castro's recent takeover in Cuba being reported on the car radio, the hail clattering on my windshield, the dinner Jan was preparing.* I was surprised to suddenly find myself in our driveway, the engine turned off, trying to collect my thoughts. *How could I break the news to Jan?* I slammed the door a little harder than intended but did no discernible damage. *Good thing Jan talked me into buying the station wagon instead of the convertible I fancied.* I walked over and kicked a tire: *You babies are gonna have to carry me and my family nearly 1500 miles. Hope you're up to it.* Dinah Shore, one of our TV favorites, had been throwing kisses for Chevrolet for months; however, in real life, the Ford salesman gave us a really good deal on buying the 1959 model just before the 60s came out.

Darkness was overtaking twilight. Jan turned on the light above the sink. My breathing accelerated at the sight of her through the fogged window; I enjoyed watching Jan stir about in the cozy kitchen. It filled me with memories of the things we had been through since our elopement to South Carolina during college, eight years before. Jan was the sweetest, most honest and loving woman who had ever come into my life. Once again, I was about to ask her to set out on yet another uncharted adventure.

Jan was always kinder to people than they were in return, kinder than she should be, I often reprimanded. There was one thing sure: she loved me. In the words of Edgar Allan Poe, "This maiden, she lived with no other thought, than to love and be loved by me." She loved me more than I deserved, gave me more than I could give back, trusted and relied on me with an innocence that was sometimes burdensome. I repeatedly agonized: *I wouldn't be able to live up to her expectations.*

The recessed light above the kitchen sink shone down on her luminous red hair, which she wore swept-up into a bun, the way I liked it. Her radiant milk-white skin, her rosy cheeks and red lips, shimmered through the misty windowpane over the kitchen sink as she moved about. No wonder this Irish-American beauty, this Janet Lee Fitzsimmons, had been chosen as "Dream Girl" of my fraternity at Carnegie

Tech. I stood for a moment more, then walked through the kitchen door.

"Oh, darling, you're home, good! You're five minutes late. I was worried. Dinner'll be ready about 6:15 as usual. I had to haul the kids around after my bridge game, so I'm running five minutes late, too. By the way, maybe you should mow one more time before snow starts. This warm fall has kept everything growing. I noticed Jack and Julie's and the Cosgrove's lawns look so neat."

Jan hardly looked up from the kitchen sink as I gave her the usual evening peck on the cheek. I went into the powder room, leaving the door ajar so I could hear.

She continued to babble. "Norma picked us up for the bridge game in her new four-holer Roadmaster. Is that a Buick? A really nice car. All these new 1960 names for cars are driving me crazy. Whatever happened to just plain Fords, Oldsmobiles, Cadillacs, and Plymouths? By the way, I think mine needs something. It sputters and coughs—kinda embarrassed me on Main Street."

"*The damn carburetor,*" I mumbled to myself.

"What are you doing?" she said, sticking her head around the door. "*Oh!* Guess I'd better close this door; Julie may pop in. She's getting Jack one of those new power lawn mowers for Christmas, hopes it'll take the strain off his heart. Did you notice the Johnsons across the street are having their house painted again? Just a touch-up I guess; it's so late in the year. I wish old Mr. Remsky would paint *this* place. It sure could use it. Are you okay in there? You seem awfully quiet. When you go outside check on Tammy. She's in the playpen on the side porch, make sure the light's on. She wanted to wear her new snowsuit so she's plenty warm. The Cosgrove's hired-girl has been keeping an eye on her. Wouldn't it be nice if we could afford a girl? Bob, if you're out of the john, will you please get that phone? I think it's Alice saying she's sending Timmy across the street. The street's getting so busy since it's been extended to that awful new subdivision, I don't think a four-year-old should cross alone. Was that Alice about Timmy on the phone?"

"Yes, I'm going out to meet him now. I'll be back in a couple of minutes. Then I want a moment of your time please. *Please!* I have something really important to tell you."

"Humm...thought there was something. You're so quiet."

I stepped out onto the front porch to see if Alice had started Tim across. I glanced up and down the street, subconsciously casing our upper-middle-class neighborhood. *We're really in it,* I thought, *at least we've got all the symptoms. We're caught in the one-ups-man-ship contest.*

"Here he comes, Bob," Alice hollered from her curb.

"Thanks a lot, Alice. I know he had a wonderful time."

Timmy scampered across the street. "Daddy, guess what they're gonna build? A swimming pool at their house!"

"Oh, really?"

"Yep, and they said me and Tammy can swim it in anytime we want, even if she's only three!"

"Boy, that sounds really great! Tim, please go around to check on your sister in the playpen. I want to go in and talk to mommy for a few minutes."

"OK, oh boy, oh boy, I don't have to go in the house yet! Dum dee, dum dee dum,"

Tim hummed, trotting merrily around the side of the house.

I walked into the room. Jan rambled on, "The Hubbards asked us to the buffet at the Guyan Country Club. Do you think *we'll* ever be able to afford the Country Club?"

"Probably not."

"Oh, oh well. Should I get a new dress for the buffet?"

"Better not."

"Then what'll I wear? That Anne Fogerty thing?"

"Good, the cleavage one."

"Oh."

"Jan, today I decided *absolutely* to quit my job."

"Oh? *Oh!*"

"You're surprised?"

"A little. I thought you were going to tell me you had *already* quit. You were so quiet."

"You're not undone?"

"Undone? I'm delighted and so relieved. I thought you'd never do it."

"God, I know. Making the decision is worse than doing it!"

Jan reached over and put her hand behind my head. With her other hand she shook a finger at me, "I told you so. I told you you'd never be happy if you got out of television. Oh! Lordy, when are you going to tell Mr. Blenko?"

William Blenko, Sr., the founder and owner of the world-renowned Blenko Glass Company, located in Milton, West Virginia, had elevated me to manager of the Stained Glass Division.

"That's the problem. I'm not sure. I don't think I'd better tell Mr. B. before I get my Christmas bonus. Needless to say we'll need that money to cover our travel and moving expenses. Taking that radio job in New Orleans is going to mean less money for a while." I paused, considering. "Remember, they want us both, so we'll have two salaries. Even so, we'll probably have to live in a small apartment, no built-in-kitchen, no closet space, no wall-to-wall."

"No lawn to mow," Jan chided.

"We may even have to sell one of the cars."

"Goody, let's sell mine! It's always in the repair shop anyway. Besides, I haven't been on a city bus for years and I understand they still have streetcars, way down yonder!"

"Are you taking me seriously?"

"Yes, but I refuse to be forlorn. I'm really delighted. We have so much more to gain than to lose. Since we left TV we've felt squelched. You've been unhappy with your job, and I've been unhappy for you. I've gotten wrapped up in clubs, bridge and keeping up with 'The Joneses.' You know that's not me. The Junior League is even breathing down my neck. And as for you, I think you're just plain psychologically pooped out. Why else are you tired all the time. You never were when we used to dash madly around the WSAZ-TV studio. I haven't seen you really sparkle since you did your last commercial."

"What about our friends like Lindsay and...?"

"Lord knows, Bob, we can always write to them from 'The Land of Cotton,' tellin' them all how fabulous everything is. Frankly, if we stay in this neighborhood much longer, something's got to give, the date book or the bank book!"

"What do you mean?"

"Bob, you may be earning more now but we're enjoying it less. So, we get the ranchyest wagon, the pineyest den, and the fertilizeyest lawn. Are these the things we really want?"

"Good Lord, I don't know whether to answer or to weep."

"Ah ha, because you know the answer! You worked for the last two years for things you didn't really want! Right?"

"Well, lady, *you* win the box of Snickers."

"And to continue, Mr. Anthony, he did it all for little me!"

I pretended to wipe tears from my eyes. "Yes, Sir, I did it all for her and the children and did they appreciate it? No, Mr. Anthony, they did not."

"Print that! Real tragic quality!" laughed Jan. "Don't call us, we'll call you."

"Hey, lady, I can also do magic, tap dance, tumble, sing folk, play my zither..."

"Ah ha, Sir Robert, you're beginning to sparkle! Let's hear you say W-W-W-W. Your elocution teacher told you you'll *never* be a radio announcer unless you can say W!"

I reared up in dread. "Suppose the station in New Orleans doesn't like our work?"

"Then we'll find something else. Don't worry, combined we're the greatest magicians, tap-dancers, announcers, tumblers, zither-ers, and folk-ers in the world!"

"Jan, remember. It's *only* radio."

"OK, Mister Gloomy, can TV be far behind when you're so cute? And wait 'till they get a glimpse of me!"

"I think women must have more stable psyches than men."

"Why?"

"Since we left TV two years ago, you've become an adjusted hausfrau, while I've become a stupefied, commuting zombie. I think it's really dangerous to commute by car if you're unhappy. You just make your way home mechanically staring blankly ahead into the traffic. You think of all the things you want to be, or ought to be, or should have been."

"I hate to annihilate your gloomy reflections. I can smell the dinner and I think that's Tammy crying."

Jan got up to look out the window. Watching her move across our comfortable living room gave me pause: *Is the grass greener on the southern side? Is New Orleans our answer?*

"Bob, you'd better run out there quick to see what's happened. I think Timmy just ran his trike into the Cosgrove's dog! And goodness, Tammy's having a tizzy. The neighborhood will think I'm an unfit mother."

Popping up to head for the door, I whirled around in glee, and with a lusty grab, flung Jan into the air, amazing her with kisses.

"Good Lord, the dinner's burning!"

"So am I, and it's settled! *New Orleans* after the first of the year! Just in time for Mardi Gras!"

As I dashed out to check on the kids, Jan stuck her head out the door, hollering like a fishwife, "What was it your great-grandmother Aupagnier always said?"

"In *Nouvelle Orléans* there's only one place to live, *Le Vieux Carré!*"

"You mean, the French Quarter?"

"Yah, honey, I've heard about it *all* my life."

"Bob, when did your great-grandparents leave New Orleans?"

"Gosh, just about a hundred years ago, right after the Civil War!"

It was only natural that Jan and I, and the two children, would have some regrets about leaving our friends and the security of our home for the past five years. Huntington and its environs had been very kind to us during our years as television personalities; Marian and Bill Blenko had been like parents to us during my time at the glass company. We had made many close acquaintances, though few intimate friends, most of whom had moved away to greener pastures. Ann and Bill Romaine had packed up for New Orleans, and now, we, too, would fulfill our yearnings to move on.

We held a garage sale at our big red brick house to shed things too heavy or useless to move economically. Our greatest forfeiture was a wonderful glider that had graced our front porch. That glider, with its comfy cushions and rhythmic gait, had been a hand-me-down from my parent's home, Hedy-Lee Farm, in Painesville, Ohio, where it had earned a reputation as a special spot to spoon. *Oh, if that glider could talk,* I thought, as a young couple struggled to load it onto their pickup truck, *it would tell how my mother's eighteen-year-old hired girl gave me an exploding sexual thrill by unzipping my fly and fondling me late one summer afternoon when I was sixteen.* On a platonic level, I had sat several evenings with my mentor and junior high school English teacher, Phyllis Brooks, plotting a career in "The Theatre" or public speaking. The subject of radio, or new-fangled TV, was never even considered.

After the sale, only our dearest treasures remained. Jan and I commented on how freeing it was to let things go—not an easy task, however liberating. How Dao De Jing!

The moving van arrived at 7:00 A.M., and the house was stripped in no time while Jan and I packed as much as we could, either into or on top of our station wagon. I took great care to create cozy spots in the back seat for the children, using their favorite pillows, blankets, and stuffed toys.

By late morning, the house swept and bolted, and the moving van long departed, the neighbors waved us off, checking to see if the tires would go flat from the weight once we were all in the car. We bounced down out of the driveway, scraping our back bumper. The shocks carrying the load sprung the wagon back into a relatively horizontal mode, motivating our friends to cheer wildly and motion us on. Wiping a tear from her eye, Jan never looked back. Through the rearview mirror I could see the neighbors scatter toward their homes. I turned the corner and lost sight of our house.

We had hardly crossed into Kentucky before the kids started complaining: they were hungry, thirsty, itchy, and had to tinkle. And there was the ever-present question, "When are we gonna get there, daddy?"

In spite of the cozy places I had fixed for them, Timmy and Tammy seemed to be extraordinarily cranky. Tammy kept whimpering and Timmy nagged at her to be quiet. We concluded their irritability was due to leaving their home and abandoning their friends.

When getting back into the car after the second toilet stop at a filling station, Jan whispered, "Tammy has bumps on her arms, stomach and legs. The welts look as if fleas or ants have bitten her."

As Jan and I discussed the problem in the front seat, Timmy, standing in his usual position—straddling the driveshaft—leaned over to say that he was feeling itchy all over. Maybe it was just nerves. We had all been through so much getting ready to move, it wasn't surprising we would have some sort of stressful manifestation. The added turmoil and dust was enough to give all of us the itches. But now that we were on our way, I suggested if everybody would just calm down and take their little rest, all would be fine and we would be in Tennessee before too long.

The farther we traveled, the fussier the kids became. Little red pimples were popping out all over them. Some of the bumps oozed a little puss, seriously aggravating the children. As the day passed, we realized the children must have either the chicken pox or measles, so we decided to make no unnecessary stops. We were disappointed to miss Mammoth Cave; however, the kids were fascinated by the Wigwam Tourist Court where we spent the night. Our cabin was shaped like a tepee and almost as drafty as a real one, with bathroom facilities dating back to the Cherokees.

During the night, the children became more and more uncomfortable. Jan insisted I get up and go out to search for *Doctor Spock's Children's Medical Book*, somewhere under the fold-down seats. So, at three o'clock in the morning, under the dim light of the rickety reading lamp clamped to the head of our bed, Jan concluded, according to Spock's description of pustules, the children must have chicken pox! None of us got much sleep.

In order to stay on schedule, we headed out very early the next morning to reach New Orleans by nightfall. Snugly packed in, Timmy and Tammy waved goodbye to our wigwam with the wish our home in New Orleans would be as interesting. We all nibbled on glazed doughnuts and chocolate milk Jan and Tammy had bought while Timmy and I gassed up. Before we were half an hour on the road, Jan and the children had fallen asleep.

Invaded with anxiety, I felt alone, overwhelmed by the realization of my total responsibility for the destiny of my little family. *Had my great-grandfather been consumed by similar fears as he headed north? A sense of urgency engulfed me. Their safety and security was now my obsession. They clung to me in trust as we sped south to a whole new life.* My eyes teared.

This overwhelming insecurity was banished as my superego assumed command: *you are a well-educated devoted couple, able performers experienced in both New York and local television. You have made the right decision. You will succeed!*

I pulled a hand from the steering wheel and wiped it across my cheek. My tears were as real as the burning in my stomach. *Anxiety, and cheap doughnuts, had given me a severe case of heartburn,* I reckoned.

Glancing in the rear vision mirror to check the highway behind me, my eyes caught sight of our sleeping angels. How beautiful and how absolutely vulnerable. Tammy looked like an antique Dresden doll, the ones with little chubby round faces and wisps of black hair falling over their foreheads. The car hit a rough spot in the highway, causing the kids to readjust their positions and their blankets. Tammy eased her thumb into her mouth, slipping farther down under the covers. Timmy opened his eyes for a moment to check the scenery, then closed them again. The morning sun danced across his handsome little face, bringing to mind the remark of one of my parents' friends: "That child has a kind and sweet countenance, he's going to have many, many friends."

Jan rallied slightly, opened her eyes a bit and looked over at me, "Everything okay, honey? You aren't getting too sleepy are you?"

"No, no, I'm fine. You know I enjoy driving."

She reached over and danced her fingertips gently along my thigh. Grasping her hand gently I glanced in her direction; we smiled at each other knowingly, she giggled and drifted back into sleep saying, "Keep your eyes on the road, honey, our lives are in your hands."

She looked so peaceful and relaxed, seemingly unaware of the strain, excitement, and the hard work ahead, getting our apartment settled once we arrived in New Orleans. Jan was never afraid of hard work. Her years of tap-dance training and growing up on a farm had earned her a trophy as "The Healthiest Girl in Belmont County, Ohio." In my opinion, her greatest asset was her accessible sweetness and her naïveté, which was often disarming. I reached over and put my hand on hers; she didn't stir. I found myself praying softly, thanking God for this challenging opportunity.

Jan and the kids continued to sleep as we sped across the Tennessee-Alabama state line and on to the outskirts of Birmingham. I pulled into a big truck stop, the kind that sports a restaurant, restrooms, diesel fuel, pinball games—the whole caboodle. While I was filling up with gas, Jan took the kids to the bathroom. They found a table in the slightly sleazy coffee shop where I slipped into the pea-green naugahyde covered booth next to Timmy. The waitress set down four glasses of ice water and gave Jan and me white paper menus incased in well-fingered, yellowing clear plastic. The children watched the wet glass tumblers skitter across the greasy Formica tabletop.

The waitress pulled a pad and pencil from the pocket of her purple uniform. "How y'all doin?" her husky voice bellowed through a pleasant grin.

Startled by her Tallulah Bankhead voice, we looked up and smiled.

"Fine, thank you."

"Well, well, well," she said. "See y'all got the chicken pox."

"Why, I don't know!" Jan replied. "You think it's the chicken pox?"

"Yes, Ma'am, ah know the chicken pox when ah see it! Ah've got five kids myself. Fact, one of 'em's got the chicken pox raht now. Ah think everbody in the South's got the chicken pox raht now."

"Is that right?"

"Yes, Sir, it's sure enough goin' round, an' there's nothin' you can do bout it, Sir."

Placing both of her calloused hands on the table, she leaned way over to Timmy and Tammy. "Y'all are two of the prettiest little younguns ah ever did see. Now, let me give you some real good advahce. When those little thangs start in to itchin', don't you scratch 'em 'cause you're goin' leave yourselves a whole lot of scars. You don't want to mutilate y'alls pretty faces, do ya?"

The children recoiled.

"How can you tell the difference between chicken pox and measles?" Jan asked.

"Ah don't know, Ma'am, ah just *know*! Chicken pox just look different an' ah can tell you, *them's* the chicken pox what they got!"

"What can we do for them?"

"Well, Ma'am, not much you can do 'ceptin' keep the kids quiet. Try to keep their fever down and make 'em rest." She glanced back at Timmy and Tammy. "And make sure they don't scratch those little ole yallah thangs!"

She leaned way over the table once more, nose to nose with the kids. "Now don't y'all scratch them pesky thangs, *heeah?*"

Timmy and Tammy sat wide-eyed and deathly still. Jan thanked the waitress warmly.

"Tell you what ah'm goin' do, Ma'am. Ah'm goin' fix up a little pack of ice an' put two cloth napkins in it. Don't tell the boss. When those kids start in to gettin' a little fever, you just take those cold napkins out and you put 'em on their foreheads and that'll cool them down *real* nahce. Ah know y'all must be travelin', 'cause nobody ever stops here lessen they goin' on a *real* long trip."

We explained we were moving to New Orleans.

She laughed heartily kidding us, "Wish to the Lord above I could slip into y'alls car 'cause, Noo Orleens, that's one place ah can sure tear loose!"

The conviction in her eyes assured me that she knew what she was talking about.

Due to construction of an enormous super-highway in Birmingham, I got lost three times trying to get from U.S. highway 31 to U.S. 11. Our problem was that we couldn't understand what anyone was saying. Directions like, "Go clean through yonder lahght an' lay a raht to Bessmah" or "Y'all cain't git theyah from hee-ah!"

Eventually, quite by accident, we found ourselves on the Bessemer Road driving past belching, open-hearth steel furnaces, which, I guess, is exactly what several people had told us to look for. At any rate, we followed highway 11 endlessly through towns with exotic names like Tuscaloosa, Eutaw, Boligee, and Toomsuba, plus other small cities new and strange to us: Meridian, Laurel, and Hattiesburg. After a toidy stop in Poplarville, Mississippi, we left the car windows open to enjoy the peculiarly warm, humid January weather.

Emerging from my reverie, I was still nervous from our recent Bogalusa experience. I was relieved to see a marker indicating the Pontchartrain Causeway, now only three miles straight ahead.

"Tammy, Tammy, we're almost there," Timmy cried, shaking Tammy from her thumb-sucking doze.

From the narrow, shadowy, pine-sheathed state highway we burst forth into a clearing. The last miles of the road leading to the Causeway were a broad boulevard laid out in a direct course toward the bridge. The woods had been cleared back from the ditches on both sides of the highway for at least a hundred yards, imparting the feeling that someday this was going to be a major thoroughfare. Hovering just above the treetops on our right, the dying western sun created long sabre-like phantom shadows that took turns striking the side of our vehicle. Louisiana seemed intimidating and mysterious.

The smile of the toll taker, leaning out of his booth at the entrance to the Causeway, was a welcome relief. As I handed him my dollar toll, I started to ask, "How far to—"

He politely interrupted, "It's twenty-four miles to the south shore, then six more miles to Canal Street. This is the longest bridge of its type in the world. It was opened on August 30, 1956, under the administration of J. J. Holtgreve, Bridge Chairman and General Manager, a joint undertaking of Jefferson and St. Tammany Parishes. The speed limits are posted. Drive carefully, sir, and have a nice trip, y'all."

Accelerating onto the Causeway, I commented, "Good heavens, such a spiel!"

The kids peered out the right-side windows.

"Yippee, it feels like we're on a speed boat," Timmy joyfully yelped, glad to leave the boredom of the last few miles behind. "Now, *this* is fun!"

"When do we git to the udder thide?" Tammy muttered, without removing her thumb.

"In about a half an hour, sweetie."

"How long is that, mommy?"

"Not very long, dear."

"Aw wight," Tammy replied, contentedly slipping back into her pillow.

The setting sun threw a scarlet cast across the January sky and painted the surface of the lake a crimson so vivid that the surface looked sturdy enough to drive upon. The sky and water changed hues many times during our trip across the bridge. Speeding toward New Orleans, I grew breathless. A sensation of trepidation surged through my body, ending in my brain. *My God, what have we done? What have I done? In search of new fulfillment, I have uprooted my entire family and dragged them more than a thousand miles from their nearest friends and relatives. What if we fail? What have I done?*

But once again, I managed to dismiss all negative thoughts.

Jan reached over and touched my hand. Our eyes met. I think she was having similar misgivings.

"I love you, Bob Carr." She leaned over and kissed me.

"Yuk, what are you doing?" came the remark from the back seat.

"Mommy and I are kissing. You want to make something of it?"

"Yuk," was the weakened reply.

The winter sky had turned to dark burgundy; the Lake had taken on the look of black velvet, with the exception of a path of garnet streaming toward our car from the drowning sun on the western horizon. The hue, reflecting onto Jan's face, gave her the appearance of a well-lighted movie star. How beautiful she was. I breathed heavily in appreciation.

The 12-mile marker whizzed past. Ahead in the distance, a few city lights began to glimmer on the lake's south shore.

"Look, children, there's New Orleans!"

"That's New Orleans?" Timmy asked.

"Yuk, it looks so far." Tammy then asked, for what we hoped would be the last time, "When do we get there?"

"Let's turn on the radio and see if we can get WWL," Jan suggested. "What's the number, Bob?"

"870."

When we finally located the station, the CBS network news was wrapping up with an announcement that Coca-Cola was going to bottle its beverage in aluminum cans for the first time. Question: would the public feel safe drinking from cans? Fred Hammond came on with brief local news about the building boom on the West Bank and the need for additional levee protection, plus a weather wrap-up. Vince Alletto followed with drive-time chitchat and mellow music.

"I can't believe we'll be on the air in a week with our own program," Jan agonized. "It scares me to death! WWL is so famous my Uncle Bill could hear it in the South Pacific during the War. I'll be so nervous, I don't know if I'll have anything to say!"

"You will, honey."

"I hope so. Oh, my God, I hope we've done the right thing!"

"We have," I reassured, although I could feel a chill rush through my loins.

"Listen, *listen* to the radio," Jan interrupted.

Vince Alletto had begun a promotion for our new radio show. "They'll be coming your way weekdays on WWL at twelve noon with tunes and topical tips for the housewife. Jan and Bob Carr are a young, married couple, who will keep you entertained throughout the afternoon with guests, handy hints, family tips, and music. Join Jan and Bob Carr, New Orleans's first on-the-air married couple, starting Monday, February First, and now, here's Peggy Lee with her latest hit, *Fever*."

"Oh, my God…oh, my God."

"What's the matter, Jan?"

"I hope we'll be ready. I hope New Or-*leens* will like us."

"New Aw-leans is bound to like us."

"Oh, my gosh, New Aw-leans. See what I mean? I can't even say the name of the city."

Timmy leaned over the seat from behind and put his arms around his mother. "You'll be ready, mommy, and if you're not, Tammy and me, we'll help you get ready."

We bounced heavily past the south shore tollgate as we dropped with the roadway down the side of the levee into the suburb called Metairie, which someone had told us during our earlier visit means "dairy farm" or "pasture land" in French and is often pronounced "Metry" by the natives. No matter from which direction a highway arrives in New Orleans, it must cross over a levee or a flood wall, ultimately descending below sea level into the city often likened to a saucer floating in a pan of water.

I stopped at a filling station to phone Ann and Bill Romaine, informing them we were on the outskirts of the city and to review the directions to their house in the French Quarter. Ann and Bill were the reason we had come to New Orleans. We had worked with Bill at WSAZ-TV in Huntington for several years and had become close friends. Bill and Ann had struck off across the country a year or so ago to find a job and a city they liked. New Orleans was the place they chose. Now ensconced as the Program Director of WWL Radio, Bill had hired us to be a "bright new image" for the station. Both extremely attractive, they were an interesting mix as a couple. She was a lovely blond with impeccable manners, very Junior League, while Bill, though from a fine old upper-crust New York City family, bordered on the bohemian. Though he put on the appearance of an Ivy League businessman by day, his heart led him to sing at beatnik coffeehouses in the French Quarter by night.

In the excitement of finally being in New Orleans, we lost our bearings and ended up on Tulane Avenue, one of the main commercial thoroughfares.

"Bob, we're on *Tulane Avenue*! I thought you said Ann and Bill told you *not* to get on Tulane Avenue because you can't turn left on Tulane Avenue!"

"Jan, that's silly. There's bound to be a left turn somewhere."

We kept driving toward the river, knowing the French Quarter was somewhere off to our left; sure enough, at each intersection, a traffic sign boldly instructed, *No Left Turn*. We continued on, more than twenty blocks, passing such interesting street names as Telemachus, Genois, Gayoso, Dorgenois, Derbigny, and Villere.

"Jan, I feel like I'm in a foreign country!"

"What worries me is how we'll ever learn to pronounce all these strange names."

"Look, look, Jan! We're free at last! There's a left turn arrow, and look at the name, Liberty Street!

"Liberty! Hallelujah, free at last," we both chuckled, enjoying well-needed relief.

Once on Canal Street, we knew we could find our way to Bourbon Street and Bill and Ann's house.

A few weeks earlier, Jan and I had flown to New Orleans finalizing our jobs and renting a French Quarter apartment. The historic French Quarter with its beautiful architecture had delighted us, the broad bend in the Mississippi River, as it sweeps past the city, had left us in awe; however, the antics along Bourbon Street, named after the Royal Family of France, had astonished us.

As we turned off Canal Street onto traffic-clogged Bourbon, I wasn't fully prepared for the effect the unfolding spectacle would have on the children. The sounds, the sights, and the smells along Bourbon Street were different from anything they had ever encountered. The experience was an incredible stimulation to their senses. They bounced from one side of the back seat to the other, trying to see it all at once.

"Daddy, look at the lady in that big picture," Tammy shrieked, totally forgetting about her thumb and blanket. "She's only got her panties on!"

The door next to the blow-up photo of Blaze Starr swung open revealing a gyrating stripper. Timmy yelped, flinging himself forward until he nearly fell out the window. Tammy burst forth with a piercing screech and then buried her head, ostrich-like, in her pillow. Moving at a snail's pace behind the ogling passengers in the car ahead of us, we passed several more strip places. Tammy kept her head nestled deep in her pillow. To Jan's consternation, Timmy had pulled himself out of the window and perched his derriere on the back seat windowsill so he could hang onto the topside luggage rack with both hands.

"Daddy, can I sit on top of the car?"

"No, indeed!" Jan quickly rebuked.

"Timmy, I think you can see enough from where you are. Just hold on tight to that luggage rack, please."

"Alright, daddy, but I can't see up on the balconies."

The traffic was bumper to bumper. The barkers in front of the various nightclubs were boldly trying to hustle pedestrians into their particular joints. We eased past the Famous Door and got a generous earful of New Orleans Dixieland Jazz.

Suddenly, a midget sporting an overly tall top hat darted toward our car from the narrow sidewalk in front of the Old Absinthe Bar. He approached Jan's open window hawking a Night Club Tour. She said, "No, thanks." He persisted, so she rolled up her window. He then stuck his face in the back window, but when Tammy looked up at him with her pockmarked face, he immediately fled.

The traffic began to move a bit faster. Timmy was ecstatic. Still sitting on the windowsill, he was by now holding onto the luggage rack with one hand, the other arm fully extended with an open palm to catch the breeze. With his eyes darting hither and yon, Timmy's outstretched hand unexpectedly collided with the posterior of a buxom, peroxided prostitute.

Startled, she whirled around. "What the shit do you think yer doin'?" she bellowed. "My ass is my bread and butter. Black and blue it don't sell!"

Timmy slithered down into the back seat and closed his window.

Tammy looked up from her pillow, "When do we get there?"

"Honey, we're here," Jan said, hoping to console her. "This is New Orleans. We're here at last!"

Tearletts welled in Tammy's eyes for a few seconds as she took a deep breath and held it until her face puffed up, turning so red that it looked as if she would pop every pustule on her little pocked face, then exploded into an avalanche of tears.

"Baby, what's the matter?" Jan asked.

"I don't *wanna* live here, if this is here. I wanna go back to Wester-ginia. I wanna go home!" she wailed.

"This *is* home, Tammy," Timmy blurted.

Tammy buried her head in her blanket once again.

Once we passed St. Peter Street, the traffic began to thin out. We crossed St. Ann.

"Look," I said. "Look, Tammy, there's Mrs. Romaine and your friend Liza on that balcony."

Liza had been born two months after Tammy while Ann and Bill still lived in Huntington.

I tooted the horn; they waved wildly. Frail Liza looked as though she might fall between the wrought-iron rungs of the railing. Timmy got so excited he climbed out the window and sat on the top stash of suitcases strapped to the luggage rack. Wiping her eyes, Tammy waved timidly. Leaning over the railing, Ann hollered orders for us to park across the carriageway entrance in the no-parking zone, adding that Bill was on his way down.

Their apartment took up the entire second floor of the ancient three-and-a-half story brick town house, which, rising against the night sky, looked even more enormous than it was. Flush with the street, one of the immense green paneled carriageway doors swung open. Bill emerged with outstretched arms that caught Timmy as he jumped from the top of the car. Bill and Timmy had always had a strong affection for one another. A lover of children, Bill was sensitive, artistic, and strikingly good looking. He longed to be a full-time musician and singer of his own plainsongs—similar to Gregorian Chants.

Jan hustled out to give Bill a kiss as I jockeyed into the rather limited no-parking zone. Bill came around to my side, and leaning through the window, gave me a big bear hug, then reached into the back to embrace Tammy.

We had called Ann and Bill from Nashville to tell them Timmy and Tammy had become sick with what might be the chicken pox, meaning we couldn't stay at their house, as originally planned. Their baby girl, Emily, was only four weeks old. Jan didn't want her, or Liza, exposed to the children's disease.

"I don't think you should hug the children, Bill," Jan instructed. "They might still be contagious."

"I'm not going to get anything," Bill shrugged. "Liza has been waiting all day to see Tammy, so let's set Tammy up on top of the car with Timmy so she can see Liza up there on the balcony."

Tammy and Timmy stared somewhat bashfully up at Liza. Not one of them could think of a thing to say.

Bill continued, "It's time for Ann to nurse the baby, so I'll ride over to your apartment with you. You'll need some help carrying up your things. Then I'll come back here and babysit while Ann walks over with some dinner for y'all."

Our apartment was located on Dumaine Street between Decatur and Chartres, just three blocks away from the Romaines' and half a block from the French Market. Jan and I felt fortunate to have found an apartment in the French Quarter whose owner would accept children. It was on the second floor with a balcony overlooking the street. In its entirety the apartment was barely large enough for our family.

We were lucky to find a parking place almost in front of our building. To show the kids their new home, I pointed up to the balcony in front of us, which was lighted from the glow of a simulated antique streetlamp nearby. Their expressions reflected their astonishment.

"But daddy," Timmy asked, "where's our front yard?"

"That balcony, that's your new front yard. It'll be lots of fun. You and Tammy can watch all the people go under you along the sidewalk."

"And you can even see the big boats on the Mississippi River from up there," Bill added hastily, trying to appease their solemn, doubting countenances. "By the way, Bob, technically that's not a balcony. A balcony is cantilevered. What you have is a gallery. It extends across the sidewalk and has iron posts to hold it up. Also, in New Orleans, they don't call it a sidewalk: it's a banquette. Not to worry, you and Jan will learn all that jargon soon enough."

"Oh, Lord, I hope so," Jan sighed as she wrestled the key from the depths of her purse and we opened the wrought-iron gate protecting the enclosed patio from intruders. Timmy and Tammy nestled close to Jan as we toted some of the suitcases along the shadowy passageway leading to the patio and the antiquated, circular stairway beyond. Bill suggested we leave the suitcases in the patio for a few minutes until we had gone up, unlocked the apartment, and turned on a few lights.

"When is your furniture due?" Bill asked, as we struggled up the steep twisting stairs.

"Either tomorrow or Saturday. It depends on how long it takes them to pick up a partial load somewhere in Mississippi."

We reached the top, pausing to breathe.

"Bob, look, I think our front door's partly open!"

"Was someone supposed to meet you here?" Bill asked.

"No. We got the key from the landlord, Mr. Cresson, when we were here last month."

It was nearly nine o'clock. The children were restless from travel and the added irritation of chicken pox—plus Jan and I were exhausted. The stair landing was dimly lit, making it pitch black inside the apartment. I cautiously pushed the ajarred section of the narrow French door wide open and peered in. It was like an inkwell. I edged my way inside through the darkness, trying to find a light switch. My nose was struck by the foul smell of the place. Without warning, something soft brushed swiftly against my trouser leg, causing me to cry out. The reverberating sound of my yelp in the dark room terrified me and startled into action five or six sleeping cats that slithered past my legs, out the door, and down the steps.

The sight of the animals panicked us all, setting off a chain reaction of one scream after another. Tammy started crying, Jan gasped, Bill chased the last cat down the stairs and Timmy *broke wind!* We all erupted into tears of laughter, relieving the tension—except Tammy, who chose tears of despair. Jan picked her up and comforted her against her bosom.

Edging with care further into the living room, I flicked on the overhead light. The timid quartet behind me clamored in through the half-opened French door. We stood awestruck. Apparently, a covey of cats had been living in the apartment for several days. The smell of cat poo was nauseating. The brightness of the light also triggered an army of roaches into action; they dove between the floorboards and scrambled under the walls. It was more than an exhausted Jan could bear. She began to cry, followed by Tammy. I too, was about to cry, when I recalled an amusing alliteration Jan and I had learned in speech class at Carnegie Tech.

"Jan, remember, 'The cats that crept into the crypt and crapped and crept out again?' I think we've found those creepy crapping cats' crypt!"

Jan laughed through her tears and in our tired and nervous state, we *all* began to laugh. For a brief time our laughing bordered on hysteria. It all seemed surreal and terrifying.

"Let's open the French doors onto the balcony or the gallery or whatever and let some fresh air into this *God-forsaken place!*"

Under the kitchen sink Jan found an old dustpan, which I used to scoop up the cat dung. Jan, Bill, and Timmy began to drag up our belongings. I posted Tammy out on her 'front yard,' the gallery, to keep an eye on the car from above. Jan was aghast at my judgment, though too weary to worry.

After our earthly treasures had been toted up the winding stairway and were safely inside the apartment, Bill left for home, allowing Ann the opportunity to come over with the dinner she had prepared. We had no furniture, so Jan knelt on the floor and made up the mattress as if it were an ancestral bed. We would all have to cuddle together. What better way to feel loved and secure?

Ann arrived with a delicious meal, the name of her pediatrician, and a plan of action for the next day. Jan and I, so tired and weak, were amenable to anything. Ann spread a linen tablecloth over a couple of boxes pushed together and set out the dinner, complete with Spode bone china and sterling silverware. Jan and I looked at the oasis in wonderment.

"Ann, you've always had impeccable taste!"

"Thank you, Bob. A little ostentatious maybe. I thought it would give y'all a lift and a glimpse of how things will be after you're settled in. I called Dr. Henry Simon at home and made an appointment for the children to see him in his office at ten o'clock in the morning. I'll take them there so you can be in the apartment in case the moving van arrives."

Ann excused herself, but not before insisting we eat before the food got cold. We all dashed to the gallery to wave good night. The kids tucked their tiny feet between the rungs and folded their arms along the railing. We all watched as Ann walked up dimly-lighted Dumaine Street until she was out of sight. Timmy and I pulled the shutters closed behind us and went back into the apartment to *dine!* With no curtains or shades, I closed the louvers to keep out tomorrow's morning sun. The bedroom was just inside the gallery, facing the street.

Following dinner, we changed quickly into our jammies and nestled onto the makeshift bed. Well after midnight, we all lay still for several moments.

"Mommy, daddy, we din't say our prayers," Timmy exclaimed.

"An you din't tell us a thtory, daddy," Tammy added.

"Dear children, you lived your story today. Someday, you can tell your own children about your travels south!"

"What about our prayers?"

"You two say the prayers for all of us," Jan suggested through a yawn.

Just about the moment we all sleepily said, "Amen," someone kicked over a garbage can on the street directly below our room. Startled, we simultaneously rose from the mattress, then fell back in a quaking heap.

"What was *that*, daddy?"

"Just somebody falling over a garbage can, nothing to worry about, kids. Let's go to sleep."

We clung tightly to each other. Slowly I could feel a calmness come over us as one after the other we fell asleep. Just before dozing off, I wearily reviewed our day's journey down through Mississippi, in and out of Bogalusa and across the Causeway. I thanked God we were safely in bed together. I fell asleep thinking how this move would forever change all our lives. This was a day to try our mettle and we had survived.

All four of us plummeted into a profound sleep. Our physical and mental exhaustion was so acute that our entwined bodies lay absolutely motionless on the mattress, our muscles lapsing into a state of blissful eight-hour lethargy. Nothing short of Beelzebub's wrath thrashing the damned of Hades could have awakened us.

Somewhere in the drowsy dream-world state, between insensibility and stupor, my mind, responding to a clamorous earth-shaking noise, suddenly leapt into reality. In frenzied fright, I rose from my pillow, dragging the bed covers and my family with me. We clung together, trembling even more than we had the night before. Groggy, crazed, disoriented, we huddled petrified on our sleeping pallet, clumped like the subject of a sculptor's consanguine still-life.

The menacing noise stopped as unexpectedly as it began, causing me to wonder if it were only a moment of delirium. Then, there it was again! This time, louder and more intense then before, shaking our very room. Clutching one another in terror, we became as one. Bricks seemed to fall from the outside wall and strike the gallery floor just beyond our bedroom door. Then, silence. Bizarre earthquake? The racket started once again. Finally, in command of my full wits, I realized this was no earthquake noise but rather a man-made sound.

Pulling away from my frightened family, I eased open the shutters; morning brightness flooded the room. The pain in my contracting pupils subsided momentarily.

Squinting through my sleepy haze, I could see a maze of fallen plaster chips from which dust was ascending up a sunbeam.

"What is it, Bob?"

"I don't know."

I stuck my head cautiously out between the shutters into an unknown world. To the left, where the noise seemed to originate, I spied a frightful apparition standing atop a ladder, propped against the building adjoining ours. It looked like a thing from outer space holding a Buck Rogers ray gun; a dusty jump suit and masked helmet covered it. *It* didn't see me. I pulled back into the room. The noise began once again.

And once again, Tammy began to cry. "I wanna go home!" she bellowed over the noise.

Timmy stood up, dropping the blankets from around him and shouting through the din, "Tammy, this is home!"

Jan shuddered. "Timmy, *stop* that!"

"Stop what, mommy?"

"Stop scaring Tammy."

"Well, this *is* our new home, isn't it?"

"Timmy, mommy just means that Tammy isn't used to it yet."

"I'm not used to it either," shouted Timmy through the clatter outside. "But I'm not crying."

The noise stopped.

I stuck my head out, yelling through the dust to the being on the ladder, "Hey, what're you doing?"

The deafening noise obliterated my words. This time I could see what was happening. The apparition was holding a jackhammer to chip the stucco coating off the brick of the adjacent building. Having the truth revealed was a great relief; nonetheless, awakening out of a deep sleep to such a racket had been most unsettling.

Before we had a chance to reckon further with the fracas outside, *inside* the doorbell rang with such ferocity, it created the falling domino effect: startled, Jan screamed, which caused Timmy to jump, prompted Tammy to cry, and me to despair. Suddenly, I realized it must be the movers. I pulled on my pants over my pajamas and dashed down the stairs to the front gate.

"You Mr. Carr?"

"Yes, you the movers?"

"Yeah, we're ya' movers. Where in the hell are we gonna unload? Ther' ain't no place to park on this narrow street and that idiot up on that ladder is droppin' rocks on our hay-eds. Thank God, I got my cap on!"

"Let me come out and take a look."

I turned the knob on the iron gate. It wouldn't open. I twisted, shook and pulled at the gate. I couldn't move it. I felt like a caged animal. The moving man tugged on it from the other side to no avail.

"Mr. Carr, we cain't unload iffen we cain't git in yer house."

A wave of panic descended over me. "Just a minute, I've got it. Don't go away, I'll go up and get the key from my wife and be back in a flash."

The moving van, designed to carry several partial loads at one time, was enormous, nearly half as long as the block of Dumaine Street between Chartres and Decatur. Like a whale in a creek, it floundered in the middle of the street, blocking impatient motorists.

The moving man explained that their dispatcher was supposed to have put up *No Parking* signs along our side of the street, where cars normally parked, so the van would be able to park and unload. Apparently he forgot.

"Why don't you pull up on the sidewalk over on the other side of the street, where there are no cars?"

"We tried that, the goddamn police ran us off...said the weight of our van would bust up the sidewalk, or whatever he called it. These French Quarters is a pain in the ass! I'd oughter get back to the van with the driver so those bastards stop tootin' their friggin' horns. I'll be back as soon as we find a goddamn place to park and unload."

As the moving van pulled off, the apparition with the jackhammer descended his ladder. He lifted his headgear, revealing a cheerful black face, shook off some dust, and took a deep breath of fresh air.

"Are you finished?" I asked.

"Will be 'bout fifteen minutes. Den ah be goin' in da coht-yard, foh da rest of da day."

"That's great, because movers are bringing in our furniture and I was afraid some of your cement would fall on 'em."

"You gimme fifteen minutes, sir. Ah be gone, ah *be* gone, ah promise dat."

I was relieved to take part, finally, in an amiable conversation. Making my way back up to the apartment, I discovered a button on the wall of the passageway to the patio that, when pushed, released the gate lock from the inside. *Smart*, I thought. *Sorry I hadn't discovered it earlier.*

Jan had put Timmy and Tammy into the bathtub so they would be ready when Ann picked them up for the pediatrician. Jan and I rolled up the mattress and shoved all the suitcases into the closets so the movers could put down the rugs and set up the beds. I noticed the guy on the ladder had stopped hammering on the wall and went out to take a look. Climbing down the ladder, he saw me and took off his helmet.

"Mistah, ah bees finished. Sorry foh all dat dust on yo gallery. Guess you can sweep it off now. Ah's done."

"Hey, Mister Carr," someone hollered from below.

I was surprised to hear someone call my name. I didn't think anyone knew me. It was the moving man.

"Hey, Mister Carr, I'm down here!"

I leaned over the railing, feeling suddenly like a New Orleanian. "Did you find a place to park and unload?"

"Yeah!"

"Where?"

"*Jackson Square!*" he replied with extreme aggravation.

"Good Lord, that's three and half blocks away, isn't it?"

"You bet your sweet ass! It's gonna take us longer to unload than we thought!"

"I'll be right down. Wait a minute. I'll walk to the van with you."

The first thing off the van was our refrigerator. I followed the two movers as they toted it from Jackson Square, along Decatur, around the corner on Dumaine, to our building. Then they squeezed the dolly carrying the refrigerator through the long, narrow, flag-stoned passageway to the foot of the winding staircase. They were about to give forth a few choice four-letter words when they looked up and saw Jan and the kids peering over the banister.

"This is going to be a pisser of a day!" one mumbled under his breath. Ann who always seemed to be in the right place at the right time—with the right food—suddenly arrived with breakfast rolls, juice, coffee, and hot chocolate for the children. Once they'd had their fill, she whisked them off to the pediatrician.

The movers reminded us we were supposed to pay them in cash or by money order before they finished unloading. Our banker in Huntington had told us the best way to transfer our money was with a bank draft, which would be honored anywhere. Alas, such is not the case in New Orleans. No one, in any bank, would cash our West Virginia bank draft. It was only $500, but it was our life's savings, $300 of which was to go to the movers. The movers, who were about half-finished, sat down on the winding stairway to rest, and emphasized that they must be paid before they could continue. Prior to the days of credit cards, there was only one way to solve the dilemma; we signed the entire bank draft over to them. The overpayment would be returned sometime the next week from the main office. We had just enough cash left in our pockets to buy groceries!

By the time all of our belongings from the seven-room house were packed or stacked in our four-room apartment, we were exhausted.

Ann returned with Tammy and Timmy cheerfully licking lollipops given to them by Dr. Henry Simon, who said they were fine and healthy; however, they would look wretched for a few days. Tammy constantly picked at one festering eruption on her forehead, which the doctor said would leave a scar if she persisted. Unfortunately for Tammy, the doctor was right.

"Dr. Simon is our first friend in New Orleans," announced Timmy proudly.

"His office is up in the air like a big tree house," added Tammy.

"And he has lots of tin soldiers and French Army hats."

It was dark by the time I rearranged the boxes and furniture. We were all tuckered out. I set up our folding lawn chairs on the gallery so we could sit outside and eat hamburgers while enjoying the balmy January night. Tammy snuggled onto my lap; Timmy joined Jan on the plastic mesh chaise. The sights and sounds were strange to us. The scuffling of footsteps and hushed voices passing on the sidewalk just below were alien to anything we had ever known. Timmy jumped up to peer over the gallery railing every time a car passed. Even Tammy sprang to her feet at the clatter of an approaching horse-drawn carriage. Looking toward the river, across the cupolaed rooftop of the French Market, we could occasionally catch a glimpse of a ship's running lights atop its mast. And way in the distance, beyond Canal Street we could, on our tiptoes, spy the Greek temple sitting majestically atop the Hibernia Bank Building. It's perched there as if dropped in place by a latter-day Greek God of architecture to create a perfect crowning finial for the city's tallest neoclassic skyscraper. The temple, we learned, effectively masks the reserve water supply for the building's fire protection. High overhead, the Big Dipper was a familiar and comforting sight. Suddenly, a star fluttered loose from the Milky Way. It blazed brightly for a few moments and then died before falling quietly into the Mississippi.

"That means good luck, daddy," Timmy said confidently. "It means me and Tammy, and you and mommy, are gonna have good luck in New Orleans."

"I hope so."

"It *does*, daddy, it *does*!"

"Thanks for your confidence, honey. I think it also means it's time to go to bed."

Jan inserted, "When the sky starts falling down, Henny Penny, it's time to go inside."

"Oh, mommy, that's silly. The sky's not falling down."

"Nevertheless, Timmy, tomorrow's going to be here all too soon. Let's get you guys settled into your bunks so you both get a good night's sleep. Tomorrow will be filled with lots of new experiences."

Tammy was nearly asleep as I carried her carefully through the French door that led from the gallery directly into the children's room. As I strained to place her up on the top bunk, her eyes eased open slightly, and she smiled and remarked that it was cozy to be back in her own bed. With that, she squinched up into a fetal ball and passed into slumber. Timmy crawled into the bottom bunk, kicked off his cowboy boots, gave a gasp, and fell asleep with his clothes on. Jan gently slipped off his Wyatt Erp trousers, pulled the blanket up over him, and kissed both children good night.

"I'm exhausted!" Jan said.

"Come get into bed."

"I can't find my nighty."

"Never mind your nighty. I'll keep you warm!"

I lifted the covers and she cuddled close to me. We kissed. My lips left hers and wandered down her throat to her breast, as my fingers traveled down her stomach.

"My God, not tonight. I'm nearly asleep already," she pleaded.

"Don't you want to christen our new bedroom?"

Her hand ran from my knee up along my thigh. She seized me gently, kneaded me briefly, ultimately loosening her grasp as she fell asleep.

I lay throbbing for a brief time, then relaxed. In the moments before I fell asleep, I thanked God for the strength and good fortune he had bestowed upon us.

Our life in New Orleans had begun.

Bob and Jan leaving for New Orleans to finalize their jobs, 1959

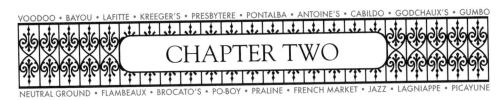

WWL Radio, "This is Bob and this is Jan for Luzianne."

Ann found us a wonderful black lady named Mercedes (she promounced it *Mer-sa-dees*), who would be able to stay with the children for several weeks until we could hire someone permanently. Mercedes, in her middle fifties, had lived her whole life on a plantation near St. Francisville, Louisiana. She was wonderfully large and gentle—"the middle chile of twelve siblings." She was in the city for a couple of months, "stayin' by her ahntie's, for a time, and glad to pick up some extra money, to help her ahntie along." With the pressure of the children off our shoulders, we set out happily toward WWL Radio, located two floors above the famous Blue Room of the Roosevelt Hotel. Our first day on the job was to prove exhilarating.

From our Dumaine Street apartment, we strode along Chartres Street with its rows of galleried eighteenth-century buildings, pressed snugly one against the other. Cutting across in front of St. Louis Cathedral, we found it interesting that many pedestrians on the sidewalk made the sign of the cross as they passed the main entrance of the church. Walking through Pirates' Alley caused our hearts to beat faster. The name alone conjured up thoughts of New Orleans's fascinating and sometimes turbulent history. On Royal Street, Jan was tormented by not being able to stop and shop at the myriad of enchanting stores but was thrilled by future possibilities. A cool, clammy late-January breeze swept down Canal Street, chilling us while we waited briefly for streetcars to pass.

"Bob, Ann told me this is the widest main street of any city in the United States."

"Yah, and I'll bet the hottest to get across in the summer!"

"Look at that department store, G-O-D-C-H-A-U-X; I wonder how you pronounce *that?*"

"God-shawcks? Oh, God, I don't know. I hope they're not one of our sponsors."

We pushed our way into the shiny solid brass revolving door of the Baronne Street entrance of the famed and fabled Roosevelt Hotel. The glamorous lobby, stretching a full block from Baronne to University Place, was paved with thick floral carpet and capped with the soft glow of Bavarian crystal chandeliers. Shops lined this famous Valhalla-like reception hall where my former boss, Bill Blenko, once told me that the loveliest women in the world linger. Ornate signs pointed out the Fountain Lounge, the Plantation Room, the Sazerac Bar, and the Blue Room. Bell boys stationed at regular intervals bowed slightly as we passed. We felt as if we were

walking the Yellow Brick Road to Oz as we made our way quite breathlessly, and with some trepidation, toward the elevators at the far end of the great arcade.

For years, WWL had been broadcasting from the Roosevelt. With its fifty-thousand-watt clear channel, it was heard with regularity halfway around the world, making both *it*, and the Roosevelt, internationally famous. Mulling this over, we had both become apprehensive. Jan eased her hand around mine as we stood staring at our reflections, peering back from the highly polished brass elevator door. Our images disappeared as the door rolled back, allowing a group of chattering tourists to exit. The uniformed elevator attendant stepped out into the lobby, nodding courteously as he motioned us in.

Still holding hands, we disembarked on the third floor. We timidly made our way through the double glass doors into the reception area of the radio station to be greeted by the sweet smile of the lovely, Southern-voiced Mrs. Stark.

"You must be Jan and Bob Cahr. We've been expectin' you. Bill Romaine and Mistah Vath, our manager, are raht down the hall, first door on the raht. May ah say that you two children are even more attractive in person than in your photographs."

"Thank you very much," I chuckled.

"Ah hope you don't think me too fohward?"

I leaned toward her. "Oh, no, I could listen to you talk all day, you have such a beautiful voice."

She blushed.

Looking cheerfully confident, Bill came striding up the hall to greet us. He took us to meet John Vath, the General Manager, who had given him permission to hire us. No easy task, since the station had a policy prohibiting the employment of husbands and wives, which we thought odd, since it was owned by Jesuits of the Catholic Church.

Mr. Vath, a kind and perceptive gentleman, received us warmly. He explained we were an innovation to the city's airwaves and hoped listeners would take us into their hearts. The station had recently discontinued the long-popular and highly expensive *Dawnbusters* show, a New Orleans institution. Although not carried on network radio, it was heard by a large and faithful audience due to the station's kilowatts. The program's format had been somewhat like the more famous *Don McNeal's Breakfast Club*, broadcast nationally from Chicago. WWL's television division had in turn produced *Dawnbusters* for a short time, but it turned out to be a dawn-*Bust* when transferred to the television screen—vastly more costly and complicated to produce than ever expected. And with two of its regulars, Al Hirt and Pete Fountain, becoming nationally famous with outside recording contracts, the tab for local advertisers was prohibitive. The O'Dair Sisters, who had been the darlings of the AM program, split up their singing act when the show died.

A new day of radio was on the horizon; Mr. Vath had hired us to be part of it. *God, were we scared!*

Events moved swiftly once we went on the air. Bill counseled us on social contacts for interviews designed to draw listeners to the station and ingratiate us to the public. Announcers Fred Hammond, Jimmy Steel, and Vince Alletto were especially thoughtful in helping us over the difficult pronunciations of people, places, streets, and things peculiar to Noo Aw-yuns, as many of the politicians pronounced it. We found out early on, in New Orleans, one drinks Burgundy wine on Bur-*gun*-dy Street. Many ride the St. Charles Streetcar (never trolley) Uptown to Ly-ola (Loyola) and *Too*-lane (Tulane) Universities across from Audubon Pawrk.

Morris Trahan, an account executive with WWL, and Peter Mayer, a young advertising turk, took a liking to us and started selling our show. Our first big account was for a coffee company. Pete and Morris asked us to look at the fact sheet and then ad lib a few spots. What came out each time was, "Hi, this is Jan and, this is Bob for Luzianne Coffee, etc. etc. etc." Peter felt something was wrong; the copy just didn't play.

"I've got an idea, kids," Peter said. "Bob, be less gentlemanly; change around the order of your names once and let's see what happens."

We started. "Hi, this is Bob—"

"And this is Jan—"

And together we said, "for Luzianne!"

"That's perfect, you've *got it!*"

From that time on we started every radio program and hundreds of commercial spots with "Hi, this is Bob and this is Jan."

Our two-hour daily program consisted of chitchat on a wide range of child-rearing or marital topics, for which we did research or drew from our own experiences. We had a couple of regulars like Mrs. Francis Senter, "The Flower Lady," who gave advice about the planting and care of wonderful New Orleans subtropical flora.

One day we were anticipating an on-air visit from Coco Chanel, whose *parfums* were being touted at Masion Blanche on Canal Street. Mademoiselle Chanel did not appear but rather her representative, a flashy and gregarious woman dangling a diamond encrusted cross in her cleavage, with 'the' perfect French accent to do justice to the *eau de toilette* product line. She pushed a small (very small) vial of No. 5 in Jan's direction, mentioned Coco had introduced it in 1921, and asked her where she would wear it.

"Everywhere," Jan replied.

"Non, non, Madame, where would you place it on your bow-dy."

Jan blushed.

I suggested behind each ear.

"Oh, Monsieur, be more lavish. The ears, yes, but then de throat, de elbows, behind de knees, everywhere you hope to be keest!"

Jan's Irish complexion fired up even brighter.

I saved the day by telling her I had brought my mother Chanel No. 5 when I returned home from serving overseas in the army of occupation.

She pushed a small vial of *Cologne du Monsieur* in my direction. It toppled onto my lap, popped open and trickled down my trousers, stinging my thigh. Smothering our giggles, I quickly cued a commercial. What came up was the roach exterminator jingle, "Miller the Killer, Miller the Killer, he kills 'em all!"

Our program also played recorded music, and there were daily interviews with local guests and famous stars, some of whom were appearing at the Blue Room two floors below.

My first celebrity interview was Sophie Tucker, the famous and outrageous sex symbol of vaudeville, night clubs, and movies from silent to talky. She was starring at the Blue Room for the umpteenth time. Billed as "The Last of the Red Hot Mamas," Miss Tucker didn't wish to venture from her gracious hotel-provided suite to the radio studio because, according to her, "Only mad dogs and Englishmen go out in the noonday sun!" Rather, she insisted that I and my recording equipment come to her suite on the top floor. Louis Benedetto, our engineer, accompanied me.

We were greeted by a crisply uniformed black maid who ushered us into the suite's bedroom, where the full-figured and amply busted Miss Tucker was stretched out on a damask-covered chaise. Bedecked in a pale blue negligee, she held a Roosevelt-engraved water glass replete with what appeared to be straight whiskey. Even in the muted light of the heavily curtained room, her brightly tinted blonde up-sweep glowed.

"You gorgeous young thing, come on over here, Baby, and sit yourself down by me so we can get intimate."

I could feel my eyebrows rise; my cheeks flushed. I glanced at the maid, who smiled, rolling her sharp bright eyes. I searched for eye contact with Louis; he was busy mumbling about the need for an electrical outlet. I perched modestly on the far end of the chaise.

"Bob," Louis barked, "ask Miss Tucker where there's a hot socket I can shove this plug into."

Sophie Tucker almost rolled off her chaise with laughter at hearing Louis's question. "Honey," her crusty voice bellowed, "I don't hear so well, Baby, but I heard that! Hey, Baby boy, come on over closer, right here, so we can get a little chummy."

The damask chaise squeaked as I slid across its surface.

"For a minute there, Baby, I thought you let a little toot!" She laughed broadly again, throwing up her hands. When they came back down, one landed on my thigh.

Louis thrust a hand mike toward me. "Bob, try testing."

"I always do," replied Miss Tucker. "I always do!"

I was so rattled, I couldn't think of a first question.

Chuckling and rubbing her jewel-adorned fingers lightly up and down my thigh, she said, "Can't you think of anything you want to ask me, Baby?"

"How old are you?" I blurted out.

She didn't flinch. "Baby, we never ask a lady her age, but I'll tell you this, I was around before your daddy ever grabbed your mamma by the ass!" She laughed uproariously.

Discreetly, Louis looked the other way to avoid my embarrassment. Slipping the earphones over his head, he cued me, "Take it!"

"Hear that, Baby? You gotta take it while you can get it. Life is a ball, with only so many bounces, so ya gotta take it when it's offered!" Looking at me quizzically, she continued, "Carr, you must be Scotch Highlander, with those rosy cheeks and cute turned-up nose." She tweaked the end of my nose with a long, red false fingernail. "Speaking of Scotch, Baby, reach over there for that decanter and ice cubes, and freshen my glass."

I looked at her ancient leathery face, layered with pancake makeup and slathered with lip rouge, and became so flustered that I let an ice cube drop from the tongs and skitter haphazardly across the carpet. As I leaned over to pick it up, she reached out and patted me on the behind. "Baby, that's what I call some cute buns!"

I broke out in a cold sweat as I uttered one inane question after another, figuring at any moment she was going to work her roving fingers into the fastener on my Talon zipper. After an eternal fifteen minutes, we left.

Sophie Tucker must have enjoyed a good laugh that afternoon, thinking about how she nearly scared the pants off a cub interviewer. When, several years later, I read of her death at the age of 78, I realized the world had lost a great humorist. I chuckled wistfully at the memory of the torture she had enjoyed putting me through.

For Jan's "first," the station selected Joan Crawford. Though world-famous as a movie queen, Crawford was, at this point in her life, pushing Pepsi Cola. Her forth husband, Alfred Steele, President of Pepsi and the man single-handedly responsible for the brand's phenomenal growth against Coke, had recently died of a heart attack. Instead of being left a rich widow, Miss Crawford was left liable for Mr. Steele's multitude of debts—the result of *her* ostentatious life style. The word was out: Joan Crawford, always a tough cookie to interview, was even tougher now, in her sorrow. A press conference had been set up next to her suite at the Roosevelt. The room was appropriately lit to flatter Miss Crawford and was filled with fresh red and yellow roses, per her request. Each press person had to wait his turn.

We had been instructed that Miss Crawford would allow only one person to speak to her at a time; the fact Jan and I were a husband-and-wife team cut no weight. I stood in the anteroom with Jan as Joan chewed up one interviewer after another. Jan was becoming extremely apprehensive. Suddenly, a Pepsi man ushered her briskly into a chair directly facing *Joan Crawford—Movie Star*. Temporarily obscured by an oversized hand mirror, she reapplied lipstick to her ample mouth and fluffed her lengthy faux eyelashes. Apparently pleased with her paint job, she abruptly tossed the mirror to an aide, narrowly missing the top of the Pepsi bottle placed advantageously adjacent. Looking straight at Jan, she inquired tersely, "What do you wish to ask, my dear? Let's get on with it, I'm growing weary!"

Jan was petrified. Highly allergic to roses all her life, she gave forth a muffled sneeze.

With her long, fiery-red fingernails Miss Crawford clawed impatiently at the silk brocade upholstery on the arm of her gilt-edged chair; the sound of the fingernails scraping along the fabric seemed deafening to Jan, who, trying to gain composure, sat speechless for a moment.

"Wasn't your real name La...La Sewer?" popped out.

In the anteroom, I covered my face to shield my embarrassment for my wife.

Glancing at the aide holding the mirror, Joan remarked, "That's the most irrelevant question I've ever been asked! LeSueur—Lucille Fay LeSueur! *Now*, young lady, don't you have a question relevant to my career?"

Recalling my previous prompting, Jan asked, "Did you ever dance in a movie, other than 'Rain'?"

"Well!" Joan Crawford's head inclined. "My whole career was based on my dancing skill. It's obvious, my dear, you've never seen my early films!"

"My grandmother said I was too young, at the time, to see films of that sort," Jan replied timidly, trying to be polite.

Miss Crawford's heavily painted eyebrows arched expressively, "Next question!"

"Did you drink Pepsi Cola before you married Mr. Steele?" was destined to be Jan's final query.

Joan glowered, then nodded to her Pepsi aide, who eased Jan out of her chair. Still fully within earshot, Joan remarked, "That girl has a fascinating voice quality, but from which Louisiana ooze did she emerge—and what cretin counselled her on her interviewing skills?"

So much for our association with Miss Joan Crawford, and so much for our taste for Pepsi.

Of the many celebrity guests we interviewed during our days at WWL, the most engaging was Archbishop Fulton Sheen. His piercing, electric-blue eyes mesmerized us, as they did millions of his faithful viewers. Bishop Sheen was so exhilarating and brilliantly intelligent on his broadcasts that we were reticent about meeting him in person, especially considering the outcome of some of our former celebrity encounters. We were further impeded by the fact that we were not Roman Catholic; however, since the station was owned by the Jesuits of Loyola University, we had little chance to avoid an interview.

Late in the afternoon we were shown to his tenth-floor suite, where we sat briefly in an anteroom with a large window overlooking the city. Lights were beginning to click on in some of the buildings. A stream of light gushed along Canal Street, iluminating the street lamps mounted on giant green cross-shaped poles.

"Gee, Jan, think of all those Catholics who would give their souls to be here waiting to visit with Bishop Sheen!"

"We're so fortunate, Honey, we get to do some wonderful things."

The click of a door latch preceded the appearance of a priest dressed in a black cassock. "The Bishop is ready to see you, Mr. and Mrs. Carr."

The Bishop stood up as we entered the sitting room of his suite. Extending both hands in a gesture of welcome, he looked like the Jesus of children's Bible storybooks, except that he was dressed in bright crimson, signifying his station. His hands were warm and soft. He held tightly to our fingers longer than, initially, seemed comfortable. Commanding our attention, he smiled. "I am so pleased to meet you." He motioned to the sofa. "Would you like to sit together on the couch, across from me?"

"Yes, Sir," Jan replied uneasily. "Thank you, Sir, Your Highness, Your Honor."

My knees buckled at Jan's remark.

The Bishop chuckled. "Don't be nervous my dear, we are all children of God."

"Excuse me, Sir. There's no microphone," I said. "I thought you were supplying the recording equipment."

"Dear children, what we say here is between the three of us. What you wish to tell your listeners tomorrow is your prerogative."

I felt spiritually undressed as his steel blue eyes seemed to penetrate our innermost thoughts. He didn't wait for us to speak, but inquired about our marriage, our children, and our work. He was genuinely interested in our responses.

"Does anything worry you, my son?"

"It concerns me sometimes that we have so much and are so happy when millions have so little and are so miserable. I wonder what contribution we're making to the betterment of society."

"My boy, I know you're sharing your marriage and love with hundreds, indeed, thousands of listeners everyday. You're giving them inspiration by offering them the example of a moral way to lead their lives. You two have great influence. Use it wisely. Tell me more about yourselves."

"I'm sorry to say we're not Catholic," Jan confessed.

Her candor again caught me off guard. "Oh, don't be sorry, my dear. Do you believe in God?"

"Oh, yes, Sir. I believe in God."

"Do you know Jesus?"

"Well, yes, Sir, I know Jesus is the Son of God, who came to save us."

The Bishop spoke, "My dear child, you are a member of the Holy Catholic Church Universal, so fear not that you are not a Roman." The Bishop smiled, "You are one of God's children."

We talked for nearly a half-hour. As we got up to leave, Jan asked spontaneously if he would pray for us.

"My prayer for you two is that through your example, you will bring others to know the Lord. I am sure that's your destiny."

We bowed to him slightly and shook his hand, as we backed reverently out of the room, not knowing we could have knelt and kissed his ring. We walked silently to the elevator, savoring our very special experience.

Our life at WWL Radio was a revelation. After having spent five years on television in West Virginia, we were pleasantly surprised at how much we enjoyed radio. After the complexities of TV, we felt liberated by the newfound freedom radio presented: no director, floor manager or cameramen slowing our pace or giving frantic cues. Just the smiling face of our engineer.

Bill, as our Program Director and immediate supervisor, gave us free reign in choosing guests and deciding on our commentary, though he retained rather strict control over the music we played. Rock and Roll was making great inroads into all music; however, WWL had resisted the sound until Bill became P.D. Even then, his decision to program the new beat was often overridden by manager John Vath. Since Bill was our friend as well as our boss, he pressed us to try out some of the new-beat recordings rejected by other station personalities.

A new young singer on a promotional hype tour across the country was scheduled as a guest. Although unknown to Jan and me, Brenda Lee had been a child star for some time in Country and Western Music. Now, as a teenager, she was just crossing over into Pop and Rock. She appeared all by herself at our studio door on the appointed day, just as we were about to go on-the-air. We were totally unprepared for her diminutive size and her childlike demeanor. She didn't seem to be more than four foot ten. I gathered up two telephone directories to put on her chair so she could speak into the mike. Brenda was shy and very plainly dressed. While she spoke modestly about her current release, she was enthusiastic when she told us about a soon-to-be-released "platter" she had just cut back home in Nashville, which we would receive in a couple of weeks.

After the interview, the engineer played the song she had been sent to tout; it was pleasant but rather nondescript, much like Brenda herself. I remember thinking: *Brenda Lee, what an introverted, mousy little girl, hard to believe she could have a dynamic singing voice.* Less than a month later, during our program, our engineer called from the control booth into our studio saying Bill had just brought in the new Brenda Lee recording as a substitute for the Rosemary Clooney we had programmed. We said, "Okay," and the song was fed through our speaker as we closed our mikes.

A cadence of slow rock beat issued forth. Da dum da dum da dum. I could see Jan wince as the beat continued. Brenda Lee broke in over the beat, whining with great exuberance, "I'm sorry, so sorry...I made you cry last night." When the engineer opened our mikes at the end of the record, Jan exclaimed, "What was *that?*"

"Honey," I said, "that was Brenda Lee's newest record, the one she told us about when she was here last month."

"I think its awful! It sounds like Rock and Roll."

"Honey, it's not Rock. It's just part of the new beat."

"It *still* sounds awful to me." Speaking directly into her microphone, she continued, "I suggest you listeners write or call and tell us what *you* think."

"Honey, it's time for us to join CBS for the network news."

Bill stuck his head in the door. "Jan, don't criticize the station's music policy on the air."

Then he closed the door. It swung open again as Mrs. Senter, the Flower Lady, backed in with an armload of freshly cut flowers from her garden, which she invariably brought to us when guesting on our show. We had one more hour of program ahead of us.

When the program ended, Jan made haste straight to the control room. I switched on the intercom. Jan was asking the engineer for the recording of "I'm Sorry." Disk in hand, she marched directly into Bill's office. Recognizing her state of exasperation, he cut short his phone conversation.

"Well, Jan, Mrs. Stark on the switchboard says a lot of people have called to say they don't like the Brenda Lee record."

"Good for them!" Jan roared. "Here's what I think of it." Wham! Jan smashed the 45-record over the miniature Eiffel Tower paper weight on his desk.

"I've got five more copies," Bill said calmly, retreating back against his credenza as if to avoid further confrontation.

John Vath and I arrived at the office door at the same moment. "What seems to be the problem?" John asked politely, as was his style.

Jan began to cry. "I don't want our program ruined with that junky music. We've worked too hard to build an audience." Sobbing, she caught her breath. "We don't want to drive them all away."

John put his arm around Jan. "That's all right, dear, you won't have to play that record on your program anymore. We'll schedule it on the *Sid Noel Show* instead."

Jan had taken one of her many stands to keep the "Bob & Jan" image unblemished.

To tell the truth, I liked "I'm Sorry" and most of Brenda Lee's records, but I suppressed my opinion to keep peace until Brenda Lee finally became a household name on all popular music stations.

Several years later, Brenda was once again a guest on our program. This time she was starring at the Blue Room. I told her privately about the commotion "I'm Sorry" had caused. She got a kick out of the story. That night, Bill, Ann, Jan, and I saw her show. She is an incredible performer: quiet and shy off-stage but dynamite once the klieg lights flash on.

After several numbers, she announced, "Now, Ladies and Gentlemen, ah'd like to sing a medley of mah most recent hits, dedicatin' the first one, as a peace offerin', to Miss Jan Carr and her Program Director, Bill Romaine."

The Blue Room's Leon Kelnor Orchestra started the beat. Brenda drew the hand mike close to her mouth, looked straight at our table, and began to sing, "I'm sorry, so sorry…." At the end of the song, Brenda pitched a kiss in our direction; the four of us lifted our glasses in a toast to the dynamic God-given voice and the kind thoughtfulness of the diminutive star.

*   *   *   *   *

We occupied our little apartment on Dumaine Street for four-and-a-half months. Though we found the space very charming, Jan and I realized that the children needed more than the gallery as a play yard. We walked the streets of the Quarter seeking *For Sale* signs. Sunday mornings were spent scanning the *Times-Picayune* real estate listings, *Houses for Sale Below Canal Street*. "Below Canal" refers to property down stream or down river from Canal Street, the major thoroughfare bisecting the city. The French Quarter occupies the first thirteen blocks of land below Canal Street, so named for a planned canal, never built.

Sunday mornings were spent perusing the paper so that Sunday afternoons we could call about prices or visit open houses. There was very little on the market in the French Quarter in 1960, and what we found was always out of our price range. The few available houses were either too tiny or too dilapidated to be of interest. It became clear that we needed a real estate agent to help us find a place.

One day we wandered into the office of Marilyn Tate, a realtor whose signs proliferated throughout the *Vieux Carré*. Mrs. Tate was not in; nonetheless, a young man, Jeff Biddison, listened to our wishes patiently and with great resolve.

"You know, Mr. and Mrs. Carr, buying property in the French Quarter is very peculiar. Prices are high and banks and homesteads are very hesitant to extend loans on old houses, especially in the Quarter, which of course is a real shame because there are so many treasures that need to be saved. I'll be happy to help you look."

Jan and I were overjoyed at his interest.

"One other thing," he said, "are you sure you want to raise your children in the French Quarter?"

"Oh, yes," we chimed in unison.

"It's so historic," Jan continued, "we'd like the children to be part of it."

I spoke up. "We want the children to grow up realizing there are many different kinds of people in the world. The Quarter's a potpourri of humanity. We like that."

Jeff added, "Yes, artists and actors, drifters and debutantes, French aristocrats and old Italian families, and of course, young couples renovating houses and lots of single people."

Jan paused, thought for a few seconds, then asked, "Do you think some of those people are homosexual?"

Jeff smiled and gently answered, "I suppose so. Will that make a difference?"

"No, some of our dearest friends are like that, I think. I never could figure out what they do!"

Blushing, I quickly responded, "I wouldn't worry about it, honey."

Jeff chuckled at my embarrassment.

During the next couple of months, we looked incessantly at houses throughout the Quarter, finding nothing. Jeff showed us several places along Esplanade, the grand old avenue of the French-Spanish Creole aristocracy. Esplanade runs along the outer limits of the French Quarter, from the Mississippi River to the commemorative equestrian statue of Confederate General P.T.G. Beauregard overlooking Bayou Saint John. This natural bayou was the Tchoupitoulas Indians' canoe route into the old town of *Nouvelle Orléans*. We loved Esplanade Avenue with its imposing old mansions and rows of camphor trees, which when sniffed at close range smelled like rubbing liniment. Yet the Avenue seemed somehow a little too removed from the action of the French Quarter.

We were so depressed by not finding anything in the Quarter that we spent one whole Sunday looking at model homes in the suburbs of Metairie, Algiers, and Gretna. This made us even more depressed. The kids loved the newly built houses we looked at in the subdivisions, causing Jan and me to feel there was something wrong with us and our values. How could we want, so much, to live in a part of town many locals referred to as filthy, shabby and populated by deviants? We decided to give up our search for a while trying to distance ourselves from our dilemma.

One day, Jeff phoned us at the radio station. We were still on the air, so our colleague and newfound good friend Margie O'Dair took the message. Jeff had just heard of a house in the Quarter that might interest us. It was being probated in an estate, and though not yet on the market, he knew the heirs and had obtained their permission to show it. It would probably be in our price range; however, we might not be interested because it was located on Bourbon Street.

We had asked Margie to join us, since she was our expert on the Quarter, having grown up there.

"Did he say *which* house it is?" Jan and I asked repeatedly of Margie, as we strode briskly along.

"No, no," she kept repeating. "He only said it could possibly end up in your price range. *But* you might not be interested since it's located on Bourbon Street."

"I hope it's not too close to a queer bar," Jan lamented.

"Well," I chided, "it may be a toss-up who'll be our new neighbors—drunks, strippers, beatniks, Christian fanatics, or perhaps a straight macho wife-beater!"

"Bob, I'm getting scared. I hope we're doing the right thing." She reached out to hold my hand.

It was a warm, sunny May day, the kind New Orleans wears so well. Instead of the air being filled with humidity, it carried the fragrance of jasmine and honeysuckle. When the three of us trudged into Marilyn Tate's office, Jeff was on the phone with a client. Mrs. Tate offered us refreshingly cold iced tea, allowing us to catch our breath.

Hanging up the phone, Jeff ran his hand though his abundant light brown hair; his handsome, sensitive face grimaced in bewilderment. "Those damned homesteads are such a pain in the rear. They have absolutely no understanding of the historic value of lending money to restore a French Quarter building. Damn, damn, damn!"

He jumped up. "OK, come on along with me. One of the lawyers will let us in. God, I hate dealing through lawyers!"

Once out the door, we continued down Bourbon Street until we encountered a hollow-eyed elderly gentleman in a crumpled three-piece Haspel seersucker business suit waiting in the scorching sun. A wilted Panama hat shaded droplets of sweat trickling down his flaccid face. His brown and white saddle shoes were planted firmly on the granite stoop of the house, affording his feet a few inches of merciful shade.

"I'm Jeff Biddison. Are you Mr. de la Houssaye?"

"Yessir," he replied. "Ah have the keys."

Jan and I looked up at the house. It had shutters, balconies, wrought iron work—everything we'd dreamed of.

Mr. de la Houssaye spoke slowly and softly in a cultured Uptown drawl. "Ah can't fancy why anyone in they-a raht mind would want a rundown ruin lahk this, in such a Gawd-forsaken neighborhood as the ramshackled *Vieux Carré*!"

He struggled with half a dozen keys until the ancient lock finally yielded, permitting Mr. de la Houssaye to nudge open the front door with the help of his rather frail shoulder. Stepping from the bright warm afternoon sun into the cool, dim, and musty stillness of the house compelled us to squint until our pupils readjusted to the new surroundings. When my eyesight returned, I was able to make out the great front hall. My breath quickened at the scene.

I whispered to Jan and Margie, "Look at the beautiful stairway and the high ceilings! I love it already!"

Mr. de la Houssaye spoke, "Gawd damned hovel, in my opinion. The floors are a sight, the ceilin's fallin' down, and that stairway—an invitation for a heart attack!"

Mr. de la Houssaye warily eased himself onto a dusty Victorian settee that still resided in the long stair hall.

"Y'all wander around to your heart's delahght." He waved his fragile hand. "Jiss take care y'all don't fall through any rottin' floors!"

"Wouldn't you like to look around with us, sir?" Jan inquired.

"Dahlin', ah live in a Lakeview ranchhouse an' can see no good reason to tahr myself out climbin' through a place lahk this! Much obliged; nonetheless, ah'll jiss sit raht here and pass a rest."

We prowled through the house discovering one interesting room after another. There were double parlors with matching marble mantels. The dinning room had an antiquated gas chandelier, which appeared to be still operative. There was a small room with shelves from floor to ceiling, which looked as though it had served as a pantry or office. The room we assumed to be the kitchen consisted of only bare walls, several windows, a pump, and a dirt floor.

Jeff, always the optimistic real estate promoter, pointed out, "Gee, Jan, this could really be great with a little imagination!"

We discovered a funny little servants' stairway so completely filled with old *Times-Picayune* and *States-Item* newspapers and assorted ancient periodicals that it looked as if it had been used as a repository for the literary castoffs of some longtime disabled second-floor resident. Moving back to the front of the house, we made our way up the front steps, which sloped graciously to a second floor hallway identical to the one below. The staircase continued on to the attic.

Huge bedroom doors seemed to be everywhere.

"Oh, look, Bob, this could be our bedroom, and there's a place a bath could be built," Jan exclaimed.

"And look here, everybody," I indicated, "it opens right out onto a balcony over Bourbon Street."

"You'll hear the tourists kick over every garbage can in the neighborhood," Margie kidded.

"Yah, and we'll pour scalding water or molten lead on the vassals below," I exhorted, "just like Quasimodo at *Notre Dame* in the Middle Ages!"

"You'll be lucky if there's any water at all in this house," Margie teased once more.

We continued along the hall, with Jan instructing, "This can be Timmy's room, and this could be Tammy's, and this can be a room for live-in help."

"You sure have some grand ideas, honey."

"Grand ideas for a grand house, dahling, or at least it was once."

We looked in a couple of small rooms in the back wing, which Jeff and Margie referred to as the slave quarters, a term Jan and I still had to come to grips with, though the expression was used widely, even in newspaper ads, to describe that section of a house or building where enslaved house-servants once lived.

After investigating the attic, we jabbered enthusiasticly as we descended the stairs. Our chattering startled Mr. de la Houssaye, who had dozed off, apparently overcome by the warm, dusty, stale air permeating the house.

"Sooo, what y'all think?" Out of respect for the ladies he rallied to his feet.

"We love it," Jan and I bubbled enthusiastically.

Jeff butted in abruptly, "They think it's awful, then again—has possibilities!"

Mr. de la Houssaye pursed his lips, smoothed his rumpled seersucker trousers by pressing his flattened hands down along his fly, then patted the insides of his thighs, as if to cool his crotch. He reached for his hat as he spoke, "Ah think you young people need some guidance. Mah advice is that you oughta consider buyin' in Gentilly or maybe Metry. Gentilly would be nice if you ever have children."

"But we already have children," Jan blurted.

"Good Lawd." Shaking his head, he mumbled something like "it takes all kahnds!"

"I'll call you tomorrow, Mr. de la Houssaye," Jeff said, "after I've had a chance to discuss this property with Mr. and Mrs. Carr."

"Good Lawd! Maybe, jus' maybe, they'll come to their senses bah then. Maybe the problem of financin' a place lahk this'll keep 'em from makin' a horrible mistake, a horrendous mistake! Yes, the lack of financin', maybe that will be the remedy."

His voice drifted off as he shook his head in disbelief, rather like an accountant shakes his head when he discovers a mathematical error.

We bid *adieu* to Mr. de la Houssaye on the banquette in front of the house. He donned his hat, turned toward Esplanade, and disappeared around the corner.

"*How much,* Jeff?"

"I think it's in your price range, if you can get the down payment."

Jan and I were so excited we could hardly speak. We just stood and stared up at the house. We crossed over Bourbon Street to the other side and stared at it some more.

"What do we do next, Jeff?"

"Go home and eat!" he chided. "Tomorrow, I'll talk to de la Houssaye about the price and call around to homesteads about a loan and interest rates. You check with your folks about down payment money."

Jan wasn't content until she got her father on the phone back home in Colerain, Ohio. "But, daddy, it's just perfect, and it's right in the center of the historic section of old New Orleans, and you always said when we wanted to buy a house you would help us with the down-payment."

Jan was doing a rather successful job on her father. Dad Fitzsimmons, a mild mannered widower of many years, loved his two daughters deeply. He had never been to New Orleans so could only guess, from his Midwestern experience, what the historic area of New Orleans might be like. Jan neglected to mention the Bourbon Street location.

Daddy ultimately acquiesced to Jan's wishes, consenting to send us the same amount he had given her sister and brother-in-law, several months earlier, to purchase a split-level ranch house in the suburbs of Hartford, Connecticut, replete with its landcaped lawn. *If daddy only knew!*

The next morning, before our radio show, I anxiously phoned Jeff. He told us the heirs, who had been blocking the sale, were now ready to get rid of the place. Our price was right, and our down payment would be sufficient, if he could find a homestead that would take the mortgage. Of the eight calls he had made, no one wanted to even discuss property in "the Quarters," the term disdainful lenders used to refer to the area. He told me to tell Jan he would keep trying and not to lose faith; however, my heart was heavy, and Jan was in tears, until moments before we went on the air.

Our program opened with the Jack Jones upbeat rendition of "Wherever we go, whatever we do, we'll always do it *together*!" The music and lyrics gave us the lift we needed to get through the first hour of our show. The lyrics were so meaningful to us that we decided to make this song our radio theme.

During a station break, Margie stuck her head into the studio to announce that Jeff had called. "He thinks he's found a homestead to take the loan! You're to meet him at Mutual Homestead on Tulane Avenue at 3:30."

This was to be our first major loan, an enormous step for us. Terrified, we sat before the loan officer, who patiently, and rather sternly, explained the twenty-five-year terms.

My God, I thought, *I'll be over fifty before this is paid off.*

The loan officer continued, "Now, if your father, Mrs. Carr, sends you the amount you mentioned for the down payment and the C.A.B. gives your property a good appraisal, we should be able to strike a deal."

"What's the C.A.B., Sir?"

"Oh, that's the Central Appraisal Bureau. They appraise all property. We can give you a loan for eighty percent of their assessed value."

"What happens if the C.A.B. assessment is below the figure we talked about today?"

"Then, we'll not be able to give you a loan, unless you can come up with more cash."

"Oh!" we sighed, dumbfounded.

"But it's such a beautiful old house!" Jan explained, hoping to convince him by her optimistic air.

"Yes, ma'am, I'm sure it is. Still, I have found those old places in the Quarters are often rat- and termite-infested and quite dilapidated. So, Ma'am, we *must* rely on the C.A.B."

We spent an agonizing week and a half waiting for the results of the survey. Each day, Jan or I would call the real estate office, and each day Jeff or Mrs. Tate would caution us not to get our hopes up; appraisers, they warned again, don't take too keenly to Quarter property. In fact, many New Orleanians would like to see the French Quarter bulldozed to the ground and sprayed with disinfectant.

In the middle 1940s, just after the Second World War, there was a movement in the City Council to level the first three blocks of the Quarter from Iberville to Conti Street to make way for new retail space, offices, and parking. The plan was voted down in the Council Chamber by a slim margin, saving an untold number of historic buildings from demolition. Loving the Quarter as we did, it was hard for us to fathom how so many people failed to appreciate its historic, cultural, and commercial value to the city.

One evening, during this period of anxiety, we took the kids out to Fiorella's, a cheap po-boy sandwich shop down by the docks on Decatur Street. Jan and I ordered oyster po-boys fully dressed with extra ketchup, horseradish, and Tabasco. The kids said "yuk" to that, sticking instead to overcooked roast beef with—as we New Orleanians say—"my-o-nezz."

Sometime during the shank of the night, my fully-dressed oyster po-boy combined with my mounting anxiety over the house deal began to send off shock waves deep in my stomach. About 3 A.M., anticipating an attack of diarrhea, I slipped quietly and quickly from under the bed covers, clad only in my T-shirt, a carry-over from college days. I made my way hastily across the pitch-black room and vigorously swung open the john door. I narrowly missed Jan, who, unbeknownst to me, was sitting on the throne under the same affliction. Startled by my presence, she let out a terrified gasp so ear-piercing that I emptied my bowels onto the floor.

"How *wretched!*" Jan exclaimed.

"*Wretched* is hardly the word for it. *Shee-ty* is more like it. This has to be the shee-tiest experience I've ever had! This is hideous!"

In spite of myself, I began to laugh. Jan began to cry, then laugh through her tears.

"It's *wretched!*" she exclaimed again as she fled the scene, leaving me to clean up the damage.

"Where do you get old English words like wretched at a time like this?" I moaned in despair. She was out of earshot.

After a shower, I fell into bed. We slept soundly into Saturday morning until the phone rang.

"Bob, Bob, is that you?" Jeff asked from the other end of the line. "You sound awful!"

"It's me, it is I," I reported groggily.

"I'm at the office, just opened the mail. Looks like you kids bought a house! The C.A.B. is gonna be okay!"

I deliberately tightened my anal muscles to keep from having another accident.

"Bob, are you okay?"

"Yah, yah, I'm gonna be just fine, Jeff."

"What is it Bob, what is it?" Jan prodded, hearing a change come over me.

"It's okay! The C.A.B, it's okay!"

Jan began to cry in relief.

"Are you all right, honey?" I asked.

"Yes," she sobbed. Then she began to laugh. "Just don't you repeat last night's performance!"

"I won't, I put on *two* jockey shorts!"

Hiking up the bed covers, we threw our arms around each other and lay in a rapturous embrace until the kids, awakened by the phone, hurled themselves on top of us.

"What are you doing, mommy and daddy?"

"We're hugging each other, 'cause we're so happy."

"Well, why are you tho' happy?" Tammy asked, lisping as usual through her missing tooth.

"We're so happy because we're going to move to a house all our own like in Huntington," Jan explained.

"Where we gonna move to, mommy?"

Timmy quickly and authoritatively replied, "To Bourbon Street, booty-ah booty-ah. Heaven's sake, Tammy, haven't you been hearin' mommy an' daddy talkin' about that house on Bourbon Street, booty-ah booty-ah!" Timmy twisted and turned like a hoochee coochee dancer; Tammy broke into tears.

"What's the matter, honey?"

"I don't wanna move to Bourbon Threet an' become a thripper," she wailed plaintively.

"You won't be a stripper, honey," I assured her. "We'll make sure you become a sweet, Southern Lady, with a big hoop skirt, just like in the movies, okay?"

"I guess tho'," she replied, popping her thumb into her mouth while still heaving an occasional melancholy sigh.

Jan hugged her snugly.

Consumed with anticipation about our new house, renovation sugarplums danced through my head.

Hedy-Lee Farm Painesville, OH where Bob grew up

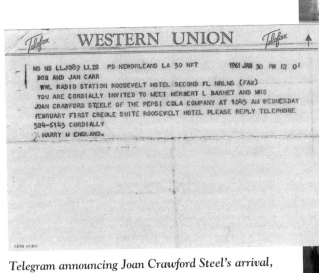

Telegram announcing Joan Crawford Steel's arrival,
1961

Bob& Jan at WWL-Radio, 1960

Seated at the Roosevelt Hotel's Plantation Room at a 1960 broadcast with Bob and Jan are local businessmen Walter Newberger, Allen Greenwood, Al Widmer, Bill Deane, Walter Bouché, William Songey and Wade Brownwell.

Timmy and Tammy enjoying their first Easter in the French Quarter, 1960

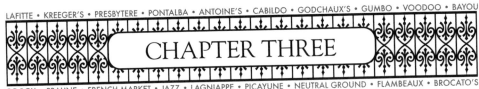

CHAPTER THREE

Olympia Washington, a Gift from Heaven

No matter where one chooses to buy a house, he runs the risk of eccentric neighbors. In the Quarter, however, eccentric neighbors are all but guaranteed. Of course, walls and iron fences protect one from physical contact, but vocal and visual contact are almost impossible to avoid. For instance, the day we moved into our house on Bourbon, we were greeted by one of our neighbors in a most startling manner. Standing behind the closed shutters of the open window in what was to be Timmy's room, we overheard a woman apparently hollering at us, or someone.

"You goddamn son of a bitch, why the fook don't you come out here where I kin see you? For Christ sake."

Jan looked aghast, while I, apparently the only one who knew what some of the words meant, couldn't help being intrigued. Although all the windows that would budge were open, we had left the shutters closed to keep the house cool and secluded from view. I peeped between the shutter louvers, a favorite habit of many Quarterites, in an effort to find the source of the racket. The second-story balcony of the house next door, with its long, floor-length French windows, was plainly visible across our courtyard. As I adjusted the louvers to get a better look, I totally understood the Rodgers and Hammerstein line, "Nosey folks will peek through their shutters and their eyes will pop."

Mine certainly did.

For there, half in the window and half out on the gallery, stood a haggard wench with a bottle in one hand and a broom in the other. She had the look of Lady Macbeth in her wilder moments, but the costume was quite different. *What a picture!* I thought. *How very Tennessee Williams: a balcony, a hag, a bottle, a broom, and a virtually transparent shorty-nighty. No virtuous Juliet, this one!*

As the woman continued cursing at a high pitch, Jan scrambled for a better view. Our combined weight was more than the shutters could bear. Without warning, they burst open banging against the sides of the house. The hag registered shock. I suppose the two of us did look rather preposterous, mashed together, hanging out of a second-story window with our eyes flashing wonderment.

As she drew her hands over her most vital parts, readily visible through the sheer shorty, she curtsied demurely, saying, "Oh, y'all must excuse me. You're not who ah expected."

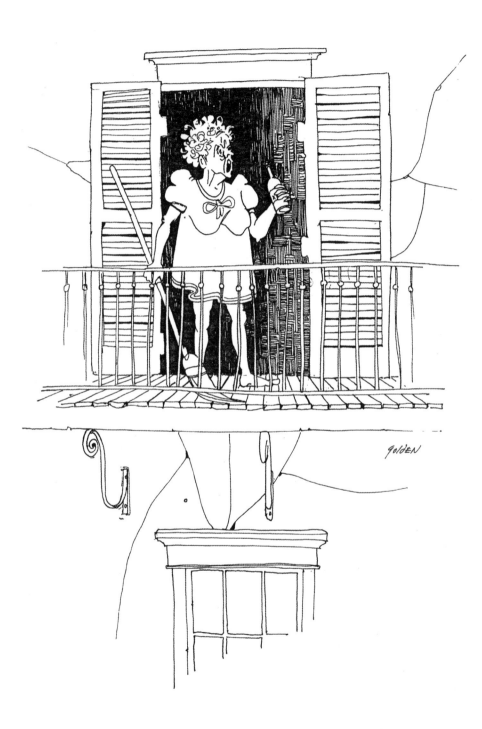

With that, she retreated through the French windows, never to be heard from again.

Jan and I always felt a little sad about that, for we thought we had discovered our own impious Blanche DuBois. We suspected, by her disappearance, she had been hauled in by the vice squad, surrendered to AA, or laid to rest in St. Louis Cemetery near other famous ladies of the evening.

Moving so soon again to a new place was very difficult, largely because we have always moved on a shoestring, doing most of the work ourselves. When Beverly and Jim, my sister and brother-in-law, helped us move by trailer to a college apartment in Pittsburgh, Beverly got pinned for half an hour between a couch and a newel post on a winding staircase to the third floor until we could locate extra help to release her.

Another time, we almost lost our lives, as well as our worldly possessions, when the trailer we were pulling came loose. It dropped down on the safety chains and began to head across the median of the Pennsylvania Turnpike, pulling the car along with it.

At times like those, we envied men who worked for large corporations that covered all their moving expenses and headaches. We were in New Orleans only six months and moving again! Ah, but this time, for the *first* time, it was to our own house, even if, to some unenlightened eyes, the house in question was a Bourbon Street wreck.

New Orleans is, of course, a tourist center. So it shouldn't have come as a surprise to us when a never-ending flow of visitors began to descend upon us from various parts of the country.

"Can you imagine Bob and Jan living on Bourbon Street in New Orleans?" was the chatter amongst relatives and friends.

We were never quite sure whether our out-of-state guests came to visit *us* or to gape at our bizarre environs; however, we were certain, once they'd been to *our* house, they would not soon forget their visit.

To live in the Quarter and be mistaken by the hawking barkers along Bourbon Street as a tourist is a mortal wound. On the other hand, to be pointed out by a tour captain to a busload of air-conditioned visitors as a typical Quarterite or Creole-type is met with great pride by us, "the natives," a group to which we finally felt we belonged.

Having settled into the house, we were able to continue one of our favorite after-dinner evening rituals, a jaunt over to *Café du Monde* at the French Market for coffee and beignets. It was an on-foot excursion for Jan and me but a Radio Flyer little red wagon ride for the children.

"Daddy, I'll get the wagon out o' the slave quarter an' bring it up to the side gate," Tim called from our makeshift kitchen.

"Timmy, you gotta fix us a cozy pwace in the wagon. I'll get the pill-wos and the banket to keep us comfy," Tammy yelled from the landing on the back stairway. In a short time, from the second floor balcony she hollered, "Hey, Timmy, you weddy? Catch!" She shoved the pillows over the balcony railing.

"Hurry up, Tammy, I'll make you the cozy place while you get Tate and Medea."

Medea was Tammy's three-and-a-half-foot, life-sized doll, which seldom wore clothes, *not because she's a fripper*, according to Tammy, *but because she doesn't have no arms left to hold them on*. Tate, on the other hand, was about two inches tall and Tim's favorite Teddy, given to him by his adopted *Vieux Carré* aunt, Marilyn Tate.

"OK, Tammy, push 'em over, I'll catch," Timmy commanded.

Over the rail went little Tate, followed momentarily by Medea.

On a prior evening, when Tammy had just shoved Medea off the balcony, we received a frantic call from the new young tenant in an apartment over the sidewall, declaring one of the children had just pushed the other off the second floor balcony. She explained she didn't know whether to call *us* or an ambulance. I thanked God, *and* her, for calling *us* instead of the emergency service. And I went on to explain to her about Medea.

Timmy, Tammy, Tate, Medea, a blanket, and two pillows were huddled in the wagon, ready to go. Opening the side gate, I pulled my little cargo out into the real world of Bourbon Street, booty-ah, booty-ah, as the kids loved to say. The courtyards and patios of the Quarter offered a solitude and fragrance that differed from the streets, which displayed a pungent scent and undulating pulse all their own.

"Daddy, please, please, can't we go *way up* Bourbon tonight?" Tim pleaded.

"Yah, daddy, pooeez, pooeez," chimed Tammy.

"Well, I don't know..."

"Oh, please, daddy, remember Tammy won *last* time."

We had a little game going. About once every two weeks, we would walk all the way up the Bourbon strip on one side and back on the other. From the wagon, the kids would count as many strippers as they could spot through the swinging doors. The one counting the most got an extra beignet at Café du Monde.

Jan, not particularly pleased by the game, still gave in to my whim. Actually, she loved to watch, as much as I did, the expressions on the faces of the Midwestern tourists when, straining to see the strippers, out-of-towners occasionally stumbled over our little family outing. The shock of seeing us pulling along a wagonload of dolls and children provoked a wide variety of comments.

"Look at *that*, can you imagine!"

"Isn't that *sweet*?"

"Do you suppose they're the parents? Wonder if they're married?"

"Now isn't that just *awful*, think how demented those children will be!"

"Oh, well, you can't expect much more from beatniks and communists."

"Only in New Orleans!"

One night on the way home from our Café du Monde trip, Jan and I ran into one of the couples who lived in the building next door to ours. They were sitting at the bar just inside Lafitte's Blacksmith Shop. We wanted to see them for a minute about some vines that were clogging our gutters. I edged the wagon up to the front door under the gas lantern so we could keep our eyes on the children who had fallen asleep. Medea was hanging half out of the back of the wagon with her hair nearly trailing on the ground. Tim was resting comfortably against her, while Tammy, sucking sporadically on her thumb, was propped half-erect against Timmy's knees and partially covered by the blanket.

We stepped just inside Lafitte's to speak to Jerry and Gladys. As usual, the Blacksmith Shop was dimly lit with red table candles; no one passing by outside could see us. It hadn't dawned on us that the children looked as if they were all alone in front of the bar.

We realized there was a traffic jam on narrow Bourbon Street when we heard automobiles honking. Some well-meaning lady, whose car brandished an Iowa license plate, had made her husband stop in the middle of the street so she could find a policeman, "to save those dear babies." I found it impossible to convince her I was the father and the children were completely happy and would stay that way, especially if she would keep from waking them up. She was even more upset when neighbor Jerry stepped outside in his bikini bathing trunks. Jerry and Gladys were actually on their way to a pool party in the next block.

At this point, with the taxi drivers and assorted motorists showing increasing impatience on their horns, Tim rallied briefly and said, "Daddy, I counted more strippers than Tammy!" Then he lapsed back into sleep.

The lady from Iowa was so undone, *she* collapsed back into her Chevy Impala, demanding that Elmer, whom we assumed was her husband, get her out of this den of deviants!

* * * * *

Growing up in Ohio, Jan and I had always attended public schools, so it seemed natural that we would educate our children in the same manner. We arranged a meeting with the principal of William Frantz Public School about ten blocks away on St. Claude Avenue, just outside the Quarter. The school secretary ushered us into the office of the principal, a pleasant, full-faced man in his late forties. We gave him the details of our life and the expectations for the children. We were taken back when he suggested a private school might be a better option. He told us the civil rights storm was boiling and when Washington mandated integration in the New Orleans school system, violence could break out.

His prediction came to pass several months later; federal marshals drove little first-grader Ruby Nell Bridges, a black child, and her mother, to that same Frantz School. Other area schools were also integrated, but little Ruby Nell was alone at Frantz. *The Picayune, States-Item* and the broadcast media made much of the volatile unfolding story. Even Norman Rockwell depicted the ruckus for the cover of the *Saturday Evening Post*. Jan and I were brought to tears as we watched TV's coverage of angry whites catcalling profanities at the brave and stoic six-year-old. We fretted over how we would have handled ourselves if Timmy and Tammy had been students there. Our hearts were heavy for many months.

The Frantz principal had given us an alternative, and with a certain amount of guilt, we took it. He told us he had heard good things about a small private school in the 700 block of Esplanade Avenue.

We couldn't bring ourselves to jeopardize the children's safety or gamble with their education, so we made a decision that would forever affect our children's lives.

"This is Timmy, he'll be in kindergarten, and this is Tammy, she'll be in nursery school." Jan was speaking to Miss Edna, the headmistress and owner of *La Petite Ecole*. The little school was located in an 1850s Creole townhouse on the Uptown side of Esplanade Avenue, between Royal and Bourbon. Miss or Mrs. Edna Wilson, I never quite knew which, was a lovely, lean, Junior League-ish looking woman who had created and for several years operated *La Petite Ecole*. She had gained considerable acclaim as an educator not only in the *Vieux Carré* but throughout the rest of the city as well.

The success of the school was based on its warm, touchy-kissy attitude and rather free and loose classroom approach—*loose* in the sense of careless abandon, not so much in the moral sense, although I occasionally wondered who was touching and kissing whom, and *where*, not so much in the geographical sense, but in the anatomical sense. In fact, Timmy came home from school three times with his fly open, throwing Jan into hysterics. Having grown up in a family with only a sister, she was poorly schooled in the goings-on of little boys. I tried to explain to her it was probably the result of one of two things: either he had been playing doctor in the patio behind the school after classes, or, most likely, he had forgotten to zip up as he dashed out of the boy's lavatory, after straining on tip toes, trying to steady his stream into the wall urinal almost out of the reach of a kindergartener.

"Of course, Jan, there's always the chance that he was playing with his…"

"Oh, Bob, that's a horrible thought. Stop at once!"

"Well, boys will be boys! I remember when I was a kid, my friend Leo Hill, the sixth of nine children and the only boy, would leave his fly open just so his mother would pay attention to him."

Timmy always made friends very quickly. In less than a week he had organized a gang of pals: Pierre, the Creole from Esplanade, the Avenue of fading aristocratic Creole mansions; Kelvin, the suburbanite, from newly developed Pines Village; and Mark, the downtowner from the Ninth Ward, a voting district downstream from the industrial Canal where people speak in a New Orleans accent, famous as an immediate cousin to Brooklynese.

Timmy, Pierre, Kelvin, and Mark became habitual friends. Each of the four pals had something different to contribute, but they all loved to play soldier. Timmy was the only one of the gang who did not have to be car-pooled to and from school. Since the boys lived several miles apart, occasionally the mothers would arrange an overnight stay. If they were coming to our house, *Mercedes*, still with us temporarily, would pick them up at school. When she arrived at the front stoop of the school, she would invariably engage in a boastful conversation with some of the other black maids about her babies. "They bees the most darlin'est chilrin ah ever did know!"

* * * * *

The day Olympia came to work for us was the kind of day when miracles are made. There was a presence about her the moment she walked into the house. She was lean and tall, well over six feet. *Watusi, I* thought, as I looked up into her astute eyes, her dark brown face punctuated by an engaging smile, her pleasant Southern voice and gentle though firm manner leading me to believe this woman was going to be a part of our children's history.

With Jan and me both working, it was essential to have someone with the children in whom we had total confidence, someone who would care for them not as hired help but as a part of the family.

As Yankees, Jan and I were finding it rather difficult to adjust to some Southern ways.

It was 1960, and even though schools, buses and streetcars had been desegregated, many customs still existed that we found strange and hard to accept. Sometimes even the terminology seemed to be a repugnant.

We had told some of our newfound friends and business associates we were looking for a woman to take care of the children.

"Oh, you want a maid!" they'd say.

In our Ohio upbringing the term "maid" had been reserved for people who worked in hotels or household employees of the very rich. It was difficult for us to use the term "maid" when referring to our own life. Somehow, the thought of hiring a maid put us into a category in which we didn't feel quite comfortable. Although we had noticed numerous of our friends referred to their hired woman as "my maid," it seemed even more surprising to us when those friends' *children* referred, very possessively, to the hired woman as "My maid."

The term "the maid" seemed palatable—that is, it seemed like a description of a person doing a job, even if it wasn't quite the job we intended—but the addition of the possessive pronoun had connotations that we wanted nothing to do with. Whomever we hired, I never wanted to hear the children refer to the woman as "mine" or "my maid."

Jan and I sat down with Olympia around a small table in the front parlor to discuss working for us. Olympia's discerning eyes darted around the room surveying the grandeur *and* the unrestored aspects of the house. Jan was more nervous interviewing Olympia than she had been during her brief encounter with Joan Crawford.

"Mercedes has told us you're like a sister to her and a wonderful woman. Do you know anything about caring for *little* children?" Jan asked nervously.

Olympia's smile grew wide, and her dazzling teeth and eyes sparkled brightly in contrast to her bronze face.

"Mizz Cahr, ah done raised up many a chile, some mah own and some others. I'm not an educated woman, ah come up on a farm, but there's one thing ah knows about, and that's about mindin' chilrin. And, ah can say this, ah'm proud o' those chilrin ah raised up! They never gave me one ounce o' trouble, not my own and not those o' other people. You love 'em and they gonna love you back."

Jan's eyes grew bright with interest.

"That's quite a record," I interjected. "What's your secret?"

"Like ah says, Mistah Cahr, *love*. That's the basic. But, ah guess there's more to it then that. You gotta be steady wit chilrin, ah means like bein' reg'lar. If you're gonna be stern, you gotta stay stern. You cain't be playin' games wit chilrin all the time. They'll find it out, and they'll take 'vantage of ya. Best thing ah ever loined from my Ahntee, who raised me up in the country, was when ya says somethin' ya stays by it, or ya don't speak it at all. Ya gotta be honest and steady wi' chilrin. *That*, an' *love*, they the most 'pohtant 'gredience!"

"You sound like a mighty wise woman."

She laughed audibly as she relaxed slightly into her chair. "Well, Mistah, nobody ever tole me ah was wise befo'." She laughed again. "But, people have said ah know somepin' 'bout raisin' up chilrin. Ah won't say it's always easy. My oldestest boy, who now stays in California, well, he gave me some big grief, but he's fahn now. Then there was the Gervais chilrin. That oldest boy, he was some difficult, an' he's fahn now. Ah'm really gonna miss that boy. Sorry they had ta move back over to the Mississippi Goff Coast."

Obviously captivated, Jan asked, "Does that mean you would be available to come to work for us?"

"Yes, Ma'am, I'd be 'vailable, bu-ut…" She stretched the word into two syllables and glanced down.

"Bu-ut, what?" Jan asked, so captivated by Olympia that she found herself mimicking her pronunciation.

"Well." Olympia glanced back up at us. "Ah wouldn't be 'clined to go to work any place where ah din't have a chance ta git 'quainted wit those chilrin who gonna be in mah care."

"The children are at nursery school right now."

"Well, ma'am, 'at's too bad."

"I've got an idea," I said. "I was just about to go pick up the kids at school. If you have the time, why don't you walk over to the school with me? I'll introduce you to Timmy and Tammy and let you walk them back home. That way you can chat with them while you're walking along and it will give me a chance to run over to the hardware store to pick up a couple of things I need for Saturday. When we get back here, you and Mrs. Carr and I can spend a few minutes together, before you go home to think about it."

"Ah'll do that. Yes, Sir, ah'll do that," Olympia cheerfully replied, showing a healthy enthusiasm.

I was elated. *This woman is much wiser and more intelligent than her lack of education at first revealed. She is like Jan's grandmother, who though not afforded the opportunity of higher education, had learned brilliantly through life experience.* Grandma, the eldest of five, had to quit school to take care of her siblings, while her widowed mother, whose husband died of pneumonia after the Civil War, was forced to work as a housekeeper for a rich family on the hill to make enough money to feed her children. Like Grandma, Olympia had learned the niceties of life through a kind of trickle-down social osmosis.

Olympia and I walked down Bourbon Street to Esplanade. The afternoon sun glared off the colorful facades of the mishmash of hundred-year-old buildings.

"Mistah Cahr, ah never did spend much time in these French Quarters. It's a kinda strange place. All these houses 'long here, nice as where you stay?"

"Gosh, Olympia, some are and some aren't, I guess."

We turned right toward the school passing in front of the Baptist Mission with its array of bedraggled, stoop-settin' winos. Olympia's glance registered consternation.

"Most colored people don't spend too much tahm in 'the Quarters'. Fact, people by my house tell me dey got some o' the strangest white people in the French Quarters they ever did see!"

"I suppose. You know it takes all kinds of people to make up the world."

"Yes, Sir, an' that's fo' sure, all *kinds* o' people. Don't make me no mind, long's they ain't mean. Cain't stand no mean people."

As we approached *La Petite Ecole*, a burst of children flooded through the front door. Vehicles lined Esplanade, driven by parents carpooling their children away from the Quarter to the suburbs: Gentilly, Metairie, and Lakeview. *La Petite Ecole* had become one of the *in* places to send young children. It was considered a school of free spirit where 'The Arts' were stressed. Training in French was mandatory, even in toddler classes. The course of study appealed to young suburban parents who hoped that someday, by virtue of their social and educational credentials, their children would find their way into the "proper" Mardi Gras organization or private club.

Tammy came running out. As soon as she saw me, she dashed to my side, threw her arms around my pants' leg, and immediately put her thumb in her mouth. Olympia, towering above me, leaned over to say hello. Tammy frowned, sucking harder on her thumb.

"Hah, Mizz Tammy. Ah'm Olympia. Can you shake mah hand?" Olympia stretched out her big brown hand.

Tammy's arms squeezed tightly around my leg; her little fist plunged deep into her mouth.

"Tammy, can't you say hello to Olympia? She's very nice and she might come and stay with us."

Tammy held tight, backing around behind me, away from Olympia.

"Daddy, daddy," Tim hollered from the front door as he and another youngster came dashing over.

"Daddy, daddy, you remember my friend, Pierre? His grandfather was a general in the war 'gainst the Yankees, an' he wants me to come over and play Saturday. Can I go? Daddy, please, can I go? He's gonna show me part of his grandfather's 'federated uniform. Can I go? Can I go?" he persisted, jumping up and down.

I felt a bit uneasy at the mention of the Civil War in front of Olympia.

"Where do you live, Pierre?" I asked.

"Out Esplanade near City Park, but it's too far to walk from here, Mistah Carr."

"Okay, I think it'll be all right. Why don't you have your Mommy call Mrs. Carr to make sure?"

"Okay, Okay," he replied, dashing off and into the back of an eight-passenger station wagon.

"Timmy, this is Olympia. Olympia…" I paused, realizing I didn't know her last name. "Excuse me, Olympia. I don't know your last name." *Had I dehumanized her by not asking her last name much earlier?*

"Well, Sir, ever'body mostly calls me Olympia, septin' at my church where ah be Mizz Washington."

"If you come to work for us, don't you think the children should call you Mrs. Washington?"

Olympia smiled a big grin. "Lawd, Mistah Cahr, those chilrin call me Mizz Washington, ah'd be 'barassed to death."

Tammy still had her arm around my leg; Timmy, however, greeted Olympia with an enthusiastic smile. "You gonna be me and Tammy's *maid?*"

I winced.

"Why, ah don't know, Mistah Timmy. We gonna see 'bout dat."

"Timmy," I interrupted, "I have to go to the hardware store and mommy's waiting at home, so Olympia's going to walk you and Tammy back to the house."

Tammy swung even farther behind me, so far that she pushed between my legs and came out on the other side, bumping into Olympia's highly-starched white uniform, which crackled like a brand new grocery bag.

Olympia stooped down beside Tammy and looked her straight in the eye. "Chile, that looks like the best-tastin' thumb anyone ever nursed."

Tammy plunged the thumb even farther into her mouth, almost covering her whole fist.

"Can ah take a look at dat thumb, Mizz Tammy, an' fine out what tastes so good?"

Tammy scowled; Olympia responded by turning on her biggest smile. Tammy slowly pulled her fist away, revealing her wizened thumb, which she turned around and pointed up toward Olympia.

"Umm, dat thumb looks *some* good. Ah tell ya what, baby, you walks home wi' me an' ah'll show you how to put that thumb in some jella and make it taste even better, lahk candy!"

Olympia reached out her long arm and took Tammy by the hand. Tammy acquiesced. Olympia reached out her other hand toward Timmy.

"Oh," he said, "you don't need to take my hand. I'm old enough to walk by myself. My friend Mark never takes *his* maid's hand, and we're the same age."

"Fine by me," Olympia replied, "how'ver, you make certain you stays by mah side."

Tammy slowly eased her other arm from around my leg as I pulled away. "Okay, kids, I'll be home in about 15 minutes. You show Olympia the way back to the house."

Later, Olympia related in vivid detail what had transpired on their walk home from school: The three of them started toward Bourbon, Timmy jumping over each crack in the sidewalk along the way.

"Whatcha doin', boy?"

"Step on a crack, ya break your mother's back!"

Trying to avoid a crack, Tammy stumbled suddenly, catching herself around Olympia's long, slender leg.

"That's all right, chile, you hold on an' we'll try ta miss all them cracks. You likes school?"

"Gynastics," Tim was quick to reply.

"What'sat, boy?"

"Gynastics. You know, like tumblin' an' somersaults." With that, he rolled over in a somersault on the sidewalk.

Olympia reprimanded him gently. "You gonna hurt yo'self on that *cee*-ment. 'Sides, you got yo' good clothes on, young man. You jiss wait'll you git home to do those ackabatics."

"Okay," Timmy consented drolly.

At Bourbon Street the trio turned toward home.

"You lahk schoo', Mizz Tammy?"

Tammy garbled an answer past her thumb.

"Chile, ah cain't understand you wi' that thumb in yo' mouth. You gotta take that thumb out yo' mouth so ah can know what you sayin'."

Pulling her thumb out of her mouth, Tammy responded, "I like thissors."

"Thissors! What they be teachin' you in that schoo'?"

Timmy butted in. "She means *scissors*; they take scissors and cut out the A B C's so they can learn their alphabet. Tammy likes it, but me, I thought it was kinda boring myself."

"S'not boring!" Tammy said emphatically, looking across the front of Olympia's starched uniform.

"Well, it's boring to *me!*" Timmy rebuked. "Gynastics is a lot more 'citin'."

"You lahk anything else in schoo', Mizz Tammy?"

"I like Kitchen Time."

"Yuk!" Timmy interrupted. "That's *really* girls' stuff."

"What's Kitchen Time?"

"That's when we peetend we cook."

"You lahk to cook?"

"Uh huh. I peetend it all the time."

"Well, maybe ah can show you how to cook fo' real."

"Can you cook pralines?" Tammy asked.

"Shore ah can cook prah-leens, and ah can cook red beans an' rice, an' gumbo, an' all that good stuff. Ah'll show you how to cook all those good things."

"Lympia, you really know how to cook gumbo?" Timmy asked.

"Bin cookin' gumbo all mah life."

"My mommy cooked gumbo one day. She put okra in it and it was so slimy, it looked like snot."

Olympia chuckled.

"Timmy, you're not 'sposed to say snot," Tammy chastised.

"Well, it *did!* It looked just like *green* snot. Made me sick to my stomach. Mommy said we had to eat it 'cause she spent four hours makin' it. I was really worried 'cause I thought we was really gonna have to eat it. Then daddy came home, looked at it, and said we'd all go out to Bud's Broiler for hamburgers, 'cause that stuff looked like slime!"

Olympia laughed again as the threesome approached Barracks Street.

"Timmy, you take my han'."

"Why I gotta take your hand?"

"'Cause we gonna cross the street an' *you* gonna hold onto my han'."

Her voice commanded authority. Timmy reached up and took hold of her hand and held onto it until they reached the other curb, where he immediately shook lose. They walked silently for several steps.

Timmy looked up and said, "You know, I can walk across the street all by myself. I'm old enough."

"Ah'm shore you can; how'ver, when you wi' *me*, you hold my han'."

"Oh." Timmy mulled it over for a few moments. "Mark's maid doesn't make him hold *her* hand when *he* walks across the street."

"Chile, ah cain't speak for Mark's maid," Olympia flashed back, "how'ver, if ah'm gonna be yo' maid, *you* gonna hold my han'! An' that's the way it's gonna be, dahlin'!"

Tammy squeezed Olympia's hand even tighter as they crossed the last street. Once across, Timmy broke loose, ran to the front door and rang the doorbell. Jan opened the door just as Olympia and Tammy were catching up. In the front hall Timmy stood defiantly with his arms folded across his chest. Olympia came up the front steps with Tammy still hanging on tightly to her large hand.

"Mommy," Timmy asked pointedly, clearly for Olympia's benefit, "if Lympy is my maid, do I have to hold her hand when I walk across the street?"

Olympia glanced down at Timmy to make eye contact, waiting for Jan's response. Jan, well aware of Timmy's tactics, knew her answer could very well be the pivotal factor in Olympia's decision to take the job.

"Timothy, if Olympia is here to take care of you, you're supposed to do what she says because *she* will be the boss."

"But, mommy, that's not fair. Mark's maid don't make him hold her hand when he walks across the street."

"It doesn't make any difference about the woman who takes care of Mark. If you're with Olympia, and she wants you to hold her hand to cross the street, you hold her hand. She's the boss. When you can show her you can walk across the street safely by yourself, I'm sure she'll let you do it."

Olympia looked both satisfied and relieved at Jan's response.

"Lympy's gonna show me how to cook, mommy, and she told me if I showed her my thumb, she'd show me how to make it taste really good."

"Really?" Jan replied quizzically.

"Oh, Lawdy, Mizz Cahr, ah don't mean to take anymore o' your time, but do you have any jella in the kitchen?"

"I don't know. Come on out and we'll see."

Reluctantly, Timmy followed them into the kitchen. He was still sizing up Olympia, not yet sure whether he was going to take to her stern measures. Jan found a box of Jell-O, which Olympia carefully opened, emptying nearly half the package into a tiny bowl.

"Now, Miss Tammy, put that thumb o' yours in your mouth and get it nahs and wet."

When Tammy pulled out her thumb, Olympia took her hand and put the thumb down into the Jell-O powder and rolled it around. "Alright, chile, now put dat thumb in yo' mouth."

Tammy did as Olympia instructed; she grimaced at the bittersweet taste.

"Now don't dat taste *some* good?"

Tammy nodded affirmatively without removing her thumb.

"I wanna do that, too," Timmy insisted.

"Well, boy, wet yo' thumb an' stick it in that powder."

Jan decided it looked so good she did the same thing.

I walked in from the hardware store and was startled to see the *three* of them, all standing with their thumbs in their mouths. "What're you *doing?*"

"Daddy, look." Tammy held up her purple thumb. "This is 'licious."

I couldn't resist sampling it myself. The taste reminded me of how, when I was a kid, we used to put Jell-O powder into a shot glass and then stick our tongue into it and suck on it for hours.

"Well, Olympia," Jan said. "I guess we've kept you long enough."

"Yes, Olympia, I hope you had a chance to get acquainted with the children on the way home from school. Why don't you call us tomorrow?"

"Who's gonna pick the chilrin up from schoo' tomorrow?" Olympia asked.

"Gee, I don't know. We haven't thought that far ahead."

"Well, Mistah Cahr, if it'd be aw-right wit you and Mizz Cahr, *ah'll* be most glad to pick up da chilrin."

"Sounds good to me. All right with you, honey?"

"That would be wonderful!"

Tammy threw her arms around one of Olympia's long, dark legs. Timmy, on the other hand, reserved his enthusiasm for now.

"What about pay, Olympia? How much do you charge?" I asked.

"Whatever you think is fair, Mistah Cahr."

"But, Olympia, you need to give us an amount."

"You can't put a price on love, Mistah Cahr; when ah comes here to tend yo' babies, they gonna be *our* babies, what you pay me not gonna make any difference. You an' Mizz Cahr good people, I can see that. You'll be fair."

We never had any further negotiations. Olympia was about to become an indispensable part of our family.

Thanks be to *Gawd*, Olympia took charge of the house and the children. During the first week, Tammy clung relentlessly to her side, one hand clutching the hem of Olympia's uniform while she pressed the other to her lips and savored her Jelloed thumb.

Timmy, meanwhile, maintained his distance. His aloofness was soon shattered by Olympia's announcement that she was taking the kids fishing after school. The three of them would have a picnic supper on the Lake Pontchartrain floodwall, where she could teach Timmy everything she knew about catching fish. Blessed by the gods with a talent for dealing with children, Olympia easily won over her unsuspecting victim.

With the kids away for the evening, Jan and I relaxed over TV dinners in our sparsely-furnished front parlor. Our heavy work schedule at the radio station had given us precious little time to do much house renovating. We loved our house passionately, every cracked crown-molding, every chipped wainscoting, even the sluggish toilets, with water reservoirs hung high above their worn and splintered oak seats.

Jan startled my calm with a burst of enthusiasm, nearly causing me to topple my flimsy TV table, exclaiming, "Bob, let's have a big party before we fix up the house! That way, all of our curious friends can get a look at the *before*."

"Honey, are you sure?"

"I'm positive. That way, everyone can see what a wreck it is now. A year from now, if it's still a wreck, they'll be used to it; although I hope in a year it will look like a partially-restored mansion. Besides, we've made so many new friends and acquaintances, it's time we entertained. We owe lots of different people."

"You have a point, honey. At least now our friends' expectations won't be too grand. Okay, let's do it. It'll be great fun! Lordy, remember the electrician warned us not to use too many lights at one time, until we upgrade the electric power."

"No problem, women always look better in candlelight, anyway. Let's make it a real Southern dress-up affair."

"Dinner jackets?"

"That might keep some of the fellows from coming - but at least cocktail dresses."

"We better start looking up phone numbers."

"I think it would be more fun to send out printed invitations, something unusual."

"Great idea, honey. How about something a little *risqué*, like "The Madam Jan, along with her consort, Bob, requests the pleasure of your desires at the opening of her new *house* on Bourbon Street." Or maybe "You are invited to the House of Desire on Bourbon. 8 o'clock till. RSVP your desires."

"Honey, whatever you want," Jan replied with resignation.

For several weeks we had been dickering with the plumbers about the cost of replacing the pipes and fixtures in the bathrooms. Money was always a consideration, but the sewer-pipe terminology in New Orleans plumber dialect perplexed us both. "Terlet" we translated to toilet. But having to pay nearly a hundred dollars for "zinc" seemed outrageous. After much discussion, Di Cristina's head plumber brought us a pamphlet which showed the "zinc" we would be buying. We were astonished and relieved to learn that "zinc" was New Orleans-speak for *sink*. Once we made ourselves understood to one another, we told the plumbers to start the project as soon as possible.

However, the unexpected happened the very morning of our party. While Jan and I were still at the radio station, the plumbers came to the house and ripped out every pipe in sight. Jan and I arrived home to find Olympia in a dither.

"Mizz Cahr, by the tahm ah caught on to what those plumbermen was up to, it were too late to stop 'em, but they left me 'structions on how to flush the commode. Jis fill a pail o' water at the spigot by the front gate, 'cause that's the onlyest water runnin', then haul it upstairs to keep by the commode. After a person's relieved therself, they pour that water into the commode till everthin's gone! But Mistah Cahr, they's jis one problem, how you gonna keep enough water on hand durin' da party, to keep da commode flushin' proper-like?"

"Gosh, Olympia, why didn't they fill up the bath tub before they tore out the pipes?"

"I axst 'em that, Mistah Cahr. They said they fo' got, till it were too late."

"Damn," I muttered, trying not to let Olympia hear me. She never used profanity.

So to fill the tub, Timmy, Tammy, and I performed a bucket brigade from the front gate on Bourbon Street to the bathtub on the second floor. Alas, the buckets had to be sand-pails so the kids could handle them.

"Timmy, you take the first lap along Bourbon from the faucet to the front door. Tammy, you hold the door open, and I'll take the pail up the stairs to the tub."

The two kids looked on this activity as a lark and were amazingly efficient for three- and five-year-olds. A little less spilling and a little more concentration could have cut our time considerably; however, the children's efforts were most gallant and a good training exercise.

Disregarding the schooling of rich ladies in the proper etiquette of Emily Post, our parties have been most successful when we invited a cross-section of society. That way, one may congregate with one's own peers or stand back and make cracks about unknown and unfamiliar guests. In New Orleans, a host is able to bring together a larger variety of invitees than in most cities. The Beat Generation Quarterites, who usually shunned razors, launderettes, and employment, were almost always available on a moment's notice for liquor at *your* house. Since they were often self-appointed experts on a wide variety of local and worldly subjects, their most important role was to keep the conversation going, for they were always either talking or being talked about. I recall one spacey guest who talked to himself in our peer mirror for half an evening. Later in the week, he phoned to ask, "Who was that kind and intelligent chap I met at your house?"

There were the "restorer" types, usually an older and more genteel group that made the preservation of the Quarter its life's cause. A few of these were a must to mingle with the Uptowners and Suburbanites who were convinced that the Quarter was filled with nothing but strippers, queers, beatniks, and old Italian holdovers from the Sicilian immigration of the early 1900s.

The Uptowners were from the *fahn-old families* along oak-lined State Street and St. Charles Avenue. This group claimed it would consider living in "The Quawtah" if doing so weren't guaranteed to make *grand-mère* and *grand-père* roll over in their mausoleums. One had to be aware the Uptowners might consider attending a Quarter party to be "slumming."

Some of our best friends were Suburbanites, yet we didn't want our daughter to marry one! Our showbiz friends, a must, were difficult to classify. They ranged from *prima donnas* to "queens" who could be counted on for grand entrances and exits. Broadcaster friends were unreliable guests because they were usually working, making personal appearances, or sleeping. Foreigners, doctors, and professors, added a little class, but they weren't any more dependable than the broadcasters, though foreigners and professors could be counted on to eat you out of house and home.

We had discovered that the easiest, cheapest, and classiest way to give a big party was to start at the American Rent-All Company. Rather inexpensively, we could fill our dining room with silver, crystal, and china for the night. Instant class! And we could even "charge it, please."

American Rent-All's grand silver champagne fountain would serve as our centerpiece. It would be filled with the *Beverage de la Maison*, 2/3 sauterne and 1/3 soda. When the party was off to a sparkling start, we could switch to 1/3 sauterne and 2/3 soda for a little bubbly. The expensive catered *hors d'oeuvres* would be doled out sparingly, but we kept chips, dips, and nuts well-stocked. In the final analysis, it wasn't the eats or drinks that made or broke a party, it was the interaction between the guests.

With Timmy and Tammy ushered off for the night to friends Uptown, which they considered "the country," Jan, Olympia, and I braced for our guests. Jan was setting out each and every wedding-present ash tray and coaster we possessed, endeavoring to preserve some unblemished areas on the furniture; I was double-checking the ice, something I always forget until the last moment; Olympia was cautiously lighting the last of the 48 candles in the various chandeliers and sconces, when the first guest rapped on the front door.

"I think the house looks gorgeous," Jan remarked, with an admiring sigh, "in spite of cracks in the walls and lath showing through some sections of the ceiling."

"And the paper half-stripped from the walls," I added.

Through the soft shadowy candlelight we glanced around lovingly at our home. *How beautiful, how elegant, how like the Créole days!*

The first arrivals rapped again; I tugged at the front door, spying Maurice and Claudine through the beveled glass.

"It's stuck," I groaned. "Maurice, push!"

Finally the door flung open, bearing Maurice and, unfortunately, the doorknob, into our home. It was a shame that they were the first guests; Maurice was a business friend from the suburbs whose wife we had never met.

Following a muddled "Hello," Maurice handed me the recalcitrant door knob.

Looking around, Claudine asked, "Are you sure it's safe for us to be in this place? I've heard these old houses in the Quarters are riddled with termites and ready to fall down."

Jan smiled reassuringly as Olympia removed Claudine's fake fur stole. We showed them through several rooms. They were as polite with their "oohs" and "aahs" as we were weeks later when they showed us their six-room, yellow brick rancher on *a slab* in Gentilly.

Oh, God, will the next guests ever come before we have to show the bathroom? Luck was with us; Olympia announced Bill and Ann.

Olympia was in charge of stocking the food and champagne fountain. Early in the party, while she was in the kitchen restocking the shrimp bowl, one of our friends added a fifth of vodka to the first batch of punch. Before we realized what lethal drinks we were serving, it was evident the party was slightly over-launched!

"Bob, your father always said to serve the first couple of drinks strong to get things going, then slack off."

"Honey, we've been serving Mickeys for the last hour without even knowing it. I'm afraid they're beginning to take effect!"

Jan and I stood in the archway between the double parlors amazed at how large the party had become. We had anticipated ninety to a hundred, but we looked out now on what appeared to be two hundred souls, plus a sprinkling of atheists who displaced the same amount of cubic inches and frequently consumed somewhat more than the standard Christian serving of booze.

About two hours into the party, Jan cornered me in the dining room.

"Thank heavens we have plenty of room," I whispered to her.

Jan smirked. "Uh huh, and we have plenty to drink, too, if they don't notice it's plain soda."

"What do you mean, honey?"

"The sauterne's all gone, so Olympia and I added vanilla and rum extract to the soda, and they're still drinking."

"I doubt if they notice or care. Many of them carry flasks."

Cocktail parties are fun because the conversation is always vigorous, though often inane. It can be very interesting just to mingle and listen before chiming in, if and when you're so inclined.

"I don't believe in abortions. I do believe in birth control."

"I believe birth control leads to extra-marital relations."

"How do you know?"

"Nothin' wrong with havin' sex, if you don't have to worry about being knocked up."

"How vulgar!"

Jan popped her head into the group. "I second that, that's really vulgar." She then moved swiftly toward the front door to hail farewell to some departing Uptowners.

"Of course, we have a divine little Creole Cottage just behind Miss Dixie's Musical Barroom."

"Isn't that where all the faggots hang out?"

"I don't think I know what you mean."

"Faggots, queens, isn't that where all the queens hang out?"

"Oh, no, I don't believe so. I never see any debutantes there. They seem to cater only to men. The queens I know have their affairs, only at Antoine's."

Evidently our phone had been ringing. Someone's arm was holding the phone receiver high in the air. I pushed through to answer it.

"The Quarters might be a fun place to visit, but to think they're raising their children here."

"Isn't that a shame?" someone whispered.

I was just getting hold of the wandering phone receiver when I overheard the previous conversation. "As long as you folks are whispering anyway, would you please speak a little softer? I'm trying to hear my children on the phone."

Timmy and Tammy wanted to assure me they had said their prayers and brushed their teeth, in that order. Also, Liza and Emily, their buddies, were fine. I had backed into a closet with the phone in order to hear. I emerged in the middle of:

"I hate those damnable dogs constantly crapping on the sidewalks."

"I wouldn't *have* a dog!"

"No, not in the Quarter."

"God, one of the funniest things I've ever seen was these two dogs hung-up right in front of St. Louis Cathedral."

"I heard."

"How shocking and just before Mass."

"How carnal!"

A lady in lavender exclaimed, "Yes, we use our patio a great deal."

"You're so lucky."

"Do you have one?"

"No, but we do have a gallery on Dumaine Street."

"Of course, that's nice."

"It would be if the fish market odor weren't so strong. Every Friday we have to burn our charcoal grille, whether we cook or not, just to cut the smell of dead fish!"

I recollected how much Jan and I disliked that smell. Tammy always referred to Friday as "P.U. Day."

Olympia passed near Jan with the last of the catered *hors d'oeuvres*.

"Next week, we're going to Del Prado."

"Where?"

"She means Mexico City."

"Oh!"

"I can't face *May-hee-co* again, so John is planning another dull Mediterranean Cruise."

"No travel for me, there's too much right here in good ole Norlens."

"Man, ya oughta face it, New Orleans is a friggin' hot hole this time of year!"

I smiled because I had seen Jan sidling up to that group, but she quickly sidled away when she heard that last remark. Spying me, she asked, "What are you smiling about?"

"Oh, nothing, just you!" Changing the subject, "Look at Mary and Corrine over there. They're frantically lambasting Carmine, that artist from Jackson Square. They are so housewife-ish."

"Well, I know what I like."

"Me, too, and I like to be able to tell what it is! That abstract stuff, I could do that."

"If you're gonna paint a woman's breast, why not make it look like a woman's breast?"

"I guess some artists think they can improve on God."

"Well, artists are kinda bizarre."

"Uh huh."

"What do you do?"

"I'm an artist."

"*Oh!*"

Jan sent me to check the toilet water supply in the bathroom.

"Zat new fountain in zee Jackson Square, eet eez terreeeble."

"I rather like it."

"I don't tink zey shood have named it ahfter De Gaulle."

"Why?"

"Look at zee mess he made in Algiers."

"Algiers? *Algiers?*"

"Non Algiers, Louisiane, cherie, Algiers, Nord Afrique."

I reported back to Jan that the bath tub was still nearly full, but for some reason, there was a huge fish floating in the tub.

"I'd never wear imitation fur myself."

"But you sell it to your customers."

"Do you think it will ever replace real fur?"

"God, no, do you think stainless will ever replace sterling?"

"I'm sure you can tell *this* isn't machine-made mink."

"Sure can. It's mink-dyed muskrat!"

I moved on before the fur flew. I didn't smoke at all and my mother only smoked at fashionable affairs to look sophisticated. I was always first to be affected by a smoke-filled room. I asked Olympia to switch on the ceiling fan in the back parlor while I tugged at several ten-foot-high French windows to help clear the air.

"Huey Long gave this state a great deal."

"Yah, a great deal of graft."

"He built our skyscraper capitol."

"Yah, where he got shot dead!"

"He *was* better than his brother, Earl."

"Now, Earl had a fabulous personality."

"Yes, and he owed it all to liquor and God knows what!"

"Fund raisers, fund raisers, give, give, give."

"Such a bore!"

"*We* never give anything."

"If they all belonged to the Community Chest, the Cancer Association for instance..."

"Oh, doctor, that reminds me, I've been meaning to ask a physician, why do Jewish women have less cancer of the uterus?"

"Sweetheart, you can't *break* what you don't *use!*"

The breeze from the ceiling fan blew out a bevy of candles, but no one seemed to mind the near-darkness. Only Olympia was worried because wax had dripped down one wall.

"Never mind," I consoled, "all that old flowered wallpaper has to come off anyway."

With a sigh of relief she headed toward the kitchen.

"When I first came here, I didn't think I could stand them."

"They *are* rather creepy."

"They don't mean you're dirty."

"They're horrible; some even fly!"

"Y'all talking 'bout roaches?"

"Hell, roaches *are* Norlens, sorta like the State Bird."

"An' *that's* the truth!"

I went to check the commotion coming from the dining room. A frayed extension cord rubbing against the base of the silver champagne fountain was emitting an electric shock with every drink. It didn't seem, however, to be driving away any well-charged guests. I fixed it quickly with a handy Band-Aid, thanking God no one was electrocuted.

"*We* belong to the Patio Planters."

"Must be interesting."

"Oh, it is, Percy and I just love to grovel in the dirt."

"Personally, I prefer bromeliads."

"The patios *are* interesting, but how do you solve your parking problems?"

"Easy for us, we don't have a car!"

Eventually I grew weary of the smoke and chattering. Although I love to get ready for parties, I have a short attention span for drivel. I hadn't had a chance to talk in-depth to one individual, and, worse still, no one had offered to talk to *me* for more than two minutes. Finally I eased down into a chair.

"*We*, of course, live in the Garden District, can't break the family tradition."

"*We* live Uptown near Tulane University, on Audubon Boulevard."

"The Quarter is so convenient."

"If Andre and I were braver, we'd live here; it's truly a piece of history, tradition lies on every doorstep."

"Yah, an' plenty of drunks, too!"

Jan approached my resting place. "Bob, are you sure you're not drinking too much?"

"I'm fine."

Off she went before she heard me complain I was ready for bed.

Nestled between two groups, and sitting on the floor directly in the center of the front parlor, was Tony Schwartz, alias Antoine Du Barré, a sort of Ivy League yogi who often embarrassed or delighted the girls, and some boys, by curling one leg up under himself while propping the other behind his collar bone. Jammed into his overly-tight continental trousers, a position rendering him anything but private. And there he was, center stage, locked like a huge still-life pretzel.

"Look, Jan, he must have added something new," exclaimed Margie. "I notice he keeps flinging his head to one side."

"I can't watch."

"Neither can I, makes me ache."

Some minutes later, when Jan was checking the remnants of the chips and dips, she noticed Antoine was still locked in position. Jan drew back when she became aware of a large, ugly scar on the side of his neck and shoulder. She pulled David and Monique next to her to point out the scar. David reached out with his hand, then drew back in surprise.

"Ouch! Something's hot!"

"What?"

"Why, it's that goddamn chandelier!"

"What?"

"Look, it's hot wax. It's been dripping off that chandelier and the damn fool doesn't even know it. He must be nuts!"

"No, David, he's in suspended animation."

We had envisioned the party more as a viewing than a house warming, though several people brought gifts. Swishing his way stealthily through the mob with apologies and pardons, latecomer Mr. D'Evereaux of Patio Planters toted a five-foot-high *Philodendra Paficus* straight from the front door to the back patio. The plant's gunny-sacked ball dribbled dirt along the way as the mammoth *Paficus* leaves merrily slapped drinks out of people's hands.

"Fabulous plant!"

"I'll bet it's worth a hundred dollars."

"*Hardly*, darling."

Trying to pick up bits of dirt as we went, Jan and I eagerly followed Mr. D'Evereaux and his balled shrub out into the patio. Fortunately there was still an old 1930's washing machine next to the slave quarter that graciously accepted his gift. In our anxiety to find a home for Mr. D's plant, we'd not noticed the merry version of "crunch hopscotch" taking place in the patio.

"It's fabulous fun!"

"Look, when I turn on the flashlight…"

"Come on."

"Join the fun and see how many cockroaches you can crunch before I turn it off!"

"Aw, come on."

"Ick, no, the sound makes me sick!"

"Be careful you don't hurt yourself."

"The bandages are what make me look so bad."

"I could never stand to get my nose bobbed."

"It's that long needle between the eyes and those awful black and blue blobs afterwards that turns my stomach."

"Is there any more shrimp?"

"Are Dick and Charmaine still in the closet?"

"I heard he *came out*. I don't know why he's crying."

"Guess he lost his lover."

"Let's all go up on the front balcony and sing Christmas Carols."

"But it's not Christmas."

"Who cares, those are the only songs everybody knows!"

"We all know Governor Jimmy Davis's song."

"You are my sunshine, my only sunshine..."

"It's after one o'clock."

"The *Vieux Carré* Commission should have more control."

"Look what happened to Greenwich Village!"

"Quiet, quiet, quiet everyone, Dirk is on the stair, ready to recite."

Dirk, a sensitive and delicately-countenanced recent graduate from Loyola Drama School, brushed back his shoulder-length hair, struck a limp but authoritative pose, and recited his latest ode:

A Moment in Time
by
Dirk Van der Garde
My soul has drifted through infinity a millennium of years.
And now, takes this precious moment to connect with you.
Your kind and gentle love brings me to the brink of tears.
With you, I dare to be myself, you have alleviated all my fears.
I don't know who I am, or who I want to be.
But having felt your love and warm embrace,
Cheers me on to my eternity.

"How inspiring!"

"What does it mean?"

"Who cares!"

"The music's too loud."

"It's two o'clock or so."

"I'm tired."

"Don't slide down, the banister won't hold you."

"Wheeeeee!"

"Didn't think it would hold you."

"What's the dirtiest word you know?"

"Kumquat!"

"Ugh."

"We have to drive to the suburbs."

"Pity."

"Please, please. No! I said, *No!*"

"What'cha, frigid or somethin?"

"Keep your filthy hands to yourself!"

By that point, I was exhausted and hoping more than anything that everyone would just go home. I moved to the hall by the front door and sat on the hall-tree seat, ready to help guests out and down the front steps. Jan, who never fades at parties, appeared arm-in-arm with a bubbling guest.

"Thank you, veddy, veddy much, Mr. and Mrs. Cahr. The Consul General and I have had a most lovely evening. It's so interesting to see how Amedicans *really* live."

Jan poked me; I rose and stumbled back, graciously bowing and trying to look alert. Just then, Marilyn hollered from atop the stairway, "Did you see what we brought you?" She held up the huge pink fish, about two feet long.

"What is it, a king-sized goldfish?" I yelled.

"No, silly, Pete went deep-sea fishing off the Gulf Coast. It's a red snapper. We brought head and all; it's been in the bathtub. Good god, it's really slippery. Oops!"

The fish slipped out of her hand and slithered briskly down the twenty-five steps, giving the Consul a good nudge as it glided to a halt at Jan's feet. At that, the General and his madame hustled out the front door onto Bourbon Street. Jan was flabbergasted by the episode. I was just numb. Suddenly, a chant escalated from the parlor.

"We want, Cha Cha Cha…"

"We want, Cha Cha Cha…"

"Have you heard this new album, *Music to Strip By?*"

"Man."

"Wow."

"Go gal."

"Quel beetch!"

"Put on Chubby Checker. I wanna Twist."

A tough-looking blonde, who I guessed had come with one of our actor friends, had started to shimmy and shake. Gyrating seductively, she tossed well-timed bumps and grinds hither, thither, and yon!

"Who *is* that, Jan?" I asked.

"Don't know. She's a little much for the Uptowners."

"I know. I wish they'd *all go home!*"

The music ground to a crescendo as she swished a final bump and grind. Then, surprise, off came the blonde tresses!

"My God, it's *Dirk!*"

"Can Mardi Gras be far behind?"

"Must we go?"

"It's three thirty or so."

"Let's go to a Decatur Bar."

"It's too far."

"Anybody want a beer?"

"Come on, dear."

"It's four!"

"I don't think you know the score."

"Don't fall asleep."

"You creep!"

"Oh, hum."

"You bum!"

"Don't get mean."

"But, deah, I've never beeen."

"It's five!"

"I know a Dixie dive."

"Come on, let's all go."

"Sorry, but Jan and I really must say, *no!*"

Jan and I, alone at last!

"Honey, no wonder Creole mansions get run down so fast!"

North Pole Denizens Sunbathing in "the Quarters"

Ann and Bill invited us to join them and several couples they thought we should meet for dinner at the famous Brennan's Restaurant on Royal Street. With our busy moving and work schedules, we hadn't had time to enjoy up-scale eateries. To us, entering Brennan's was magical: the ambiance, the cordial staff, and the fragrance wafting in from the patio mingled with the pungent aroma from the kitchen. The other guests were having cocktails in the patio by the fountain. Bill introduced us around. The first couple we met was John and Renna Godcheaux. At last, we could find out the proper pronunciation of their name! He said "god-shaw" and she said "god-show." We were learning the incongruities of local articulation while imbibing local libations: Jan, a Ramos Gin Fizz; me, a Sazerac, with its pungent licorice flavor I loved.

We were seated at a table for eight, that special table in the corner next to the patio window. The conversation went from The War Between the States to "When in the hell ya gonna get over that, and let us move into the 20th century!" The interchange of words was extremely impassioned; suddenly everyone stopped and looked up at the imposing lady who approached our table.

"Good evening, I'm Ella Brennan. I hope you're being well taken care of. Since I know the rest of you, this must be Bob & Jan Carr. I enjoy your noontime radio patter. WWL's finally getting it right, so refreshing to have a real married couple on the air in this city of family traditions. Since it's your first meal here, I suggest Turtle Soup or Shrimp *Remoulade*. Then, for an *entrée*, Trout *Meuniére* or a Filet, Créole style." She shook our hands. "Keep coming, we love celebrities here. We'll put you right back at this same table."

I turned back to the others, "I can't believe we just met the restaurant icon of New Orleans and she was so amiable."

"And, Bob, she even listens to our show. That's scary!"

Renna Godcheaux spoke up, "She's a shrewd businesswoman with her finger on the pulse of the city."

John chimed in, "She and her late brother, Owen, two Irishmen from the Channel, have turned this Creole-restaurant-town on its ear and are making a fortune."

We walked home exhilarated by our dining experience, aware that opinions here ranged from ante-bellum to Martin Luther King but unaware we would eventually

become good friends with the Brennan family.

Our radio show was over by one o'clock, which meant we usually got home a little after two and began working on the house. For several days we had insisted the children play outside in the patio after school because we were trying desperately to varnish all the downstairs floors we had painstakingly sanded. Olympia was away for a week on a church retreat, so the kids clung to us incessantly. They would run in and out and in and out for one thing or another, grinding dirt into the raw wood. I was getting really testy with the children over their *tramp, tramp, tramp.*

Jan suggested they learn as many new things about the patio as they could, planting thoughts of pirates and Indians who might have buried treasures there in years past. On the first day they discovered an old hand-blown wine bottle, a rusty hinge, a half-decayed wooden coat hanger from the Palmer House, which must have come down from Chicago on the Panama Limited, and a piece of chinaware they were certain one of Lafitte's pirates had eaten from. On the second day, they dug up another piece of china, a second rusty hinge, and a leg bone from that pirate who ate off the china, or so they claimed. On the third and fourth days of their exile from the house, they became attracted to the two ten-foot ladders I had propped up against the patio wall.

Since moving into our house we had naturally gotten acquainted with some of our next-door neighbors. Our block was laid out in such a way that several patios backed up against ours from other streets; we had no idea who some of the neighbors were over the walls, as most stood at least eight feet high. Once the kids grew weary of playing archeologist and rooting in the treasure-laden dirt, they began looking onward and upward, up the ladders toward more interesting discoveries. Our children had always loved to climb, so we didn't particularly worry as they scurried up and down the ladders playing fireman and rescue squad, plus sundry other ladder games. Finally, they became interested in something or someone on the other side of the wall, and we hailed their preoccupation as a chance to finally finish applying the last coat of varnish to our treasured heart-of-pine floors.

At dinner, Tammy told us they had met Mrs. Santa Claus and Tim spoke of Miss Snow Ball.

"Who else did you meet?" Jan asked.

"We don't know all the ladies' names," answered Tim.

"How many ladies were there over the wall?"

"Oh, about sfix or sfeven," reported Tammy.

"You oughta see 'em, daddy, they all have beautiful long hair."

"Yah, like frippers."

"Like *what?*"

"Like frippers, mommy, on Bourbon Street, booty-ah, booty-ah," she replied, grinding away and twisting like an exotic dancer. "Bourbon Street, booty-ah, booty-ah."

"Bob, that's terrible! You go out there this minute and take down those ladders!"

"Oh, mommy, Tammy's only 'magining things. 'Sides, she likes to get you riled."

Nearly a week passed; the kids still seemed fascinated by the ladies on the other side of the wall. When the kid's friends came over, they would all climb the ladders and sit on top of the wall in a row, like a gang of tomcats.

Jan began to fear that maybe Tammy's theory was true. I, on the other hand, was a little worried that our kids and their friends might be bothering the neighbors. So, at Jan's insistence, I eventually climbed the ladder to see for myself who lived on the other side of the wall, and also to inquire whether the children were being bothersome. In most neighborhoods, when you want to peek at the folks next door, you merely steal a glance; however, in the Quarter, it's not always so easy, especially if you don't want to get caught. And after our experience on moving day, I felt some trepidation.

Jan was kidding me as I sneaked slowly up the ladder. She shook it just enough to give me a scare, as she pointed out a distant police siren. "If they haul you in as a peeping tom, for heaven's sake, don't use your right name. What would our listeners say? Remember our image!"

"Sh-Shhhh," I whispered emphatically. "Just be quiet."

"Okay!" she hollered back, still teasing.

I edged my head up over the wall to see into the patio; there was the sound of muted music.

A bit too loud for my nerves, Jan asked, "What do you see?"

I hunched down quickly, "I don't know."

"What do you mean, you don't know?"

"I don't mean anything."

"Well, then, what did you see?"

"I didn't see anything *yet*. And I never will if you won't be quiet! Now, shhhh."

I crept up one more rung on the ladder and finally got a good look at the lovely patio on the other side. The back part of the house and the slave quarter apartments opened onto a beautiful oval swimming pool. The patio lay in the shadow of the main house; the area was heavily planted with many varieties of tropicals, accented by beautiful crepe myrtle trees. Jan wiggled the ladder slightly, nodding me on up. I scowled back at her as I moved up a couple more rungs. I swung around so I could see the part of the patio directly beneath the wall.

Oh, my God! There they were, at least three of the children's pals: Donder, Blitzen, and Mrs. Claus, perhaps? Not worrying about chilly arctic winds, they were stretched out full-length at pool's end in the only strip of sunshine left on the patio. I'd never seen so many luscious boobs at one time and nipples screaming for pasties! I felt flushed. They were clothed in nothing but Coppertone, or maybe Sea and Ski, or could it be Sun and Fun? Al Hirt's *Sugar Lips* was playing on their poolside portable radio.

Before I had a chance to get a really *good* look, Jan shouted, "Is anyone home over there?"

Startled, I lost my balance, and in an attempt to catch myself knocked a piece of brick loose from the wall. It tumbled into a clump of Birds of Paradise right next to one of the frippers. Before I could secrete myself, she looked up, slowly removing her sun-blinders, and to my surprise, and relief, said, "Haah."

"Haah," I answered back, waving almost as if I were tipping my hat, "I just wanted to see you!" *A rather inane statement under the circumstances.*

She eased the situation by saying, "I'll bet you're Timmy and Tammy's daddy, aren't you?"

"Yes, Ma'am, I am," I said proudly but meekly.

"They sure are cute kids. I hope you don't mind us talkin' to 'em."

"No, no. As a matter of fact, that's why I'm here. I mean, up here! Ha, ha. Jan and I...she's my wife. Anyway we want to make sure the children don't bother you—oh, and you, too," I added, glancing sheepishly at the other two "ladies" stretched out on their backs. Neither of them had made a move to cover their dusky triangles with even their hands. They all smiled at me so pleasantly that I self-consciously smiled back. Not knowing what to say, I blurted, "I see y'all's crepe myrtles are in full bloom!"

"Say, aren't you the Bob of Bob and Jan on radio? I recognize your voice."

"Yup, that's me. Ha, I mean us!"

She sat up, shading her eyes (*but nothing else*) from the sun!

I could feel the ladder shaking from below. "In fact, Jan's right down here," I said, pointing toward our patio and thinking to myself: *What a stupid thing to say, and thank God, Jan can't see them!*

"Geez, I'm glad to meet ya. I hear y'all's commercials in my dressing room sometimes; y'all got me to buy that Luzianne coffee ya sell."

I grinned. "Yup, we're Bob & Jan for Luzianne. Where do you work?"

"Around. We're all exotics. Mae works at the 500, she backs-up Kitty West, ya know, Evangeline the Oyster Girl. June and I work at the Sho-Bar."

"What's your name?"

"My name's Ernestine. Isn't that hideous? But I go by Snow Ball. Why don't you and Jan come by the club some night? It'll be drinks on the house."

"Thanks, we'll try." I felt Jan shake the ladder again. "I guess I better get down. I hope the kids don't bother you."

"No, not at all. It's okay with us if it's okay with you."

I convinced Jan the children had not bothered the neighbors. However, knowing what I knew, I suggested to Jan, so the children wouldn't wear out their welcome, that we stash the ladders somewhere else for a while. I didn't tell her until much later that our neighbors didn't wear bathing togs to avoid suntan lines. *After all, why create an issue?*

Four or five days later, the subject of suit-less sunbathing came up. It seems, while Jan and I were at the station, Tammy and Olympia had a go-around about sunbathing in the nude; by the time we got home, they were both in a lather.

"But, Mizz Cahr, Tammy be wantin' to take her sunbath in the backyard and she won't wear no clothes 'cause, she say, you're not supposin' to if you want to be a dancer. Well, ah cain't take kindly to that chile bein' nekked in the out o' doors. It's jis not proper, Ma'am."

Tammy was sitting over in the corner sulking, sucking her thumb, and holding her "banket."

"Aw, Tammy, why're you so sad? Tell mommy."

"I don't want to wear any froze."

"Why not, sweetie?"

"'Cause the nice frippers over the wall don't wear froze to get tan, so I don't want to wear froze, too. 'Cause I want to take dancin' lessons." With that, tears began to trickle.

"Oh, Bob, what'll I do?"

"Let her take her froze off and go sunbathe."

Olympia looked hard at me, her eyes flashed and her brow furrowed. "Mistah Cahr!"

Jan broke in, "I can't, I just can't let her."

"Oh, for Lord's sake, who's going to look at a naked three-year-old? And besides, nobody can see in the patio anyway."

Jan and Olympia both stood tear-cheeked as I trotted the smiling Tammy out for her sunning, *au naturel*.

Tammy's sunning ritual lasted only fifteen minutes. Timmy and his friend Pierre came home unexpectedly, surprising her in all her glory. She never asked to do it again. Perhaps Olympia's supplications had something to do with it.

The number of strippers actually residing in the Quarter is rather small, considering the upper end of Bourbon Street, near Canal, is devoted mainly to the art of undressing. Most of the dancers like to get away from it all, so they live elsewhere, like Gentilly or Metairie. One of our friends who left the Quarter for the suburbs "for the children's sake" was shocked to learn that her suburban neighbor, across the street in River Ridge, not only ran a strip house on Bourbon Street, but specialized in an audience participation sex show known as "The Carnal Cavalcade." If you were *fortunate* enough to receive an invitation priced at one hundred bucks, you were eligible to participate in any form of unusual sexual activity that might be your cup of tea! If you were the shy, wall-poesy type, you could enjoy being a *voyeur*.

When Jan's friend Geneviéve (pronounced the French way) would talk up the virtues of River Ridge and how great it was for the children, Jan would pipe up with, "Well, we may have a few strippers over the wall and in the Royal Street A&P, but at least there aren't any pimps in the block!"

I thought once more, *Jan has come a long way from her grandparent's farm in Ohio*.

* * * * *

The French Quarter was fertile ground in which to raise one's children to believe in God. So many alternatives to venerate Him are expounded either by the varied and silent historic edifices like St. Louis Cathedral, St. Mary's Italian Church, and the Ursuline Convent, or vocally by the street-people selling a wide variety of religions.

The children were always fascinated by Mike Stark, the wonderful beatnik-style Baptist preacher who roamed the streets of the Quarter with bright red hair streaming down from his otherwise bald pate. He moved almost as if motorized beneath the voluminous batik moo-moo covering his rotund body. His appearance was most portentous as he glided about, but offering him a pleasant glance or a cheerful hello brought a warm and pious response. As the beatnik population of the Quarter grew in the Sixties, he mediated for many of the lost young souls who had found their way into a nightmare of drugs. His Church was in the gutters, alleys, and deserted rat-infested patios of the riverfront. During our evening strolls with the little red wagon, we would see Mike meandering through the French Quarter tending to the needs of his street people.

There was also Bob Harrington, self-proclaimed Chaplain of Bourbon Street, who preached the Gospel at bars and strip places. Occasionally he would bring a B-girl to "know the Lord." A fine-looking, burly man with the demeanor of a riverboat gambler, he wore a dark blue serge suit accented with a red tie, red socks, and a red handkerchief, which he declared represented the blood of the Risen Lord Jesus Christ, spilled on our behalf. For many years, Reverend Bob maintained an office and a Chapel in the 200 block of Bourbon Street tucked between a strip joint and Galatoire's, the venerable dining Mecca for old-line New Orleanians. An intoxicating orator, he built a national following through evangelistic broadcasts. On numerous occasions he was a captivating guest on our radio show.

The children's religious training started shortly after we got settled into our Bourbon Street house. Jan and I both had been raised in religious WASP families; however, we had strayed away from the Church during our early married life. Now, we both strongly felt the children should be raised in a Christian way, which I guess we thought was the "American Way," whatever that meant.

And whatever it meant in the majority of the continental U.S., it was certainly something different in New Orleans, especially in the French Quarter. American history in New Orleans doesn't spring from the pilgrims, the Mayflower, or the Boston Tea Party: it stems from the Creoles, the Cajuns, the African-Americans, the Battle of New Orleans, and, of course, the long and difficult Yankee occupation in the 1860s.

For the unlearned, it might be well to point out briefly that the Cajuns or Acadians are those folks forced by the British out of Nova Scotia in 1760 because of allegiance to their French Catholic heritage. They came to settle along the Gulf of Mexico in what is now referred to as Acadia in the southwest portion of Louisiana. Towns with such French-inspired names as Thibodaux (Tee-bo-*dough*), Abbeville (Abbe-*veel*), Lafayette (Lah-fah-*yet*), Bayou Teche (Bah-you-*tesh*) and St. Martinsville (Sa-martin-*veel*) grew and prospered. Until the advent of English-speaking television in the 1950s, the only language spoken was eighteenth-century French. St. Martinsville is where you will find the statue of the heroine of Longfellow's poem *Evangeline*, which most American children discover is required reading to either enjoy or suffer through in junior high. The Cajuns are country people whose ancient form of spoken French amazes visitors from France. When speaking English, their accent sparkles with a peculiar lilt. The reversal of word order, outlandish mispronunciations, and final syllable emphasis make it simultaneously a delight to hear and a struggle to understand.

Creoles are totally different from Cajuns, although they share a French heritage. In New Orleans there are French Creoles (my great-grandparents Aupagnier), Spanish Creoles, French-Spanish Creoles, and black Creoles; however, contrary to most Yankee belief, all Creoles are not black or of mixed race. In fact, no blacks are *Créole* in the finite meaning of the word. New Orleans Creoles are those people, or their descendants, who came to Louisiana from France or Spain in the eighteenth or nineteenth centuries to settle the land. Creole Cooking, Creole Architecture, and Creole tomatoes are their heritage. Many of the Creole slaves, who were often fair-skinned due to interracial liaisons, chose, when freed, to continue to call themselves Creole. Ultimately, a whole sub-society of black Creoles grew to prominence in New Orleans.

Mathilda Bonét, who sometimes tended the children to spell Olympia, was such a Creole. She had delicately chiseled features with a lovely tan complexion, spoke in a softly modulated voice with an accent that was one part Scarlett O'Hara Southern, one part New Orleans Brooklynese, and one part street tough. Mathilda was a religious person in the finest sense. She had an air about her that let you know she was a lady.

"Lord have mercy, Mistah Cahr, but I've been blessed," she used to say, "even if ah am a widda. The Lawd, He's been fine ta me. 'Course ya know, there's *aw-ways* somethin', Mistah Cahr!"

"You're absolutely right Mathilda, there's always someone or something that can give you grief, if you let it!"

The children loved the way Mathilda would always make the sign of the cross upon her abundant bosom whenever they passed in front of Saint Louis Cathedral, a custom the children quickly latched onto.

"Thanks be to Gawd, Mistah Cahr. It pleases me to assist in y'all's chilrin's religious trainin'. Mistah Cahr, you just gotta git those chilrin their catechism so they can make their first communions. Sure don't want 'em stuck in Limbo!"

Mathilda's concerns haunted us. Both Protestant, we felt our best strategy would be to send the kids around the corner to Sunday School at St. Mark's Methodist Church on Rampart Street, a street made famous by jazz musicians. The street, however, was actually named for the embankment of earth, surmounted by parapets, defending the outer limits of the early village.

"If Sunny School is hard like real school, I don't wanna go!" protested Timmy. "I have enough of that kinda stuff all week!"

"Do they have recess?" questioned Tammy, as Jan pulled the petite blue-and-white Mitty blouse over her head.

"They don't have recess, dummy, all you do is hear some old lady tell ya 'bout Jesus!"

"Timmy, that's not true," Jan retorted, now struggling with shiny patent leather Mary-Janes over the white socks covering Tammy's chubby little legs.

"Ya mean ya don't learn about Jesus?" Timmy demanded.

"Yes, you learn about Jesus, but not from old ladies."

"Nana is an old lady and she's fun," Tammy countered.

"Yah, but Nana is our Grandma and that's different. Besides, she doesn't talk about Jesus. She talks about Cadillacs!"

"Okay, kids," I interrupted, "end of discussion! It's time to head out for St. Mark's."

Stepping out of our Creole Mansion onto Bourbon Street on a Sunday morning was always fraught with surprises. Our street is like the chameleons we find in our patio, green one moment, brown another. Saturday night Bourbon Street is noisy red and gaudy gold; on Sunday morning it's silent, bathed in fresh sunlight, pink, and azure blue, save for the discarded refuse, both human and tin, which has found its way into the gutter under the cloak of the darkest hours of Saturday night.

"Daddy, that man looks really dead!" Timmy exclaimed, jumping down from the granite stoop to the sun-bathed pavement of the banquette.

"Pee yoo!" Tammy complained, "he smells worse than the fish market on Fridays."

"He smells like whiskey ta me!" added Timmy, authoritatively.

"Tammy, Timmy, shh!" I hushed. "Let me see if he's all right." I bent down to find out if he was dead or alive. "Hey, Mister, are you okay?"

"Go away, Buster, I'm sleepin'!"

"But, you're in the gutter. You might get hit by a car."

"Or the Desire bus," Timmy chimed in.

"You could get killed laying here," I added.

"Just lemme sleep. I wanna sleep, damn it!"

"Daddy, he said a bad word," Tammy scolded.

"Look Mister, don't get upset. I'll pull you up onto our front steps. You can sleep there while we're at Church."

"*Bob!*"

"Well, honey," I said, shrugging my shoulders, "if we're going to be Christians—"

"I guess you're right."

"Do you think he needs some water?" I asked Jan, as I tugged him up the steps and out of the sun, with very little help on his part.

"Ya got a beer?" he mumbled.

"*No!* We'll see you later!"

Hastening the children away from the scene, Jan instructed, "Okay, let's get on our way to St. Mark's or we'll be late."

The kids skipped on ahead up Governor Nicholls Street.

"Jan, let's not get too involved at church, let's just play it cool or the next thing we know, we'll have the preacher and half the congregation over to visit us."

"Timmy, Tammy, watch for the cars on Dauphine street. Wait until daddy and I get there," Jan hollered, before turning back to me. "All right, Bob, I'll do as you say."

Without notice, Timmy and Tammy screamed and sprang back from the iron patio gate they were passing. In the process they almost fell into an open sunken garbage receptacle.

"Don't get yourselves dirty," Jan beseeched.

I chimed in, "Calm down, you two, you're getting too hyper."

"That li'l rat dog almost scared my pants off," bellowed Timmy.

Tammy giggled, thinking what that might be like in the middle of the banquette!

"That little dog always barks when we walk past this gate," I said. "You should be used to it by now. So calm down, you're going to get all sweaty."

"He doesn't have anything else to do, daddy, let's see if we can pet him."

"*No*, Timmy!"

"Oh, mother!"

"She doesn't want you to lose a hand, Timmy," Tammy said protectively.

"Oh, *Lord!*"

"*Timothy!*" I rebuked.

Peachy Villere pushed her shutter door open and stuck her head out to pick up the Sunday morning *Times-Picayune* off her stoop. Peachy, one of the sweetest and friendliest ladies in the neighborhood, always had a kind word and a smile. Her husband, Henri, of French Creole decent, was proprietor of the pharmacy on the Uptown-river side of Rampart Street and Esplanade Avenue.

In New Orleans, there is no north and south, nor east or west, as the old hymn says; rather, every direction is given by using Canal Street as the dividing line. Uptown is up river or up stream from Canal and Downtown is down river. Riverside is toward the Mississippi and lakeside is toward Lake Pontchartrain. The Villere's Creole Cottage is on the Uptown side of the street, at the Uptown riverside corner of Governor Nicholls and Dauphine.

"Y'all look lahk a picture in your Sunday best," remarked Peachy. "Y'all going to Mass?"

"Well, we're on our way to St. Mark's Methodist Church," Jan replied, almost apologetically.

"Oh my, I hope they don't have any trouble over there again this Sunday. I must say, that preacher is mighty brave."

As Peachy stepped out of her doorway onto the stoop, the children noticed she was wearing one very unusual shoe. They couldn't help but stare at it.

"Think ah'll walk to the corner with y'all to get a breath. It's such a gorgeous morning, can you believe—but, y'all better get on your way or you'll be late for Mass, or y'all's *church*, I mean!"

She walked along beside us; the children were intrigued by the one big shoe and her limp, which seemed to cause her no concern.

"Think this is as far as I'll go. Bye, y'all, and God Bless." She patted Tammy on the head but Timmy lunged forward to escape her loving touch.

The kids skipped on ahead to the middle of the block, then abruptly stopped and came running back. Almost simultaneously, they asked, "Why does Miss Villere wear that funny shoe?"

"She has a club foot."

"A club?" Timmy questioned.

"Kids, let's keep walking."

Jan took the children by their hands. "She has a crippled foot. She was born with it, I think. She has to wear a special shoe on that foot to help her walk."

"That's better than crutches like Tiny Tim, huh, mommy?"

"That's right."

"Seems like sometimes people don't get borned just right," remarked Timmy. "Why does God *do* that, mommy?"

"I'm sorry, I can't answer that. But what's the best thing you noticed about Mrs. Villere?"

He speculated for a minute. "She's always real nice."

"And she smiles a lot," added Tammy.

"You see then, it doesn't make much difference if you have a lame foot, wear glasses, have red hair like me, or dark skin like Olympia. As long as you are friendly, kind, and smile, people will like you."

Timmy pondered that thought for a couple of moments. "Mommy, you sure are smart!"

Although we had been walking on the shady side of the street, I was glad when we arrived at the church; the rays of morning sun were beginning to reflect off the buildings, adding heat to the humidity.

St. Mark's Church, with its lovely colonnade and patio along Rampart Street, was painted a soft mint green. It is a fairly creditable reproduction of a mission church one might find in Florida or the Southwest, making it a bit architecturally foreign to the *Vieux Carré*.

"Daddy, look at all the people standing on the neutral ground in front of the church."

In New Orleans, the grassy area in the center of a boulevard or parkway is referred to as the neutral ground. Apparently the term comes from the days when, just after the Louisiana Purchase, Canal Street became the boundary between the Creole part of town (*Vieux Carré*, old square, or the French Quarter) and the American Sector, where the U. S. settlers were boisterously taking up residence. The land in the center of Canal Street was *terre neuter, zone neutre* in present-day French.

"Daddy, are those people looking at us?"

As the four of us started up the rather imposing front steps of the church, we heard shouts from across the street. The children scampered up to the landing in front of the main double doors. Jan and I glanced around to see if we were being summoned. We became aware of what was being shouted. Blasting at us from the crowd in rhythmical cadence came, "Niggah lovahs…Niggah lovahs…Niggah lovahs!"

"What'll we do?" Jan asked worriedly.

"Keep on going," I instructed. I hurried to pull open one of the large wooden double doors.

"What are they saying, daddy?" Timmy asked.

"Nothing!"

"But, daddy, they're saying *somethin'!*"

An elderly white gentleman dressed in a dark suit emerged from nowhere; as he shoved a program leaflet in my hand, he welcomed us with a cheery, though somewhat toothless, smile. "Y'all're newcomers. How nice," he said in a warm and encouraging manner. "Just sit anywheres. We may not have all that many today."

The Church was austere, almost barn-like, and seemed overly bright as the sun streamed through the purple and milky-white opaque stained glass windows. The two years I had worked for Blenko Glass had taught me to appreciate high quality hand-blown stained glass. This place of worship was no *Chartres* Cathedral!

The eight or ten robed members of the choir processed into place singing gleefully, if not too harmoniously. The service had begun. The Minister of the Church, the Reverend Andrew Forman, was a bookish-looking young man. He stood up to speak; pausing first, he bowed his head, seeming to recite some prayers to himself.

As his sermon unfolded, we came to understand about the people across the street on the neutral ground.

"There are those among us who call themselves Christians and yet do not know what it means to be their brother's keeper, or to love one another, as He loves us. I say to you, this is wrong. If Jesus were here in the flesh today, he would be saddened by our brothers and sisters who stand outside our Church and jeer because we have seen fit to welcome, into this house of our Lord, a colored family, a family who lives in the shadow of this very building. A family who, instead of crossing town to worship Jesus Christ, our risen Lord, has asked to be a part of our body in Christ. I cannot do less than accept them under the sheltering wing of the faith, hope, and charity of this congregation. We are called to serve Jesus, not always easy, sometimes it means to hang with Him on the Cross."

I was impressed by the likeness of his words to a speech by Saint Paul to the Corinthians.

During the remainder of the service I found my thoughts constantly harkening back to the demands being asked of us, of *me*. I agonized as to whether I would, or could, live up to those demands, if my feet were put to the fire. And there was a fire raging just outside the church. I considered myself a man of moral convictions. *But what,* I deliberated, *makes an honorable man brave? How strong will one be when he is called upon to sacrifice life, property, and even family safety, to remain true to his convictions? Where, or from whom,* I pondered, *does he receive his strength?*

The service ended with Reverend Forman offering his final blessing. His benediction was delivered from behind the rear pew. As the congregation of thirty-five or forty rose to leave, the two ushers flung open the double doors leading to the main Rampart Street entrance. The Minister stepped outside onto the raised front landing about to receive the first of the exiting parishioners, when a half-bushel of soft, stinking garbage landed on his shoulders and slithered down his black ministerial robe. Seemingly undaunted, he shook the slop from his robe and stepped back into the vestibule, pulling the double doors firmly shut. As he regained his composure, he asked us to remain inside for a few minutes so that he could go out and reason with the hecklers.

A quiet nervousness came over the group. Suddenly, we could hear what sounded like rocks or stones being hurled against the side of the building. Someone urged that we stay away from the milky glass windows, lest they be shattered. This ruckus took place so fast that none of us was frightened, but it quickly occurred to me: *This is how the Alamo fighters must have felt blockaded in the San Antonio Mission.* I'm sure it was the architecture of the building that inspired my imagination.

Before we had time to panic, the Reverend Forman pushed open one of the double doors and once again stepped out to face the crowd. In a calm but authoritative voice, he appealed to them, "Let my people go!"

The crowd responded in silence. He told them no police had been called or would be called, so long as the congregation could leave safely. The crowd on the neutral ground remained silent.

After a few minutes the minister asked us to file out of the church if we wished. He felt no harm would come to us. A few frightened souls stayed in the church, but the rest of us scurried down the steps and hurriedly set our course for home. Only a few weak catcalls could be heard from the hecklers as Rampart Street quickly disappeared behind us. Jan took Tammy by the hand, I took Timmy and we made fast tracks for home. The drunk we had left on the front steps was gone.

As I pushed my backside against the door, closing it firmly, Tammy broke the tension by asking, "Is Sunday School always like that?"

"Honey, we didn't even get to Sunday School today, but I assure you, it's not usually like that!"

Late in the evening, I walked over to the church to see if there was still a crowd; no one was in sight. There had been slight damage. Some of the crashing we had thought to be stones was bottles of liquid creosote that had broken against the side of the church, marring the pale green stucco walls by running down the façade, forming jagged, unsightly scars. The Reverend Forman chose to leave the marks there for many months as a record of man's inhumanity to man.

The next morning, when I walked to the bus stop at the corner of Royal and Ursulines Streets, Forman's sermon still echoed in my mind. It had been nearly a year since the Federal Government had ordered the enforcement of integration in schools and public transportation. *How long would it take people to become color-blind?* As the Desire Bus approached, I could see through the windshield that it was crowed with passengers all the way up to the driver's seat. Along with a couple of others, I stepped up onto the bus and pressed my way through the cluster of people in order to deposit my seven cents' fare. A rippling effect of readjusting bodies, caused by acceleration of the vehicle, thrust me toward the back of the bus. I was surprised by what I saw.

This particular bus originated in the Desire Project, a mostly black public housing development, then makes its way through a white, blue-collar neighborhood known as the Upper 9th Ward.

For nearly a hundred years, or at least as long as there had been public transportation in the South, the custom had been to have designated areas posted for the seating of whites and blacks. A moveable sign, stating *White* and *Colored*, would be shifted forward and backward according to the available seats. If the sign were moved back, whites would sit on seats formerly occupied by blacks, but whites would never sit *next* to a black on the *same* seat. Not only was that not done, it was against the law. Although this humiliating and often embarrassing practice for both races had now been revoked, the custom did not die easily. Many whites were still finding it repugnant to seat themselves next to blacks. And many blacks were fearful of sitting next to whites.

What I saw in the back of the bus both amazed and amused me. When the empty bus began its journey from the Desire Project toward its destination at Canal Street, black passengers had sat *one* to a seat, all along the windows; by the time the bus made its way into the white neighborhood, the only seats left were along the aisle, which meant that if a white person took a seat, he or she would *have* to sit next to an African-American. Thus, the reason for the front of the bus being so crowded, was that not one white had opted to sit next to an African-American. It was an interesting standoff that presented me, a former Yankee boy and recent graduate of Andy Forman's sermon, a challenge.

Somewhat timidly, I eased myself into a seat next to a middle-aged woman dressed in a freshly-starched white uniform. I set my gaze straight ahead, as did she. I could feel her robust body inflate and contract and hear her breathe heavily, as if releasing pent up anxiety. Folding my arms across my chest, I tried to dispel my own anxiety and to give the appearance of being in control. Still, I felt awfully alone as I staved off stares from the White passengers who had turned around to look. I felt my mouth go dry and found it necessary to force saliva around my tongue. To avoid any eye contact, I focused my eyes on an advertising poster for Luzianne Coffee. What kept running through my mind was: *This is Bob and this is Jan for Luzianne. This is Bob and this is Jan for Luzianne. What would Jan have done in this situation? I know what the Reverend Forman would have done.*

The bus lumbered along, making stops at Dumaine, St. Peter, St. Louis, Iberville, and finally Canal Street, where everyone piled out in front of Wools-worth's, as many New Orleanians call it. The whites left by the front door and the blacks exited through the rear. I was in a quandary for a moment, but finally followed the other whites out through the front. Because I had paused to consider my departure route, I was the last one off. The bus pulled away leaving me choking in a cloud of exhaust fumes, which the now-retired Desire Streetcar—of Tennessee Williams fame— would never have done. I was about to step off the curb to cross Canal Street when I was stopped and spun around by such a force that I almost lost my equilibrium.

A large, red-faced white man grabbed hold of my necktie and pulled it up the side of my head like a noose, cutting off my breathing and blood flow. Four or five other burly guys moved in to surround me. I felt my eyes bug out.

"You ass-hole Niggah lover, think you're a pretty fuckin' smart ass, don't cha? Well, if ya know what's good fer ya, ya better not set next to no more Niggahs or you'll git your smart ass beat off!"

He yanked my tie up a little tighter and gave me a slight knee job in the groin, causing me to burp and reach down to protect myself. They all laughed boisterously, disappearing quickly into the rush hour crowd. There was no doubt I had gotten their point. Passersby were either ignorant of my plight or chose not to get involved. I pressed a fist against my groin for a moment to help relieve the pain and leaned against a fire hydrant trying to regain my composure.

Although I wasn't physically injured, by the time I reached the neutral ground of Canal Street, I had tears in my eyes. My firsthand experience with violent bigotry left me emotionally shaken and spiritually wrecked. I made a choice not to tell Jan or anyone else about the incident until I had sorted it out in my own mind, which would involve a great deal of soul searching. My greatest fear was that I would not be brave enough to take a stand and sit down on the bus again the next morning.

The next day I arose earlier than usual after a sleepless night agonizing over how I was going to get to work. I left the house telling Jan a little white lie; I told her I had to be at the station ahead of my usual schedule to confer with Bill Romaine. The truth was, I had decided to walk to the station to avoid having to face the bus; however, instead of taking the direct route up Bourbon Street, I found myself detouring via Rampart Street, where I stopped and stood across the neutral ground in front of St. Mark's Church. The penetrating morning sun distorted the color of the defacing creosote, which had trickled down the side of the church on Sunday; it glistened like great wounds. I buried my face in my hands and rubbed my eyes fiercely to rid them of the sun's glare. I paused for a moment with my eyes still closed; those creosote spots appeared to me like gashes of blood on the hands of Jesus. A warm turbulence encircled me for a moment like a wrap. I was bewildered. The whole episode was over so fast that I wondered if it had happened at all.

When I opened my eyes, I realized a bus was standing at the curb with its door open, waiting for me to board. Giving it little thought, I pulled myself up the steps and pushed my way in through a group of white people to pay my fare, as I had done the day before. Again this bus, like the Desire Bus, was lined with blacks sitting along the windows. My heart leapt. I hadn't even intended to ride a bus this morning, but suddenly, here I was. Right next to where I was standing sat an elderly White woman holding what appeared to be her grandchild, seated beside a black lady. I couldn't take my eyes off her; she was the *only* white person sitting. When I looked at her, I didn't see just an old lady with a kid on her lap, I saw a Madonna and Child. Suddenly, and without reservations, I slipped into the seat behind her alongside a middle-aged black man dressed in clean coveralls. I glanced his way after I had settled into my seat. We made eye contact.

"Good morning," I said, a bit hesitantly.

"Yasir, good mornin', sir," he replied with a smile.

"Goin' ta work?" I asked rather rhetorically, in my assumed leveling accent.

"Yasir."

That was all there was to our conversation, but it was enough to put us both at ease. The bus stopped at Dumaine. Two young white women in their late twenties pushed aboard through the crowd. From their dresses and high heals they were probably clerks at one of the department stores, either Maison Blanche or Krauss. The bus lurched forward and with nothing to hold onto, they went stumbling down the center aisle, grasping for a seat to keep from falling; before they realized what they had done, they were sitting *and* sharing seats with African-Americans. Although they kept themselves positioned close to the aisle, they did stay put even after realizing their position. The bus made one more stop before reaching Canal Street. An elderly white man teetering on a cane made his way into the bus. Without hesitation, he sat next to a black lady who appeared to be in a nurse's uniform.

Something quite amazing had happened on that brief ride, a ride that I never expected to take. I was changed and so were others. Never again on a New Orleans bus did I fear to sit next to whomever I chose.

* * * * *

I was watching John Chancellor's critique of JFK's inaugural speech on NBC. His memorable phrase, "Ask not what your country can do for you, ask what you can do for your country," intrigued and disturbed me. Being our first Roman Catholic President, he was of special interest in our Catholic city. The titter of some Protestants was that the Pope would soon be running our country from the Vatican! My concentration was broken when I heard Olympia ring for dinner.

Each evening at dinner, the children vied for the honor of saying Grace. This evening it was Tammy's turn.

"God is great, God is good, and we thank him for our food; by His hand we all are fed. Thank you, God, for our daily bread. Amen."

Timmy butted in, "Daddy, why must we thank God for this food? He didn't buy it."

"Well, eh, you see, God makes it rain and controls the sunshine. That way seeds grow into corn and wheat, and grass can grow so animals can eat, and we can eat the animals."

"Daddy," Timmy interrupted, "why don't we eat wolfs and bears and lizards?"

"Yuk!" squeaked Tammy, "that's gross!"

Tim continued to reel off animal types, "and bunnies, and squirrels, and dogs and cats..."

Tammy's eyes pooled with tears. Chokingly, she cried out, "You're not 'spostah' eat bunnies and dogs and animals like that."

"This gumbo's got crabs and roaches in it!"

"*Timothy*! Stop teasing your sister *now* or you're going to leave the table," I reprimanded.

"Everybody here is so dull, no drama!" Timmy grumbled, half under his breath.

"I'll drama your behind if you don't stop pestering Tammy!"

"Well, daddy, you're the one who said we eat animals."

"Timothy, let's drop the subject." Jan instructed, somewhat pleadingly. "It's difficult enough to get Tammy to eat anyway, so please don't upset her stomach with all this gross talk. Olympia worked very hard to make this delicious gumbo, so please eat!"

Tammy had always been a finicky eater. "Angel Child" that she was, she was extremely stubborn about food. Sometimes at dinner she would sit with tears dribbling down her plump rosy cheeks, defying our suggestions she should eat her dinner like a "good little girl." Usually we just gave up in despair by the end of the meal and let her leave the table whether she'd eaten or not. After all, she was a chubby little thing, always had been; however, we were concerned about nutrition.

One night, when Olympia had prepared some extra tasty trout *Meuniére*, I insisted Tammy eat every bite.

After only two bites, she shoved the plate away. "Yuk, that's all I'm gonna eat of *that* stuff!"

"You are not leaving this table until you finish your dinner: trout, okra and rice," I insisted. (In New Orleans, rice is more popular than mashed potatoes; personally, I prefer potatoes!)

She looked me straight in the eye and squared off. A stalemate was underway.

"Tammy, you're going sit here until you're twenty-one years old if you want, but you *will* eat your dinner!"

She sat straight up in her chair, hands folded in her lap, and without saying a word, shook her head mechanically from side to side like a carved figure on a Bavarian cuckoo clock.

"Tammy, you've got a really long time to go if you don't eat until you're twenty-one!" Timmy interjected. "You'll be an old lady like mommy!"

"Timmy, please leave Tammy alone."

"Bob, don't you think she could eat just half?"

"No! I'm determined that for once in her life, she is going to finish her dinner!"

Olympia appeared at the door to clear the table.

"Oh, Tammy, mah li'l angel dawling, you dint like yo dinner?"

"Olympia, please leave Tammy's plate where it is, I think she's being a slow eater this evening."

"Yes, Sir, I sees." Olympia looked lovingly at Tammy. "Dawling, ah be savin' you some of that good pecan pah ah made. You jis eat up, chile!"

"Thank you, Olympia," Jan intervened, "please serve the pie to the rest of us."

"Yes, Ma'am, and some *café au lait* like regular?"

Jan, Timmy, and I finished our pie as Tammy sat quietly defiant with her hands folded; her tears had ceased. Upon leaving the dining room, Timmy scampered up the back stairs to his room in the *garconniere* (a *Créole* term for young men's or bachelor's quarters, pronounced gar-son-yair). As Jan and I adjourned to the front parlor, I reminded Tammy she was to finish her dinner before she ate any pie. Out of the corner of my eye, I could see Olympia listening carefully from her post in front of the kitchen sink.

"It makes me ache inside to leave Tammy all alone in that big dining room," Jan said, "but I guess she has to learn to eat what's best for her."

Jan and I sat in the twilight for nearly half an hour discussing our next day's broadcast when Olympia stuck her head in to announce she had finished the dishes and was leaving.

"Mizz Tammy still be sittin' at da table. She bees a mighty stubborn li'l lady. She's some set in her ways. Wun't s'prise me none if she be raht there in da mornin', but ah hopes not. Yes, Sir, ah hopes not. Night, y'all!"

Some ten minutes after Olympia left, there was a creaking on the front stairway, and then the obvious, firm closing of a door on the second floor. I quietly snuck halfway up the long staircase, just far enough to get a glimpse of Tammy's closed bedroom door. I eased back down the steps and went directly to the dining room table to check Tammy's empty plate. *Ah ha, victory*, I thought! *At last, Tammy knows who's boss around here and what's required of her.*

Feeling quite smug and victorious, I went back into the parlor to finish program plans with Jan, who was pleased with the results, though she felt I had been overly harsh.

"If we're going to sit there and say, 'God is great. God is good, and we thank Him for our food', we damn well better know how valuable the food is!" I said.

"Okay, Okay. Enough preaching, Father Carr. Let's finish looking over this bio on Danny Thomas. Remember, we pre-record his segment tomorrow since he's on a tight schedule."

After finishing preparations for the next day's program, we started upstairs, when Jan asked me to check the dishwasher. Olympia had complained that sometimes it turned off and didn't run through its complete cycle. Seeing the dishwasher was functioning properly, through habit I checked to see if there was any last-minute garbage. Tilting open the top of the garbage can, I could see it was empty save for a neatly folded paper napkin in the bottom of the Schwegmann's Giant Supermarket shopping bag that Olympia used as a liner. The napkin looked strangely clean and neat; intrigued, I unfolded it to find the remains of Tammy's dinner. My first reaction was rage, but I was also amused by her bold defiance. I folded the napkin and put it back. Though I hated to face an encounter, this act of disobedience on Tammy's part could not go unpunished.

I bounded up the stairs with such an explosion that Jan thought I was being chased. Jan watched quizzically as I bounced to a halt at Tammy's door and knocked.

"She put her dinner in the trash!" I whispered to Jan, then raised my voice, "Tammy, are you in there?"

"Uh huh."

"May I come in?"

"Uh huh."

I opened the door on an almost dark room. A cool breeze from the river danced across the balcony through the louvers of the closed shutters. Jan stood in the doorway bracing for what might come next. Tammy was stretched out on the coverlet of her tester bed like a mummy. Arms folded across her chest, she stared at the canopy over her bed. I could see her jaw was clenched and her lower lip was tucked securely up under her nose. Tears were trickling down both cheeks. Without saying a word, she rose from her bed, swung her feet off the side farthest from me, cut a wide swath around the room, passed through the door to the hall, just missing Jan, and proceeded down the long stairs.

"Where's she going?" asked Jan.

"I have an idea. Let's wait a minute and then go see."

After what seemed like an eternity, we followed her. The house was almost dark, and the downstairs always seemed a bit spooky to Tammy if we left her there alone. She wasn't in the hall, the parlor, or the dining room. In the almost totally dark kitchen, we could hear the sound of sobbing over the swish-swash of the dishwasher. On the floor, next to the garbage can, with the napkin neatly unfolded on the red brick floor, sat Tammy, quietly eating the final remains of her trout *Meuniére*.

Jan and I stood in the shadows wiping away our tears.

* * * * *

We were always amused when tourists spotted our family trekking through the Quarter. Many of them looked at us with amazement, assuming us to be beatnik parents, dragging our children through a life of degradation and deprivation in the defiled French Quarter. Little did they know that during the day, we represented the sacredness of family life to our Monday-through-Friday listeners. Our family was, indeed, sacred and holy to us; however, to me, there is a certain excitement in flirting with the seamy side of society. *After all*, I thought, *how could I ever know for sure what was right and good, if I had never come in close contact with what some people consider evil or sinful?*

I wanted to be sure that I, and my children, would always judge people on their own merit and not by the house they live in, the car they drive, the clothes they wear, the way they pronounce their words or their ethnic background. Well-educated people in fine clothes, backing their expensive cars down the driveways of their lovely homes, very often perpetrate the crimes of cruelty, injustice, jealously, hatred, bigotry, and intolerance. And even beyond that, I guess I took delight in suckering judgmental people into making quick and inaccurate conclusions about *us*. I liked knowing in our hearts that we were not what they may have at first assumed.

On many a family walk to Jackson Square, toting the kids behind us in the red wagon, we would pick up a huge muffaletta sandwich, the invention of the Central Grocery on Decatur Street, along with several Barq's sodapops. The children enjoyed spreading out a blanket in the square, on the thick spiky St. Augustine grass on the far side of the bandstand, where we could savor both music and seclusion. The children also loved to chase the pigeons that congregated around, and often pooped on, the statue of General Andrew Jackson mounted arrogantly on his rearing stallion. Lying on a blanket in the shade of a live-oak tree under a cloud-speckled sky, surveying the array of historic buildings that encircle the square named for the man who defeated the English in the Battle of New Orleans gives one a feeling of being *in* history, not *after* it.

Jackson Square, or *Place d'Armes*, as the French originally called it, had, since the founding of the city, been a center of military, political, religious, and social activity. The Louisiana Purchase was signed, and the document still housed, in the Cabildo building just across Pirate's Alley from St. Louis Cathedral, the oldest cathedral on the Mississippi.

Living in the Quarter could be likened to living in a field of varied wildflowers. Some are beautiful while some are not; some bloom brightly and of long duration, while others pale and fade quickly; but they all add to the uniqueness of the bouquet. The Square is the vase that, for a time, brings the blooms together in an ever-changing arrangement.

On our outings to the Square, we often encountered an ancient woman whom we referred to as "Madonna and her plastic baby Jesus." The stooped and weathered Madonna seemed to have but two missions in life as she trudged along: one, to feed the pigeons; the other, to attend Mass. An apparent recluse, the old soul lived in a dilapidated Creole townhouse on Chartres Street near Dumaine. The building was shabby and dreary, an odoriferous blight to the block. If the exterior of the place, replete with hanging baskets of dead ferns alongside scrawny cats occupying the decaying balcony, were any indication, the inside must have been in a total state of clutter and filth.

The old woman would step forth onto the banquette in a tidy yet tattered three-quarter-length white eyelet dress accessorized with a white broad-brimmed straw hat and white gloves. Grossly smeared chalk-white polished shoes completed her ensemble. Departing her doorstep, she quietly tugged her plastic baby Jesus in a two-wheeled wire shopping cart with one hand, while in the other she clutched a large, white, wooden crucifix, which lay across her bosom. She said not a word, but went straight to her work, praying and feeding the pigeons. Numerous times I tried to make eye contact or obstruct her given path to induce an encounter for the purpose of making conversation and offering assistance. It didn't work. She was adamant in her determination to avoid all social contact.

Her beat was a path from her home to the square to scatter breadcrumbs, then on to the Cathedral for prayers and supplications before returning home. From whence her breadcrumbs came, we could only speculate. One day, when the Madonna looked particularly bedraggled, Jan felt we should stop to ask if she needed anything. This proved futile. She became quite hostile and rebuked us fiercely, leaving Jan crushed.

After some months of not seeing her on her rounds, the *Times-Picayune* reported her death. Eloise Lopez Arollo Samakintos had been discovered in eternal rest surrounded by hundreds of loaves of stale, rodent-infested bread, still clutching her crucifix and Jesus doll.

* * * * *

Although we continued to go to St. Mark's Methodist Church, Timmy and Tammy became more and more intrigued by what lay behind the great facade of the Cathedral at Jackson Square. A wonderful celebration held annually in the shadow of Jackson's statue since 1946, the Christmas candlelight caroling service sponsored by the Patio Planters Association of the French Quarter had become a tradition with us. Hundreds of people of all types, and of many religious persuasions, turned out annually to make "a joyful noise unto the Lord" on the Sunday eve before Christmas. The tolling of the huge St. Louis Cathedral bells at seven o'clock summoned the multitude.

Church groups, rowdies, friends, and jovial New Orleans families with flocks of kids poured in from Metairie, Gentilly, and Uptown, jamming traffic as they descended on the Quarter. These Suburbanites were joined by hundreds of Quarterites moving in a happy frenzy along the streets and banquettes in anticipation of raising their voices to God in a holiday fa-la-la.

The four iron gates in the fence that surrounds and protects the square were pushed open as the seventh reverberating bell-tone died. In near silence, the waiting throngs politely pressed and jostled through the narrow openings. Song sheets and hand-held candles, doled out by Patio Planters volunteers, were lit one from the other by the carolers as they hastened toward the dais singing "O Come All Ye Faithful." It was a moving experience for "all God's chillin'."

From a temporary rostrum in front of the equestrian statue of Andy, the Archbishop of the Roman Catholic Diocese of New Orleans welcomed "the faithful," many of whom were not Roman Catholic but certainly felt a devotion to Christmas. The mayor, or a city councilman, got in a few good words and hopefully gained a few votes for himself or the administration; and then, just as everyone began to get restless and to doubt the longevity of his or her flickering candle, already singeing the hair on one's hand, the song leader stepped forth. For the next hour the sacred and joyous songs of the season filled the air and warmed the hearts of the carolers.

There were always a few hee-haws and giggles when the choristers exuberantly hit the words "don we now our gay apparel." Some "straights" self-consciously glanced around to see who in the crowd might be a "homo," and many gays took gleeful delight in the invocation of gaiety. It was a great time to witness veneration to the Lord by the wide variety of human beings God had unleashed upon His earth.

Following the caroling, it was tradition to adjourn to someone's patio, weather permitting, or perhaps his parlor, to enjoy a toast to the Holiday Season with a hot and hardy cup of *Café Brulot*, accompanied by freshly prepared pralines, beignets, or *callas tout chaud*.

Pralines, always pronounced prah-*leens*, were made traditionally with the fall crop of Louisiana sugar and pecans (pee-*cahns*). *Beignets* (ben-*yeas*) are square, puffed-up Creole doughnuts, found twenty-four hours a day in the French Market at *Café du Monde*. And *callas tout chaud* (*calah*-lez too-*show*) are sweet, deep-fried rice cakes, originally cooked following the Louisiana rice harvest. Today, callas are seldom found except in the kitchens of private homes and usually at the Coffee Pot on St. Peter Street. *Café Brulot* (cah-*fay* broo-*low*) is a pungent blend of cloves, cube sugar, orange, and lemon rind, flamed with brandy in a silver bowl. Like an inviting noel fire, the flaming concoction evokes "oohs" and "aahs" from the spectators. To quench the flame, dark roast coffee with chicory is poured into the bowl. It is a brew that tantalizes the taste buds. Superstition has it that if the hostess can peal the oranges and lemons in a single cut without breaking the rind, good fortune will follow the imbibers.

Café Brulot is found on the menus of some New Orleans restaurants and hotel dining rooms including Antoine's, Arnaud's, Brennan's, Broussard's, Galatoire's, and the Royal Orleans Hotel. It is interesting to note that all the aforementioned recipes grew out of foods abundant at Louisiana harvest time, including oranges and lemons, from the warm rich land immediately down river from New Orleans, plus the tangy spices imported through the city's port.

With Jackson Square and St. Louis Cathedral as a backdrop for many pleasant activities of our lives, the children repeatedly wanted to know what went on inside that building during Mass. We had overheard Timmy telling Tammy, "Me and Pierre went in there one day, they've got a big huge cross up by the stage and Jesus is hanging on it. I never seen him look so bad. And they got all these red candles burning for spirits, and there's humongous statues of Joseph and Mary and other Catholic people. Pierre's uncle, who's a minister or somethin', told him they're Saints!"

Pierre, now Timmy's closest friend at school, had an uncle who was a monsignor. This made Pierre the religious authority in his peer group. Born into a Creole family, he was very serious about his religious commitments. If, on a Friday or a Holy Day, he would stay over for dinner and we happened to have meat, he would respectfully abstain. Once, when Timmy's birthday fell a week before Easter, I took a group of the boys to the Orpheum Theater for a juicy afternoon thriller. Following the movie, we set out for home on foot to have birthday cake and gifts. Turning onto Bourbon, the boys all dashed ahead sneaking looks at the blow-up photos of shady ladies, posing in their G-strings. Each time they stopped in front of a photo, they snickered embarrassedly and then dashed on to the next full-busted blow-up. I was chuckling at their antics when I realized that Pierre had never left my side; he was clinging to me like a fly to fly paper.

"Pierre, are you all right?"

"Oh, yes, Mister Carr, I'm fine."

"Don't you want to run on ahead with the rest of the gang?"

"Oh, yes, sir, I'd like to, but..."

"But, what?"

"You see, sir, it's Lent. I'm not s'posed to look at those naked ladies during Lent. I gave it up!"

"Pierre, I am very proud of you, *very proud!*"

That young man taught me a great deal about sacrifice and forbearance, which I shall not forget. As we walked along in the heavy heat of the afternoon sun, passing in front of The 500 Club strip joint, the naked lady posters struck me as more tawdry than usual. I took Pierre by the hand, as if to protect him from the lusty, busty ladies' leers and lairs, but I felt in truth, Pierre was *my* protector.

With so many Catholic friends, I thought it was time we learned more about that particular brand of religion. My mother had been Catholic as a child; she gave it up when she married my dad. All she ever told me and my sister about her Catholicism was how she learned to play the piano quickly because the nun would wrap her fingers with a ruler if she hit the wrong key.

"Jan, the kids have so many conflicting stories about Mass and Catholics, and what goes on in the Cathedral, I think we should take them to a service there next Sunday. There's suppose to be a special Dixieland Jazz Mass that I'd love to hear!"

Bent on hearing the Jazz Mass, we decided to take the kids, even though the

Roman Catholic Church was foreign to us. For me, one of the nicest things about going to a Catholic Church is that nobody bothers you. At least at St. Louis Cathedral, there seems to be a call to be with God. From the moment you push open the ancient swinging paneled doors in the foyer, with the little square peep-holes though which timorous tourists peek, until you step back out into the worldly hustle of Chartres Street and Jackson Square, there is a commanding holiness. This three-hundred-year-old sacred edifice serves as a sanctuary where quiet worshippers pay little concern to gawking tourists or other pious persons as they go about their business of genuflecting, lighting candles, fingering their rosaries, or making the sign of the cross while murmuring their petitions.

"Jan, we'd better get going," I yelled up the front stairs, "if we're going to get a seat."

I shouted up to Timmy in the *garconniere*. "Come down *now*. We're leaving!"

"*Daddy*, I'm right here behind you."

As I turned around, I could see he was wiping syrup off his white shirt, which had dripped from the *pain pardou* (French toast) we had eaten for breakfast.

"May I help?"

"I'm spotless 'cept for this spot but my suit coat'll cover it. See?"

"Okay, let's go. Jan, where are you?" I called again, sounding a bit irritated.

"Don't rush me. I can't find Tammy's hat. Darn it, you know we can't go to a Catholic Church without a hat. It's against the rules or something. Just wait one minute. I found it!"

Tammy bounced down the steps, tying the pink ribbon under her chin so that her floppy-brimmed straw hat would stay in place. Suddenly she caught the toe of her shoe in the new carpet I had not yet fully tacked in place, causing her to descend the last six or eight steps sliding on her knees, almost as if she were crouched on a toboggan. As she came to a complete halt on the bare pine floor, we all held our breath in silence, waiting to see, first of all, if she was hurt and, secondly, if she was going to cry. I'm not sure which was our greatest concern. Tammy was known to cry at the drop of a hat and her hat had definitely dropped, slipping back off her head, tightening the pink grosgrain ribbon around her throat. Without uttering a word she picked herself up, dusted herself off, and readjusted her hat.

She didn't utter a sound until Timmy spoke up. "Tammy, look at the blood on your knees!"

She bent over to see, and then burst forth with a scream that almost shook the antique banister from its mooring.

"Oh, my baby!" Jan yelled from the top of the stair. "Are you all right?"

Tammy screamed again.

"Tammy, you're so dramatic," Timmy reprimanded.

Another scream.

"I'll go get you some Band-Aids," Timmy said, scampering toward the back bathroom.

"Oh, my God, we'll never get to church now," I moaned.

"Yes, we will, I'll get a wash cloth and wipe off her knees and then we'll go."

Tammy continued screaming.

"Tammy, it's not that bad," I said, which only made her shriek louder.

Jan came down the stairs with a cool, wet washcloth as Timmy emerged with a box of Band-Aids. Jan touched the washcloth to Tammy's skinned knees, inciting one final violent outburst. The appeased victim eased down on the bottom step, allowing Timmy to place a Band-Aid on each knee. With a clean tip of the washcloth, Jan wiped away Tammy's tears, and we were, *at last*, headed for Jackson Square.

In spite of the dramatics on the staircase, we got to the Cathedral just before Mass commenced.

"You gotta curtsy before you go into your seat," instructed Tammy. "That's what my friend Sandy told me."

"Yah, and ya gotta put holy water on your face, too, when ya walk through the door or they won't let you in, 'cause that's what me and Pierre did," Timmy informed us.

"Yuk, I don't wanna put that yucky water on *my* face if ever'body's hands was in it."

"Ya better do it, Tammy, or they might not let ya in. *And,* ya better make like you're drawin' a cross on your chest, too."

"Stop scarin' me with all that stuff."

"Yes, Timmy, stop scaring Tammy and hurry along," Jan urged.

The children were so distracted by going into the church they didn't notice we had not taken advantage of the holy water in the vestibule; however, we did genuflect slightly and timidly as we entered a pew about one fourth of the way down the long center aisle leading to the magnificent high altar.

Timmy pointed. "See that big cross? That's Jesus hangin' there."

"Shhh, we must be quiet. Listen to the beautiful music."

"It doesn't sound like church music to me," Timmy said.

"It's special New Orleans jazz music."

"It must be Catholic music," Timmy sighed.

As the congregation knelt, Jan and I slid self-consciously onto the kneeler, beckoning the children to follow.

"I can't, my Band-Aids will come off!"

"All right, you just sit there."

"They're talking in a funny language. I don't understand nothin', daddy. Is that American talk?"

"Shh, Timmy, it's Latin. They speak Latin."

"Is that Catholic talk?" Tammy asked.

"Yes, dear."

"Pierre's Catholic and he don't talk like that," Timmy muttered.

"Please, be quiet," I pleaded.

The service continued.

In a loud, hushed voice, Tammy asked, "What's that smell, daddy?"

Timmy whispered, "Something's on fire, look at all the smoke!"

"That's incense."

Timmy sprang to his feet and blurted, "Why are they ringing those bells? It *must* be a fire!"

I reached up and pulled Timmy down by the shoulder. "There's *no* fire. The bells are to let everyone know this is a very holy time."

"How do you know that, daddy?"

"I just know."

"Oh."

I could see the exasperated look on his face and then his proverbial question, "Why they gotta have smoke, daddy?"

"It's a way of blessing the altar."

"That don't seem very religious. You always taught us not to play with fire. That smoke's gonna make me choke!"

Tammy whispered, "What's the Holy Spirit he's talkin' about?"

Jan explained, "It's part of God. I'll tell you later."

"Why are they ringing those bells again?"

"Because it's still a special holy time, so please fold your hands and pray like mommy and Tammy!"

"Tammy's not praying, she's poutin' because she can't kneel!"

"Okay. Just ignore her."

Members of the congregation began to rise and form a communion line in the center aisle.

"Bob, what do we do now?" Jan queried nervously, glancing at me across the kid's heads. "We aren't suppose to take communion in a Catholic church. They won't let us."

"How will they know?" I whispered back.

"I don't know, but *they* know."

"We'll just sit here piously. Look, other people are staying in their seats, so we're not going to be all that conspicuous."

"All right," she sighed with relief.

"When do we get in line, daddy?" Tammy asked quietly and confidently, her big brown eyes peeking up from under her hat.

"We aren't getting in line, honey."

"Why not?"

"Just because, dear."

"Because we aren't Catholic, silly," Timmy whispered loudly in Tammy's ear. "Pierre said ya gotta be Catholic ta do that stuff, besides he said what ya get up there is a piece of bread that's suppose to be God's skin and when ya eat it, it sticks to the roof of your mouth!"

"Yuk!"

"Children, *please!*" pleaded Jan.

An older lady, several rows ahead of us, who had been wrestling with an active two-year-old child, probably her grandson, stood up and moved from her pew toward the aisle to queue into the communion line.

Timmy broke forth with a rather sudden and forceful outburst, "Mommy, daddy, look at that lady!"

Moving out of the pew, she had slung her grandchild over her shoulder while genuflecting—no easy balancing act on the slippery black and white marble floor. Unbeknownst to grandma, the flailing child had somehow gotten a firm hold on the hem of her rather loose fitting, rayon dress. The woman began to move reverently up the aisle, unaware that her grandbaby was tugging on the fabric of her skirt. The child kept pulling until the whole backside of granny's garment was in his tight little fist, exposing her rather scanty underpinnings, consisting merely of nylon hose supported by a black satin garter belt. The more-than-ample flesh of her derriére quivered with each innocent step toward the high altar. In a state of complete guilelessness, the unlikely Madonna strode with babe in arms toward the Lord's supper.

"Bob, go pull that lady's dress down!" Jan instructed, beckoning me out of the pew with her hand. "You're on the aisle!"

"I can't."

"Why not?"

"I just *can't*, and I'm *not*."

Timmy and Tammy started to giggle as the lady proceeded further up the aisle. I began to giggle myself. Two gentlemen, moving from their pews, genuflected respectfully and fell into line behind her, but in embarrassment, kept their distance, which gave the entire center section of the Cathedral the opportunity to gaze upon the lady's fanny.

As the eyes of various members of the congregation fell upon the scene, they reacted predictably with a double take and then a glance around to see if anyone else was enjoying this incongruous episode. So struck with the humor of the scene, I almost laughed out loud. I strained with every muscle of my being not to cry out. I closed my eyes and recited the Lord's Prayer; even then, I was helpless. All I could visualize was that lady's white skin, flashing between her garter belt and the top of her nylons. I worked so hard trying to repress my laughter, I started to ache and shake.

"Daddy, why are you shaking?" Timmy asked.

"Stop!" I said, unable to speak further without an outburst.

"I'm not doing anything."

"Why is daddy crying?" Tammy loudly whispered.

Tears flowed uncontrollably. When my eyes had cleared and focused, my gaze fell upon a man about five pews ahead who had his arm out-stretched, pointing at the woman in amazement. I could contain myself no longer. As I began to giggle uncontrollably, Tammy and Timmy began to parrot my reaction. Trying to break the spell, Jan glanced at me fiercely, which only compelled me to become more uncontrolled. I slipped into a kneeling position, laying my forehead on the back of the pew in front of me, slowly regaining my composure, then reprimanding the children, hoping to calm them. Just as I glanced toward the front of the church, our lady was turning away from the priest. His reaction at seeing her backside so disoriented him that he bumped the altar boy, almost causing him to drop his paten. This was more than I could bear. I fell back onto the kneeler and wept openly.

Thanks be to God, the jazz trumpets were filling the sanctuary with sounds akin to those of the Archangel Gabriel. Grandma returned to her pew; after genuflecting dutifully, she placed junior on the seat next to her, adjusted her skirt and resumed her devotions, never knowing the agony she had put me through. *God takes care of His own*, I thought reassuringly. With a great sweeping gesture, the priest made the sign of the cross, bestowing his final blessing on the congregation. We sat for a few moments composing ourselves while worshippers began to shuffle out.

The aforementioned lady came down the aisle pulling her unwilling two-year-old by the hand. Passing our pew, she glanced at me and smiled. She startled me as she leaned over and whispered, "I've heard you and Miss Jan on my radio and I've seen you and your beautiful family in the neighborhood. Gawd Bless!"

I smiled back politely, but I was thinking, *Lady, you have no idea where I've seen you!*

As we stood to leave, Tammy wanted to light a candle.

"That's very sweet," Jan said. "As we light it, think of someone you love and miss very much and this candle will be for them."

"Okay, mommy, I made my wish, but I can't tell 'cause it won't come true. Now, gimmie that funny match thing, so I can light it by myself."

"Bob, do you have any change?"

"Here, honey."

Tammy squeezed a coin into the ancient mite box.

"Timmy, do you want to buy a candle?"

"Heck, no, daddy. I'd rather have a pistachio sno-ball!"

Family gathering on grandparents' farm in Colerain, Ohio, 1955. Jan, Grandpa Franke holding baby Timmy, Bob, Grandma Franke, Dad Fitzsimmons, sister Carol and husband Jesse Carroll

CHAPTER FIVE

From Radio to TV for a "Second Cup"

The ratings on our noontime WWL-radio show had become the highest in the market for our time period. Jan and I were thrilled, and for the first time since our arrival at the station, we felt secure in our acceptance by the community. Management was equally happy about our ratings but on the other hand very concerned about the sluggish ratings in the early morning. Ever since the station had decided to discontinue the popular but immensely expensive *Dawnbusters* show, a tough battle for listeners was being waged solo by Sidney Noel Rideau, a young, local humorist, who had created for WWL-TV a weird, disorderly, but adored mad scientist known as *Morgus the Magnificent*. Morgus was the filler act during the extended commercial breaks of the late night horror B-movies. *Dr. Alexander Momus Morgus of the Higher Power* had become insanely popular with fans of all ages. But on weekday radio mornings, Sidney Rideau became yet another character known to his listeners as Sid Noel. He received slow acceptance from the disoriented, and sometimes unhappy, former *Dawnbusters* listeners.

Bill, our program director, so positive about the co-host concept the station was pursuing with Jan and me, asked me to extend my schedule to include the drive-time slot with Sid in the morning. I would serve as his straight man and side kick. Flattered and delighted, I saw it as an opportunity to stretch my personality in a direction untried in my on-air relationship with Jan. Sid was an extremely versatile and talented guy with a fertile mind for outrageous ideas. He was used to working alone and I found it difficult to get him to accept me or let me enter into his on-the-air dialogue. Either he resented being saddled with me or he considered me some sort of a threat to his individuality. Of course, he was a native and I was an outsider.

His first thaw toward me came during a surprise snow storm, the first in ten years. The storm hit New Orleans during a frigid January night in 1961. Sid concocted a scheme whereby we would sell our early-morning listeners shares of stock in a ski-lift on Monkey Hill in Audubon Park. Although man-made Monkey Hill is the only hill in New Orleans, we asked listeners who were stranded at home by the snow to call in and pledge money for the hasty construction of the ski-lift. Sid and I were truly surprised when the phones began to ring, ring, ring. We had thousands of dollars in what, I am sure, were pledges as bogus as the scheme itself.

By 8:45 A.M., fifteen minutes before the program signed off, we got a call from the good-natured parks commissioner saying the snow on Monkey Hill had melted. Alas, we had to announce to our audience that our plan was a failure, the city would be left without a ski-lift and the pledges would be considered null and void. The ski idea may have been a failure, but the audience and the WWL sales staff loved Sid and Bob together, and from then on, so did Sid.

When French President Charles DeGaulle was about to visit New Orleans, Sid fantasized an idea: we could install huge electric fans above Canal Street to blow the scent of hot French bread over the motorcade to make the General feel welcome. We were once again stirring our audience to buy stock shares, this time in the fan business. The giant fans would be installed on the rooftops of stores like D.H. Holmes, Godchaux, Kreegers, and high above the Maison Blanche building. While caught up in announcing this outrageous idea, I suffered a slip of the tongue and inadvertently announced that we were hoping to welcome President DeGaulle with the scent of hot French *bed!* From then on, Sid and I were good friends.

Singer Margie O'Dair, who had accepted a position in the promotion department of the radio station by day, continued to pursue her singing career at night spots around town. She also performed occasionally on the Mississippi Gulf Coast at the fabled frolic spot of New Orleanians, the Broadwater Beach Hotel in Biloxi, owned by the fabulously wealthy Mr. and Mrs. Joe Brown. Jan and I learned quickly from our Gulf Coast listeners that Biloxi is always pronounced Ba-*lux*-ee by Mississippians and well-traveled Southerners.

Margie's magnetic personality, disarming directness, and air of *savoir faire* had attracted us to her immediately. The adversity of losing her spotlight and taking an office job must have hurt her enormously, but it was never evident. Jan and I marvelled at her humility and tenacity. She was loved by everyone, especially her co-workers and members of the Roosevelt staff, who admired her not only as a star but as a kind and affable person. She happily introduced us to everybody. Margie may have been attracted to the two of us because of our enthusiasm for the French Quarter as a place to live and raise our children. She herself had been raised in the Quarter along with her two sisters. The French Quarter was her jewel and she fancied anyone with a fondness for it.

At one of her cocktail parties we learned the interesting dichotomy of local drinking habits. Margie, who had no patience with race prejudice and gender bias, engaged a young, somewhat effeminate black friend, to work as bartender for her party. As a struggling artist, the young man needed to augment his feeble earnings by doing various odd jobs. Margie, a modest drinker and a devout practicing Catholic, never dreamed that James, a devout and practicing Baptist, had been taught by his grandmother to never touch alcohol, and consequently, had never mixed a drink.

We arrived early for the party so Jan could help Margie put out chips and dips. Margie and James were in a slight confrontation over how to mix a cocktail as the guests began to pile in. To add an air of class to the cheap whiskey she had purchased from Schwegmann's Giant Supermarket—that vast paradise of middle-class New Orleans shoppers—Margie had poured the various liquors into antique decanters. James got the party off to a rousing start by mistakenly substituting gin or vodka for water in the mixed drinks. The party peaked within an hour. The jovial and slightly rowdy revelers dumped their drinks of Bourbon or Scotch, laced with gin or vodka, into paper go-cups, as locals are want to do, and raucously rambled down Decatur Street, past the French Market, to *La Casa de los Marinos*.

La Casa, as it was affectionately called by those in the know, had become the *in* place, where, as the lyrics in "Basin Street Blues" state, the elite meet: black, white, brown, sailors, salesmen, Uptowners, Downtowners, wealthy, scruffy, straight, and gay—a true cross-section of New Orleans. The *Merengué*, the newest rage and the dance of the house, seduced the smoke-saturated crowd into a sensual undulating mass. Spanish was mumbled over the high-volumed juke box, enhanced by three live bongo players of diverse color, sweating profusely as they beat away on their tom-toms. Each time a record ran out, someone dropped in another nickel and lit another cigarette. The music never ceased; Jan and I danced nonstop like there was no tomorrow. During one of the brief breaks, a little Spanish-speaking fellow came up to Jan and asked for the next dance; she looked at me for guidance.

I shrugged, indicating approval. "Maybe you can learn a few new steps," I whispered in her ear.

The music started. Jan and Elpanzo were off into the throbbing throng on the smoke-filled, dimly lit dance floor.

This was my opportunity to call home to see if the kids were okay. I pressed through the tightly-packed gyrating crowd to find a pay phone.

"It's by the dressin' room," the bartender instructed.

I understood, remembering that in New Orleans, the restroom is usually referred to as the "dressing room." Down a long dark corridor, the phone was attached at waist height to the wall opposite the men's room. I could barely see to deposit my nickel; there being no chair I had to stoop over to dial; in order to hear or be heard I practically had to bury my head into the receiver. I cupped my hands around my face to make myself understood. From what I could hear, all was fine at home. The kids had said their prayers and were dozing off. I was placing the receiver on the hook when I felt someone's hand reach between my legs from behind and firmly grasp my entire private parts! In disbelief for a few seconds, I couldn't move. I coughed slightly, feeling as though I had just re-experienced the G-I scrotum test. An arm reached around my waist, embracing me as a soft, squeaky voice whispered something in my ear. I squirmed around, releasing myself from his grasp, coming face to face with a pale, fleshy fellow in his mid-forties, not much more than five feet tall.

"Oooh, excuse me, doll, I thought you were someone else," he shrieked, wriggling with pleasure. "Oooh, but you're cute too, honey boy!"

"I am?" I choked.

"I'm certain we know each other," he giggled. "I know all the Ken dolls in town! I'm Tru Capo—"

I fled from his creepy clutches to find Jan. Fighting her way through the shifting bodies, she sprang into my arms.

"Where have you been?" she pleaded excitedly. "I've been searching for you desperately!"

"And I've been looking for *you!*"

"Let's get out of here!"

"Is something wrong?"

"Yes!"

Waiving goodbye to Margie, we set out toward home. A heavy, wet winter fog had rolled in off the river a block away, forming mysterious shadows as it danced around the old-fashioned street lamps. To avoid the dampness, we ducked under the balconies and galleries flanking the ancient buildings along Decatur; the shifting fog curled in under them like taunting ghosts in pursuit.

"Jan, what's the hurry?"

"That creepy little Spanish man kept pinching me on my rear-end and snuggling his head between my breasts. Uck, I feel dirty."

"Oh, is that all? Honey, wait'll you hear *my* story!"

We went to *La Casa* many times, always being careful who we turned our back on or with whom we danced!

Margie was delighted to share *her* French Quarter with us. To know her was like knowing the countess of some small duchy or principality in Europe. Her black hair, milky-white skin and flashing, dark green eyes made her look every bit the part of New Orleans Creole aristocracy in spite of the fact that she was actually Irish through and through. Her family surname was Boyle; however, she and her sisters thought the name Boyle too harsh. As the result of a listener contest, they took the name O'Dair (which also sounds Irish), made up from the letters in the word r-a-d-i-o. When Margie strode through the streets of the Quarter, she reaped smiles and greetings from everyone who saw her passing. Shopkeepers would tap on their display windows to attract her eye, and little old Italian ladies in their black babushkas waved hospitably from second- and third-floor balconies.

Timmy and Tammy had immediately taken to her. She loved children and had a talent for treating them as equals, never once speaking down to them. She became "Aunt Mawgie," as she would say in her slightly New Orleans Brooklynese accent.

A favorite evening for the children consisted of buying lemon ice and hard anise cookies at Brocato's Italian ice cream and sweet shop, then making our way past the Cathedral, on through Pirates Alley, to the ancient four-story *Le Petit Salon* mansion, where Aunt Mawgie lived on the top floor. Once inside the huge iron gate, Timmy and Tammy invariably made a mad dash up the three-and-a-half flights to Margie's apartment. On mild evenings the huge twelve foot double-hung parlor windows were flung open, allowing complete access to the narrow balcony, resting perilously on iron scroll braces some forty-five feet above St. Peter Street. The view was breathtaking. To the right, over the flood wall, could be seen the Mississippi River beyond Jackson Square, while to the left, through a maze of galleries dripping with wrought-iron lace work, nestled the A&P Store on the corner of Royal Street; in the middle of that block, sharing the sidewalk with Pat O'Brien's famous bar and patio, stood the venerable Preservation Hall. Only three doors to the left, Tenneessee Williams wrote *A Streetcar Named Desire.* And directly across the street, towering above the old Arsenal and the Cabildo, lay St. Louis Cathedral, whose twin spires pierced the sky.

The children, dangling over the wrought-iron rail for long stretches to amuse themselves, had little realization they were suspended over history. From time to time they would dash into the parlor to announce the passing of a ship on the river or the unruly antics of drunken or rowdy tourists staggering beneath their imperious perch. Margie's zestful appreciation for life and its wonderous treasures gave our family a desire to sample new things with great relish: art, theatre, music, food, and people of all ilks and persuasions. These, she preached, were all gifts needing only to be savored to be enjoyed and understood. Her influence alone seemed justification for our choosing the French Quarter as the place to raise our children.

Through Margie, we met Betina and Larry Johnson. Larry was the Director of *Le Petit Théatre du Vieux Carré*, the Little Theatre of the French Quarter, the oldest continuing community theatre in the United States, founded in 1916. Located next door to Margie's, it offered a variety of activities for the theatrically inclined. Jan and I gravitated naturally to the theatre, so it was no surprise when Jan announced plans to attend readings for the next show; she was overjoyed when she landed one of the leads, along with Margie, in a Noel Coward trilogy. A problem arose when we found my schedule at the station had been changed temporarily. I would be filling in for Dick Martin, the famous nighttime mellifluous-voiced WWL Blue Room announcer, while he was on vacation.

"I can't take the part if you have to work in the evenings. It'll put too heavy a burden on Olympia."

"Why don't you check with Larry Johnson? They have a small child; I'll bet he won't care if you take Timmy and Tammy with you as long as they behave. Take along some coloring books and pillows. After all, it's only two nights a week that I won't be home."

The arrangement worked beautifully; Tim and Tammy looked forward to it and Larry was pleased to see we were exposing our kids to "The Theatre." By virtue of Jan's role in the play, we gained entree into the local theatrical crowd. A feeling of déja vu ensued when we encountered local actresses Lynn Goldman and "Miss Linda" Mintz, soon of Romper Room, both fellow alumnae. We fondly reminisced about our happy years at Carnegie Tech Drama School where our lives had been touched briefly by George Peppard, Sada Thompson, Nancy Marchand, Frank Gorshin, Mariette Hartley, Ray Kaplan—who became Ray Danton—and hundreds of other talented fellow students.

Later in the season, when Larry was casting *Life With Father*, he immediately thought of Timmy for the part of Harlen, the youngest child. Jan and I discussed the possibilities and ramifications with five-year-old Timmy, now enrolled in kindergarten.

"Timothy," I instructed emphatically, "I have to impress upon you, if you get the part, you will have to spend a lot of time learning the lines."

"*And* it means," Jan added, "you'll have to go to rehearsal almost every night for the next six weeks. And I think it will be important for you to take a little nap after school each day. I don't want you to get too tired."

"I *won't*, mommy, I promise. I think it'll be lots of fun. Anyway, you was in a play an' worked all day an' took care of Tammy an' me an' you din't git tired. So, I giss I won't git tired either."

The first night of rehearsal, Timmy and I set out on foot toward *Le Petit* (or *Lah Piteet*, as locals say) five blocks away. Tim was no longer nonplussed by living in the Quarter, but this night, he seemed to be discovering things he had never noticed before. He was full of questions as we headed up Royal Street.

"Daddy, why do these houses have wire lace? Where do strippers come from? Were they ever children? How come it costs more money to ride in a horse carriage than a regular taxi?"

Turning onto sparsely-lighted Pirate's Alley, Tim let go of my hand and charged ahead, brandishing an imaginary sword and bellowing, "Look out, I'm Jean Lafitte, the pirate!" He didn't get more than twenty feet before he stubbed his toe on one of the age-old, hand-hewn, stone drainage gutters criss-crossing the alley. I couldn't help but smile as he pulled himself up and asked in all seriousness, "Daddy, how come New Orleans has such bad streets?"

"Come on, Tiimmy, we don't want to be late for the first rehearsal. After all, if you want to be in a real play, you must be on time and behave like a professional."

"What's a professional?"

"Well, er, ah, a professional is a person who does a job and gets paid for it."

"How much do I get?"

"Well, ah, you don't get money, you get experience and pleasure."

"Daddy, I think I'd rather get money!"

"Maybe someday. Come on, now, we don't want to be late."

Jan and I had wanted Timmy to be in the play not because we wanted him to become an actor but so he could meet new people, discover new surroundings, learn a new area of discipline and become a bit more independent. We were always anxious to expose the children to knowledge-stretching activities.

In the words of one of our sage teenage baby sitters, "If you know a lot about a lot, you'll want to know a lot more!"

Or, maybe better-put by my favorite fictitious role model, Auntie Mame, "Life is a banquet, but some poor sons-o-bitches are starving to death!"

At the theatre door we were greeted by a twelve-year-old. "You must be Harlen in the play. I'm going to be Whitney, your bigger brother. Let's go back stage and see who's in the Greenroom!"

"Daddy, what's the Greenroom?" Timmy whispered.

"It's where the actors wait when they're not on stage."

They trotted off, leaving me with the impression that this was definitely not Whitney's first theatrical encounter.

In his capacity as executive director of *Le Petit* and director of this particular production, Larry Johnson came to the lobby to discuss whether or not I should stay for rehearsals. We agreed it would be easier for Larry if I disappeared, leaving him in full command; I was relieved. I hadn't been looking forward to sitting through six weeks of rehearsals. Fortunately, one of the cast members was able to drop Timmy at home after each session.

When Timmy arrived home that first night, he told us the director would like me or Mommy to call if we were still up.

"Hello, Larry, did anything go wrong?"

"No, Bob, I was just surprised."

"What do you mean?"

"Well, I handed Timmy a copy of the script, but I didn't realize he can't read. I've never directed anyone who couldn't read. I was caught off guard, forgetting how young he is."

"Do you want to get someone else for the part? I'm sure we can make him understand."

"No, no, it's not that. I just wanted to tell you we've already taught him many of his lines and the blocking. He's a really quick study. Why don't you or Jan come to rehearsal tomorrow night and mark down all the blocking, so you can go over it with him. The way he's going, he'll know his part before anyone else in the cast."

So *we* did and *he* did!

To anyone's recollection, Timmy, at five years of age, was the youngest speaking actor in the long history of *Le Petit*.

The script for *Life With Father* requires that all members of the family have flaming red hair. During dress rehearsals, the Technical Director sprayed Timmy's hair with a red, gummy powder, which had to be washed out each night. It was a mess, and Jan was afraid Timmy would catch cold washing his hair nightly for the next three weeks during the cold, rainy season.

"Let's just dye it red and solve the problem," I suggested.

"Bob, it'll ruin it!"

"Good Lord, women have been dying their hair for centuries, I don't see how it can hurt!"

"I hope it won't hurt him psychologically, I don't want to make him queerish!"

"Give me a break! It takes more than that to make somebody queerish. After all, your hair's red; his Aunt Carole's hair's red; his Uncle Jesse's hair's red. In fact, he had red hair when he was born, so he really comes by it quite naturally. I'll explain it to him."

The next day after our radio show, Jan and I sallied up to the hair dye counter at Maison Blanche department Store. We were greeted quite aloofly by a well-tinted and cosmetized beauty of some sixty-odd years.

Intimidated, Jan hemmed and hawed, so I spoke up abruptly, "We want a batch of your reddest hair dye. We're going to dye our kid's hair fire engine red!"

"I beg your pawdon, sir," replied the cosmetologist, causing a chink to appear in her pancake base as she vociferated, betraying this haughty hussy was actually blue-collar Irish Channel stock.

"That's right, we want to dye our kid's hair flamin' red," I reiterated gleefully. Jan squirmed with uneasiness.

"I'm sorry, Sir, I just cannot do that," asserted the clerk. "I cannot sell you dye for your child's hair."

"You mean there's some law against it?"

"Oh, no, Sir, I just can't! It just don't seem right somehow. I suggest you apply our fabulous rinse or a fashionable aerosol spray color."

I held my ground, "No, we want a bright red dye, D-Y-E!"

"I'm sorry, sir, I just can't sell it to you. I must take a firm stand, I just cannot be responsible for helping ruin y'alls daughter's hair!"

Ah! My chance for a victorious closer on the heels of defeat. "The dye isn't for our daughter. You see, we live in the French Quarter. It's for our *son*! And he's only five years old!"

The chink in her pancake became a crevice!

We heeled around and marched across Dauphine Street to arch competitor D.H.

Holmes department store (*Homes-ez*, in the local vernacular). Jan suggested that if my mind was really made up about the dye-job, and she knew it was, it would probably be better for *her* to ask for it this time, as if it were for her hair.

Once at the cosmetic counter at Homes-ez, I turned my back discreetly. Jan requested something considerably brighter than her own red hair.

The clerk winked, "Gonna jazz yourself up a little for 'im, huh, dawling?"

Jan handed over the charge-a-plate. I turned around and grasped the package.

"You know what this dye is for?"

"Your lady," the clerk giggled.

"Oh, no, for our little boy. He's five and he has to have red hair."

"Oh, my Gawd!" she blurted. She stamped the sales ticket with the charge-a-plate and asked, "Your address, Mrs. Cawr?"

Jan supplied our Bourbon Street address.

The clerk furrowed her brow and looked up at us through her curled, crisply-coated Maybelline lashes. She seemed to be thinking that people who live in "the Quarters" are all beatnicks at heart!

Timmy looked like a Titian cherub with his new color, a masculine image of his mother. Even after the play closed, we let it stay red as long as possible. Jan and Tammy had tears in their eyes the night I gave him a crew cut. It just wasn't seemly for a boy to run around kindergarten with dish-water-blonde roots showing.

Timmy's life in "The Theatre" was grand. In fact, he looked forward to it so much that he would come home from school at noon and pop into bed for his nap without even being asked—a miracle in itself. He became a sort of mascot at the theatre. Everybody catered to him. On opening night he had cake and candy bars, even a nip of champagne. He spent much time in the Greenroom learning to play blackjack and poker and also adding theatrical jargen to his vocabulary: *proscenium, flat, hit, wings, cue, upstage, downstage, gay, fag, queen,* and *queer.*

Walter Persiveau, an acquience of ours reading for the next production, sashayed on gossamer wings into the Greenroom during a performance of *Life With Father.* According to Walter, Tim was so involved in putting together a puzzle while waiting for a cue that he didn't look up to see who had approached.

"Hi, Timmy, what're you doing?"

"Puttin' together a puzzle, sir."

"Oh!"

"What're *you* doin', sir? Readin' for the next show?"

"Yes, as a matter of fact, I am."

"Hope ya get the part."

"Thanks, Timmy."

Never looking up from his puzzle, Timmy added, "Well, just one thing, sir. If you get the part, don't let 'em put any of that eye makeup stuff on you. They put it on me—made me look like a little fag! It'll make you look like a bigger fag!"

Walter thought it was hilarious.

* * * * *

Startling the tourist is nothing new in the Quarter, but it took Timmy and Tammy's callow business ingenuity to get doubletakes from the neighbors and locals. The children had earned a considerable amount of money toward summer camp, doing commercial spots for the prestigious home-based Whitney Bank, but they still needed a few more dollars to meet their goal.

"Mommy, daddy told us how once when he was our age, he had a lemonade stand to make money, so please, pooeeze, can't we, can't we?"

"Wait till your daddy gets home."

When I got home from what I thought was a hard day at the radio control board, Jan, along with Timmy and Tammy, confronted me with the children's proposition.

"Daddy, daddy, pooeeze, pooeeze," Tammy begged.

"But, Bob, on Bourbon Street?"

"Why not? There's every other kind of enterprise!"

"But—"

The kids screams of joy overwhelmed any further protest.

Two afternoons later, to the consternation of Jan *and* Olympia, we swung open the front gate to expose a rude but adequately-equipped lemonade stand fashioned from wooden orange crates, skirted with old bedroom curtains, and topped with a piece of clean white oilcloth. Although the *Vieux Carré* Commission holds authority to approve all signage, the kids forewent the usual channels and boldly attached lemonade posters to the front of the house and several lamp posts.

As Jan and Olympia watched nervously through the louvers of the shutters, I thought: *If the Vieux Carré Commission doesn't get them, the board of health will!*

"Look, their first customer!" Jan shrieked. "Oh Lord, it's a motorcycle policeman."

While Jan, Olympia, and I hovered undercover behind the shutters, the kids not only charmed the policeman but sold him two glasses of lemonade to boot. As a tip, he sat each of them on his motorcycle for a moment, giving them an extra special thrill. Once we saw that they had established themselves, Jan and Olympia went to the back of the house to check on the red beans and rice Olympia was especially preparing for our close friend Lindsay Morris, arriving from West Virginia. I watched the kids for a couple of minutes while they served two perspiring tourists, then followed Jan and Olympia to the kitchen.

"Mistah Cahr, you lef' those chilrin out on dat banquette all by demselves with their lemonade *an'* their money?"

"Olympia, they'll be just fine."

"Well, that's foh you to surmise, but me to find out!" Olympia scurried out carrying an additional pitcher of lemonade while mumbling, "Ah swear to Gawd, ah *swear* to Gawd...the things that man let's them chilrin do! Lord have mercy."

I was on the phone with Moisant International Airport checking Lindsay's arrival time when Olympia charged back into the room in a tizzy.

"Ah swear to Gawd, Mistah Cahr, those chilrin makin' *some* money. The driver of the Desire bus stopped to git hiself a lemonade, an', can you believe, ever'body in dat bus reached out da windows to git some too! I sware, dat be a sketch!"

"That sounds great, Olympia. They seem just fine."

"Yes, ma'am, Mizz Cahr; how'ver, there be a drunk who wanted those sweet chilrin to let him pour his cheap whiskey in a glass o' their lemonade!"

"Did they let him?"

"Mistah Cahr, you gotta be crazy. Ah run that wino half the way down Bourbon Street to da Baptist Mission where he belong!"

"Olympia, you're fantastic, a real mother hen!"

"Don't know 'bout that, Mistah Cahr, but those *mah* babies an' no wino gonna mess wit mah babies, *no way!*"

Olympia carried a kitchen stool down the side patio and planted herself discreetly behind the giant green elephant ears that grew wild beside the house, keeping her vigil until the children ran out of lemonade and enthusiasm.

The children's venture into entrepreneurship had left them exhausted. It wasn't long before they settled in for a little nap in anticipation of Uncle Lindsay's visit.

This was Lindsay's very first sojourn in New Orleans. He and Jan and I had become fast friends when, as advertizing manager for Bradshaw-Diehl department store in Huntington, he had purchased time on our WSAZ-TV show. Lindsay, sensitive, creative and well-connected socially, clung to his rather poor-paying position for the contacts it offered him in the artistic echelons of the community. Income from his real estate holdings allowed him to entertain generously both at the Guyan Country Club and at his smartly-decorated home near Ritter Park. Since he had never been to New Orleans, we wanted to pick him up at the airport, but he insisted on taking a taxi. The children were anticipating his visit even though Tammy had only a vague memory of who Uncle Lindsay was; so much had happened in the months since she had seen him. Timmy remembered Uncle Lindsay for the gifts he had always given him. As a toddler, Tim would entertain himself for hours rearranging the pots and pans in Lindsay's kitchen cabinets. The disorder caused Jan concern, yet Lindsay endlessly doled out patience in abundant quantities.

I was on a ladder in the bathroom putting up new wallpaper when the doorbell rang. Although Olympia was approaching the door from the kitchen through the front hall, Tammy and Timmy were determined to get there first. They jumped to their feet and dashed to the top of the stairway; Timmy, climbing astride the banister, slid down as Tammy ran screaming behind him, "Wait for me...wait for me...wait for me." Before Olympia was even able to get to the front door, both kids had undone the guard-chain and swung the door open. There stood Uncle Lindsay, half-hidden behind an armful of packages. The cabby was just pulling away after unloading Lindsay's designer suitcases onto the Bourbon Street banquette.

On her way down the stairs, Jan was calling to me to come down off my ladder. The kids had been enthusiastic about Lindsay's arrival, but the actual sight of him caused them to timidly back off into each corner of the vestibule, affording Olympia an unobstructed view.

"Ah guess you gotta be Mistah Uncle Lindsay, the chilrin been waitin' on you all the day long," Olympia remarked, lavishing her warm grin. "Now jis look at them, they lahk two li'l mice hidin' in the corner."

Olympia guided Lindsay up the front steps with the packages. Though perceptive, Lindsay was never demonstrative, giving each of the kids a little peck on the forehead while following them into the front hall. Looking up at Jan coming down the stairs, he roared, "I can't believe this place; it's unbelievable, incredible!"

"You mean the house?" Jan asked.

"*No*, I mean that drive up Bourbon Street. It's incredible! I've never seen so many strange people and queer bars in my whole life."

"Lindsay, not in front of the children!"

"Jan, how could those little kids know what I am talking about?"

I hung over the banister and shouted, "Hey, Lindsay, I'll be down in a minute. I've gotta wash wallpaper paste off my hands."

He looked up the stair, waived, and shouted, "Someday you're going to kill yourself, always remodeling houses, climbing ladders and doing all that physical stuff."

Jan gave him a hug and closed the front door. The kids rifled through the gift-wrapped packages he had placed on the floor. Jan reintroduced him. "Olympia, Tammy, Timmy, this is Uncle Lindsay."

Olympia looked him over scrupulously. "He's even better-lookin' than you said, Mizz Cahr."

I bounded down the stairs in my swim shorts, which I normally wore when I was doing hot work around the house.

Lindsay, I could tell, was giving me the once-over.

"Like my outfit?"

"If I were you, I'd be damned careful going around half-naked in this neighborhood."

"Lindsay, everybody knows I'm a father and husband!"

"Well, I hope those swim-shorts have a cast-iron lining."

Jan interrupted, "Lindsay, where's your suitcase?"

Always a little absent-minded, he replied, "Why, oh, I don't know. I guess out on the sidewalk."

Yup, there sat his suitcases, all by themselves right out on Bourbon Street. Thankfully they hadn't taken up feet and walked away.

"This house is unreal," Lindsay said, "I can't fathom it. What an awesome place. The ceilings have to be ninety feet high."

"In reality they're thirteen. I know, because when Jan and I push a four-by-twelve-foot piece of sheetrock up against the wall, it fits right on top of that 12-inch baseboard."

"I can't believe you and Jan are doing all the work on this place. You're going to kill yourselves someday."

"You're gonna sleep in my room, Uncle Lindsay," Timothy announced. "Your gonna sleep in my room and I'm gonna sleep in Tammy's room."

Jan explain we had only three livable bedrooms. The other three still had falling plaster, exposed lath, and plenty of dust.

"How was your flight?"

"Fine, no problem. What's that long bridge across the Gulf or whatever, I could see from the plane?"

"That's the Causeway, across Lake Pontchartrain. New Orleans isn't on the Gulf, we're ninety miles from the Gulf."

Timmy added, "That Pontchartrain Causeway is the longest bridge in the world."

"Really? We flew right along the bridge and then landed."

"West Virginia's still there?" I asked. "How's everything in Huntington?"

"All your friends asked to be remembered, all your friends at WSAZ-TV. Your friends out in Milton, at the Blenko Glass Company, wonder how things are going for you in New Orleans. They're all still amazed you picked up and moved so far south."

Timmy interrupted, "I want to take Uncle Lindsay upstairs to show him my room."

Tammy pulled her thumb out of her mouth just long enough to say, "I want him to thee my dollies."

"Mistah Uncle Lindsay gotta be frightful hongry after that long airplane trip all the way from the North, ah got some good red beans an' rahs an' andouille sausage already for him," Olympia interrupted, exiting to the kitchen.

"What was *that*? Was she speaking English?"

"Olympia has cooked you some red beans an' rice and *andouille* sausage."

"What do you mean, red beans and rice?"

"Well," Jan explained, "this is Monday. In New Orleans, Monday is the day we eat red beans with rice."

"Red beans *and* rice? Isn't that a little starchy? And why Monday?"

"In the old days, Monday was wash day," Jan explained. "The lady of the house soaked the red beans Sunday night and let 'em cook all day Monday while she did the washing."

"Still sounds like more starch on the table than in the clothes! And what's that other stuff, some kind of sausage?"

"That's *andouille* sausage, pronounced *on-doo-ee*, spelled a-n-d-o-u-i-l-l-e. It's a Cajun sausage made out in the country. It's good an' spicy; you'll love it."

"You an' Bob told me on the phone I'd feel like I was coming to a foreign country. That feeling has already started."

Timmy began tugging at Lindsay's biggest suitcase. "Timothy, that's too heavy for you. I'll take it up."

"No, Uncle Lindsay, I'm strong. I'm real strong. I'll take it all the way to the top."

Lindsay, noticing the stair rail, remarked, "That's a handsome banister."

"There are two-hundred-and-one rungs from here up to the third floor!"

"A third floor…you have a third floor in this house?"

"You bet your aching muscles we do."

"We'll show you the whole house," Jan added.

"Timmy, don't hurt yourself with that suitcase."

"No, Daddy, I'm not hurtin' myself."

Timmy, bumping the suitcase up the steps, apparently loosened the lock, for all of a sudden the suitcase popped open, sending Lindsay's clothes tumbling down the stairs.

"Oh pooh," Timmy said. "Pooh, pooh, pooh!"

"Timothy, don't say that."

"I'm sorry, mommy, but it wasn't my fault!"

Lindsay spoke up, trying to help Timothy out of a tough situation. "That's okay, Timothy, the lock's broken on that suitcase anyway, don't worry about it."

The clothes, toiletries, and a couple of magazines had tumbled halfway down the staircase. We began to gather things together and put them back.

I picked up a newspaper that had fallen at my feet. "Oh, is this the *Huntington News Register?"*

Lindsay snatched it quickly out of my hand.

"What is that newspaper?"

"Oh, nothing. Let's look at the rest of the house."

Lindsay helped Timmy get the suitcase to the top of the stairs and into the bedroom.

Timothy was very proud of his room. "Uncle Lindsay, these are my bunk-beds and over here, is my desk and this is where I keep all my clothes, and here are all my drawings. Daddy and I walk down to the river and watch the boats, and when we come back home, I draw them." Timmy, pointing at an artist's easel, proudly remarked, "And that's what I drew, see?"

Lindsay dutifully admired the rude drawings.

It was an especially balmy night so the windows were wide open, with a gentle breeze blowing in just enough to rustle the curtains. Lindsay walked out through the windows. "I can't believe you have a balcony. This whole place is magical."

Tammy pulled her thumb out of her mouth. "I have a magic balcony too, Uncle Lindthay."

We all joined Lindsay on Tammy's balcony facing Canal Street. There was an almost unobstructed view of the New Orleans skyline.

Lindsay pointed. "What's all that?"

"That's Canal Street, Uncle Lindsay."

I added, "Canal Street is our main street; those buildings just beyond it are the tallest buildings in town. The white tower is the Hibernia Bank building. They light it up in different colors for holidays, and that one with the big red sign, looks like it's at the far end of Bourbon Street, is the American Bank building."

"What's that over there?"

"Oh, that's the spire of St. Louis Cathedral."

"I just cannot believe I'm here. It really *is* like being in a foreign country, I feel like I'm in Europe."

"This isn't Europe, Uncle Lindsay, this is New *Aw*lins, some people say New Or*leens,* but we say New *Aw*lins."

Lindsay patted Timmy on the head approvingly.

We showed Lindsay the house from top to bottom, took him to our bedroom, showed him our balcony over Bourbon Street, and in the back patio pointed out the old slave quarters. He was amazed we used the term "slave," a word he thought repugnant in today's 1961 society.

"The words 'slave' and 'slave quarter' were hard for Jan and me to get used to also. It's just a part of the New Orleans vocabulary."

We finally ended up in the dining room. The kids had gotten tired along the way, so Olympia had helped them change into night clothes and told them they could come downstairs and listen to the conversation if they both curled up with their blankets on the old Victorian chaise lounge. Lindsay, Jan, and I sat at the table.

Olympia leaned in through the kitchen door. "Mistah Uncle Lindsay, you like a Red Hot or a Barq's?"

He hesitated as if he were again hearing a foreign language. "A what?"

"You like to have a Red Hot or a Barq's to drink with yo' red beans and rice?"

Still perplexed, Jan explained to him: a Red Hot is a soft drink, red in color with a cherry flavor, and Barq's is a popular New Orleans drink, pretty much like root beer.

In a quandary, he replied, "Do you have any *bourbon* here on Bourbon Street?"

"Oh, yah, I forgot," I said. "I'll fix you a bourbon on the rocks. Olympia doesn't like to make alcoholic drinks."

An expression of relief came over him. Bourbon was something he understood, a little *too well* from time to time.

As we sat at the dining table we talked about a variety of things: Huntington, our move down and the number of exciting things we were doing. The kids fell sound asleep so Jan and I carried them up to Tammy's room. Lindsay wanted to help; however, he'd always been self-conscious about handling the children. Eventually Jan started to get Lindsay headed to bed, explaining that we had to be at the station early in the morning, so wouldn't see again him until we got off the air.

"That's fine, Jan, I'll sleep late anyway. But now, I'm going to change my clothes and go out."

"You're going out, *now?*"

"Jan, I didn't come all the way to New Orleans to stay in my room, great as it is."

"It's kinda late!"

I walked in with a bourbon refill.

"Bob, tell Jan it's all right for me to go out. I'm a big boy, even if I am from hillbilly country. I just want to cruise around a little bit and get my bearings."

Jan gave him a goodnight peck on the cheek and started upstairs. At the front door I explained the peculiarities of our antique lock and noticed he was clutching the newspaper he had earlier jerked out of my hand.

"So, what's so special about that paper?"

"It's a newspaper that lists the interesting or unusual establishments around the country, the restaurants, hotels, bars, and so on."

"Gee, I didn't know there was such a thing. Any places listed in New Orleans?"

"A couple. One on Bourbon Street I passed in the taxi, Lafitte's In Exile, I think."

"Not that place on the corner of Dumaine and Bourbon? It's queer!"

"Really?"

"You probably mean Lafitte's Blacksmith Shop on Bourbon and St. Phillip."

"I'll check 'em out."

Concerned, but wishing him well, I handed over a small tourist map of the French Quarter, the key to the front door, and then off he went into the night.

Lindsay stayed for a week. He fell in love with the French Quarter before returning home to eventually quit his job and move to New Orleans!

* * * * *

The clatter of high heels striking the pavement of the banquette in front of our house reverberated through the triple-tier brick wall, heralding the dawn of Mardi Gras day. These were not just any high heels, but glamorous spiked pumps in sizes 12 to 16, gracing the nimble tip-toes of drag-queen tootsies marching like lemmings toward their watering hole, which in this case was Miss Dixie's Bar of Music, or the environs of Bourbon and St. Peter Streets, where they could, not too prudently, display their jewels, gowns, coifs, and painted faces.

The click-clack of high heels always causes me to recall my first Mardi Gras, when Bill Romaine and I ventured out early in the day to see the developing sights while Ann and Jan stayed behind with the children. Bill thought it would be fun to see the gathering throng at Miss Dixie's Bar of Music, though he had never dared go inside during the two years he and Ann had lived on Bourbon Street. Miss Dixie Fasnacht, a clarinetist and astute businesswoman, was the musician-proprietress of what, since 1949, had become the number one cufflink-set homosexual bar in the city, probably the South. Locals referred to Dixie's as the kind of place where Uptown and Downtown, straight and gay men, celebrities, and regular folk rubbed shoulders. I had never been in such a bar; we thought it would be a lark. Bill suggested we might get a glimpse of Tennessee Williams or some Hollywood star letting his guard down in the Queen City of the South.

It was early February and unseasonably chilly for New Orleans. Though the city's streets were already filling with crowds of people, many of the revelers had chosen to huddle in various bars and clubs to keep out of the cutting wind that sometimes blows in from the northwest during the winter. Dixie's was packed like a tin of male sardines: all ages, all colors, and all degrees of gaiety! I was flabbergasted.

We pushed our way through the melee of undulating bodies swilling drinks and swaying to the beat of Mardi Gras music. Edging his way through the crowd ahead of me, Bill kept turning around to observe my reaction. He yelled over the clamor that he'd heard the best costumes would be in the patio. I nodded, indicating I would follow. He pressed on; I was absolutely surrounded and immobilized. I was trying not to make eye contact when abruptly someone—I couldn't figure out who—had taken a firm hold of my crotch. Not just a nudge, but he had a grip on them that gave me the creeps; I pulled away, yet he held tight. I'd lost sight of Bill and became flushed and embarrassed. I didn't know which of the guys, pressing in on me from all sides, had me in his grasp. He let go, so I made haste, using my shoulders to slice through the throng. I cupped my own "jewels" as I made my getaway, realizing what had happened was just part of the game everyone was playing. Now, I could relate to Jan's plight on a crowded bus in Rome some years earlier. I finally caught up with Bill in the patio and asked if he'd had an experience like mine. He had not; however, someone had French-kissed him on the back of his neck. He was scowling and still wiping it dry with a handkerchief.

It was chilly in the patio but not windy, thanks to the enclosure. The area was encircled above with a balcony accessed by a spiral staircase. Despite the cool temperature, men in all forms of dress and undress were dangling over the railing to display their wares. Several were adorned in drag with waist cinctures so tight that Scarlett would have swooned. Numerous guys were decked out as cowboys in ten-gallon hats, five-gallon codpieces, and chaps that left little to one's imagination, especially when their wearers lopped their bare butts over the rail. One exceedingly *grand dame*, perched precariously above and crowned with a towering headdress, wore huge feather-adorned wings that lovingly embraced his entire being. The crowd taunted, "Spread your wings. Spread 'em!" He eventually complied with a great sweeping gesture, revealing his completely naked body bathed in gold save for a festoon of grapes haphazardly fastened to a flimsy jock strap.

This bizarre scene seemed unreal, as from a Fellini movie. My brain was whirling. I thought I might black out, as I had once done during an Army physical when everyone had to strip for a "finger-wave exam." Someone put an arm around me; I thought it was Bill trying to steady me. It was *not!* I looked groggily into the face of my embracer. She kissed me heartily, pressing her gyrating pelvis into mine. I could feel her lipstick smear on my lips as her tongue pushed its way against my teeth. I resisted. She pulled away, flung both arms into the air and shrieked at the top of her voice, "*Gotcha, baby!*" She broke forth with a roaring guttural guffaw that filled the patio. And then *I realized the she was a he!* Everyone was laughing riotously except Bill, who grabbed me by the hand and dragged me to an exit. We fled through the kitchen onto St. Peter Street, where the crowd had grown larger and more boisterous. Bill smirked at me as we leaned against the hood of a parked car. Spitting into the gutter, I ran my wrist across my lips, wiping away the leftover lipstick. I had been baptized into the tactile and sensually veiled world of New Orleans.

Mardi Gras is the day; Carnival is the season, although the terms are used interchangeably (incorrectly) in New Orleans. Mardi Gras, French for Fat Tuesday, is *not* a religious holiday. It is a hedonistic celebration occurring the day before Ash Wednesday, when the 40-day season of Lent officially begins and Catholics must fast and do penance. Mardi Gras is a day to eat, drink, and be merry before the lean days ahead. Away from New Orleans, it would be referred to as "Shrove Tuesday." I think someplace in the Midwest they flip pancakes on Shrove Tuesday!

Carnival commences on the eve of Twelfth Night or King's Day, a religious holiday celebrating the three wise men's visiting the Christ Child. It's the twelfth night after Christmas and celebrated in New Orleans by baking and eating king cakes, circular rings of coffee cake sprinkled with colored granulated sugar and containing a hidden tiny, plastic baby that represents Jesus. The guest who gets the baby is obliged to give the next party, and so it goes until Mardi Gras. Twelfth Night is also the kickoff time for the multitude of grand balls presented by the various clubs, or "krewes," as they're called in New Orleans. Krewe members take their traditions very seriously. The most prestigious krewes are Comus, Momus, Proteus, and Rex.

Ann had arranged invitations for Jan and me to attend the Rex Ball, held Mardi Gras evening at the Municipal Auditorium. The invitation was *veddy, veddy* pompous, printed in grand swirls of green, gold, and purple—the official colors of Carnival. His Royal Highness, Rex, commanded our presence at his ball. When I asked Ann, who was always most proper, if it would be anything like the festivities at Dixie's Bar of Music, she scowled at my impudence!

The invitation proclaimed the dress code as strictly formal. Bill snidely indicated that this meant a tuxedo for me and long gown for Jan. He reiterated, with further sarcasm, that thus gussied-up, we would have the honor of sitting in the balcony, as krewe members reveled joyously whilst they presented their debutante daughters to the *crème de la crème* of society on the main floor. Invited plebeians—that was us—would be privileged to watch from above in reverent awe!

Jan still owned a long gown, but I had donated my seldom-used-since-college tuxedo to the Salvation Army. Bill had one; however, he was a half-head taller than I. However, he had an idea in which Ann put little faith.

Accepting Bill's solution, we left for the ball, Jan in a long gown and me dressed in my darkest charcoal suit with a tux shirt, studs, black tie and cufflinks. Because it was cold and damp, Bill and I reasoned I could wear my raincoat as I passed security at the front door and no one would be the wiser. Was I wrong!

We looked smashing as we approached the main entrance, Jan wrapped in her silver fox shrug and I in my black raincoat. We held our heads high; Jan passed through the door as I showed our invitations to the attendant, who looked down indifferently. Jan pushed swiftly ahead into the crowd. I, too, moved ahead with some difficulty as the attendant put his hand firmly on my shoulder and with brute force pulled me back toward him.

"*Sir*, you are not properly attired. Please step outside and clear the doorway!"

I was mortified; Jan was inside and I was outside. How was I to find her? I pressed my face against the window of an adjacent door, searching for a glimpse of her. Nothing! Several guests pushed me aside as if I were a vagrant. Barred outside, I felt like Stella Dallas! I tapped frantically at the window when I saw Jan scurry across the vestibule. Several people turned my way, looking rather annoyed as I pointed in Jan's direction. One kind, though slightly tipsy gent tapped Jan on the wrist of her long glove and motioned toward me. She looked at me in amazement; I beckoned her to come out. She pressed against the door's releasing-bar and slipped out, causing the attendant great consternation. But the act was done.

In an embarrassed frenzy, we fled back to Ann and Bill's to confess that our sinful plan had failed. Bill insisted: if it's a tux they want, I should put on *his* ill-fitting one and return to the ball *post haste*. Emotionally exhausted, I did as he insisted. Although Bill's pants were bunched over my shoes, the attendant let me pass muster.

We had endured this ruckus just to sit in the balcony. Once there, we were impressed by the spectacle but dismayed by the amount of money it represented. Little did we realize, just two years hence, we, too, would be sitting on the main floor involved in the ritual of a Carnival ball.

Ah, but how did that door attendant know so quickly that I had not been wearing a tuxedo when he seemed to be staring down so apathetically? One such attendant later explained that he always looked down at a gentleman's trousers to make sure there was a satin stripe and no cuff!

* * * * *

Jan and I received an extraordinary amount of fan mail for our WWL radio show, much more than from our 1950s television viewers in West Virginia. Perhaps the radio audience feels a greater intimacy with the performer, who is surely enhanced by the imagination of the listener. This amplified visualization can be extremely creative, allowing the listener to develop fantasies of great familiarity that make the performers a more intimate part of their imagination than the images that they see and hear on television.

Favorable fan mail is always flattering. Occasionally we would accommodate people requesting a radio station visit to view a broadcast. We received such a letter from a woman in Amite (ah-*meet*), a small strawberry-farming community some sixty miles north of New Orleans. Her letter went on to say that Jan had the most wonderful voice and sweet manner she had ever heard on radio, reminding her of her mother, who had died when she was a child. Since Jan had also lost her mother when she was young, this letter touched her heart. The woman was planning a trip to the city and would love to watch a broadcast. In return, she would be glad to help us with any work that had to be done. There wasn't anything she could do, nor did we want any help, but the letter was so heartwarming that Jan invited her to pay us a visit.

A few days later, Mrs. Stark, that affable Southern-speaking switchboard operator who always took great pride in screening guests, called from the reception room.

"Jan, dahlin'," Mrs. Stark whispered into the phone, "there's a most peculiar young woman here at the front desk claimin' to have an appointment to see Mizz Jan Cahr an' view her radio broadcast. Surely, dahlin', this person can't be one of you-ah guests. Should ah send her away?"

"Where's she from?"

Mrs. Stark continued to whisper. "Amite, dahlin', least ah think that's what she said. She's got a voice like a baby crow!"

"Oh, yes, Mrs. Stark, that's the young lady I invited. Just send her to the viewing room."

"Well, dahlin', if that's what you really want!"

We were busy announcing "Handy-Hints for the Day" with a homemaker consultant when the young woman appeared outside the massive window separating us from the viewing room. Mrs. Stark was right, the young woman was odd-looking, but then, her features appeared a bit distorted through the double soundproof plate glass. We motioned for her to sit in one of the many chairs seldom used since the death of *Dawnbusters*. She looked disappointed until she realized she could watch and at the same time hear us through the monitor.

Mrs. Stark was right, I thought once again. This person is most peculiar and exceedingly obese. Her colorless waist-length hair was pulled back into a ponytail, revealing an austere, oversized face adorned with a straight, hard line of unplucked eyebrows across her forehead, almost obstructing her piercing eyes. Could this be a guy in drag?

As we conversed with our female consultant, the young woman from Amite cocked her head and stared up at the monitor mounted on the wall. Having never seen Jan in person, she was apparently trying to figure out which one of the two ladies was Jan. When she separated Jan from our guest by hearing her voice on the monitor, she stared intently at Jan without looking away for a moment. Jan was busy babbling through the interview, asking our guest about some new product called "Teflon," which was supposed to help the weary housewife get cupcakes out of the pan without sticking!

Meanwhile, I remained distracted by the young lady outside the window, whose strange penetrating stare focused intently on Jan.

Our Handy Hints segment lasted, between commercials, about thirty minutes; the young woman continued to focus on Jan. When the station joined the CBS Network for the top-of-the-hour five-minute newscast, Jan thought it would be nice to invite the young lady into the studio. After all, she had come all the way from Amite.

While I worked through the commercials and music for the next hour, Jan ushered out the Teflon lady. Through the window I could see Jan greeting the Amite girl and inviting her into the studio. She was absolutely entranced by Jan, hanging on her every word and following her every movement as she clumsily edged her enormous frame through the door.

"Bob, this is Pearl," Jan said, eyeing me apprehensively.

"Hello, what's your last name?"

She acknowledged me hesitantly, responding with, "Jis call me Pearl."

Her eyes fixed on Jan, she began, in a crow-like voice, to flatter Jan with niceties. "Miss Jay-an, thank you, thank you for allowin' me to come into your lahf, there ain't nobody in the world lahk you, Miss Jay-an. Ah'm more an' thrilled to be in N' Orleans an' sit in the same radio studio with Miss Jay-an, ooo-eee!"

Jan seemed flattered, but it was obvious that some of Pearl's faculties had been left back in the strawberry patch. True to form, Jan was very sympathetic toward Pearl, who seemed harmless enough, though rather pathetic. She sat quietly in the studio as we interviewed our next guest, a Department of Agriculture representative who had come on the show to extol the succulence of Louisiana strawberries.

Following our program, I went into the control room to discuss tomorrow's show with the engineer as Jan and her visitor moved into the lobby where they could talk for a few minutes. Intrigued by Pearl's odd voice and country accent, Jan grew more interested as her story unfolded. Pearl also grew up on a farm, but unlike Jan, who was raised by loving grandparents and a kind father, Pearl's father was an angry and verbally abusive strawberry farmer who permitted his grown daughter to come to New Orleans only once every six months or so. Jan began to realize this visit to the city was very special for Pearl and, by necessity, quite brief.

To Jan's relief, Pearl excused herself after a few minutes. "Ah gotta git the Greyhound back before Pawpaw misses me!"

"Doesn't it take two hours to get to Amite?"

"Yes, Miss Jay-an, ma'am, you're raht, it does. An' that's why ah gotta git goin'. Ah told Pawpaw ah was sick an' cain't pack strawberries today. Ah gotta git home an' inta bed 'fore he gits in from the field or he'll git ugly."

She reached out and took Jan's hand, shook it fiercely, and looked directly into Jan's eyes, for moments longer than was comfortable. "Miss Jay-an, ah've never been so thrilled in mah life. Oh, my God, to meet a real radio star like you! You have the voice of an angel an' you're the most beautiful woman ah've ever been next to." Pearl backed away, apparently to get a full-length view of Jan. Folding her hands across her breasts, she sucked in a deep breath. Then, exhaling a commanding sigh, uttered, *"Ah'll be back, Miss Jay-an!"*

I met a perplexed Jan in the hall.

"Bob, I've got a strange feeling about that girl, somehow she seems obsessively interested in me!"

"After all, darling, you are wonderful," I teased. "Maybe she's thinking of you as a mother figure!"

"I'm not that much older," Jan rebuked.

"Perhaps on radio you sound more mature, darling."

"Bob, be serious!"

Several days later, Jan received a touching thank-you note from Pearl; she had arrived home safely before her father. She emphasized that she was thrilled Miss Jan had been so nice to her. "After all, ah'm a nobody." Her closing line, "As soon as ah can sneak away, ah'll be back!" left Jan apprehensive.

Indeed, she did come back, every Tuesday for the next four weeks! Each time she begged Jan to let her help with any chores that needed to be done; there was nothing, but Pearl kept pressing. It had become irritating and disconcerting; we wanted to discourage her. Jan braced herself to take action to end Pearl's visits.

Following a Tuesday broadcast, Jan invited Pearl into our office and closed the door. "It has been very sweet of you to offer your assistance, but actually the management of the station frowns on people coming into the studio to watch programs on a regular basis. We'd love for you to visit, but it's company policy and, well, you know how *that* is?" Jan stammered, trying to get her point across.

When Pearl began to get the drift of Jan's meaning, she looked so utterly stricken that Jan asked her to sit down. The delicate wicker chair groaned and crackled under her massive weight. Jan took refuge by seating herself on the other side of the coffee table, which held a stack of our publicity photos. Grasping at straws, she picked up a pen to autograph a picture, hoping it would help to pacify Pearl. Jan signed the photograph "From the two of us with our very best wishes, Bob & Jan" and handed it to Pearl.

She looked at it for a moment, then emitted a long, guttural sigh of chagrin. "Oooooh, Miss Jay-an, please, please, please...*please* don'tcha have a pitcha of jis yourself?"

"No, I'm sorry, I only have photos of Bob and Jan."

"Please, Miss Jay-an, please. Please, sign me one from jis you. Sign it: From Miss Jay-an with love."

The request was peculiar, but Jan was willing to do anything to get her out of the place. Jan signed the photo and handed it to Pearl, who clutched it reverently against her voluminous bosom.

"Oh, Miss Jay-an, ooooh, this is the most wonderful thing ah ever got in mah lahf!"

Jan eased herself back onto the small sofa, trying to get the courage to tell her not come to the station again. "It would be nice if you dropped us a line from time to time, but please, please understand we can no longer have you come to the station and watch our broadcast. As I said, the management frowns on regular visitors."

Tears clouded Pearl's penetrating eyes before exploding onto her chubby cheeks. Sensing trouble, Jan tried a few comforting words. "I'm really sorry, but you must understand we just cannot have regular visitors."

Pearl gulped a deep breath that ballooned her face like a dirigible. "Youuuu don't like me. Youuu don't like me. Youu never did an' you don't want me 'round ja, do ya? Yer jist like the rest o'ma family. Nobody wants me 'round 'cause ah'm big an' fat an' ugly!"

"No, no, it's not that at all."

"Yes, it is! Youuu don't want me!"

"Pearl, you don't understand," Jan stammered, trying to gain control. "I like you very much. You are very kind. You're such a darling, lovely person who wants to be helpful."

Hearing the endearing words Jan babbled, Pearl sprang up, "Oh, Miss Jay-an, ah do love you!"

"Don't you understand? I'm married!"

"Don't make no mind, Miss Jay-an, we kin still have our own kinda kinship."

"Kinship, what kinship?"

"Our very own kinship, jis you an' me! Ah don't pay no mind what people think no more. They always sayin' dumb crap about me anyways. You bin nice to me, ah love you, Miss Jay-an, with all ma heart."

Jan stood up to take command. "You are *not* a failure unless you allow yourself to be, *but* you have to understand. I have a husband, children, a whole family. I have *no* room for anyone else in my life. Please, you must leave!"

Pearl sat motionless for a few brooding moments, wiping her cheeks with the Kleenex Jan had given her. Regaining composure, she picked up the press photo and tore it in half, letting my face flutter to the floor. The half containing Jan's face and signature she stuffed into the top of her dress. "Ah'm gonna be *awraht*. An' ah *ain't* comin' back!"

With one last piercing glance at Jan, she cocked her head, turned, and walked out of our office *and* out of our lives. Jan fretted over the young woman's condition for days.

* * * * *

Despite our encounter with Pearl and sundry irksome kooks, Jan and I thoroughly enjoyed most of our "adoring" fans and the fan mail, which was encouraging, supportive and helpful. Our eighteen months at WWL radio were both exciting and rewarding. We had joined the station with the hope that one day we would also be featured performers on WWL television; however, that hope vanished with the news WWL channel 4 had hired a beautiful blond bombshell for a morning show. An even worse blow was to learn that John Vath, our boss, whom we truly admired, was leaving for a new challenge *and* joining WSMB radio, our archrival. On top of that, Bill Romaine won an audition to become the shill-personality for a meatpacking house. He was about to become the "King Cotton Kid," hero to thousands of hyperactive, snotty-nosed kids throughout the Gulf Coast region of south Louisiana and Mississippi. Our new station manager was an insufferable, egotistical yahoo with no managerial sensibilities to speak of. Finding ourselves in an intolerable situation, we turned our attention to channel 6 WDSU after hearing reports that they were interested in airing a new morning show to compete with the channel 4 enterprise.

The channel 6 ploy was to broadcast from a remote location somewhere in the French Quarter. We immediately began making inquiries as to the validity of the rumors. WDSU-TV writer and producer Al Shea, with whom we had become friends through our mutual interest in *Le Petit Théatre*, urged us to put together an audition on kinescope so that the management of WDSU, already familiar with our radio style, could observe our TV personalities. Although we had studied the art of portraying characters in drama school, our television careers had always demanded that we play ourselves. In our audition we chose a *potpourri* of vignettes that reflected the natural personalities of "Bob & Jan." The outcome of this audition would be a determining factor in shaping the future of our careers and even the future of our stay in New Orleans. It was surely the most important thing to happen to us since moving to the city.

We were exhilarated to be back in a TV studio. Jan and I breezed through the audition but cringed during the playback, seeing several things we would have done differently; however, Al, John Domec, the director, and several of the engineers from the control room came into the studio praising our inventiveness and uniqueness.

One of the engineers remarked he seldom watched with interest what appeared in his viewfinder but stopped to watch us because we aroused his curiosity. "I haven't seen antics like that since Dick Van Dyke was on staff."

Jan and I were heartened by these advanced reviews but had to wait nearly a week and a half for the opinion of station management. Al, who had inadvertently become the mediator between us and the station, called to tell us our years of TV experience in West Virginia and our decision to present a miscellany of activities that best reflected our personalities had paid off. The television camera, so penetrating and intrusive, captured something about the two of us that appealed to A. Louis Read, the general manager of the station. The program for which we were hired would be called *Second Cup*. It would originate live from the roof of the Royal Orleans Hotel, located next door to WDSU on Royal Street. The roof garden of the hotel commanded a panoramic view overlooking the French Quarter, the Mississippi River, and the tall buildings along Canal Street. Additionally, we would have our own radio program.

We were thrilled beyond composure. The pain from such overwhelming joy was a seldom-felt malady, sending our central nervous systems reeling out of control. Our cure was carnal, found between the sheets of our four-poster bed.

* * * * *

A few weeks later, glued to the TV set, I watched the evening network newscast with John Cameron Swayze. I was intrigued by the coverage of the inauguration of George Wallace, the new Governor of Alabama. The marching bands, decked out in Rebel uniforms playing Dixie, seemed surreal. Wallace was taking the oath of office beneath the white-domed capitol in Montgomery, where Jefferson Davis had been sworn in as President of the Confederacy a century ago.

"Let us rise to the call of the freedom-loving blood that is in us, and send our answer to the tyranny that clanks its chains upon the South," Wallace trumpeted. "In the name of the greatest people who ever trod this earth, I draw the line in the dust, and toss the gauntlet before the feet of tyranny. And I say, segregation today, segregation tomorrow, segregation forever!"

My thoughts harkened back to my Aupagnier great-grandparents who must have read a news report in the daily *Picayune* that carried a similar message from newly-sworn-in President Davis. Now I was seeing this same rhetoric telecast in 1963.

Jan and I were now Southerners, Southerners by location but not by conviction. And I reminded myself: *New Orleans is Créole, not Southern! One must travel north or east from New Orleans to get to the South.* In short, I tried to make justifications in my mind for bringing my family way down yonder to "Looisiana."

The doorbell startled me.

"Bob, would you please answer the door?" Jan shouted down the stairwell. "I'm helping the children with their homework and Olympia is cooking dinner. With that old exhaust fan running above the stove, she can't hear the doorbell half the time."

"Okay, are we expecting anyone? I'm in my Italian bikini!"

"I don't know. Maybe it's Rivet delivering my wig for tomorrow's show. He'll love you in *that* outfit!"

"Thanks a lot, dahling!"

Approaching the front door I could see, through the finely-etched ruby-and-crystal-flashed window glass, the profile bust of a woman. The shadowy figure once again raised her finger to depress the bell.

"Coming, I'm coming!"

Unlocking the huge cypress door, I swung it back just far enough *not* to expose my lack of clothing.

"Hi, may I help you?"

"Oh, hah, ah'm Stella, Stella Golden, from ovah there. Ah mean, up there in the next block of Boybon Street."

She seemed rather nervous at meeting me.

"An' this is mah little goyl, Carrie. She jis made four. We met a couple of weeks ago at mah husband's art studio on Royal Street, when you and Miss Jan were on yor way home from the TV station. He does watercolors."

"Oh, oh yes. He's great. What's your name again?"

"Stella!"

"*Stella!* Oh, yes."

I stood staring at her as my mind wandered for a minute. *I can't believe there's a real live Stella in New Orleans. Could she be the one Tennessee Williams wrote about?* I was particularly intrigued by her flawless New Orleans Brooklynese dialect. Having studied accents during college, I thought, *What a great candidate for Professor Henry Higgins!*

She continued, "Anyway, ah jis thought ah'd drop bah to say hello and tell ya we have two little children. They go to St. Louis Cathedral School over on Dumaine and…"

My mind wandered again: *Very attractive reddish brown hair, handsome chiseled features. Her classic nose was prominent but more delicate than those of the nine muses of Greek mythology whose names had been bestowed upon the New Orleans streets located just above Lee Circle.* I particularly noticed the way her Krauss budget-store housedress clung intermittently to her well-endowed figure. I refocused my attention.

"An' ah'll borrow that Zatarain's. You can't cook shrimps without it, and Miss Madonna's at the corner is all out of it."

Apparently she had been asking me for something during the time I was staring at her in a daze.

"What is it you want to borrow?"

"A li'l bag of Zatarians. You know, crab berl."

"Oh—oh, you mean crab *boil?*"

She looked at me quizzically. I thought: *We're operating in the same language but on slightly different frequencies. Besides, who am I, a Yankee, to correct her perfectly adequate New Orleans vernacular, even if I am a speech specialist? Furthermore, she was much too attractive to alienate during our first meeting on the door step.*

As I pulled the door fully open to invite them in, I revealed myself clad only in my bikini. Stella's eyes descended the length of my body. Taking little Carrie by the hand, they backed down one step.

"I know this is a hellava strange way to greet guests, but, you see, I've been out washing down the damn shutters in the patio. Y'all call 'em blinds in New Orleans."

"Oh, ah see," she said, retreating one more step but not taking her eyes off my bathing suit.

"You and your little girl, Carrie, come on in while I go ask my maid if we have any crab boil in the pantry." *Oh, God, I can't believe I said my maid!*

"*No!* No, we'll wait raht here on the stoop."

"Okay, just a minute." Dashing down the hall, I called back over my bare shoulder, "Now don't y'all go away."

Olympia was up to her elbows in turkey gumbo.

"Mistah Cahr, how come you be answerin' da doh like *dat*. Ah swear to Gawd, you be scarin' yo fans off dressed that away. They gonna be thinkin' you Tah-zun da ape man. An' no tellin' what dose fancy boys along the street be thinkin'. Now here's yo pack a Zatarain's foh dat lady. An' here's our biggest dish towel foh yo naked body." Shaking her head in dismay, she continued her scolding as I wrapped the towel around my waist and dashed back to the front door.

"Ah swear to Gawd, Mr. Cahr, you sumpun else. Ah swear to Gawd!"

I handed the crab boil to Stella, who had, by now, retreated to the safety of the banquette.

"Here you are. I hope it's big enough."

"Oh, it's big enough all right. Your Zatarain's, it's jist the raht sahz package!"

"Mommy, look, he's not as nekked as he was!"

"That's enough, baby. We gotta go now." Stella took Carrie by the hand and urged her toward home. "Thanks a-gayn for the crab berl."

"That's okay. Say hi to Stanley!"

As I closed the front door, Jan came down from her homework session with the kids.

"Who was at the door, Rivet?"

"No. Stella, the wife of the artist on Royal Street, the one whose water colors and sketches we like. Is his name Stanley?"

"Heavens, *no*, it's Rolland. Rolland Golden...sounds musical, doesn't it?"

"Oh, my God!"

"What?"

"I just told her to say hello to Stanley. She told me she was Stella. All I could think of was *Streetcar Named Desire*. She'll think I'm a complete ass."

"Speaking of rear-ends, I don't think you should open the door in your Italian diaper! You want to get raped right on Bourbon Street?"

"Jan, you're such a prude."

About a week and a half later, we received a hand-delivered invitation to an opening at the Patio Art Gallery, a showing of the latest works of Rolland Golden.

"I'd really like to go to that opening," Jan said. "I absolutely love his sketches of the French Quarter."

"Fine, let's go."

"I hope the artist's wife recognizes you with your clothes on!"

"She will!"

"What do you mean?"

"She's seen me on television."

"How do you know?"

"I could tell."

"How?"

"Just by the way I shocked her in my Gorizia bathing suit."

"You did that on purpose?"

"Maybe!"

"Why?"

"I just like to see how people react."

"You're gonna get in trouble someday."

"I doubt it."

"Why?"

"Because I'm basically a prude. And besides, behind all the glitz, I'm really chicken."

"I'm glad you're not chicken with me!"

I took Jan in my arms and bending her back Valentino style, planted a sumptuous kiss on her lips. I lost my footing, causing us to collapse in a giggling heap on the parlor floor. We continued to kiss, romping and rolling on the carpet. I nuzzled Jan's neck just below her ear.

"Mr. Cahr, this is unseemly in the parlor, especially with Queen Victoria lookin' down at us from that carving on our settee!"

"Just close your eyes!"

"But I can smell Olympia's gumbo simmering on the stove."

"I'm simmering, too. Feel that!" I nuzzled her more seriously.

"Mr. Cahr, there's a time for everything an' this isn't the time or place for such carryings on. Meet me later on the balcony outside our boudoir! But for now, you may call the chilren to the dining room, sir."

"Lawd have mercy, it pleasures me *so* when you talk Southern!"

* * * * *

The Patio Art Gallery was located in the rear of a three-and-a-half-story Creole townhouse on the riverside of the six-hundred block of Royal Street, a block of particular architectural interest. The early French and Spanish Creole settlers of New Orleans built their large houses flush with the street. The ground floor was commercial, with the family residing in the upper stories. Jan and I entered the townhouse by passing through the long flagstone-decked carriageway leading to a courtyard, which, it turned out, served as the main gathering spot for most of the guests. The tiny gallery, hidden even farther back into the compound, was on the ground floor of the three-story slave quarter; a gentle hum of conversation greeted us. The setting seemed almost artificial, vaguely suggestive of the Saenger Theater on Canal Street, which, like so many theaters of the twenties and thirties, depicted a Spanish courtyard. The perfect starry sky overhead was of such cobalt blue that it appeared as if frescoed on a gigantic suspended ceiling. Every once in a while, trade winds from deep in the Gulf collide with the dry air of the Plains States, producing such a wonderfully balmy evening in New Orleans that it makes one feel, indeed, God is taking a special interest. This was such a night.

We edged our way into the crowd seeking either the artist, his wife, or a familiar face. Pressing on toward the gallery, we could overhear the guarded voices of two overly-gesticulating sibilant gentlemen who seemed to recognize us.

"I ssay dahling, is-sn't that…what's their names? You know, from the TV?"

"Oh, yess, Bob and—"

"And Jan from channel 6. She lookss thinner than on TV."

"I didn't know she had such *gorgeous* red hair! I wonder if it's hers or one of those Mister Rivet dye jobbies?"

"Donno, but wonder if they're as happy as they look on TV?"

"I hope not, 'cause I could drag *him* under my coverss anytime!"

"You better not let your lover hear you ssay that."

"Oh sshee-yt ssilly, he could care less anymore! He's got himself a new young trick. Ah'm juss ssick!"

I grabbed Jan, my defender, by the hand and pulled her along. Someone who looked familiar emerged from the narrow French doors that led into the crowded gallery.

He smiled. "Hello, aren't you—"

"Yes, Bob and Jan Carr."

"I thought so. I'm Rolland, Rolland Golden. I'm so glad y'all came."

He was immediately open and friendly. At this point we couldn't realize Stella and Rolland would become lifelong friends and he, in time, an internationally-renowned artist.

"We have plenty of cold bee-ah. Lemmie getcha a couple."

It seemed fitting that this artist would serve beer at his opening exhibition. Beer made a statement about him and his art that wine or champagne could never do. The direct and tenacious personality emitting from his waterfront good looks belied his expressive sensitivity and insecurity. His eyes darting around the courtyard, he called for his wife over the crowd: "Stell-ah!" With the back of his hand he brushed perspiration from his forehead as his fingers gently ruffled through curly, fawn-colored hair, lifting the dampened strands from his brow. "Steh-*lah*," he called one more time.

"Rolland, ah'm *comin!*" She appeared in a simple, cool, cotton dress. "Oh, hello. You look so nah-ce."

Although I knew she meant the remark for Jan, I couldn't help but reply, "Gee, thanks. I didn't think you'd recognize me with my clothes on!"

Stella blushed slightly. "Rolland, why don'cha show Bob and Jan into the gallery, even though it's kinda stuffy in there. The ceiling fan seems to have died. Ah'm gonna see about the other guests."

As we followed him he beckoned us closer. "Ah've gotta tell y'all a secret about Stella. A couple of years ago she fell in love with the guy in the Coca-Cola signboard poster over the soda fountain at the Royal Pharmacy. Now she's really embarrassed 'cause she heard it's *you* in that picture. Is that true?"

Jan and I looked at each other and chuckled. I got red in the face as Jan explained, "Bob did that Coca-Cola shoot back in 1953. It was all over New York for a while, but we never expected to see it still being used. That's really an hysterical coincidence."

"Oh, for God's sake, don't tell Stella ah told yah. She'd kill me!"

Suddenly, out of nowhere, a Southern belle engulfed him. "Rolland Golden, ah sway-ah, your paintin' becomes bettah with each brush stroke. My darlin' husband, Jack De Cells, an' ah, jis wanna bah ever-thin in sight."

"Well, thank you very much. Bob and Jan, I don't think you've met Betty and Jack De Cells."

"Y'all have ta git to know each othah," remarked Stella, passing out more Dixie beer.

"Yes," said Betty, "we should all stick togethah, since we all have children who must be protected."

"Yes, and we all have husbands," Jan added.

"Who also need protecting!" I smirked, glancing around at the others to see if they caught my gist.

"Oh, Bob, shh!" Jan sputtered.

Betty's attention and exuberance toward Rolland gave Jan and me a chance to steal off into the gallery to view the exhibit. We had been quite taken with some of Rolland's sketches printed weekly in the *Vieux Carré Courier*, the local newspaper of the Quarter.

It was here, in this small slave quarter art gallery, that we truly fell in love with Rolland's work. There were delicately painted watercolors so intricate that we wondered how he could achieve the separation of colors. Jan was particularly moved by his seemingly contradictory subject matter, while I was struck by bright, sun-drenched sunflowers, speaking out loudly in the foreground of several paintings backdropped by somber Southern cypress buildings and fences. Rolland's finite sense of composition especially appealed to us. Jan pointed out the depth Rolland achieved and how important it was to look behind the obvious for yet another visual thrill.

"Well, dahlin'!" came a rather loud, effete, and effusive voice. "There's Pete Fountain. Can you believe that rug?"

Jan and I turned around to see who was being so rude. It was the same "dahlin'" who had remarked that I could slip under his covers anytime. Our glances crossed briefly. I gave him an icy stare, but he winked at me; I couldn't help but smile as I looked away. Pete and his wife walked toward us. Jan gave him a big hug and kiss on the cheek and thanked him for being a featured guest on our show the previous week. (The telecast from the windy roof garden of the Royal Orleans Hotel had caused Pete a bit of hairpiece concern.) He introduced us to his wife, Beverly, an absolute delight.

In a bubbly manner, she asked, "Did you hear that creep cast aspersions on Pete's toupee?"

"That was impolite," Jan agreed.

"Pete's getting so fed up with wearin' a hairpiece, ah think sometahm he's gonna just shave it *all* off!"

"You can believe it, Bev!" Pete replied.

"Beverly," Jan interjected, "Pete told us you have two boys our Timmy's age. Maybe they can come over and play sometime?"

"Pete's strange about the boys. He doesn't allow Kevin and Daryl in the French Quarter, even though his club is on Bourbon Street!"

"Really?"

"He thinks it's too racy."

"Pete, didn't you and Rolland grow up together in the Irish Channel?" I asked.

"Yup, in old Victorian double cottages. I guess that's wah ah understand Rolland's work so well. We have so much in common, not only in our backgrounds, but bein' artists in our New Orleans. Rolland, man he *lives* his art, he's beautiful!"

We all moved out into the courtyard. Stella was right. It was stuffy without a ceiling fan to stir the air.

"Aren't you Bob and Jan?"

"Yes," we responded simultaneously.

"We ahr Vivian and Stephen. We have a little boy who gets frightfully lonely and thought, perhaps, yah maid and owah maid could get togethah some aftah-noons so the children could play collectively."

"That would be wonderful. Bob and I are always looking for children in our neighborhood. Where do you live?"

"On Orleens nee-ah Burgundy."

Vivian and Stephen were just putting the finishing touches on a restaurant-bar, *Le Boeuf Gras*, that they had opened on St. Peter Street across from Pat O'Brien's. Steve was a physicist at the NASA space plant in New Orleans East, but he had worked side-by-side with Vivian to get the place up and running. Vivian, a beautiful redhead from the delta country of Mississippi, dripped honey with her chatty magnolia accent. Steve's dark, masculine looks were made more interesting by his quiet, sensuous manner. They invited us for a drink so they could show us around.

Six couples left the reception and paraded into the restaurant past the long bar. The bill of fare at the cafe was designed to feature twenty different kinds of steakburgers. We all started creating beefburger recipes, giving them exotic names: the Romanoff (a burger topped with sour cream, chopped egg, and caviar); the Rajah (a burger cooked in curry and topped with chutney); my offering was a Nutty Buddy (a burger topped with peanut butter, relish, and ketchup)—not totally my invention but something I had learned to eat as a youngster at Walt's in Beloit, Wisconsin.

After the fun of creating a menu for Stephen and Vivian and sampling a variety of drinks, we all paraded home along Bourbon Street. Stopping to say good night in the shadow of the Convent of the Holy Family, we chattered boisterously about our wonderful common ground, the Quarter, and our common problem of finding playmates for our children. Above the mayhem, someone was heard to say, "Lets start a club for our kids."

"Sort of a French Quarter family group?"

"The *Vieux Carré* Parents Association" was another suggestion.

"No, that's too hifalutin-soundin'."

"French Quarter Parents Club?" Jan suggested, somewhat timidly.

"That sounds good, real direct," someone responded.

And so, the French Quarter Parents Club was born on the corner of Bourbon and Orleans one Saturday night as the great Saint Louis Cathedral chimes tolled twelve. A couple of weeks later, an organizational meeting took place at our house. It was decided the purpose of the club would be to help build family relationships, to foster the camaraderie of our children, and to further their knowledge of the historic area in which they were privileged to live.

Two meetings a month would be scheduled, one solely for parents to socialize and discuss any problems concerning the welfare of our neighborhood or the preservation and wellbeing of the Quarter. Mothers and fathers, on a rotating basis, would plan and supervise the alternate meeting, primarily for the enjoyment of the children. It was further decided that the fathers would take the children on most of the outings since they had less opportunity to be with their kids.

A committee of mothers arranged our first outing with the children on Saturday two weeks hence, with the understanding that several volunteer fathers would go along to supervise the group. Jackson Square and its environs was the target. What better place to start, since it was the hallowed founding ground where, in 1718, *Jean Baptiste Le Moyne, sieur de Bienville*, established the city? He named the settlement *La Nouvelle Orléans*, in honor of the regent of France, *Philippe, Duc d' Orléans*. It was laid out around the *Place d'Armes*, now Jackson Square. In spite of the bragging of my great-grandmother Aupagnier, and some of the current descendants, most of the first residents were French convicts, German indentured servants, and African or Haitian slaves. American Indians, traveling between the Mississippi and Lake Pontchartrain, had long used the spot as a portage.

Four fathers volunteered to take the children's group on their first historic sojourn. We met in the courtyard of St. Mary's Italian school, next to the Ursulines Convent herb garden.

Susie Cangelosi, wife of volunteer-father Anton, an experienced volunteer guide, consented to help as our tour narration leader. Various club mothers deposited a total of twenty-four little darlings, aged three to ten, in the convent courtyard. For the next few hours, each father had six kids to supervise.

Susie spoke briefly about the ways in which the nuns used the herbs from their garden for cooking and gained interest by breaking off several leaves and letting the children sniff the fragrance until a couple of them sneezed. But she attracted greater attention when she assumed a mysterious voice to tell the diminutive listeners how herbs were used for treating various types of illnesses from snake bites to yellow fever. After explaining to the fidgety bunch that the convent building was one of the oldest structures on the lower Mississippi, we headed along Chartres Street, taking care that the children didn't wander off the banquette.

Moving toward Jackson Square, we passed the old icehouse ruins, soon to be replaced by the Provincial Motel. In order to keep the kids of various strides together, the fathers started them singing in cadence, an old military tactic I had learned in the infantry. "Ta de tum…He played one…He played tic tac on my drum…With a tic tac paddy wack doodle all the day, we can march a long long way." And so we did, the three blocks to the Presbytere Museum.

Under the colonnade at the *Presbytére* (French for Ecclesiastical House), completed in 1813, the boys pushed forward as we gathered around the old cast-iron submarine. Susie explained that before it sank anything, *it sank!* The boys all groaned.

"Did anybody git drownded dead, Miss Susie?"

She answered politely, "No one drowned."

Inside the Presbytere, the children were fascinated by the death mask of Napoleon. A climb to the top floor gave us a fabulous view of Jackson Square and the Mississippi River as we peered out the dormer windows of the mansard roof. The roof had been added later to the original building to afford additional space and to achieve a more French appearance to the Spanish architecture.

The little girls loved the display of Mardi Gras costumes and ball gowns, but the boys began to roughhouse, so we herded them on to our next stop, the Cabildo; of course, everyone needed to tinkle. Susie, being the only mother, had to supervise the eleven little girls. All was fine until one of the antiquated toilets backed up, filling the commode so high it chilled the tender derriere of four-year-old Carrie. The thought of pee-pee water splashing along her bottom and rushing down her socks caused her to let out a scream heard throughout the entire building. Rolland, her father, and I went in and lifted her off the john so Susie could dry her off. All the little girls tittered and giggled at the thought of "daddies" in the ladies room. Fortunately, the joviality was infectious enough to inspire Carrie to stop crying and start laughing.

"Ta de tee…he played three…he played tick tack on his knee."

We were off to the Cabildo, the first city hall of New Orleans, built in 1795 by the Spanish. Marching past the front of St. Louis Cathedral, all the little Catholic kiddies made the sign of the cross as taught by their parents and grandparents, including Timmy and Tammy, taught by Pierre. The high point of the Cabildo for all the boys was the exhibit of Confederate uniforms and firearms. A quill-penned original of the Louisiana Purchase fascinated the older girls. It was hard to believe it had really been signed on this exact spot.

Once outside the museum, hearing a familiar jingle, the kids made a mad dash for the Good-Humor Man, strategically located at the main gate of Jackson Square.

Armed with dripping ice cream bars, Susie suggested we all sit on the grass in Jackson Square while she explained a little bit about the Pontalba buildings and the house we were about to visit.

"Look, see the big red brick buildings over there on the Uptown or upriver side of the Square and these matching buildings on the Downtown side? The Baroness de Pontalba built them all. Her first name was Micaela. Can you all say mi-ka-el-la?"

"Mi-ka-el-la," the children parroted.

"Very good, children! Micaela wasn't very pretty but her father arranged her marriage to the Baron de Pontalba, right there at the Cathedral, when she was only sixteen years old! But…" Susie's voice became hushed as she raised her finger and widened her eyes, a technique to assure the complete attention of each child. "After their wedding, the Baron took Micaela to his ancestral home outside Paris, France, but Micaela was lonesome and unhappy, so she misbehaved."

"Like a beatnik?" asked one of the kids.

"Well, sort of. Anyway, her father-in-law got so upset, he broke down the door to her bedroom and shouted, 'Madame, I am going to kill you!' *Bang!*"

The kids all flinched.

Susie continued to transfix the audience. "The first bullet tore off Micaela's fingers as she protectively covered her chest. He shot and hit her three more times…bang, bang, bang!"

The children cowered. The girls hugged each other protectively.

"Micaela slumped to the floor before the old Baron left the room, *but* there was one more *bang!*"

The kids jumped again.

"The old man killed *himself!*"

There was total silence.

"What happened then, Miss Susie?" asked Timmy.

"The old Baron was dead but not Micaela. She lived for *fifty* more years. When she died at the age of seventy-five, the three bullets were still inside her!"

"Did they hurt?"

"I suppose, when the humidity was bad like today. Now, let's all get up and rinse our hands off in the water fountain and I'll take you into Micaela's house right over there. It's called the 1850s House now, but that's where Micaela lived."

Rising en masse, looking like a small squadron leaving bivouac, we approached the Charles De Gaulle fountain to rinse the grass stain and ice cream stickiness off our hands. After much giggling and splashing, which soon turned into screaming, we fathers ordered the group to "*fall-in!*"

"Ti-de-den…he played ten…he played tic tac, once again…with a tic tac paddy wack." And off we marched, passing single file into the entrance of the 1850s House, the only row-house retaining its original configuration and appearance on all four floors.

Susie was busy getting the tickets while we fathers gathered the children into a group in the large ground-level room, which had originally served as a shop for the residents of the house but now provided space for a museum display area and a small gift shop.

Susie rang an antique dinner bell and raised her voice to get our attention. "Children, when this house was built over a hundred and fifty years ago by the Baroness, she even climbed ladders in her hoop-skirt to show the workmen how she wanted it done."

"Even with them bullets still in 'er?" asked Timmy.

"Oh, yes." Susie chuckled politely, pleased to know someone was paying attention. "Now let me explain for a minute about the house, then the dads can take you upstairs to the first floor."

"But Miss Susie, I thought *this* was the first floor!"

"Well, it really is, dear. You see, in the United States we call this the first floor, but in France, it's called the ground floor because it's on the ground; that makes the next floor up the first floor. Remember, Micaela was from France, and New Orleans had French customs in those days."

"It was called La Nouvelle Orléans," interjected one of the older girls, cocking her head in a self-satisfied tilt.

"Yes, you're correct. The original kitchen is back through those doors off the courtyard. The servants carried the food up the outside winding stairs rain or shine, to the dining room on the—which floor?"

"The *first*," came back the enthusiastic reply.

"Y'all are really smart. The parlor or living room is also on the first floor; from there we will walk out on the beautiful gallery through long windows to look at the square. But please, stay near your daddies, so you won't fall off. Remember, even if it's called the first floor, it's real high up in the air. Oh, one more thing. When you're on the gallery, look at the cast-iron railing to see if you and the daddies can find Micaela's initials in the iron scroll. Her last name was Almonaster de Pontalba. So look for and 'A' and 'P.'"

"Like the grocery store?"

"Not exactly, Timmy, but that's very observant. Okay, now listen. After the first floor we'll climb to the bedrooms on the second floor. There is also an attic where the servants slept, but we aren't allowed up there because it's being repaired, so stay with the daddy you were assigned to, and let's go. Brandy and Julie will go with me so I can hold their hands, because they're so little."

We reassembled in the courtyard to look at the kitchen, then ascended the creaky stairs in daddy-led groups, followed by Susie and her two little troopers.

In the large parlor the boys were fascinated by the telescope, which to me seemed just about powerful enough to see across Jackson Square to spy on one of the lovely 1850s ladies in the upper Pontalba building.

"Mistah Bawb, did they have stores a hundred years ago?"

"The stores were down on the first floor, I mean the ground floor!"

"Ah know *that!* Ah mean, stores in the skah, silly!"

"Stores in the sky? Oh, *stars!* Yes, they had stars in the sky in those days," I said, finally grasping her New Orleansese.

"Thanks, Mistah Bawb; look at those dawlin' dawls. That baby dawl is so dawlin'."

Susie pointed out a pair of binoculars, which were actually his and her whiskey flasks for the opera.

"Timmy Cawr, that is not yor daddy," rebuked Carrie, as she pointed to the male portrait over the mantelpiece in the parlor.

"Well, he looks like mah daddy."

"Mistah Bawb, is that a pick-chah of you in that big frame up they-ah?"

"No, I wasn't born when it was painted, but it does look very much like my great-grandfather Aupagnier, who was born in New Orleans in the 1840s."

Timmy smiled boastfully.

Then Carrie cocked her curly blonde head. "Well, mah grand-père was a Dussan with a plantation in La Place!"

Susie rang the little antique dinner bell kept on the great sideboard, located through the huge sliding pocket doors in the dining room. "It's time for us to go upstairs to the bedrooms. You must not get on the beds or touch anything. All right, let's go."

The little girls loved the tester beds with their enormous posts supporting elaborate canopies. Tammy spied a four-poster bed almost identical to hers.

"Where are the bathrooms, Miss Cangelosi?"

"They didn't have bathrooms."

"Wow wee, how did they pee-pee?" whispered one of the boys, inciting giggles from everyone.

"There were no bathrooms in those days. Instead, they used beautiful potties, which were usually kept under their beds."

"Yuk!" came the reply from several of the girls.

Timmy butted in again. "My daddy says in the olden days, people had a canopy over their bed an a can-o-pee under their bed!"

Everyone giggled as Timmy assumed a self-satisfied grin.

But Tammy glared at him chastisingly. "Timmy, that's gross!"

"And now, boys and girls, we're all going to meet out on the back gallery and start down the very winding and steep servant's stairway. I'll take Julie and Brandy by the hand first because they're the youngest."

We held our charges back so Susie and her two tots could negotiate the extra high and narrow steps. When the three of them got to the gallery below, Susie called up to all of us staring over the railing.

"Don't lean on the railing, kids," warned Anton. "It's very old and not very strong."

"Ooooh!" cried the children, pressing back against the wall of the slave quarter.

"I'll wait here," hollered Susie. "Start sending the children down one by one."

Three of the girls locked hands and cautiously started descending the perilous spiral stairs. Disappearing around the turn, they immediately issued an ear-piercing scream, which bounced in echoes off the old brick walls. Scrambling down the steps to see what was wrong, I found the girls pressed against the wall. Tammy was scraping something from the bottom of her shoe.

"Gross, gross, gross!" she beseeched.

"What is it? A roach?"

"Gross, gross, no daddy, it's poo poo!"

"Poo poo? That's impossible!"

"Daddy, I know poo. This is poo poo 'cause it smells like poo poo. It dun't smell like a roach an' it dint crunch like a roach. It squished!"

Susie peeked her head around the landing. "It looks like Brandy is losing something out of his diaper."

"*Yuk!*" came the distress call from the three girls.

"I'll get some Kleenex out of my purse," Susie volunteered.

Apparently little Brandy had been carrying his firm load for sometime, but as he stretched his tiny legs to the limit on the tall stair-risers, he deposited a bead of poo poo each time his diaper flashed open.

Susie worked her way back up the steps, collecting pellets in a Kleenex. Brandy's father took him down to the men's room to empty his britches. Back in the ground floor salesroom, we thanked the museum people for the rare privilege of going out on the balcony.

"Bah, bah, an' thank y'all!" everyone yelled politely as we moved out the front door onto the banquette.

"Hey, look up, that's where we were, way up there!" yelled several kids.

"Y'all come along now, we have to stay together to cross at Decatur Street."

The kids skipped along, sneaking peeks into curio shops that inhabited the ground floor of the Pontalba building.

Once across Decatur, we split into little groups to secure tables and chairs at the always-crowded *Café du Monde*. Everyone ordered—what else?—café au lait with beignets. New Orleans children, unlike most other kids in the U. S., are practically weaned on coffee and chicory served with hot milk, along with puffed-up greasy square doughnuts known by that funny French name.

We sat sipping coffee and powering our beignets with heaps of confectioner's sugar from the metal shakers. The kids took great relish in blowing the powered sugar all over each other while snickering raucously. None of us dads tried to stop them. Calm them down a bit, yes—but after all, it's a New Orleans tradition!

"Okay, kids, take the last sip of your ice water," I commanded, "and then wash off your sticky fingertips in your water glass. Be sure to dry them off with napkins from the dispenser. Hey, but *don't* drink the water after you've stuck your fingers in it!" (This old New Orleans custom would probably be considered unseemly elsewhere, but at *Café du Monde*, it's *de rigueur.*)

We reassembled our spiffy little group on the banquette and "tic-tac-paddy-wacked" through the French Market colonnade, echoing our way past the fruit and vegetable stands back to our original meeting place.

The first of many planned outings of the Parents' Club was deemed a rousing success.

Summer Stock production of "The Charm Kid" with Bob, Bill Putch and Sadie Miller, 1951

(top) Bob in an advertisement, 1954

(left) National advertisement, 1953

(bottom) Bob in one of many advertisements for Coke, 1954

THE TIMES-PICAYUNE, NEW ORLEANS, LA., SUNDAY MORNING, FEBRUARY 26, 19

Two Theaters to Open Productions Th

'Life with Father' at Le Petit

"Life With Father," Howard Lindsay's famous long-run play about the family with flaming red hair and the patriarch with a flaming temper, will oepn this week at Le Petit Theatre du Vieux Carre.

Roger Keller and Orrie Summers will have the lead in the Wednesday through March 12 production. The opening night curtain is at 8:30 p. m.

Playing the four sons in the domestic comedy will be Danny Bennett, Tim Carr, Arch Lee Wallace and Al Salzer. Tim, the youngest member of the cast, is five years old. He is the son of Bob and Jan Carr, New Orleans radio and TV personalities.

Executive director Lawrence L. Johnson said Le Petit Theatre has never before staged "Life With Father," although it has been performed by other resident nonprofessional theater groups in past seasons.

"Life With Father" established an all-time record for longevity on Broadway when it played a staggering total of 3224 performances.

Also in the cast will be Gloria Scott, Sydney Wolf, Joe Barefoot, Beline Devine, Mildred Costa, Dell Mitchell, Jane Trosclair, Cora Ann Ribaul, Walter Bougere and Robert Blomefield.

THE DAY FAMILY AT LE PETIT 'SITS' FOR ARTIST TOM CONDON
"Father" rails at "Mother" for failing to keep her accounts straight in this scene sketched from Le Petit Theatre's forthcoming production of "Life With Father." The principals are Roger Keller and Orrie Summers, as head of the Day clan, and little Tim Carr as an amused onlooker. The other sons are shown in silhouette portraits in the background.

MARCH 1, 1961

Roger Keller, Orrie Summers and Little Timmy Carr depicted by Tom Condon for The Times-Picayune *Newspaper, 1961*

Timmy (age 5) on stage at La Petite Théatre du Vieux Carré, 1961

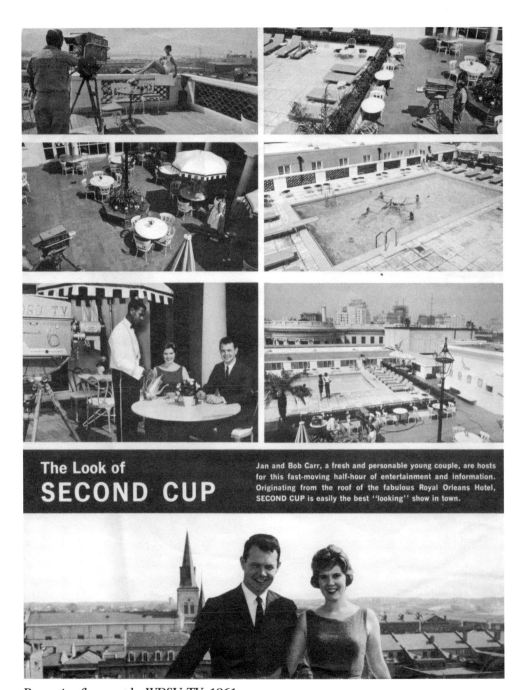

The Look of
SECOND CUP

Jan and Bob Carr, a fresh and personable young couple, are hosts for this fast-moving half-hour of entertainment and information. Originating from the roof of the fabulous Royal Orleans Hotel, SECOND CUP is easily the best "looking" show in town.

Promotion flyer sent by WDSU-TV, 1961

CHAPTER SIX

The Stork Visits Bourbon Street

We were thrilled to learn Jan was pregnant for the third time and it was equally good news when the station decided Jan could continue on *Second Cup* wearing maternity clothes. The sales department accepted the challenge to market the coming event; our first new sponsor was Maternity and Baby Lane.

This would be our first baby born in New Orleans, and its first home address would forever be Bourbon Street!

Jan's first pregnancy, which produced Timothy, was rather harrowing. She was plagued by severe morning sickness. Each morning, on the way to the TV station in Wheeling, I would have to stop the car so she could hang her head out the window to throw up. Her second pregnancy in Huntington caused her no problem, so we hoped this third pregnancy would be even easier.

Our New Orleans viewing audience loved Jan being pregnant, what with the large Catholic population and the sexy Baptists, New Orleans families have always been larger than the national standard. Jan and I, *and* our television audience, became more and more anxious for the day of delivery.

On June twenty-first, Jan arose unusually early following a sleepless night, due partly to a thunderously loud storm. After consuming every droplet of chocolate ice cream and lemon ice the refrigerator coughed up, she shook me from my contented slumber wanting to take a bath but afraid to get into the tub without my help. She looked like a great white whale as she settled into the bath crystals, foaming into frothy cloud-like billows.

"As long as I'm up, I might as well shave," I mumbled half-audibly, stripping off my T-shirt. The shaving cream spewed from the aerosol can, filling my hand. "I wonder how whales have sex?" I asked, not expecting a response.

"Do I make you think of a whale?"

Lathering my face, I answered, "Humm, just a bit."

She flung a handful of suds in protest. The froth hit me just below my bellybutton, crackling like a bowl of fresh corn flakes as it slithered down my stomach until it hung like a gossamer cocoon from the end of my penis. The sensation was stimulating. Jan chuckled, reaching over the tub to remove the suds. The tender caress stimulated me even further.

"Honey, I don't think I can take it much longer. Look at the calluses on my hand!"

"*Bob!*"

LA PETITE ECOLE   ESPLANADE AVENUE

"Do you think this kid will ever get born so we can go back to love-making?"

"Honeykins, I don't like being a whale any more than you like abstinence!" She reached over once again from the tub, flicking me with the end of her finger.

"Ouch!"

"That was just to get your mind back on shaving," she smirked, slipping deeper down under the bubble bath to relax. "It's not going to be too much longer. Just hang in there, so to speak!"

Slipping a fresh blade into my Schick injector, I began to shave.

"Do you think I acted too much like an idiot yesterday?" Jan asked, blowing gently at the suds as she spoke.

"What do you mean, like an idiot?" I distorted my face in an effort to get to the whiskers along my lips.

"I mean my interview with Bette Davis. I got so nervous talking to her that I asked some dumb questions."

"You mean when you asked her how many times she'd been married?"

"That was one."

"I suppose asking someone about their intimate life isn't the best approach when there are lots of other questions you could ask."

"Super-famous people scare me. She seemed to get so upset when I asked her if she had wanted to play Scarlet O'Hara; she barked back: 'Darling, my Jezebel surpassed Vivian's Scarlet, even if the American Academy of Arts and Sciences didn't give me that damned Oscar, which I…I had named after my first husband!'."

"I wouldn't worry about it, honey!"

"Anyway, she did scare me 'cause she was so curt. I think Miss Bette was upset because I interviewed her instead of *you*."

"We didn't want me to do both interviews. After all, me talking to Rosemary Clooney made more sense, since I can use the material on my disc-jockey show when I spin her records."

"I know, but Rosemary Clooney is more my type."

"Bette Davis is more *my* type then?"

"I think so. She likes good-looking men; look at Gary Merrill."

"I'll have to admit, Rosemary Clooney is really nice. Maybe it's cause we're both from Ohio, we speak the same language." I swung my head around the bathroom door to glimpse the clock. "Honey, I think you better start getting out of the tub, Rivet is gonna be bubbling in here any minute."

Rivet Hedderal, the premiere hairdresser in New Orleans, came to our house every morning to do Jan's hair for *Second Cup*. His weekly "Beauty Tips" appearance on the program had given him considerable notoriety and generated new business for his salon, which hummed with activity and gossip, causing his shop to prosper. Rivet usually arrived about 7:15 A.M., so that we could get to the station by eight.

I finished shaving and splashed my face with cool water. Jan stood up in the bathtub; the suds clung to her, giving the appearance of a Walt Disney snow fairy—a *big* snow fairy!

"Good heavens, I guess I used too many bath salts. How do I get them off?"

"Let me turn on the shower. I'll help you wash them away."

Adjusting the temperature, I gently assisted the flow of water, lightly rubbing her pink skin until all the suds whirled down the drain. Helping her over the edge of the tub, we embraced; her naked body felt warm against mine. Blood rushed through our systems as we kissed. I felt a jolt against my stomach.

"That's the baby!" Jan exclaimed. "It just said 'good morning.'"

We scrambled for towels to cover ourselves as Tammy and Timmy came dashing in.

"Oh, look at that big tummy," they giggled, almost in unison. "Look at that *big* tummy!"

Jan tried desperately to secrete herself behind the towel and the shower curtain.

"Let me put my ear against your stomach so I can hear our baby," Timmy beseeched. Tammy followed with the same request.

Consenting, Jan wrapped the towel around herself, trying to achieve some semblance of modesty.

"Okay, kids, you've had your listen, it's time to go back to your rooms and get dressed."

I took my shower while Jan got dressed. Rivet, who had his own key, opened the front door downstairs and hollered up, "It's *me*, dahlin's. I'll get myself a cup of coffee 'cause I can smell it brewing, then I'll be right up to tease and torture your hair."

Fortunately, I had pulled on my boxers when he popped cheerfully into the bedroom with a plastic bag of assorted fruits. Rivet, similar to Jan and her grandmother, was eternally on a diet.

"Here, dahlin', have some. I'm on my diet again; let's nibble a little fruit whilst I play with your hair!"

"I'm sure glad you shampooed your hair this morning, dahlin'. I'm trying something new; I'm gonna blow it, tease it, swirl it, and spray it."

"*What are* you talking about?" I asked from the bathroom, using the medicine cabinet mirror to comb my hair. "Sounds sexy."

"You bet your bonnet it'll be sexy," Rivet retorted, working feverishly. "Gotta do *something*, darlin', to keep people from looking at that big belly."

After he had curled her hair he began to snarl it until she looked like Methuselah's wife or Medea, raging after Jason and the Golden Fleece.

Slipping into my pants, I zipped my fly, began to tie my tie, then, glancing back over my shoulder into the mirror, remarked, "Who *is* that?"

Rivet rolled his eyes. "Bob, we're doing Jan Carr of *Second Cup*, not Miss Havisham of *Great Expectations*. I'm *not* finished. Good God, an *artiste* should never show a half-finished work of art to an ignoramus."

Rivet continued to twist it and tease it and roll it around and around until it finally turned into a Beehive, the so-called hairdo of the year, according to the hairdressers, who seemed to be the only ones who could perfect it. "Dahlin', I'm making you look like Arlene Dahl. Your hair will look so beautiful no one will ever glance at that frightful tummy."

He pushed her face close to the dressing table mirror. "Now let's have a look at your makeup. I think with this sophisticated hairstyle, we ought to have something more. Let's give you a little more eyeliner today, a little more shadow, *and* just for the fun of it, a little darkening around the nose, ah, and a little dimple in the chin!"

Happily humming along, he turned my innocent Ohio farm-girl into a television personality. "Okay, *Voila!* Kiddies. I did it! Now let's use plenty of spray net so we can keep everything in place."

He stopped dead in his tracks, and laying a finger aside his nose, blurted out, "Oh shee-it! I forgot my spray net! Jan, do you have any spray net?"

Jan instructed me to get the spray net from the cabinet under the bathroom sink. As I searched for the spray net on my hands and knees in the depths of the cabinet behind assorted washcloths, diapers, soaps, cleansers, and toilet bowl fresheners, I heard Jan cry out, "Ugh," and then, "Oh my God!"

"What *are* you doing to her, Rivet?"

"Oh my God, oh my God," she bellowed. "Oh my *God!*"

"Darlin', *what's* the matter?" Rivet questioned, stepping back in alarm.

"I think I'm having pains, I think I'm having contractions."

"*You mean birth pains?* Oh, my dear, you can't have those," Rivet squealed. "Not after I've created such a fabulous coif. We've got to show you to the world!"

"Honey, I think you're just imagining things, you've got another couple of weeks."

"Easy for you to say. Oh my God, oh my God, oh my *God*. Get me on the bed, *now!*"

As I helped her onto the bed, Rivet cradled her hair to make sure the Beehive didn't come unraveled. "Jan, dahlin', let's stretch you out here with this satin pillow under your head so we don't ruin your coif."

"Oh God, oh my *God!*" she shrieked.

"You can't have the baby today," I insisted. "You've got two interviews! There's nobody else who can take the program."

"Oh my *God*," she said, rolling over on her side.

"Dahlin', dahlin', don't jostle your hair."

"Honey, are you sure you're having contractions?"

"Are you kidding? After two babies, I ought to know if I'm having contractions. I think it's time to call Dr. Goldman."

I started to get nervous. "I can't believe this!"

"Believe it! Oh my *God!*"

I dialed Dr. Goldman and told the answering service we had an emergency and to get in touch with the doctor immediately. Timmy and Tammy appeared at the door, their faces reflecting the wonderment their eyes beheld, their mother wincing and writhing on the bed.

"What are you doing to mommy?"

"We're not doing anything to mommy. She just doesn't feel well this morning."

"Oh my God, I'm having another pain." Jan cried out in such agony that Tammy began to cry.

Rivet followed with, "Holy Mary, Mother of God, I think she's going to have the baby right *now!* I've gotta get *outta* here. Oh Christ!"

Grabbing his hair curlers, blow dryer, and bobby pins, he fled down the stairs and out the door.

"Daddy, is mommy going to have our baby right on the bed?"

"No, no, children. Tammy, stop crying! Nothing's wrong with mommy and we're not going to have our baby right now."

The phone rang; it was Dr. Goldman. Of course, the first thing he asked was,

"How far apart are the contractions?"

"I don't know, sir. Here, talk to Jan."

"Hello, Dr. Goldman, oh my God!"

They chatted a minute but all I could make out was Jan saying, "We'll be there shortly."

We heard the front door slam. It was Olympia arriving to get breakfast for the children. Immediately running into the hall, Timmy jumped on the banister and slid down as Tammy hung over the railing screaming, "We're havin' a baby, we're havin' a baby, Lympy!"

Olympia looked up. "What y'all sayin'?"

Both kids screamed, "We're havin' a baby, Lympy, we're havin' a baby! Mommy's having our baby, right now, on the bed!"

I could hear Olympia say, "Oh my Gawd! Oh my Gawd!" in cadence with Jan's, "Oh my God!"

It seemed as though the whole world was pleading for God's intervention, including me.

"Bob, quick! Put some of those things in my suitcase. We better get to Touro Infirmary, *right now!*"

"Okay, Okay!"

Olympia walked into the room, "Oh, Mizz Cahr, ah can't believe this be happenin'."

Jan had another contraction. "Oh my God!"

"Okay, honey, you're packed. I'll bring more things up later. Let's get to the car."

Timmy grabbed the overnight bag. Tammy looked on in wonderment as Olympia and I helped Jan. Clutching onto the banister, Jan began backing down the long stairway step by step. Olympia stood above while I edged around below her, making sure she wouldn't fall. Halfway down, she stopped and clutched the railing even harder.

"Are you okay, honey?"

"I think so. I felt faint but now it's letting up, thank heaven."

"What's *that?*" I demanded.

"What's *what?*

"On the *step.* The step is all wet."

"Lawd have mercy, Mizz Cahr, you done gone an' broke yo' water!"

With Jan safely in the car, I set a course for Touro Infirmary, where New Orleanians have been birthin' babies for more than a century. Fortunately, the early morning traffic was light. Even more fortunately, Doctor Goldman was there to meet us and take charge of Jan. *Oh, my God,* was I relieved!

By my watch, I realized I had twenty-five minutes to get to the station, fighting the city-bound heavy traffic. In the confusion of leaving the house I couldn't remember if I had asked Olympia to call the station. At this early date we had made no plans for anyone to fill in for us.

I arrived on the roof garden set of the hotel about ten minutes before airtime. Director John Domec and the rest of the crew were frantic, wondering what had happened to us.

"Didn't Olympia call to tell you I took Jan to the hospital?"

Everyone began explaining at the same time; the phone lines weren't working in some parts of the city because of the horrendous storm during the night. John said we were lucky to have a TV picture at all. The roof-top swimming pool was a mess; the Royal Orleans crew had been working since dawn to clean it so we could do the water ballet.

It dawned on me that the low pressure that produced the storm last night might have triggered the baby.

Blaring over the speaker came the rapid-fire directions of producer Al Shea: "Bob, now hear this *and* listen carefully, you have only five minutes till air time. You have two interviews. The one with Harnett Kane shouldn't be difficult because he's going to talk about his new book. The other one is Jerry Lewis. He was supposed to be here fifteen minutes ago but apparently they're running late; I told his manager we'd rearrange the show to put him on as soon as he got here. Then he has to rush off to another appearance. We've scheduled the water ballet in the last part of the show because the pool is still being cleaned. The swimmers haven't had a chance to rehearse, so we'll just have to wing the camera angles! *Got it, Bob?*"

"*Got it, Al!*"

"Okay, now you have less than four minutes to scramble your ass into the Holmes-es double-knit white suit hanging in the men's room, so hurry. *Oh*, and *Bob*, tell your audience about Jan being in the hospital!"

Al was the brain, pulse, and conscience of our show. Each morning he pumped life into us like Geppetto breathed life into Pinocchio.

After hustling into the suit and settling down at the umbrella table, I took several deep breaths as I glanced at the live commercial copy for Holmes department store and Luzianne coffee. The opening theme popped shrilly through the sound monitor speakers. I watched the video monitor as the camera did a wide-sweep pan, as usual, across the roof-tops of the Quarter, the central business district, showing the Hibernia Tower and the American Bank building, then finally ending on Windy McCall, our weather girl. Windy, dressed in a strapless sundress supplied by Holmes, smiled fetchingly at the camera. John directed a cross fade to a shot of the table where Jan and I normally sat together. Reggie, our floor-director, cued the Royal Orleans waiter to pour the Luzianne coffee into my *Second Cup* souvenir coffee mug. Momentarily the camera zoomed-in to a head shot of me as I lifted the mug to my lips. After I explained what a crazy morning it had been with Jan, Rivet, and our kids, John cut to the five-minute newscast back in the studio.

The news over, I did my interview with nationally-famous New Orleans author Harnett T. Kane, who had become a personal friend. Harnett, whose most famous book was *Louisiana Hayride*, was a great champion and historian of the South and one of the most outspoken supporters for the preservation of the French Quarter.

He often lamented the commercialization of the Quarter, saying, "Someday, tourists will be standing in one hotel looking out the window at another hotel across the street, without ever knowing both were once private family homes."

Harnett had been scheduled on our program to discuss and promote his newest volume, *The Romantic South*, a richly illustrated anthology describing "America's only Golden Age."

During the interview Harnett got sidetracked, as he was wont to do, and began to attack developer Sam Recile's remodeling tactics on a number of prominent and very old French Quarter buildings. Although Recile would beautifully restore the exterior of a building, he would often have the interior gutted so that extra floors could be added to the inside of the structure. Harnett ruthlessly referred to these restorations as "squashed down Creole" and future slums.

When Harnett realized Reggie was giving me a frantic wrap-up, he looked straight into the camera and pronounced, "Mr. Recile, you should confine yourself to the American Sector of the city where you're building your monstrous Plaza Tower and keep your *damned* Italian hands off the French Quarter!"

I registered theatrical shock at the "no no" word, thanked Harnett and delivered my D. H. Holmes commercial, modeling and describing the white suit. Windy was reporting the weather from the very top deck of the hotel roof when Jerry Lewis suddenly breezed in with his entourage. I had anticipated an easy interview but found out differently. He made absolutely no eye contact and talked only about the things he wanted to talk about, not answering one of my questions. Having made his statements, he got up and tersely left. Although Jerry never spoke directly to me or any of the crew, his public relations man followed him around, passing out pens embellished with Jerry's likeness. I couldn't help considering this a rather cold way to make friends and influence people, and I was left somewhat stunned in his wake and more than apprehensive about emceeing his appearance at the Saenger Theater that evening. He was the consummate megalomaniac star.

Reggie frantically motioned me over to the edge of the pool for the next segment. A film commercial break was in progress, allowing me to collect my thoughts. On cue I chatted with the swimming coach whose young teens were presenting their "Jazz-a-bell" water ballet to the beat of a traditional Dixieland recording.

While the swim event was in progress, John announced over the off-air speaker from the director's booth back at the station that a nurse had called from Touro Hospital to let me know Jan had just given birth to a baby *boy*, six pounds, two ounces. "Jan and the baby are both doing jis' fahn."

Engrossed in my program hustle and bustle, John's announcement caught me unaware. A rush of joy ran through me. I could hardly believe she had given birth so fast.

Reggie shouted directions from the other end of the pool. "We're coming out on a two-shot of you and the swimming coach, you've only thirty seconds to finish the show, so announce the birth of your baby boy. We'll fade out on the swimmers in the pool under the credits."

The red tally light appeared, "*Ladies and gentlemen,* I am now the proud father of a new baby *boy*, Jan is…"

Before I could finish the sentence, Reggie dropped his headset, dashed over and shoved me, polyester suit and all, into the pool. The swimmers began to yell and splash at me wildly. The TV cameramen scrambled to catch various shots of the mayhem while the closing theme played over the scene until the station break.

I quickly changed my wet clothes. Al Shea, like the A-number-one producer he was, had a cab waiting downstairs to speed me back to Touro. "I don't think you should drive in your weakened condition," Al chided, slamming the taxi door.

I was shocked at my first sight of Jan. Her scarlet hair, which Rivet had teased and coiffed so meticulously, radiated out from her head like Medusa's. Her smeared sophisticated make-up gave her face the asymmetrical appearance of a Picasso painting. I couldn't help but snicker.

"Good lord, you look like you've been dragged by the ankles across Bayou La Fouche! I wonder if Rivet will ever get that fright wig untangled?"

"Honey," she uttered groggily, "it's been five years, so maybe you've forgotten, but having a baby is *not* like going to a tea-dance!"

Glad to see she hadn't lost her sense of humor, I gave her a cautious hug and a long, lingering kiss on the lips, closing my eyes so I wouldn't chuckle at the way she looked.

"Honey, have you seen him yet?"

"No."

"He's *gorgeous*, really gorgeous."

"I sure hope he looks better than his mother!"

Ignoring my remark, she continued, "He's the most beautiful baby I've ever seen. I think they're washing him off right now. They'll bring him back in a few minutes."

"Did you remember to tell them not to circumcise him?"

"I don't know. Everything happened so fast I didn't tell anybody anything but I don't see what difference it makes. Even Saint Paul suggested circumcision wasn't as important as keeping the commandments of God."

"Easy for *you* and Saint Paul to say! What do women and saints know about peters anyway? You know they cut Timmy's crooked then had to repair it, and it took a while to heal. You've been plenty happy with me the way I am; I'm not chopped! I just don't want any mistakes made. After all, that's gonna be one of his favorite parts!"

"*Bob, really!*"

"I mean if they mess up his penis it could affect his whole life."

"If it's so important to you, why don't you talk it over with Henry Simon?"

"Doctors always want to circumcise. They make extra money every time they slice something. Besides, Dr. Simon is Jewish, I think, so *he's* gonna want to cut for sure. The good Lord obviously put it there to make things work better, so I don't see why it should be cut off just because the Old Testament makes some big deal out of it."

"Bob, honeykins, calm down. You're getting all upset. I'll talk to the doctors before anything's done."

I sat down in the visitor's chair beside the bed and laid my head back to relax.

"We must decide on his name," Jan muttered. "It should be something that goes along with Timmy and Tammy."

Jan, under the influence of drugs, continued to blather on about names as I began to reflect on why we had already used the names we did. Timmy was named Timothy Fitzsimmons Carr, using Jan's maiden name. We began with Timothy because we thought it sounded Irish. Tammy was Tamson Antoinette. Antoinette was my mother's middle name, a name used in her family every generation since Marie Antoinette Hapsburg, according to mother's genealogical prattle. Tammy was the diminutive of Tamson, a shortened version of Thamsonne, an old English name derived from Thomas, although my Welsh grandfather spelled it Tamcyn.

I focused in on Jan's continuing chatter.

"I think we should use Robert because we ought to have a child named after you."

I wasn't very enthusiastic about using Robert, had never been called Robert, and wasn't particularly interested in using it.

"Tim, Tam, and *Robert!*" I said. "Tim, Tam, and Bert! Tim, Tam, and Bill! Tim, Tam, and John!" Nothing seemed to scan.

All through Jan's pregnancy we expected a girl and had talked about naming her Tiffany. *Breakfast at Tiffany's* with Audrey Hepburn was a movie and an actress we both loved. On the other hand, if it were a boy we would name him Tiffin, as in Tiffin, Ohio. But now that the decision was at hand, we couldn't make up our minds. The hospital began to get antsy for a name on the birth certificate, so the next day, while I was on the air, Jan named our son Robert Tiffin.

That evening on my way to the hospital, after my appearance at the Saenger with Jerry Lewis, I stopped in at a party to brag about my new son at Lem and Mary Jane McCoy's. The McCoys had named their new baby Dillard.

"His name is Robert Tiffin but we're gonna call him Tiffin," I announced proudly.

A rather officious guest who had just returned from Great Britain grandly remarked, "Really, are you not aware that a tiffin is a small English snack?"

I looked at him blankly as he scrutinized me from head to toe.

"If your son is as cute as you, he'd surely make a tasty tiffin!" He threw his head back and laughed viciously.

At the hospital I told Jan about my party experience. She was as concerned as I. Living in the sometimes flamboyant French Quarter, we didn't want our little angel boy referred to as somebody's tasty tidbit! But we did want the name to begin with a "T." So, finally, we decided to name him Thomas. *Tim, Tam, Tom* had a nice cadence. Problem was, the birth certificate had already been filled in and there was some rule, or law, or something, that only one birth certificate can be issued per child, so I illegally hand-printed the name *Thomas* in front of the other names; thus, his birth certificate reads: Thomas Robert Tiffin Carr, which was fine with me. It gave him a range of names to choose from in his life. If he became a baseball player, he could use Tom; if he decided on acting or the ballet, he might want to use Tiffin; if a banker or lawyer, perhaps Robert would be the most dignified. The choice eventually could be his. He could even use T.R.T. Carr.

Jan and I were thrilled with our decision; it seemed so avant-garde. *But* I was less than thrilled with the decision of an intern who without proper authorization sliced the foreskin off my son's penis.

Tom was a good little baby and, according to Olympia, one of the prettiest white babies she had ever laid her eyes on. He was blessed with a shock of blond hair—a goodly amount—sky blue eyes, and healthy rosy cheeks. Olympia thought him so beautiful at the hospital that she went crazy until she could get her hands on "her" baby! Tammy and Timmy had been left in the hospital lobby, knowing they were too young to be allowed above the first floor. However, through special dispensation from the head nurse, who was a fan of "Bob & Jan," they were whisked up to Jan's room on a freight elevator. Olympia and I had to restrain and hush them at their first sight of tiny Thomas Robert Tiffin.

Being a television personality, Jan received masses of flowers and all sorts of gifts. Many were presents that our TV and radio fans had made for Tom, everything from crocheted booties to quilted layettes.

Jan's recuperation was so rapid that she was back on the air in only two weeks. *Good Midwestern farm stock*, I surmised.

Olympia loved having Tom all to herself. She hated the thought of leaving her "li'l Tom" for a long weekend. I assured her she could call collect anytime the spirit moved her. Tom had been home from the hospital for nearly a month when Olympia was to leave for Atlanta. Jan rushed home from the television station to see her off, but Olympia was fraught with anxiety and seriously toying with the idea of telling the church to go ahead without her because her baby was sick.

"Olympia, you've been planning this church trip for a whole year. Now you just gotta get going. I'm sure your Tom will be okay. If not, I promise to call Dr. Simon."

"Maybe so, Mizz Cahr. Our baby been spittin' up all mornin' long. Jis don't seem raht. You a'solutely promise not to let that li'l baby out your saht?"

"I *promise*, Olympia. I *promise*."

"All raht, if you say, but ah tell you, Mizz Cahr, ah be worryin' 'bout our baby all the tahme ah'm gone."

We didn't want Olympia to miss her long-awaited spiritual outing. She loved her church and especially enjoyed the trips to Birmingham, Mobile, and Atlanta. Various choirs sang and there was wonderful preaching. She would return revitalized and her vitality was infectious. Hallelujah!

Tom, meanwhile, continued to spit up. By morning we had a difficult time getting him to take his bottle. Jan and I took turns rubbing the rubber nipple gently along his lips, trying to entice him to suck. Unfortunately, what little amount he did swallow would soon come up. Knowing Olympia would be calling to check on her Tom, Jan pressed to reach Dr. Simon, who prescribed a Similac formula without iron.

But by nightfall, he still hadn't kept any food down. The doctor advised Jan to bring him in first thing in the morning if he didn't improve.

Early the next morning, Jan phoned to report that Tom was getting awfully listless and weak. Dr. Simon directed us to take Tom immediately to Touro Infirmary. After one look at Tom, he called in a specialist; our hearts leapt. Dr. Simon directed a nurse to inject an IV Into Tom's tiny arm, no bigger than a chicken wing. He had gotten so pale that he looked like an alabaster cherub. Jan was almost as white, her face reflecting grave concern.

Dr. Simon explained that it was an ailment happening at about this age in boy babies more often than in girls. The diagnosis was pyloric stenosis, which has to do with the muscle tightening around the valve that leads to the stomach. Consequently, food is regurgitated before ever reaching the stomach. Tom was starving! A pediatric surgeon was on her way; if her diagnosis agreed with Dr. Simon's, she would operate immediately.

Operate! I could see tears in Jan's eyes, but she was trying to retain her composure. My mind was ablaze with all sorts of thoughts. I hesitated to ask questions because I feared the answers, especially in front of Jan; I blurted out a dumb question, "Doctor, is it critical?"

"Well, whenever you operate on any young baby, the operation is critical, but this is the only known way to counteract the problem. In ninety-nine percent of the cases, it's successful, and usually there's not even a scar."

"Where do they operate?" Jan inquired in a faltering voice.

"They make a small incision just above the belly button so they can get to the muscles constricting the valve's function. Once the muscles are cut, they'll spring away, like a clenched fist being released. He'll probably be in the hospital two days. This time next week, you'll hardly know anything happened."

In what seemed like hours but probably wasn't more than forty-five minutes, a petite woman appeared wearing a doctor's white coat. Introducing herself briskly and unceremoniously as Dr. Spence, she went straight about her work. After a brief examination of Tom, she announced, "Doctor, we should operate immediately!"

Immediately! My heart seemed to stop. At the same time, I felt as if my skin was on fire. I couldn't look at Jan. I couldn't, at that moment, accept more anxiety.

I don't recollect, but apparently Dr. Simon asked us to step outside momentarily while they prepared Tom. Stunned, I don't know how we made it to the waiting room. I do remember he told us we would have a brief chance to see him on his way to the operating room.

Unable to speak but holding each other's hands, we sat outside the emergency room on a sticky plastic sofa. Abruptly the automatic doors to the restricted area flung open, allowing a large gurney to nose its way into the lobby. The contraption appeared empty except for a clump of snowy white sheets in the middle; a bottle of glucose dangled from a metal pole attached to the vehicle propelled by a dark-skinned orderly and followed by the two physicians dressed in operating apparel. The whole event seemed to be playing in slow motion. At the sight of the doctors, Jan and I arose simultaneously, cautiously approaching the gurney transporting our infant son.

Jan started to cry, "Oh my God, he looks so tiny on that great big stretcher."

To me, he looked like a prepped turkey in the middle of a great big snowdrift. Cortege-like, we lumbered along the hall. Jan would not take her eyes off Tom or her hands from the bumper-rail of the gurney. Another set of automatic doors flung open, allowing the orderly to ease his cargo into the operating room. The narrowness of the doorway forced us to lag behind.

Dr. Simon took Jan by the hand. "The best thing for you two is to go get a little rest. Dr. Spence said she would be a couple of hours. Why don't you go for a little drive or maybe a bite to eat? By then we should have a report."

We decided to go home to check on the children, who were in the care of Aunt Margie's niece. As we tried to explain Tom's condition, five-year-old Tammy started to cry, not understanding why her baby brother was still in the hospital.

Trying to comfort her, Timmy explained, "Tom's in there 'cause the hospital's where he's gonna get fixed up, so Tammy, don't cry." A mature statement for a seven-year-old.

"How're they gonna fix 'im up?"

"Well, sweetie," Jan answered, "he can't keep his food down, so he's having an operation."

Timmy, always quick to jump in, added, "That's when they cut cha open in the hospital."

Tammy's eyes glazed. "Cut cha *open!*"

She ran crying to her mother, burying her face in Jan's lap. Jan scooted her up so that Tammy's head rested on her shoulder. Gently patting Tammy on the back, Jan said, "The only way they can fix Tom is to cut him open and find out what's wrong inside; then they'll sew him up and he'll be just fine."

Tammy cried louder for a few moments. Then, trying to control herself, she began asking questions through her sobs. "They goin' to sew 'im up with a big needle like Lympy uses to sew buttons on daddy's shirts?"

"It's something like that, Tammy. Dr. Simon can sew even *better* than Lympy. You know how good Dr. Simon is."

"Will Dr. Simon give him a sucker like he gives me when I go there?"

"I'm sure he will."

Having resolved this crisis, we returned to Touro where we waited at least an hour before Dr. Spence emerged through the electric doors. Her eyes roamed the waiting room. *She won't recognize us*, I thought, *she only met us for a minute*.

"How's he doin'?" we asked meekly, instinctively fearing the answer.

Glancing down, biting her lower lip and shaking her head, she replied, "I cut a hole in it, dammit! I cut a hole in it!"

Jan gasped audibly, fervently clutching my hand.

"Oh, but he's gonna be just fine!" she said, looking up to reassure us. "I had hoped he'd be out of the hospital tomorrow, but it's those damned little intestines; they're so small I sliced into one accidentally an' had to stitch it up, so we'll have to keep him on the IV a day longer. By next week he'll be completely healed; you'll never know I took an extra slice."

Jan and I were taken aback by the way she talked so casually about slicing into *our* baby, as if he were a piece of roast beef. The doctor walked away, leaving us staring at each other in disbelief.

At that moment Henry Simon walked out of the elevator. "I understand Tommy is going to be just fine."

"We guess so," I said, "but what did she mean, the doctor, when she said she'd sliced into his intestine?"

"She told you *that?*" he inquired in amazement.

"Yes, she just told us that!"

"Damn, some doctors just don't have good public relations. But *she's* the best! Actually, it's nothing that's going to cause any harm. In a baby as young as Tommy, the intestines are so small, everything so critical, it's difficult *not* to nick an artery or an intestine. It's really nothing at all. He'll be in the hospital just a day or so longer. It's really all very normal."

Normal for whom? However, Jan and I *were* relieved by Henry's comments.

Two days later, Tom came home from the hospital to a festive welcome. Timmy and Tammy had made a big banner to hang across the front door on Bourbon Street. Olympia, home from her Revival, had fashioned and stitched a special little bonnet during her bus ride. Tom seemed happy to be back home, though I wondered if, at his age, he knew the difference. Tammy was allowed to hold him for a few moments before he was placed in his crib for a good long nap. Timmy begged to see the scar; I explained it would be several days before we could remove the bandage, so if he showed some patience, he would get the first glimpse.

The next Saturday, Timmy and Tammy spent the day painting the old red wagon, long since relegated to the attic. They wanted to fix it up, pack it with pillows, and take their baby brother for a walk around the French Quarter to help him, as they put it, "recoup."

* * * * *

Vikki Carr, the new singing sensation, was appearing at the Blue Room. A Spanish-speaking Latina gal from Texas, her recording career as a mainstream pop singer was taking off in a big way. She had that unusual mix of the girl-next-door under-girded with an undulating sultriness that was captivating audiences and *me*. I have always been stirred by a Latin beat; of course, my exposure had been pretty much limited to Cole Porter's beat of the tom-tom in *Night and Day*, Xavier Cugat's surging tempo vocalized by Abby Lane, or Tommy Dorsey's version of Ravel's *Bolero*!

Vikki was scheduled for both our radio and TV shows; radio gave us more time to chat in depth. On our three-minute TV segment, her advance man wanted us to concentrate on her latest release on Liberty records, *He's a Rebel*. During our twenty-minute radio interview, she enjoyed telling us of growing up in loving though very modest surroundings in El Paso. The eldest of seven, at age four she sang *Adeste Fideles* in Latin. Although her real name is Florencia Bisenta de Casilla Martinez Cardona, we kidded about being related.

"Hey, Senorita Carr—dona, my name may have been altered once also: one great-grandmother says it may have been O'Carra when they came over from the old country. Many Irish immigrants Anglicized their names to avoid discrimination."

"That's the wonderful thing about being an American," she asserted. "You can be whomever you want."

After our radio show we treated her to *Café Royale* and French pastry across the street at the Four Seasons. She was a delight. Over the weekend, when we attended her show at the Blue Room, she introduced us to the audience by inviting us to take a bow from our ringside table.

"Bob and Jan Carr are loved by all you New Orleanians, *but* did you know we're kissin' cousins? We go way back, *way back*. I think to Adam and Eve!"

Her blockbuster *It Must Be Him*, already released in England, was about to make her a mega star in the U.S.A.

* * * * *

Timmy came to me one day with a concerned look on his face. "Daddy, our patio is so boring. There's no place to build a fort."

"Build one behind the banana trees."

"Now, that's a dumb place! Everyone can see us, and besides, there are too many roaches." He hung his head, discouraged.

"What about the attic?"

"That's even dumber! It's like an oven mosta the time."

"Under the stairs?"

"Too *small!*" he glumly replied, about to give up on my hare-brained suggestions. "I've got it! *I've* got it!"

"*Where?*" he asked, a spark of life coming back into his demeanor.

"Guess!"

"Dun't know."

"You gotta guess! It's a fantastic place!"

"Dun't know," he shrugged, "dun't know."

"If Jean Lafitte the pirate were in our patio right now, where would he hide out?"

"Daddy, dun't know."

"Think! It's 1812, the English are attacking up Bourbon Street, where can you hide?"

"Under the house?" he tentatively suggested.

"*Exactly*, under the house. *Under* the house."

"But there isn't enough room under the house to stand up. If we're gonna have a fort we gotta be able to stand up, an' we gotta be able to have secret meetings an' stuff like that!"

"Timmy, *dig* a fort down into the ground. Get Pierre, Kelvin, and Mark to help dig a fort down into the ground, and no one will ever know it's there!"

Elation overcame him. "*Yea! Oh, boy!* And we can put in an electric light and a walkie-talkie. An' Tammy an' her girl friends an' Tom an' Lympy an' mommy will never be able to come into it." He was jubilant. "We'll start tomorrow, yippee, yippee!"

Building a fort under the house was possible because the main floor timbers are set on brick pilings that rise about two feet above the ground. This was done by our ingenious forefathers to allow fresh, cool air to circulate beneath the floor during the wretchedly hot and humid south Louisiana summers.

Timmy spent the evening on the telephone hashing out his plans and canvassing his cronies. The next day, right after school, along with Tammy, Tom, and Olympia, the boys paraded home from *La Petite Ecole* with small spades and shovels slung over their shoulders, looking ever so much like the Seven Dwarfs.

When Jan and I arrived home after a grueling day of voicing a series of radio spots, Olympia virtually assailed me.

"Mistah Cahr, those boys been hidin' from me all this evnin'!"

"What do you mean?" I asked gently.

"They done took them shovels an gone! Ah mean *gone*! Ah ain't seen um no place an' ah been lookin'. Ah swear to Gawd! Why they do me like that? Why they not sweet chilrin like Mizz Tammy an' my blessed baby, Tom?"

"Olympia, I think they're under the house."

"*Under the house!* Ah swear to Gawd, Mistah Cahr, why they down in that filthy place when they got all this huge house ta play in? Ah thought ah heard termites this evenin' chewin' on these floors! Ah swear to Gawd! Ah 'een put my sweet baby Tom up on the dinin' room table to keep him safe, an' Mizz Tammy, she already gone up in her room. She be on the bed!"

"Olympia, the boys want to build a secret hide-out, that's all. They'll be fine. But I'll reprimand Timmy for not telling you where he was, so you won't worry. After all, you're the boss!"

Olympia turned to Jan, "Mizz Cahr, ah don't know why those boys do me lahk that!"

"I know, Olympia, I think boys are harder to rear than girls."

"No doubt 'bout dat, Mizz Cahr, 'ceptin' mah baby, Tom. He's gonna be different 'cause ah'm raisin' him up right from the beginnin'!"

I changed my clothes and crawled under the back of the house. As I skittered along on my belly, pulling myself by my elbows, I could hear the boys chattering quietly over the sound of shovels. They were digging into the soft moist earth, which had lain under the house for more than a hundred years, untouched by human intrusion. Of course, I had been under the house numerous times fixing the plumbing or checking an electrical line, but the cool stillness, the dusty ground, and huge floor joists overhead, dimly visible in the fading sunlight, gave me pause.

Sprawled out full-length on the cool dirt, my chin propped on my hands and my elbows dug into the ground, I closed my eyes and let my imagination run wild. Beyond the sound of digging and mumbling voices, I could hear footsteps on the bricks and horses hooves smacking the pavement. In my mind's eye, I visualized the house being constructed.

There would have been horse-drawn wagon loads of fresh cypress lumber being delivered, unloaded, and stacked; slaves or Irish day-laborers would be busy digging nearly a hundred pits for the foundation pilings, chimney bases, and the privy. My thoughts skipped ahead to the family's first formal reception: *Carriages arriving along then-fashionable Bourbon Street, guests dismounting, scurrying up the solid granite steps we know so well, greeting their hosts with sedate "oohs" and "aahs" of the era, praising the new home.*

"Daddy, is that you?" Timmy questioned in a hushed voice, breaking my reverie.

"Yes, Timmy."

"Daddy, keep talkin' real quiet!"

"I am!"

"Scoot over here and see what we're diggin'. *Look!*"

I was amazed at the size of the hole they had dug, about three feet deep and nearly nine-by-twelve from side to side. With the two feet between the ground and the floor joists, they had a hideout high enough for them to stand in. In fact, if I kept my head between the fourteen-inch cypress floor-joists, I, too, could stand erect,

"Hey, guys, this is *great!* But what did you do with all the extra dirt?"

Well pleased with their progress, Mark announced in his ninth ward accent, "Well, Mistah Cawr, we spread it all ovah the place, see? 'Cept for that pile a good doit. We savin' that for da gawden, 'cept we hafta put it out dere at night so nobody'll know we been diggin' a secret hidin' place."

"This is terrific! I'm proud of y'all. But it's getting dark so I think you better come in. Besides, Olympia is getting worried about you. She doesn't know where you are and is quite upset because she thought y'all were lost."

"We're not lost, daddy!"

"I know you're not lost, but *Olympia* doesn't know it. So the next time you come down here, you must tell her where you're going."

"Oh, phewy, that's no fun," Timmy quipped.

"She'll tell Tammy and Tom and they'll tell everybody," Kelvin remarked exasperatedly.

"No, she won't. *Not* Olympia."

"Bet she will," Kelvin insisted. "*My maid* tells everybody everything."

"I'll talk to Olympia. I know she can keep a secret. She hasn't told you fellas where Tammy's hiding place is, has she?"

They all chimed in, "*Tammy* has a hiding place?"

"Oh, yes, boys, but that's her secret!"

Of course, Tammy had no hiding place I knew of, but I was trying to build a case on Olympia's behalf.

"Fellas, it's getting awfully dark and it's almost time to eat. We'd better get upstairs so you can get cleaned up for dinner. On Saturday I'll help you hook up an electric light."

"Mr. Carr," Pierre asked, "if we're really good, can we have an extra socket so we can plug in the old hot plate we have in our shed, so we can cook?"

"Yes, I think you can do that, but I insist you *all* remember to turn it off when you leave."

"Oh, it only works half the time, an' it dun't get very hot anyway."

"It sounds a little dangerous, Pierre. We'll check it out on Saturday."

Over the next few weeks the boys worked industriously on their hideout, refining it and then furnishing it—would that Timothy had been as diligent about his homework—but I felt he was learning about leadership and construction. He loved to be in charge; and he enjoyed creating things with his hands, which he came by naturally from me.

As young teens, my sister and I would spend three or four weeks each summer at my grandparents' cottage on the Saint Joseph River, about ten miles upstream from Benton Harbor, Michigan. To help pass the time, my grandmother took me to a shoe store to get shoeboxes. Laying the boxes on their sides, I would cut out windows and doors and use scraps of cardboard, wallpaper, and cloth to create model rooms. My sister called them dollhouses, but worrying about being considered a sissy, I referred to them as designer rooms. Later in life I entered the Department of Architecture at Carnegie Tech, and although I didn't follow that field of study, I've always had a gift for creating attractive and comfortable spaces.

Timothy, it seemed to me, had a similar knack. He had the boys line the walls with tarpaper to keep it dry and snug. Then they added carpeting, mosquito netting, and a water faucet. In order to make it more accessible, he had them dig a long trench from the entrance approach at the back of the house to the hideout so that they didn't have to crawl on their bellies in the dirt.

They were so proud of the fort once it was completed that, miracle of miracles, they invited the entire family down for a look-see. Using Pierre's hot plate, they served us slightly cooked hot dogs and canned Franco-American spaghetti; from an old cooler buried in the dirt of the sidewall, they fetched Barq's soda. Olympia, realizing her size and not wanting to soil her white starched uniform, had declined their offer to crawl under the house. She chose instead to be served in the patio under the cool evening shade of the banana trees.

The boys loved their hideout and spent many a night sleeping down there, even when Jan thought it was too hot. In keeping with the current fad, their G.I. Joe dolls were always tucked neatly into miniature pup tents lined up in regimental order beside them. Of course, we weren't aware of all the antics that went on in their hideout, but from the intermittent silences, from time to time erupting into salacious giggles filtering through the floor above, I guessed the boys might be discovering some of the wonders of their approaching manhood.

* * * * *

Jan reminded me that we were having dinner and attending Marlene Dietrich's opening at the Blue Room. Olympia would be pressed for time, so she wanted me to pick up a quart of milk and a brick of Velveeta at Mrs. Madonna's. Once in the store I realized everyone was abuzz about someone's death or was it a suicide?

"Mrs. Madonna, who died?"

"Oh, that blonde, I can't think of her name. Begins with M."

"Mamie Van Dorn?"

"*No*, not that one. You know, she sang *Happy Birthday* to Kennedy?"

"Marilyn Monroe?"

"Uh huh."

"No kidding, I can't believe it. She was fabulous in *Gentlemen Prefer Blondes*." I was crushed at the news. I loved Marilyn.

Over my shoulder, I heard a customer make a flip comment. "She shouldn't a screwed around with Bobby and John."

Another added, "Sleepin' around'll getcha killed!"

As I walked into the kitchen, Jan asked why I looked so forlorn. I told her the news, which had left me oddly despondent.

We had recently seen Marilyn with Clark Gable in *The Misfits*. Rumor said her procrastination on the movie set had caused his fatal heart attack not long before his only son was born. Now Marilyn was gone, too. *How sad. The end of an era*, I thought. I never met Marilyn, but on the screen she made me tingle. I could watch her rendition of *Diamonds Are a Girl's Best Friend* over and over.

There had been gossip that when *Something's Got to Give* would be released, Marilyn would make a swing through the South to promote the film. I had my heart set on interviewing her, but that dream was gone now.

However, through the years, I had been lucky to interview an assortment of world-renowned blonde bombshells. I had spent time with Jayne Mansfield, who would be killed on the highway as she returned for another guest appearance on channel 6. She was *not* decapitated as was first reported but crushed in a convertible when it struck a mosquito-spraying truck in the hazy dawn; one of her wigs landed on the shoulder of the foggy Gulf Coast road. Her three Hargitay children, Micky, Jr., Zoltan, and baby Mariska, were asleep on the back seat but unharmed.

When I interviewed super-busty Mamie Van Dorn, she was still living off the bad girl publicity from the sexually explicit B-movie *Girls Town*, also starring jazz great Mel Tormé, with whom Jan had lunched at a fund-raiser during college. She always remembered how he picked his teeth with his fork!

Following my interview with fellow Ohioan, vocalist Helen O'Connell, famous for her renditions of *Green Eyes*, *Tangerine*, and *Amapola*, she came home with me for dinner, bringing her daughter, who was near Tammy's age. Helen was sensitive and still beautiful. They were wonderful company. The girls played together, giving us time to hear about Helen's recent stint as the "*Today* Girl" and the battered life she had endured at the hands of one of her husbands.

By a fluke, we were asked to spend a day showing Ginger Rogers around town. She had just had a minor part in a black-and-white Magna Films version of *Harlow* starring Carol Lynley, which was released at nearly the same time as Paramount's Technicolor mega-version starring the highly-touted Carroll Baker. It was destined to be Ginger's last film, though she was about to be featured in a TV version of *Cinderella* and was contracted to star in *Hello Dolly* on Broadway followed by the title roll in the London production of *Mame*. Of course, we and the children had seen her early movies on TV.

She was to arrive at our doorstep by limousine. Olympia, the children, and a few neighbors excitedly awaited her arrival. The scheduled time came and went to the point that we figured we had made a mistake or her plans had changed. Forty minutes had passed when the doorbell startled us. Approaching the door I could discern the silhouette of two women through the beveled glass. Opening the door I encountered a very sweaty movie star whose damp, flaxen hair looked like dead straw. Only her face resembled Ginger Rogers; a lady companion accompanied her. Begging to come in out of the oppressive heat, Miss Rogers at the same time pleaded for two glasses of water. Jan and Olympia sprung into action, returning from the kitchen with water and two cold, damp wash clothes. Ginger and her assistant explained that their limo had gotten a flat tire crossing Canal Street. The embarrassed chauffer told them our place was just up the street, so they decided to walk, not knowing it was actually ten blocks and in 96-degree heat.

After regaining her composure, Ginger became the *star* we all loved in the movies. She was most engaging; the children loved her, vying to sit next to her on the sofa. Eventually, the limo arrived, and the two ladies set off to see the city with us as tour guides. Following dinner at Brennan's, we strolled the cooled-down Quarter with the limo in ever-present pursuit. Ginger, a rabid animal activist, chastised various carriage drivers about the condition of their mules, but we ended on a high note by blowing powered sugar at each other at Café du Monde. It was a delightful day for us and, we hoped, for Ginger.

I was delighted by the blondes of Hollywood but aroused by raven-haired Italians—Gina, Sophia, and Silvana Mangano.

I found myself back in the kitchen putting the cheese and milk in the refrigerator as Jan hollered for me to get dressed for the evening. She wanted us to be ready by the time Olympia returned with the children so that she could read to them before we left to see Marlene at the Blue Room and record an interview. Dinner of shrimp cocktail, filet mignon, and bread pudding with signature Ron Rico sauce, accompanied by several Sazeracs, was better than the show. Marlene's performance was stilted and tired. Word reached our table that Miss Dietrich was *not* available for interviews.

Sadly, two of my favorite diva performers, Dietrich and Peggy Lee, in their waning years on stage resembled propped-up Barbie Dolls. I mused: *The desire to perform never ends. It's almost as strong as the need to breathe.*

* * * * *

Each afternoon when Olympia and Tom arrived at the front stoop of the school, Olympia invariably engaged in boastful conversation with some of the other maids about "her baby," the most blessed, beautiful, and fairest in the land! Talk about one-upsmanship!

As a further example, Olympia told us she had taken Tom for a stroll to the Whitney Bank on Chartres Street because it was so pretty and cool inside. She claimed Tom loved to look at the lights on the glistening brass chandeliers. When one of the tellers asked her who that beautiful little blue-eyed blond baby belonged to, she replied, "Ma'am, this be *mah baby!*"

Pushing Tom's stroller, and taking Tammy by the hand, Olympia would set out from school along Esplanade, past the two 1890s Victorian cottages, the hidden house with the huge secluded front yard—very unique in the *Vieux Carré*—and onto the corner where stood a beautiful old structure built by the widow of Alvarez Fisk. A highly successful cotton factor, Fisk had presented several thousand books to the city, plus his large home in which to house them. The Fisk Free Library eventually became the New Orleans Public Library. Following her husband's death in 1855, the widow Fisk had this building remodeled into a home for herself, her three unmarried children, and assorted relatives. She continued to reside there until her death in 1887. Her heirs sold it to the McDonogh School Fund, to be used as a school for young maiden ladies. In 1922, it was purchased by the Home Missions Board of the Southern Baptist Convention. Since then, the building had continuously ministered to derelicts, drunks, and every assortment of social castoffs, all of whom seemed to eternally gather on the front vestibule steps. As the children streamed past on their way home with Olympia, invariably one of the lonely forsaken souls would smile and greet the passing parade.

"Don't cha talk to mah chilrin, you filthy ole man," Olympia remanded. "Come along, chilrin, don't pay them no mind. Y'all heah what ahm sayin'?"

"Oooh, they smell like pee-pee, Olympia."

"They drinks and they pees. An' dey go outa their mine half da time. My li'l dahling, you pays 'em no mind, no mind at all, you hear, chile?"

Olympia was like a mother fox toward the children, very positive and ever-aware. In spite of her diligence, one day just as she was about to leave for school, Tom got sick to his stomach and regurgitated on the new living room carpet. Olympia dashed to the telephone to call the school, but the line was busy. She was frantic, knowing Kelvin's mother was picking up Timmy, meaning Tammy would be left alone. The more she wiped Tom's face, the more he vomited, and the more he vomited, the more he cried. As Olympia picked him up to console him, he spewed vomit down the back of her starched uniform, half-filling one of her loose-fitting shoes!

Meanwhile, back at *La Petite Ecole*, Tammy was waiting for Tom and Olympia. In the confusion of carpool pick-ups, and knowing Olympia always was there, Willie Mae, the school maid, who watched the kids like a hawk, didn't realize that independent little Tammy had decided to set out for home all by herself.

Along the way, to amuse herself, Tammy skipped through the configuration of a leftover hopscotch game drawn on the banquette. Suddenly, Tammy found herself at the corner of Bourbon and Esplanade where she and Olympia always crossed hand-in-hand at the stop sign in front of the Baptist Mission. As Tammy stood at the corner trying to out-guess the traffic, one of the derelicts offered to take her across the street. She thought for a second, sniffed for two seconds. Since he didn't smell too bad, she decided to let him help her.

"How far ya live at, ya li'l sweetie?"

She squinted in the hot sun and looked up Bourbon Street, trying to count the blocks. "One, two, three, four, five—maybe jist four."

"Ah think ah better walk ya home," suggested the scruffy man.

"That would be real nice, sir."

"Would ja like ta take my hand?"

Tammy glanced at his rather gnarled and grubby fingers. "No, sir. For men, I only hold my daddy's hand. Thank you anyways."

When they arrived in front of the house, Olympia was just coming down the steps with the stroller, carrying a rather pale and woebegone-looking Tom.

"*Man!* What cha doin' ta mah baby girl?" Olympia lashed out at the unsuspecting man. "You git from mah baby, you dirty ole wino. An' ah ax, what you doin' on our banquette anyways? Git outa here, you!" Shaking her fist, she continued, "I'll git mah madam on you if you don't be gone!"

The man backed off down Bourbon Street as Olympia pulled the stroller up the steps and into the hall, reaching out to fetch Tammy. Closing the door, she lit into Tammy.

"Chile, don't cha know you coulda bin *snatched?* Oh, mah Gawd, what ah tell yo mother? Oh, mah Gawd, chile, sweet Jesus, have mercy!"

"He was real nice and helpful and walked me home, Lympy," Tammy retorted.

"Why jew let him walk ya home, chile?"

"Cause you wun't there, and besides, he din't smell like pee-pee, only whiskey!"

Several days later, after school, as Olympia and her charges were turning onto Bourbon Street, with the four boys marching like Confederate soldiers toward home, Tammy spotted the grimy man who had walked her home. Tugging at Olympia's hand, they approached him; he smiled timidly.

"You scared my maid the other day and I guess she scared you, too. But she's really nice," Tammy explained. "She dun't want me to get snatched 'cause she can't 'splain it to my mommy. That's why she got so mad."

The man smiled at Tammy, then Olympia. "That's okay, Sweetie, I wouldn't' do ya no harm."

Olympia smiled slightly, raised an eyebrow, turned abruptly, and pulled Tammy up Bourbon Street locked in a vice-like handgrip.

* * * * *

"Bob, we've received an invitation to a PTA meeting," Jan announced. "I *guess* it's a PTA meeting. It says all parents and teachers of *La Petite Ecole* will have a chance to meet at a cocktail reception on the Delta Belle paddle-wheeler at the Barracks Street wharf."

"I've never heard of a *cocktail party PTA* meeting. It sure doesn't sound like Painesville or Colerain, Ohio!"

"Do you think we should go?"

"It sure would be interesting to see which parents belong with some of those kids. Yah, let's go!"

We hated to arrive alone at the PTA meeting—or whatever it was—so we asked Kelvin's parents, Merle and Wilson, to join us. As further encouragement, Jan informed them that Olympia would be glad to have Kelvin and their two little girls dropped off. Merle loved the *Vieux Carré*, but Wilson, an attorney with a lawyer's mentality, had little appreciation for the Quarter, Bourbon Street, or, as he put it, the queers, beatniks, and other weird people who chose to reside there. He was a bit reticent about leaving his two little girls at our house, even though Kelvin played there regularly. Sending his children to school on Esplanade Avenue was concession enough.

I recall the first time he brought Kelvin to visit Timmy was on a Saturday morning; I met them at the front door and asked them in. He cautiously stepped across the threshold and, looking around disdainfully, inquired, "You really live here?"

A bit taken aback, I responded cheerfully. "Oh, yes, of course we live here. Once the floors are sanded, the wall paper is hung, and that huge hole in the ceiling is fixed, it'll be pretty nifty."

"It's gonna take a helluva lot to make this place pretty *nifty!*"

At that moment, almost as if on cue, Emmanuel, the wonderful old gentleman who worked for us from time to time, came in from the rear patio, approaching us along the hallway. Dressed only in bib overalls and sandals, he was very tall and very black. Emmanuel looked quite threatening until he spoke through his golden smile. He continued toward us holding a limp, blood-drenched rat by its tail.

"Finally cracked dis critter over the hayd wid a broom, then ah stomped on 'im. He *dayd* now!" Emmanuel smiled broadly, almost illuminating the hallway with his flashing false teeth.

Wilson gurgled in disbelief. Hating rats as I do, it took every ounce of strength I had to hold my composure. Timmy called from the patio; Kelvin pulled away from his father and dashed toward the back of the house, nearly wiping blood from the rat across his shoulder as he passed under Emmanuel's outstretched arm.

"The boys are going to dunk for apples in the wash tub out in the patio. Would you like to stay, Wilson?"

"*Hell, no!* I've got to get to the Metairie Country Club for my foursome. It's only twenty minutes till tee-time."

"Oh, that's too bad, we're gonna have a great time."

Admonishing me not to let the boys *drown* in the washtub, he turned to leave. I guess I looked a little peculiar to him, standing at the front doorway in my Italian bikini, wet, sweating, and barefoot after having just scrubbed down the bricks on the patio, and filling the wash-tub full of water and apples for Timmy's birthday party dunk.

Wilson's concern about his son was that even at a very early age, Kelvin was somewhat accident-prone. He was adept at getting either his whole body or one of his extremities caught or entangled in any number of openings.

The school called Olympia frantically one morning when they couldn't locate Merle, his mother. Kelvin had shoved his left thumb into the round hole in the top bracket of his clipboard and neither he, nor anyone else at *La Petite*, could get his thumb loose. Willie Mae called Olympia, who in turn called Jan, just about to go live on the *Bob & Jan Radio Show*. Jan, who offered "on-air handy hints" to listeners, suggested Olympia tell them to try cold water to lessen the swelling, then soft soap or Vaseline, and if all that failed, to call her back at noon when the radio show ended. Unfortunately, none of the suggestions worked, so the phone began to ring in the control room promptly at noon.

"Mizz Cahr, Mizz Cahr, that chile still stuck an' he *be* cryin'! The school axed me to come git 'im. What ah do, Mizz Cahr?"

"That's all right, I have the car, so I can get to school quickly and pick him up."

At the school, Jan found Kelvin sitting on the bottom step of the long stairway that led up three flights, drolly amusing himself by twisting the clipboard and his hand in a variety of contorted ways. Far from tears, he smiled when he saw Jan.

"Look, Mizz Carr, they can't get it off me, but I got outta class!"

Willie Mae came out of her office. "Kelvin, you a *big* problem to me. Mizz Cahr, what we gonna do? Ah swear dat boy tries mah nerves."

The maintenance man at the station had suggested Jan take Kelvin to the sheet metal shop on Burgundy and get them to cut it off, which they did. Kelvin ended up with a sore thumb and a good tongue-lashing from his dad.

A few months later, we were taking Tammy and toddler Tom and his teddy bear for our evening stroll up Bourbon Street in his red wagon, when the four boys came huffing and puffing up behind us just as we were about to cross the street. From their fort under the house they had heard us leave and wanted to follow along to count strippers and, ultimately, get *café au lait*-laced chocolate milk and beignets at the French Market.

Skipping along like four musketeers about a half a block ahead, they darted in and out of doorways, playing their own version of treasure hunt: at pay phones and vending machines they checked to see what change or "goodies" they could collect. On previous occasions, they had retrieved enough to pay their own way at Café du Monde, exciting them greatly.

Although the boys had run some distance ahead, Jan and I were able to keep a pretty good eye on them. We could see them dash up to a strip-joint, stop, peak in for a moment until the street barker slammed the door on them, and then scamper on to another spot. For a few moments, Jan and I tarried to give some tourists directions to Antoine's Restaurant, momentarily losing sight of the boys. Suddenly, *three* of them frantically dashed back.

"Where's Kelvin?"

"He's *caught*, daddy. He's caught!"

"Yah, Mr. Carr, he's caught all right!" Pierre and Mark chimed in.

"Where?"

"In a cigarette machine," they replied, jumping up and down.

"*Where?*" I asked in disbelief. "A cigarette machine?"

"Yes, daddy, in a cigarette machine, in that teacher's stripper place up there!"

We rushed ahead with the boys, bouncing the red wagon and its surprised passengers along the broken banquette. The marquee above the door proclaimed, *Patti White—School Teacher Turned Stripper.* Just inside the entrance, with both swinging doors propped wide open, catching the streetlight's glare, were Kelvin and the barker crouched down by the cigarette machine. The "former school teacher," spartanly clad in eight-inch heels, a G-string, and *sans* brassiere, was stooping over them from her perch atop the bar. Attracted by the commotion, Kelvin had apparently darted through the door of the club while the barker had his back turned and had shoved his arm up the cigarette machine to see if there were any loose cigarettes; he couldn't get his arm out!

Kelvin squealed as the barker pulled and twisted his arm.

The barker glanced up, "Hey, mistah', dis yo kid?"

I nodded affirmatively.

"Den git him da hell outta here before we git busted for havin' minors in dis joint. He ain't gonna loin nutten good in heah!"

"Yah, dawlin'," screeched the "teacher" from her vantage point above.

Suddenly feeling a tinge of modesty, she placed her arms across her boobs, attempting to look more like a schoolmarm. This gesture only caused her voluptuous breasts to flood over her forearms, forming cleavage of incredible proportions.

"I guess he thought this was the little red school house," I remarked, trying to be amusing.

At that point a King Kong-like gorilla of a man appeared out of the smoky depths of the joint, demanding we get that fuckin' kid outta his club!

"Yes, sir, but can I ask you just one question, sir?"

"Huh?" he remarked bruskly, surprised I had the guts to speak to him at all.

"Do you have a key to this machine? It's the only way we'll ever get him loose."

Pulling out a long gold chain, holding at least fifty keys, King Kong unlocked the front panel and dislodged Kelvin's arm.

"Mistah, tell yo kid to keep his fingas outta mah machine, and his *ass* outta mah club from now on, 'cause next time, ah'll beat the shit outta him! Hear what ah'm sayin', mistah?"

We all heard, entirely too well.

I tugged the red wagon out of the way. Tom, in fright, had scrunched down in the wagon, fervently clutching his teddy bear.

Tammy stepped away from us toward the entrance of the club; she stood straight and stalwart. Looking up at Kong, she reprimanded, "You mean, mister! You scared the dickens outta my baby brother and his teddy bear, too. Shame on you!"

Kong fled into the depths of his smoke-filled joint as I made haste to steer my little troop to Café du Monde.

We were dressing for the PTA cocktail meeting when the doorbell rang.

"Olympia, will you please answer the door?" Jan hollered down the stairwell. There was no answer. "Olympia must be back in the kitchen, you can't ever hear the doorbell back there," she muttered. "Bob, will you go out on the front balcony and holler down to Merle and Wilson. We'll be right there."

"I'm in my undershorts," I shouted from the bathroom.

"That's okay, I'm in my slip. I'm looking for my dress in this hall armoire! Lord, do we need closets," she continued to mutter.

"This will be great. Wait till Wilson sees me in my shorts."

On the balcony I leaned over the cast-iron railing far enough to see Merle and Wilson and the three kids huddled on the stoop trying to avoid the two giggling homosexuals who were passing by on their way to Lafitte's In Exile. I waited until they had sashayed on up the street. Then, in a stage whisper, I said, "Hey, down there, we'll let you in. Just a minute." By the time I withdrew into the bathroom, I could hear our kids bounding through the hall below, followed by Olympia carrying Tom over her shoulder. They all answered the door, the kids greeting one another with screams and hugs.

Finally dressed, Jan and I started downstairs. Wilson, standing by the front door, sputtered, "The French Quarter's a helluva place to find parking." And under his breath, but audibly, he added, "And a helluva place to raise a family!"

Merle, the perpetual optimist, smiled. "Wilson, dear, it's only four-and-a-half blocks away. That's not too bad for the Quarter, honey!"

Before Wilson could reply, I reached the bottom step. "It's a great night to walk, y'all! And it's only about four blocks over to the Barracks Street wharf."

"Hell, I could've just as well parked at the wharf!"

"Okay, everybody, let's go," Jan declared, hoping to lighten the mood.

Closing the front door after a dozen or so farewell kisses, I could see the kids racing up the front stairs. Just as we crossed to the other side of the street, all six kids rushed out on the front balcony to wave goodbye. As we rounded the corner, I looked over my shoulder, catching a glimpse of Olympia herding them all back inside. She was always afraid one of her "babies" would fall off—never quite sure why those balconies stayed up there anyway.

Jan grabbed Wilson by the arm, deflecting his displeasure by telling him how wonderful his children were, how beautiful the sky was, and how marvelous he was to hold her arm. I took Merle's arm as we followed along behind. At the levee we were stopped by a freight train loitering on a siding. While we stood there wondering how to get between the boxcars to the wharf on the other side, an attractive couple walked up to us.

"You going to the Parents' Club meeting?" the lady inquired.

"Yes, we are."

"Good, then we're not late. I'm Leroy Ellis and this is my wife, Judy. We have six children."

The freight train moved away while we were introducing ourselves. We crossed the tracks together, walked up the gangplank and onto the old Delta Belle stern-wheeler showboat.

"*La Petite Ecole?*" inquired a young man in a sailor suit.

We nodded.

"Next deck up," he instructed.

Cautiously, we edged our way up the creaky stairs, the "girls" taking care not to catch their heels in the metal strips tacked on each step. Directly ahead, the not-so-"Grand Saloon" was filled with men and women sipping cocktails. The air was musty, but a deck hand was scurrying around opening windows to allow a touch of breeze to cut through the heavy fragrance of mildew.

One of the fourth-graders, dressed up to look like Little Lord Fauntleroy, had been chosen to greet us, saying, rather pedantically, "Miss Edna desires that each parent sign this register, please."

"You sign for me, Jan."

"No, sir," responded Little Lord Faunt in a rather priggish manner. "Miss Edna said *each* parent must sign."

"Why is that, Lord Faunt—I mean, young man?"

"Sir, some of our children have four, even five parents. *And,* some have none, only grandparents or guardians!" he responded officiously, tugging at the crotch of his too-tight blue satin knickers. "So, Miss Edna needs each attendant's name, sir, so we know who belongs to whom."

I thought to myself: *I hope Timmy is that bright in the fourth grade, but if he's that prissy, I'll drown him!*

We all signed in and made our way to the bar, where I ordered two highballs.

"Dat'll be six dahllahs, Mistah," requested the bartender.

"Isn't that a bit pricey?"

"Pawt of it is for dah school, an' pawt is for dah bawr," he responded in perfect Ninth Ward lingo.

"I see," I said, reflecting. *How different this is from my grammar school up north!*

"Dear, dear, ladies and gentlemen, won't you please be seated in the chairs provided for you so we can start our meeting." This summons was at the invitation of Miss Edna, whom everyone felt compelled to love; she was so sweet, soft, Southern-spoken, and seemingly quite vulnerable.

We proceeded quietly to our seats as Miss Edna stood strainingly erect at a podium, her chin in the air and her head oscillating like an old-time electric fan.

A hush had almost come over the group when from the back of the saloon, we heard one of the fathers shout, "What the hell do ya mean, six dollars for two drinks?"

"Sorry, mistah, dat's da way it is," replied the bartender, grimacing in a take-it-or-leave-it manner.

"Shee-it!"

After a moment of deafening silence, someone in the group had the decency to cough loud enough to attract the attention of the irate parent. He turned around from the bar to face the stares of a hundred parental eyes before sinking into a rickety folding chair.

"And now that every one of you, dear ladies and gentlemen, is seated, let us push on hastily with this first annual *La Petite Ecole* riverboat PTA meeting. Our first order of business will be to elect a president and then, of course, other officers."

Straining once again to see over our heads and to make eye contact, Miss Edna continued, "Do ah hear any nominations for the office of president for owah esteemed *Ecole?*"

There was a long uncomfortable pause. The only sound came from people nervously sipping on their drinks, followed by the tinkling of ice, as it fell back into their glasses.

"I nominate Mister Bob Carr."

I can't be hearing that, I thought.

"Would you repeat that please, sir, so Wilmer might write it on the chalk board."

Wilmer, it turned out, was the real name of Little Lord Faunt.

"Yes, ma'am, *Mister Bob Carr!*"

A sweat-swamped feeling came over me. I turned, scowled at Jan, and whispered, while keeping my head down, hoping not to be seen, "Who's saying my name?"

"I can't see across the room, but it sounds like Wilson."

"Ugh," I moaned, keeping my head down in anticipation of further nominations, but there were none! There *was* what seemed to me a forty-five-minute silence. *Humm, payback from Wilson!*

Suddenly Miss Edna spoke up. "There being no furthah nominations, ah ask someone to move that the nominations be closed."

"So moved!" exploded from eight or ten eager and relieved parents simultaneously.

"Ah suggest we fortify our confidence toward Mistah Cahr by a unanimous show of hands."

"Jan, *don't* raise your hand!" I whispered out of the side of my mouth, seconds too late. *Oh, merd! Trés apropos for La Petite Ecole!*

"Now ah think it would be quite in ordah for Mistah Cahr to take charge of the meeting at this tahm. Let us give him a naahss round of applause. Mistah Cahr," instructed Miss Edna, stretching out her arms to welcome me to the podium.

"I think you got the wrong ma'am, man...I mean man, ma'am. I don't even know the Roberts's Rules of Order," I sputtered, trying to be jovial in my misery.

"Not to worry, Mistah Cahr," she consoled, "you know we have *no rules* at *La Petite*."

Somehow I gathered the strength to continue with the meeting, electing a lady vice-president, a male secretary, and a treasurer of questionable gender. It was brought up, and decided, that we should meet once every six weeks; we should have a fundraiser for the school; *and* we should in *no way* interfere with Miss Edna's management style or operation of the school. Miss Edna made that last proposal. *Ah ha!* A tougher sprig of wisteria than we had all thought!

After the meeting, we adjourned to the waterline deck of the vessel to watch a lusty, busty, gay 90s riverboat show, fraught with blue humor and bare-assed behinds—*just the thing for the PTA!*

It was quite dark when we left the riverboat, making our way hastily down the levee and across the railroad tracks with the aid of the glaring headlight from an oncoming freight train. Jan and I found ourselves walking next to a lean, small-boned man rather rudely dressed, with an accent; he introduced himself as Jo-*zeff*. He congratulated me on being elected president, saying in complete seriousness, he felt humbled in my presence.

We crossed over to Barracks Street behind the old U.S. Mint with Jozeff fixed to our side. Merle and Wilson had lagged back, chatting with the Ellises and others.

"Please, please," Jozeff insisted, in mid-European stilted speech. "I beseech you to stop in at our modest apartment, so I can introduce you to my dear Amethyst. She gets so lonely since we moved here from Moline, what with the new baby and our sweet little Georgette."

"Oh, thank you, but we're with another couple. We really must get home."

Jozeff swung around in front of us and stopped. We almost collided with him as he reached out and took each of us by one hand. "Oh, please, sir and lady, just for a few precious moments."

Jan and I glanced at each other. "I'm afraid not!"

Jozeff, looking at us pleadingly, gasped, emitting the type of sound you hear from a child who is trying to control the final heave of a crying jag.

"Well, just for a moment. Bob, you tell Wilson."

"Thanks a *lot*," I smiled, gritting my teeth.

Jozeff pointed toward a cheerless doorway about three buildings up Decatur Street. "We live through there."

Merle and Wilson unmindfully followed us around the corner. Jozeff pushed open the huge, creaky door, lodged between two shabby townhouses. He stamped his foot in a forceful gesture, rousing a mother cat and a half-dozen kittens rifling through an overturned garbage can, then preceded along the murky alleyway. Jan clutched my hand as we followed.

"Where the hell ya goin?" Wilson shouted up the passageway.

"We're just stopping by for a quick visit."

"Uuh uuh, *no* way," he snapped. "We're goin' home!"

Merle tossed a cheerful good-bye as Wilson elbowed her out and up the street.

"Right this way," directed Jozeff, adding in a tremulous tone, "I feel wretched that we must climb to the third floor."

We crossed the slippery moss-covered brick patio. Jan held my arm tightly during our climb around and around, up the wobbly staircase suspended from equally rickety, rotting galleries.

"We can see the Mississippi from our front balcony," huffed Jozeff, still climbing. "It's the only thing that comforts us when we get homesick for Moline."

That's in Illinois. I didn't think anyone ever got homesick for Moline.

We followed him along the rickety third floor balcony. Jan edged sideways, hugging the building, hoping not to fall off. He slowly opened the door to disclose a beautiful but wan, curly-haired little girl who threw her arms around her daddy's leg, but it turned out he was not her daddy at all. A Lithuanian immigrant, Jozeff had befriended the little girl and her mother a couple of years before, plucking them out of the street after they had been badly brutalized by her drunken common-law husband. Jozeff had married the mother, adopted the child, and was father to the baby.

"Come in, come in," he coaxed.

We moved along a sparsely-lit hall with sixteen-foot ceilings until we entered a huge room with four full-length French doors opening out onto the third-floor balcony overlooking Decatur Street. The room revealed faded tatters of its former glory, as did his wife, Amethyst, who walked in holding the five-month-old infant.

"I been awaitin' for ya, Jo-*seff*. Ya done stayed out kinda late," she remarked in a Midwestern hillbilly accent.

"It took longer un I thought," he replied, falling into her speech pattern. "Meet Mr. and Mrs. Carr. He's the president of the *La Petite Ecole* School."

She acknowledged us without saying a word, then sat herself down on one of the several wooden chairs in the huge room, still clutching the motionless baby. Jozeff scrambled for chairs, pulling them up in a half-circle near her chair to catch the river breeze through the French doors.

"Miss Edna, God's disciple on earth, accepted our Georgette *gratis*. I will get you some coffee," Jozeff said, disappearing from the room.

We stared at each other.

"Nice breeze," I said, speaking simultaneously with Jan who was saying, "Beautiful baby."

The forlorn woman sat quietly in the dim light, giving me a chance to study her unusual face. Her almost waist-length brown hair was pulled back over her ears, stressing her sharp, American Indian-like features. She undemonstratively conveyed her relationship with Jozeff, describing him as her savior. Suddenly, the lifeless infant in her arms flung himself back, letting out a monstrous scream that must have been heard on the riverfront. Jan and I each shuddered, quaking in our stiff wooden chairs. Without hesitation, Amethyst laid the baby in her lap, pulled down the front of her loose-fitting peasant blouse and tucked it up under her abundant breasts. Holding up the infant's head slightly, she slipped her right nipple into his mouth. The papoose sucked ferociously with sensuous sounds that both embarrassed me and made me tingle. Jan and I were rendered speechless.

The brief silence was broken when the five-year-old girl scampered in. She went directly to her mother, grabbed the left breast and began sucking.

Amethyst didn't flinch, Jan didn't stir, and I didn't breathe.

"Georgette, stop that," Jozeff commanded, moving into the room holding a dented and tarnished aluminum coffee pot in one hand and four diner-style mugs hooked over his fingers on the other hand. "Amethyst, she's gettin' too old for nursin."

"Gives her…her nutrients," retorted the wife.

"Don't make no mind. It's not suitable when company's here!"

Pallid little Georgette backed off, smacking and licking her lips as if she had just devoured an all-day sucker.

"I hope maybe your little girl kin come over to play with Georgette some day," Jozeff remarked, pouring the coffee.

After downing the watery Moline-style coffee and a breathtakingly beautiful view of the Mississippi, we found ourselves clinging to each other, winding our way down the precarious stairway, saddened by their circumstances. The heavy patio door thundered shut behind us, as if shielding us from their world.

Bob and Jan soliciting at a United Way fund raiser, 1964

(L to R) Reggie Hendry, Rivet, Irma Kirshberg, Bob and Jan. A New Year's Eve skit for "Second Cup," 1963

Bob and Jan prepping for a show (Note the massive hair-do), 1963

Bob and Jayne Mansfield with her children and dog, 1964

Bob and Jan at WWL radio, 1960

Bob and Jan preparing for a fashion show, 1964

Building the fort under the house, 1963

LAFITTE • KREEGER'S • PRESBYTERE • PONTALBA • ANTOINE'S • CABILDO • GODCHAUX'S • GUMBO • VOODOO • BAYOU

CHAPTER SEVEN

PRALINE • FRENCH MARKET • JAZZ • LAGNIAPPE • PICAYUNE • NEUTRAL GROUND • FLAMBEAUX • BROCATO'S • PO-BOY

Grandma's Café Brulot Christmas

Having grown up on a farm in Colerain, Ohio, a village near Martins Ferry, Jan graduated with high school honors but "starred" as a majorette. Her relatives from Wheeling, across the river, would come to see her twirl her batons! When Jan was four years old, her mother died tragically of spinal meningitis; baby sister Carole was still an infant. Their grief-stricken father moved the girls from their home in Pittsburgh to their maternal grandparents' farm, knowing they would be lovingly cared for until he could rebuild his life. The move was intended to be temporary, but the separation lasted until each of the girls graduated from college. "Daddy" drove three hours from Pittsburgh every weekend for eighteen years to be with his daughters. Grandpa chauffeured the sisters to dancing school and Belmont County 4-H until they finished high school; it was Grandma who became their surrogate mother, mentor, and confidant.

Living her entire life on a farm, Grandma was an extremely wise little woman with steely eyes. She had gleaned most of her education from newspapers, books, and her favorite radio commentators: Walter Winchel, Lowell Thomas, and Gabriel Heatter. Grandma understood politics; her twinkling eyes would sparkle through her round, wire-rimmed spectacles as she discussed world leaders and foreign affairs with remarkable intelligence and candor. She had little doubt the Democrats were responsible for the woes of the country.

Grandma was well-read, if not well-traveled. Her father, John Robert Cook, was uniformed in blue during the Civil War and "fought like 'ell" to keep those Southern turncoats out of the Ohio Valley. Consequently, Grandma had never had a hankerin' to journey very far south of the Mason-Dixon Line. But after her precious granddaughter, Janet Lee, moved to New Orleans, she began to broaden her thinking.

"I reckon New Orleans is different from the rest of the South, or Janet Lee wouldn't of moved there," she would say. "It's an important city and if my Janet Lee and her Bob like it, it must have some redeeming qualities."

After ardently studying the city's history, Grandma sent us a letter with an unexpected message: "Now that I'm widowed, I'd like to pay you a visit before I die. I've studied from those books you sent me, noticing New Orleans people are buried above ground. That certainly seems quite unnatural to me. If I don't visit New Orleans soon, I might expire during my visit and run the risk of being buried above ground in one of those tomb-towns! I don't want to be buried where my bones will get all mixed up with other people's remains in one of those walled vaults. So please let me know when it will be convenient for me to come. Your loving Grandma."

We phoned and set a December date that would allow her to be with us over the Christmas holidays. Thrilled as we were about her visit, we grew apprehensive about what she might think of the French Quarter and Bourbon Street, and so we planned a bevy of wholesome activities during her stay. Several members of the French Quarter Parents Club invited Jan and Grandmother for tea, giving Grandmother a chance to see a variety of interesting houses in the Quarter. We deliberately avoided the Bourbon Street strip between Canal and Dumaine, feeling Grandma was not yet ready to be exposed to the "professional exposers"!

Wonderful activities abound in the French Quarter during Christmas preparation. Foremost of these is the gathering of hundreds of carolers in Jackson Square on the Sunday night before Christmas. Grandma was duly moved by the city's religious fervor.

A few days prior, she had particularly enjoyed seeing Timmy and Tammy participate with the *La Petite Ecole* chorus's traditional performance at La Mothe House. It had become a tradition for Mrs. Munson, who operated the La Mothe guesthouse, to invite the chorus over at Christmastide to entertain her out-of-town guests. Following the recital, with a great flurry of charm and grace, she served potent *Café Brulot* and hot-spiced cider.

Mrs. Munson charmed Grandmother, for she too was a widow and a farm girl, though her farm had been hundreds of acres known as Glenwood plantation. After a devastating fire ravaged her multi-pillared antebellum home, she came to New Orleans at the invitation of a friend to operate the small hotel in the dilapidated La Mothe mansion. Under her supervision, the pensione prospered. She became well known as one of the most gracious hostesses and hoteliers in the city. Her hospitality and preparation of *Café Brulot* had become legend.

On Christmas Eve, Terry and Lenny Flettrich invited us to their home in the bend of Bourbon Street for some traditional Creole goodies. At dark we set out on our five-block jaunt; I pulled Tom in the holiday-decorated wagon. Grandma wondered if it was safe to walk along Bourbon Street at this time of night; we assured her it was just fine. We made a brief stop at the Goldens' to drop off a couple of small gifts for the children and to admire their tree. Stella and Rolland were on cloud nine as they had just received news that one of his paintings had sold for $500, and the benefactor hoped to arrange a gallery showing in New York—incredible news since he was turning out weekly detailed sketches for the *Vieux Carré Courier* at $10 each. Eventually, Golden paintings would sell for thousands of dollars as he became internationally acclaimed.

As we once again set our course toward Terry's, Grandma exclaimed that she had never seen such a Christmas tree. Jan explained that Stella was allergic to pine, and an aluminum tree was just what the doctor ordered. Grandma was worried that the children might get shocked by touching it or burned on the red and green spotlights illuminating it from the floor as it rotated on its turntable, creating incredible shadows on the walls. I told Grandma those trees had been selling like hotcakes at Sears-Roebuck. Jan assured her that Stella was a very protective mother.

Grandma sputtered, "Janet Lee, I never heard of such a thing as a metal Christmas tree!"

A few blocks ahead, she and the children spotted the wreaths lit in the Flettriches' windows. Terry, an innovative cook and extremely hospitable, made Grandma feel right at home. There was an array of Creole and Cajun delicacies: rum balls, rice cakes, plum pudding, and even a few Guatemalan pastries, the result of our hosts' many trips to Central America. Terry played the piano and her daughter, LoAnn, strummed the recorder as we sang Christmas carols. It was all very festive; Grandma loved it.

The kids became anxious to go home, worried Santa had come. There was a cold chill in the air when we stepped out. Bundling Tammy and Tom into the wagon, we said our good-byes, then started home. Several Christmas carolers passed by singing *Hark the Herald Angels Sing.*

Strolling along Bourbon, we pointed out several festively-decorated windows with Grandma remarking, "I can't believe how wonderful it is in the French Quarter at Christmastime."

Looking ahead toward our house, it appeared there were squad cars with flashing red lights in our block.

"What's that up there?" Jan questioned.

"Don't know, looks like police cars."

Grandma remarked quizzically, "Police cars on Christmas Eve?"

As we drew closer, we realized the police cars were standing directly in front of *our* house. Olympia was at the front door talking to a police officer.

Jan rushed on ahead, calling, "Olympia, Olympia, what's the matter? Are you all right?"

The kid's eyes were as big as saucers; Grandma turned pale. Fortunately, Tom was sound asleep. The police officer stepped back from the doorway as if he were being besieged.

"Is everything all right?"

The police officer turned, anxious to speak to a man. "Yes, sir, everything is all right now."

I spotted a man sitting in the back seat of the squad car.

"Lawd have mercy, Mizz Cahr," exclaimed Olympia. "That man done scared me half to mah death!"

"Where was he?"

"*He* be in the patio! *Me*—ah be in the kitchen, straightin' up, trying to get all da trash out. *Me*—ah opened the kitchen doh and took it out in da patio. And, Lawd have mercy. This man standing right there, scared me half to mah death. I swear to Gawd, Mizz Cahr, I almost dropped dayd—*right there!*"

"How did he get into the patio?"

Trying to catch her breath, Olympia panted, "Ah swear to Gawd, ah don't know. Mr. Cahr, ah swear to Gawd, he almost scared me to mah death. Mah heart's just goin' a mile a minute right now. Ah looks down ta set down da trash, and there's two bare feet, two *naked* bare feet, right there! Ah swear to Gawd, Mizz Cahr, scared me half to mah death. Ah look up, an' look straight in the eyes o' this man with long hair and whiskers. At first, I thought it was a wino. Then ah were so scared ah thought it might be Santa Claus. Then ah ran into the house screamin', got myself on the telephone an' called the *po*-lice. They came here and they *got* 'im! Now seems that po man fell into the gate an' pushed it open. Den the gate closed behind him an' he couldn't git hisself out."

"It must have happened when we went out of the gate with the wagon; guess we didn't close it tightly."

The gate had a spring lock on it. When it was slammed, it closed and locked automatically. But if not closed all the way, it would remain ajar.

The policeman told me this fellow was a known wino and had apparently fallen against the gate pushing his way into the patio but didn't mean any harm. He'd be booked for vagrancy. Since it was Christmas Eve and he was barefoot and homeless, jail would give him a nice warm place to stay.

Olympia's state frightened Grandma, causing Tammy to cry. Jan started singing Christmas carols, and to calm the children, she talked about Santa Claus coming down the chimney.

"I could see that man in the car," Timmy exclaimed. "He had a *long* beard. Maybe *he* was Santa Claus. Wouldn't it be terrible, Tammy, if they took Santa Claus off to jail and he couldn't deliver any presents?"

Tammy's eyes were about to well up again.

"Just kidding, Tammy, just kidding, don't cry, don't cry, I'm sure that wasn't Santa Claus."

"Timmy, you just hush yo' face!" Olympia exploded. "Don't scare yo' sister. Tammy, that weren't Santa Claus. What *he* be doin' runnin' 'round the French Quarter with no shoes on?"

We lit a fire in the fireplace, and everyone began to settle down. We sat in the front parlor gazing at the twinkling Christmas tree as Jan and Olympia served eggnog. I put our favorite Christmas records on the hi-fi: Andy Williams, Eydie Gorme, Steve Lawrence, and Frank Sinatra. We sipped our egg nog and admired the tinseled tree, staring at the lights as they blinked on and off, on and off, on and off until the weary kids headed up to bed. I assured them the fire would be out in time for Santa to come down the "chimmly," then drove Olympia home while Jan and Grandma placed presents 'round the tree.

Christmas morning always started earlier than we expected. The children seemed to be imbued with built-in Christmas morning radar, getting up at what we thought was the crack of dawn and charging rambunctiously into our room. Tradition dictated they had to make their beds and straighten up their rooms, get dressed either in their clothes or best pajamas—only then would we all go down and start opening our presents. Jan occupied the kids in the kitchen until everyone was ready. Armed with my eight-millimeter camera, I hid behind the tree so we would forever have a movie of them entering the room, spying the presents. The abundance of gifts made it look as if D. H. Holmes, Maison Blanche, and Woolco had unloaded in our front parlor. The kids started tearing their way through the gifts. Tammy's favorite was a child's size hutch given to her by a lady who owned an antique shop on Royal that accommodated Jan's antique doll dishes. Timmy particularly enjoyed his chemistry set; Tom couldn't care less—he just enjoyed rattling the paper. Grandma got her traditional housedress from us. This was all she ever wanted.

Jan and I stalked shops for that special gift for each other and gloated when we each found something really meaningful. I asked Jan to open her gift first. She unwrapped the package and looked at it strangely, showing surprise but little enthusiasm. I was hurt because I had shopped and shopped, having finally found what I thought was the perfect gift. Together, we had loved the musical drama *The Man of La Mancha*. Miraculously, I had found a statue of Don Quixote, which I purchased and hid away. Somewhat meekly, she confessed she was thrilled to receive it; now, would I please open *my* present? I tore at the wrapping; I couldn't believe my eyes! She had found the only other *Man of La Mancha* statue in New Orleans! They were almost identical; we laughed and laughed but were deeply touched that obviously we had both wanted to please each other, smacking of O. Henry's *The Gift of the Magi*. We ultimately returned one of the costly statues.

About halfway through opening presents, the doorbell rang. The children moaned at the thought of their unwrapping ritual being disrupted. It was our next-door neighbors, Bruce and Malcolm, owners of a ladies' boutique salon on Royal. The guys had been together for ten years. Loving our children, they brought over gifts: for Tammy, a little make-up kit; for Timothy, a comb and brush set; and for Tom, a colorful rubber ball with a bell inside that jingled when it rolled. They extolled our Christmas tree and regaled Grandma with the marvelous things they had heard about her. Downing a cup of eggnog, they pranced off to make their next Christmas call. As they were leaving, our next-door neighbor on the other side, M.J. Mac Clung, a sergeant in the Marine Corps, emerged from her gate to walk Combat, her Great Dane, and drop off gifts for the kids. Jan gave Combat a dog goody and Mac a cup of eggnog with a stiff shot. The children loved Combat but didn't see him very often, except when they climbed up the ladder to look over the fence to drop him goodies. He could be quite vicious, but as long as Mac was around, he was absolutely docile and perfectly tame. She sat Tom on him as if he were straddling a horse and rode him around the parlor; we all snickered. Mac chug-a-lugged her well-spiked eggnog, shook Grandma's hand firmly, and was on her way.

Continuing with the presents, Grandma spoke up. "Just a minute, Janet Lee and Bob, I've got to ask about these neighbors of yours. Those two fellows, what were their names?"

"Bruce and Malcolm."

"Well, I want to know something. I have never seen any young men like that in Colerain. Bruce and Malcolm, are they brothers?"

"No, grandma, they're not brothers; they're just good friends."

"Now, Janet Lee, they look a little delicate to me!"

"But, Grandma, it takes all kinds to make up the world," I chided.

"Bob, you're right about that but, those fellas, they look a little like those fairies we had up on the next farm. You know, Janet Lee, the ones who crocheted layettes for orphan babies. I won't say they weren't nice and all that, but they seemed a little...you know...odd."

Attempting to change the subject, Jan interrupted. "Grandma, I think you have another present there."

"Just one minute, Janet Lee, don't distract me. There's something else. That big dog, the size of a horse, an' bringin' that monster in the house! You know how I never did cater much to havin' dogs or critters inside the house."

"I know, Grandma, but the kids really enjoyed it. Didn't you think it was fun having Tom ride on his back?"

"One time, maybe, getting those fleas in the house—one time maybe—but can you imagine that woman living with that dog all the time in her apartment? She must have fleas from the floor to the rafters. I'll tell you one thing about that woman, she looked twice as tough as those two fellas."

"Grandma," I chided, "I always thought you were so broad-minded."

"I always thought I was broad-minded, too. But that woman looked stronger then our Hank, who use to scythe the hay on our back acre."

"Grandma, you've got pretty good intuition."

"I just can't say, young man, if I do or I don't. I just know what I know, that's all."

"Grandma," Tim piped up, "we can't open our presents until you open your next present 'cause it's our custom, when opening Christmas presents, we open them going around the room, one at a time, giving a chance for everyone to see the presents and share in the joy."

"Thank you, 'Tiny Tim,'" I replied.

"Humm, let's see, which one shall I open?"

"Open that one, Grandma," Tammy insisted, "*that* one, right there."

"That one certainly looks pretty enough. All right, let's see, this is from Tammy to Grandma. What could it be?"

Tammy got more and more excited as Grandma melodramatically unwrapped her package.

"My-oh-my, it's an apron, a beautiful apron."

"Yes, Grandma, an apron. Mommy bought the apron at D. H. Holmes and I put your name on it. I 'broidered your name on it. *See?*"

"Well, look at this. It says Grandma Franke, F-R-A-N-K-E, and you did all that, Tammy?"

"I didn't 'xactly do all the sewing, Grandma, ya buy those little letters. They look like you sowed 'em, but ya iron them on."

"Heavens to Betsy, it looks beautiful," she giggled.

The doorbell startled us.

As Jan answered we could hear her say, "Bruce, what's the matter, you look terrible?"

"It's Malcolm! We went back to the apartment; there's something wrong with him! I don't know what it is but could you or Bob come over to help me for a minute? Maybe you can tell me what's wrong with him."

"Sure, I'll come over." She stuck her head back into the front parlor. "I'm going next door to Bruce and Malcolm's. I'll be back in a minute."

"Honey, don't you want me to go?"

"No, no, you're opening your presents. I'll be right back."

We continued opening gifts, but I became worried; Jan had been gone nearly half an hour.

"Grandma, maybe I better go over and see if there's a problem."

Grandma motioned me out. "The children are so busy with their presents they won't miss you for a few minutes."

As I stepped down from the vestibule onto the banquette, an ambulance careened to a halt in front of Bruce and Malcolm's shotgun double house. The ambulance driver, seeing I was a neighbor, asked if this was the Bruce Darnell residence.

"It is, my wife's in there. I'll see if the door's unlocked."

The door opened directly into the parlor from Bourbon Street. Jan was sitting on the antique wicker chaise lounge holding Malcolm's head; a cold cloth covered his forehead. Bruce had removed Malcolm's shoes and was massaging his feet and legs.

The paramedic entered swiftly, attending to his work: taking a pulse, using a stethoscope to check the heart, listening to Malcolm's breathing, and examining his eyes. Still looking into his eyes, the paramedic announced, "We must get this man to the hospital at once!"

He instructed the driver to get the stretcher. Then, directing his attention toward Jan, still holding Malcolm's head, he asked a bevy of questions: "Are you his wife? Will you be going to the hospital with us? Will you be riding in the ambulance?"

Jan was so surprised she just uttered, "Uh uh."

With that, Bruce spoke up, "No, no, I'll be going, he's my—he's *my friend.*"

Trying to calm him, Jan uttered, "I'm sure he's going to be all right. He'll be at the hospital in a few minutes. I'm sure he'll be all right."

"I knew he was sick. I knew he was sick all the time. He just wouldn't go to the doctor. I kept telling him to get a checkup."

Bruce laid his head on Malcolm's chest and wailed audibly. Seeing how pitiful they were together, Jan's eyes filled with tears.

Realizing the two were lovers, the paramedic became indignant, announcing rather rudely, "Look, fella, if you don't want yer buddy to die, ya better move yer butt and let us get 'im into the ambu-*lance.*"

Bruce backed out of the way, continuing to sob as I assisted the ambulance driver and the paramedic. We lifted Malcolm onto the stretcher, releasing his head from Jan's lap.

"Oh, Jan, what am I going to do if anything happens to him? He's the only thing I have in life!"

She put her arms around him. "Bruce, he'll be all right as soon as they get him to the hospital."

"What'll I do? What'll I ever do? He's the only person I've ever loved. He's the only person who's ever understood me."

Stepping out the door, I noticed several people had gathered on their balconies or were looking through their shutters, attracted by the hubbub and flashing lights.

The driver yelled, "Hey, fella, you better get in the back *now* if you want to go with us."

Although white as a sheet, Bruce seemed to be pulling himself together.

Helping him into the back of the ambulance, I instructed, "Bruce, call us from the hospital as soon as you find out anything. If you need us, we'll come and get you or bring you anything you want, okay? Now, they want to go. Bye-bye."

The ambulance sped off. We stood on the banquette for a few minutes, stunned by the whole situation. We glanced up at the balconies draped with curious faces; shrugging our shoulders, we walked back to our front door, pausing in the vestibule.

Giving Jan a hug, I said, "Honey, you were so wonderful."

"I was so scared, afraid he was going to die right there in my lap. And I feel so sorry for Bruce; he's so much in love with Malcolm. It's so sad, isn't it? It's so sad, the kind of life they have to lead!"

"What do you mean?"

"We always knew they were roommates, but until that desperate outcry of love and affection, it was hard for me to understand they were really in love with each other, *really* in love."

"I know. It's a wonder loving relationships like that can endure under such difficult circumstances, having to be closeted from mainstream society."

"We must remember them in our prayers, and thank God that we have the family we do."

"You're right, honey." I gave her another hug. "Christmas in New Orleans is like no other place in the world!"

Entering the parlor, the kids descended upon us.

"You were gone so long!"

"We opened extra presents. Now we want some eggnog!"

"Grandma said Tom has to have his diaper changed," announced Tammy, holding her nose.

Grandma was getting on in years, but her nose could detect a dirty diaper at fifty feet.

"Those gentlemen all right?" Grandma asked.

"Oh yes, one of them was feeling sick, so the ambulance took them to the hospital. They'll call us later."

"I'm sorry I said anything derogatory about 'em, but I'm just not used to the peculiar ways of the French Quarter. Now, Janet Lee, these children are going to be getting hungry before too long; I'm going out there in the kitchen and baste my Christmas turkey before it dries out."

Jan and I were excited about Grandma's Christmas dinner. We had become so accustomed to Creole and Cajun cooking that we were looking forward to some good ole Ohio farm victuals. Following New Orleans tradition, Jan tried to talk Grandma into stuffing the turkey with oyster dressing.

"Oysters are for stew, if'n you like that sort of thing. Y'aren't gonna put any oysters in *my* turkey, I'll tell you that, my dear granddaughter."

The doorbell rang, startling Grandmother. "I'm gonna hie myself out to the kitchen, Janet Lee, and fuss with my turkey. I've seen enough of your peculiar friends for today."

Ann and Bill were at the door with their three girls. On their way Uptown to have

Christmas dinner with friends, they had stopped by for a few minutes to exchange presents. We all sat down to watch the kids open gifts while Jan offered to fetch a round of egg nog.

Bill asked, "Is the egg nog polluted with alcohol? I don't know why Jesus' birthday is always celebrated with drunkenness!"

Jan chuckled a little. "There's a bit of bourbon in it."

"I'd rather not have any then, unless you can give me some without whiskey."

Ann glanced significantly toward Jan.

"Sure, I'll give you some of the same stuff I've been giving the kids all morning."

The children opened all their presents. Liza ogled the Barbie doll Tammy had gotten from Santa.

Bill reprimanded her. "Liza, you put down that Barbie doll, *right now.*"

"That's okay, Bill," I interjected. "Tammy doesn't mind."

"I *mind!* I will not have my daughter handling a Barbie doll. They're sinful. Look at the suggestive breasts and the contour of the buttocks. That's no toy. That's a sexual symbol! I will not have my children playing with a symbol of sexual wantonness!"

"Bill, don't get so upset," Ann interrupted. "The kids are just playing with their dolls."

"The toy-makers are tainting our children's minds with these sensual dolls and other corruptions. We certainly won't have any in our house!"

"Are you serious, Bill?"

"I think the anatomical detail of those dolls is over-stimulating to young children. The ones my parents gave our girls I dumped in the incinerator."

Jan walked in with the eggnog; "You put what in the incinerator, Bill?"

"My parents had the poor judgment to give our girls Barbie dolls for Christmas; I put them in the incinerator. I will not have those creatures in my house."

Since we had been friends for years, I goaded him on a bit. "How do you feel about the Ken doll? Tammy got one of those too. I already checked him out. He's been neutered unless they ran out of plastic before they could give him a proper ying-yang."

"Bob, really!" Jan reprimanded.

Instinctively trying to change the subject and save the day, Ann remarked, "You certainly have a lovely Christmas tree."

"It *was* lovely," Jan chimed in, "until this morning. I think Santa shook every needle off when he came down the chimney. We got the tree a couple of weeks ago in the Lower 9th Ward. Bob kept holding back, thinking we could get a better buy, but finally we had to buy this dried-out thing in desperation. I think trees are shipped into New Orleans from North Carolina and Virginia before Halloween. It doesn't have many needles, does it?"

Bill drank a sip of eggnog, set it down, and then commanded, "Girls, girls, we have to go now, *right now.* Come, Ann, it's time for us to go!"

"Hey Bill, don't run off," I said. "I didn't mean to upset you."

"You have your ideas, Bob, about what's sinful, and I have mine. You run your house; I'll run my house. Thanks for the eggnog, now it's time for us to go."

Not wanting to irritate Bill further, I hung back as Jan waved good-bye from the door.

"Lawdy, Jan, I think his problems are escalating. He's not the same Bill who brought us to New Orleans! There must be a medical reason for his behavior, maybe a chemical imbalance in his brain."

"Bob, you mustn't kid him about his beliefs, it's not nice. Ann told me it's very difficult at times since he's found religion."

"I'm sorry. *I'm* concerned about our friendship. We've been like brothers but now I feel estranged. I think I'll give his psychiatrist a call. Maybe there's some way I can help. They say beauty is in the eye of the beholder; maybe sensuality and lasciviousness are also in the eye of the beholder. Those Barbie dolls strike some note he can't cope with."

"I don't know, but I'm glad of one thing."

"What's that?"

"Ann had told me the girls' grandmother was giving them Barbie dolls, so I almost gave them extra Barbie outfits, but all the really cute ones were gone. That's why I got them games."

"I'm glad fate worked out the way it did. I would have hated to see him throwing their outfits into our fireplace. I'd have been really ticked."

The phone rang. I thought it might be Bruce with a report on Malcolm's condition, but instead it was my parents calling from Painesville to wish us all a merry Christmas and to make sure the children's gifts had arrived and we had gotten their check. They always gave us a dollar for each day of the year; we usually used the $365 to pay our Christmas bills!

Jan took the kids upstairs for a nap. Tammy wanted Tom to sleep in her bed so she could give him his bottle. Tim took a nap in his own room so that he could watch his model airplanes dangling from the ceiling. I stretched out on the sofa. I was still worried about Bill but content to look over the book my mother had given me on plantation architecture while Jan picked up the pieces of wrapping paper and burned them in the fireplace. Grandma maintained her vigil over the turkey.

Bruce finally called to let us know Malcolm would be fine, though hospitalized for observation for several days. He assured Jan they would be back in their salon, hustling gowns for their New Year's customers.

Grandma's sumptuous turkey dinner was a flashback to our youth. Later, during their goodnight prayers, the children whispered they missed oysters in the dressing! Mercifully, Christmas ended on a peaceful and prayerful note—not always the case when I was growing up.

* * * * *

In kindergarten, Tammy would be picked up at noon. One of the cutest sights along Bourbon Street was Tammy, Olympia, and Kee Chin wandering home under the hot noontime sun, completely unaware of the rainbow of colors they presented: Tammy, pink and rosy with auburn-colored hair; Olympia, her crisp white uniform contrasting sharply with her mahogany complexion; and petite, almond-skinned Kee Chin, her Asian eyes a-sparkle from under her long, black, straight-cut bangs. And, of course, there was blond-haired, blue-eyed Tom in his blue and yellow plaid stroller.

Kee Chin's parents, a lovely Chinese-American couple, ran a business on Royal Street. Since they worked most of the time, grandmother usually made the pick-up after kindergarten; however, she had fallen ill for a few weeks, so Jan asked Olympia to help out while the elderly lady recuperated. Due to our busy schedules we never got to know the parents very well, but diminutive Kee Chin, a year younger than Tammy, and her baby brother, D'ai Ning, were charming, well-mannered children. I called the two youngsters Kitchen and Dining for several months until Tammy received a birthday card from them with their names spelled out properly.

My mother had given us a silver tea service one Christmas, always kept shined and displayed on our antique sideboard. Jan was teaching Tammy how to polish it, which prompted Tammy to insist on holding a "grown-up" tea party for her friends. Jan thought it would be fun and a learning experience, so at the age of four and a half, Tammy was launched into what I suspected would probably become a never-ending circle of teas. Even at this young age, our daughter had a mind of her own; she knew just *what* and *whom* she wanted at her party.

The list of girls represented a kaleidoscope of patriarchal backgrounds: a children's TV star, an importer, a lawyer, a bookie (we think), a doctor, a psychologist, daddy unknown—"Mommy" manages a gay bar! Other Dads were in oil, real estate acquisition, an artist, and a mathematician with NASA.

Tammy planned her party in the same way her parents formatted a TV show: Olympia would greet the girls at the front door and escort them to the patio, and daddy would serve cocktails on a silver tray—pink Shirley Temples or blue Dale Evanses with lots of "mosquito" cherries.

Olympia would serve hors d'oeuvres, made of peanut butter, jelly, olives, and cream cheese, as the guests greeted and chatted about doll babies and husbands. After a half hour, daddy would take pictures in the parlor while everyone still looked pretty; mommy would help everyone play "May I?" and "Gossip." Olympia was to announce, "Ladies, tea is served in the dining room."

Tammy would be seated at the head of the table and serve from the silver teapot while offering lots of frosted cupcakes, cookies, and soles (a hard, thin, flat pastry with caramel glazing, which looks like the sole of a shoe). Following the tea, the mommies would pick up the girls at the front door, and Tammy alone would bid them adieu. After all, mommy, daddy, and Olympia were the maids and butlers for the party!

In spite of the rigid rules laid down by our little hostess, the tea was a smashing success, though Jan and I were not familiar with a tea commencing with cocktails until we later learned it was "Veddy, Veddy Uptown!"

* * * * *

The French Quarter has long appealed to aficionados of art and architecture, persons of various sexual persuasions, business entrepreneurs, and beatniks. For Jan and me, it had been the perfect alternative to living and raising our family in the suburbs. When "people" told us there were no single houses in the Quarter, we found one; when they told us there were no schools in the Quarter, we found one; no children in the Quarter, we found some; and so it went. In fact, all the things we needed were available in the Quarter. Being on TV and radio daily and having had a couple of stories published about us as a "French Quarter Family," we were often asked for advice about settling in the Quarter. Jeff Biddison, our real estate agent and also a good friend, called on us from time to time to bring by clients with children who were skeptical about the existence of families in the Quarter.

Late one afternoon, he rang up to inquire if he could stop by with a couple moving to New Orleans from Wilmington, Delaware; they had two little girls about Tammy's age. Taken with the idea of living in the Quarter, they were concerned about housing, parking, schools, etc.

Paul Fabry, a Hungarian diplomat until the Soviets took over, had most recently worked for DuPont; his wife, Loulie, was a well-born native of Pennsylvania horse country. Dr. Fabry had been selected as the managing director of the prestigious trade and development organization International House. The couple would be grateful if they could come by for a brief chat.

We were always glad to help Jeff, who had not only sold us our house but had actually pitched in to help us renovate it. He and I spent one weekend in gas masks, chipping and sanding a freestanding brick chimney in the family room. With the humidity and temperature in the 90s, if we had not used masks, as Jeff insisted, we might have expired from brick dust inhalation. Bricks known as "old reds" were very soft and beautiful, but for their protection, they were usually covered with stucco. It had become the vogue to expose the raw brick, then spray them with a new transparent polyurethane product.

Jeff arrived about eight-thirty with the Fabrys, whom he quickly introduced to our children as they trudged unwillingly up the stairs to bed. Jeff and I showed them through the main floor of the house, explaining some of the remodeling we had done. After reading a story to the children, Jan joined us in the front parlor. We sipped on their imported white wine and conversed well into the night, not realizing it was the start of an enduring friendship. Jan and I were excited to hear that they had been looking at the ancient, dilapidated townhouse several doors away. After talking with us and seeing the children, they decided to make a definite offer on the house in the morning.

We explained the exasperating problem of financing a hundred-and-fifty-year-old Quarter house. Although the place would probably last another century or two, few of the old buildings met the requirements of the F.H.A. Though this situation had improved a bit in New Orleans, it was still a severe problem in many parts of the country, where well-intentioned people with moderate means were trying to rescue old homes.

We were delighted when Jeff told us the Fabrys had gotten the house up the street and would be moving in as soon as the renovation was complete. Their daughters, Lydia and Alexa—affectionately called Saga— were exactly one year apart. They were sweet, shy girls whom Tammy liked immediately. Lydia was as blonde and skinny as Saga was brunette and chubby. Jan helped get them settled at *La Petite Ecole*, and of course, Tammy was thrilled to have two girlfriends join the trek with Olympia and her brothers along Bourbon Street after school. Years later, in 1978, a group of international notables gathered in the Fabry's parlor to sign a document establishing the World Trade Centers Association, which would be headquartered at the twin towers in New York City.

One afternoon we arrived home early because our show was preempted by a President Kennedy news conference concerning a civil rights sit-in at an Alabama lunch counter. We took advantage of the free afternoon to work on the front balcony, repairing a loose fascia board. The balcony was some eighteen-and-a-half feet above the banquette. The only way to get the ladder in the proper position, so the angle wouldn't be too steep, was to place the bottom of the ladder in the gutter against the curb and lean the top of it against the outer edge of the balcony. Starting up the wobbly ladder, I realized the ladder might get hit by the Desire bus. Passing our house, the driver was usually closing the door, accelerating, making change, and simultaneously trying to steer a steady course on the narrow street. I was afraid he might not see me as he passed. Equally concerned, Jan took up a position on the bottom rung to steady the ladder and wave off the bus driver.

Scrambling up the ladder with a hammer and mouth full of finishing nails, I was startled by the screech of auto breaks a block and a half up Bourbon Street. I swung around to see what was happening as a van painted in psychedelic colors barreled down the street doing at least fifty miles an hour! Impulsively, Jan scurried halfway *up* to avoid being hit as the vehicle sped past, nearly grazing the base of the ladder.

"*Idiot!*" I shouted, shaking my hammer as Jan and I turned to watch him speeding toward Esplanade.

"The *children* and *Olympia!*" Jan screamed. "They should be crossing from school about now!"

Jan's words were interrupted by a tremendous crash at Bourbon and Esplanade. From my perch on the ladder, I could see through the settling dust that by failing to halt at the stop sign, the van had collided with something at the intersection. I could also see the heads of several people through the dispersing cloud. We dashed breathlessly to the crash scene as a crowd gathered. We saw no sign of Olympia and the children.

The psychedelic van had smashed broadside into a long black limousine, the van driver having long since fled the scene. A well-dressed man lay ominously motionless on the grass of the neutral-ground.

"Oh my Gawd, he's day-ud," a woman screamed.

"Yah, he's done *passed!*" solemnly remarked a tall, lean, black man, lowering his hat in respect.

Jan gasped as we entered the scene, followed by one of the Baptist Mission's winos, who muttered, "The devil'll get cha in the end!"

The impact had bounced the limousine over the curb and onto the neutral-ground. The dazed and disheveled chauffer staggered from the driver's seat unnoticed until he started shouting, "Mah bawdy, mah bawdy, don't hoit mah bawdy!"

We all pushed back as the driver approached the static figure, rolling him over, adjusting his clothes and meticulously straightening his tie—then approached the back of the car and tugged on the jammed rear door.

"Good Lord! It's a *hearse!*"

"Oh, Bob, this is horrible! I can't look!"

"Honey, he was already dead!"

The driver stooped over the corpse, discreetly scooped him up, and prudently slid him down through a tunnel of jostled flowers before slamming the damaged door firmly. Walking calmly to the front of the limo, he slipped behind the steering wheel and drove off as a police siren could be heard approaching.

"Well, what do we do now?"

"Let's go find Olympia and the kids," Jan urged.

"Yah, we'd better get out of here before the police come or we'll be stuck all afternoon. There are plenty of witnesses."

Two of the youngsters waiting for their carpool in front of the school told us the kids had talked Olympia into taking them up Royal Street to get snowballs. We finally caught up with them in front of the Fabrys'. The children's clothes were covered with a variety of colors, as drippings from the melting snowballs had practically marked a Technicolor trail along the streets.

"Ooo, that ice makes my toof hurt!" moaned Lydia, spilling the remainder of her snowball down the front of her pretty Hungarian embroidered blouse.

"Let me look at your toofy," I asked, pressing back and forth on several teeth. "Does this hurt?"

"That one doth!" garbled Lydia, trying to speak with my finger lodged in her mouth.

"Maybe it better come out!"

Lydia grimaced.

"Yes, honey, I really think it should be pulled. Check with your mother first. Then come over to our house and I'll take it out."

Their maid opened the door.

"Hello, Netta, would you please tell Mrs. Fabry about Lydia's loose tooth? Oh, and have her rinse out her mouth. I just had my fist in it."

Netta looked at me quizzically as she closed the door.

Jan and I heard an Olympian screech from in front of our house.

"Timmy!" Olympia screeched again. "Get yo-self down offern dat ladder, boy, 'fo you gits kilt raht here on Bourbon Street! Where da good sense ah taught you, boy?"

"Timmy, for heaven's sake," Jan chimed in.

"I'm already up here on the balcony," he hollered. "That's silly. I can't fall off the balcony, I'm out here all the time! I'll meet you inside."

After putting the ladder away I searched for my "tooth-pulling" pliers. In the meantime, in an effort to make our family room coffee table look like an operating theater, Timmy had placed a sheet over it and set a floor lamp nearby, making it look antiseptic and hospital-like. I could hear Jan talking on the phone to Loulie.

"Lydia and Saga will be right over. Loulie said pull the loose tooth if you think it best. Paul would never do such a thing. He hates the sight of blood!"

Lydia was less than enthusiastic about the whole idea when they arrived, but we coaxed her to lie down on the "operating table." Tammy acted as nurse by getting a glass of salt water, plus ice in a towel. Acting as orderly, Tom got paper towels and water. Saga's main chore was to hold Lydia's hand as Timmy adjusted the "operating light." We were a formidable team.

With great pomp, I washed the pliers with scalding water from the teakettle, sprayed them with Bactine and began to search Lydia's timid mouth for the loose tooth.

"Is that it?" I asked.

"Unh Unh," she said, producing a negative grunt.

"That it?"

"Unh Unh."

"*That?*"

"*Uh Huh*, yeth."

"*Good!* Hold *real still*. There, got it! *Look!*" I held up the tooth in a triumphal gesture for all to see.

Everyone applauded. Lydia began to cry!

"Does it hurt, honey?"

"No."

"Then why are you crying?"

"I dun't know," she whimpered, "I gheth I mith it!"

"Well, here it is! You can put it under your pillow tonight for the tooth fairy."

Tammy gave her the salt water to gargle. I gave her an ice chip to suck on and then pressed the ice-filled towel against her cheek for a few minutes. She coughed slightly, spitting up a bit of blood.

"Yuk, gross!" exclaimed Tammy.

Covering their faces, the other kids began to cry, causing Jan and Olympia to arrive on the scene.

"Mistah Cahr, what you done that li'l chile?"

"Bob, did you hurt Lydia? Lydia, did Mr. Carr hurt you?"

"I don't think tho." Lydia smiled, revealing a bit of blood oozing between each tooth.

"*Yuk!*" was the unanimous response.

"But Lydia, does it hurt?"

"No, thir," came her reply, as she sucked the blood back into her mouth, followed by a broad smile. The day was saved!

Soon she was up, out, and home again, showing her parents the tooth we had entombed in an empty mayonnaise jar.

My reputation as the "Tooth Puller of Bourbon Street" grew and spread for the next several years as many of our kids' friends turned to me instead of submitting to their parents, or their dentists, for minor extractions. I was grateful to be known as the "Tooth Puller" and not the "Tooth Fairy"!

When Olympia accompanied the children from school, she would occasionally drop them off at the Fabrys' to play for a while before dinner. Loulie was a talented painter, sculptress, and carpenter, creating some very interesting playthings for the children. They particularly loved a big dollhouse they could crawl in and out of, and there was a huge linen hammock in the patio draped from the house to a large magnolia tree, a tree that invited climbing.

The Fabrys' house also had a unique central courtyard with a staircase that spiraled to the second-floor balcony overlooking a rather dilapidated house next door, inhabited mostly by transients. The balcony offered a vantage point for the kids to sit and watch any interesting antics on the other side of the twelve-foot brick wall.

It came to pass that in the first-floor apartment they became acquainted with a young couple who sat stretched out on a sofa bed under a ceiling fan facing their window—a position they assumed because their TV set was situated just under the windowsill. During the many torrid days, the couple's window was wide open, giving the kids a bird's eye view from their perch. It further came to pass that the young man and young woman, on hot humid days, would stretch out full length bare-front naked. The kids would giggle and wave, the immodest young couple drawing a flimsy sheet across themselves as they waved back. Tammy referred to them as the "nooda people." The scenario the children had been enjoying over the wall never occurred to us adults!

Time passed, and the children seemed to have lost interest in their "balcony friends." The Fabrys invited us for a family dinner, but before eating, the children asked us to go up to the balcony to see something special. Perspiring, Paul, Loulie, Jan, and I reluctantly twisted up the winding stair. Looking down across the railing and through the window, there, stretched out on their sofa bed, were the nude "nooda people." Lying across the woman's stomach happily suckling her breast was a little "nooda baby"! Could an explanation of the birds and bees be far behind?

* * * * *

That year, Paul, as managing director of the World Trade Center of New Orleans, asked us to represent the city on a European trade mission of about thirty businesspeople and their spouses. Among them would be George Healy, the oft-feared editor of the landmark *Times-Picayune* newspaper, a cradle of news since the early 1800s. Mr. Healy regarded TV as an upstart competitor to his sacred daily. The names of TV personalities were strictly forbidden in all columns.

Mr. Reed, our station manager, saw the trip as an excellent outreach for the station and an audience-builder, while also giving "Bob & Jan" great credibility. We would have to be extremely conciliatory to George and Margaret Healy to convince them of TV's positive attributes.

Pompous and arrogant, Mr. Healy incessantly lectured our travelers on the importance of the Healy clan in Ireland, our first stop. Driving through the countryside, we saw businesses and street signs with various names of our traveling companions—Mead, Molony, O'Leary, even Fitzsimmons, Jan's maiden name—but no Healys.

While at breakfast in Galway, a couple traveling with us barged into the dining room, beseeching our group, along with the Healys, to follow them. Away we all went along the avenue, down a side street, into a lane. We stood in awe. Across the bog was a somewhat dilapidated sign proclaiming *Healy's Manure Works*.

"Hey, George, we always knew you were full of it, now it's in print!" rang out the mantra.

Mr. Healy was defanged, the trip a great success, and the names of TV personalities began to appear in *The Picayune*.

* * * * *

I have always had a fascination with Italian actresses: sultry, sweaty Anna Mangano of *Bitter Rice*, sensually sophisticated Sophia Loren, and totally gorgeous Gina Lollobrigida. Gina was in town to promote her latest flick, *Woman of Straw*, co-starring Sean Connery. Al Shea got me on the phone; he was frantic. Gina with entourage would be at the station in twenty minutes. Could I come to do the interview, which was originally scheduled for next week (someone goofed)?

"I'm supposed to fly kites with kids, *but* I'll be there!"

Miss Lollobrigida's advanceman was a raving, arm-flinging idiot who made me sorry I had left the kids; and yet Gina was so perfectly beautiful and charming that I quickly melted. The interview was fun; she had a great sense of humor about her international stardom, her silly English accent, and working with Sean Connery, whom she thought I resembled! When I asked about her alleged romances with Yul Brynner and Frank Sinatra, she rolled her mascara-laden eyes, ignoring the question. After the interview she told me I wouldn't have gotten away with those "boyfriend" questions if I weren't so Conneryesque!

I walked home about two feet off the ground. Of course, the boys were waiting impatiently on the front stoop. Timmy and his friends loved to fly kites, and I enjoyed taking them down to the river on the levee by the docks where the wind was strong. We had three kites, all of them gifts.

One was a traditionally-shaped kite sporting the words "Y'all drink Dixie Beer!" We tied a long tail on that one. The second was a huge and colorful box kite that, when assembled, stood taller than any of the boys. After much discussion and consideration, we tied a tail on the end of that one as well. The third was an Oriental kite in the shape of an enormous dragon. After a greater amount of discussion and consideration than the first confab, we unanimously decided no tail needed to be added to the dragon's already ponderous and fearsome dorsal. The boys flipped a coin to see who was going to get which kite.

Pierre was chagrined when he won the Dixie Beer draw, but he dismissed any show of discontent by bursting forth with, "Yippee, I got the beer kite, which means I'm old enough to drink!" Spotting a trashed Dixie can, Pierre darted along the railroad tracks as if possessed, then tied his newfound prize to the tail.

Dwarfed by the box kite he had drawn in the coin toss, Kelvin was so excited he whirled in circles like a toy top out of control. Toppling at the end of his clumsy pirouettes, he inadvertently flung his fist though one panel of the kite! He flashed a glance my way; our eyes connected. Water flooded his eyes, blurring his vision.

My first reaction to his klutziness was to stand there and let him suffer. Instead I said, "Kelvin, I had a feeling something like this might happen, so I brought along some Scotch tape."

Kelvin rubbed his eyes, pretending he had something in them, then thanked me with a smile and assisted me as we taped the torn spot together. I noticed he glanced longingly at Timmy, who was adjusting his prize, the dragon kite.

It was one of those beautiful, low-humidity New Orleans days with intermittent sun caused by an array of cumulus clouds drifting lazily over the city. A nice breeze was blowing off the bend in the river, just behind the French Market. There wasn't another soul on the levee. I helped the boys carry their kites along the tracks to let out the lines. One by one, the boys began charging ahead to get the kites aloft. The breeze was blowing in just the right direction, causing the kites to take off like three Viscount turbo jets. I assisted them in easing out the string as the kites soared higher and higher across the railroad tracks and up over the intersection of Esplanade and Elysian Fields. Kelvin's box kite was flying beautifully in spite of its patch. The Dixie Beer can on the tail of Pierre's kite seemed to be just the proper weight to keep the kite steady in the stiff breeze.

Timmy, who had been ecstatic when he had won the Chinese kite, was having trouble. While the other two kites were flying gracefully, the dragon wasn't taking off as it should. It would rise up, soar erratically, and then nosedive. Finally, the dragon stabilized as it seized the breeze. We let out more and more string, and unexpectedly it took a long, slow dive—down, down, down like a great dying beast.

The boys gasped. "Ahhhhhh, Oooooooooooooooooo."

The kite fluttered to the ground, landing at the front door of the Port Bar.

Timothy, devastated his kite had crashed, took off like a jackrabbit, following the fallen string down the levee, clearing five sets of railroad tracks in seconds. It was amusing to see a dragon lying dead right at the front door of the bar. Just as Timmy approached the kite, it suddenly disappeared through the door. Timmy slid to a halt and glanced back at me with a horrified look. The boys and I couldn't believe what we saw: first the dragon and then Timothy disappearing through the door of the Port Bar. We stood there for what seemed a long time with the boys tugging at their kites trying to keep them aloft while I tried to decide whether or not I should retrieve my son.

Presently, Timothy emerged from the bar, the wilted dragon lying across his arms. Heading back to us, across the street and over the tracks, he had a Barq's and potato chips in one hand and the kite in the other.

Three merchant Marines emerged from the front door of the bar waving and shouting. "So long, Timmy, have a good day, boy!"

Timmy was all smiles as he approached; we couldn't wait to hear what happened. When the kite dove down to the bar's front door, a drunken sailor thought it was a wild Louisiana alligator; realizing it was a kite, he yanked it in. When Timmy appeared, the three merchant Marines insisted he give it back. The drunk protested, so two of the sailors held his arms while the third took the kite away. Since the drunk had been so disagreeable, they wondered if they could buy Timothy a drink. He selected a Barq's. They gave him a bag of potato chips as *lagniappe* ("something extra" in New Orleansese) and sent him happily on his way.

With the other two kites still flying high, we decided to tie a tail on the dragon kite and try again. After several failures, it was finally flying steadily, but it wouldn't soar because the tail was now too heavy. It hovered about 200 feet above the ground, causing the string to sag close to the tracks. The boys were ecstatic until we heard a train whistle. The slow-moving freight chugged past, snagging the string across its prow, relentlessly drawing the kite toward the engine. Closer and closer the dragon came to the locomotive until it was impaled on the headlight. The train began to pick up speed, heading down river with Timmy in hot pursuit.

"*No, no, no,* that's enough," I shouted. "Don't do that, you'll get hurt."

"But daddy, that train stole my kite!"

"We'll get you another kite. Just think how much fun it's going to be for people to see your dragon on the front of that train when it goes through Chalmette and on down the river."

We reeled in the other kites and headed home.

The boys loved walking along the neutral ground on Esplanade Avenue. One would have thought they were in the middle of a large meadow the way they romped back and forth in the grass. I kept a close eye to see that they didn't run off the edge of the curb and fall in front of passing cars. They continued to romp and play hide-and-seek between the big oak and camphor trees.

The boys were half a block ahead of me when Pierre began to yap, "Oh my, oh my, look what happened to me!"

He had stepped full blast into a healthy pile of fresh dog crap. "Dog-doo, dog-doo, dog-doo!"

The Esplanade neutral ground was a popular place for fey gentlemen to walk their fancy dogs. One had to mind one's step, lest one would, as old timers say, "cut your foot."

Pierre had not only cut his foot, he had slid full-fledged into dog-doo right up to the seat of his pants. Kelvin and Timmy didn't want to go near him. I helped him up, took some fallen magnolia leaves and wiped the dog-crap off the seat of his pants, then pulled off his shoes and scraped them on the edge of the curb. Pierre stood scrunched up, holding his nose.

"Pierre, you stink, you really stink!" the boys chided.

"Boys, that's not fair. Stop it right now!"

Giggling, Timmy and Kelvin hid behind a camphor tree.

All Pierre could say was, "I can't stand myself, Mr. Carr, I just can't stand my smell!"

"We'll be home in a couple of minutes, then we'll get you cleaned off."

As we approached the corner of Esplanade and Bourbon, two dapper gents walking their dogs greeted us. It always amused me that the bigger fellows walked the Chihuahuas and the Shih tzus or "shit-soo," as the kids called them, and the petite guys walked the Wolfhounds and Great Danes. A peculiar sight along Esplanade, but that's the way it was.

We crossed to the banquette in front of the Baptist mission. The boys began dashing up Bourbon toward home like three runaway colts heading for the barn. I shouted ahead, reminding them *not* to go through the front door but to use the side gate.

"I know, daddy, he stinks," Timmy wailed as they ran.

I jogged behind them.

The boys dashed down the side alley into the back. Olympia was setting the table in the patio for us to have dinner *al fresco*, "al-francisco," according to Tammy. The boys ran to Olympia and started jabbering about what had happened, but before she could understand their chatter, she blurted out, "Ah swear ta Gwad, what's makin' that awful smell?"

Timmy and Kelvin were quick to tell her Pierre had dog-doo all over him. Olympia, who never shirked from a duty, ordered, "Pierre, chile, come over here. We gonna get you cleaned off right now."

Pierre resisted.

"Come here, boy!" Olympia commanded. "First, we gonna take them clothes off you. Then you gonna git yoself under that spigot over there, and after that, you goin' upstairs and take yoself a hot shower."

Pierre winced, reluctantly following her instructions. As Olympia pulled Pierre's clothes off, exposing his underwear, she turned to me. "Ah swear to Gawd, Mr. Cahr, ever' time you go out with those boys it's somethin' else, but dis takes da cake!"

"But that's not chocolate, Olympia."

"Ah knows. Ah gotta nose!"

"We had a wonderful time, Lympy," Timothy injected, trying to save me from Olympia's scolding. "I was in the Port Bar. I went in to get my kite and got a Barq's and potato chips, and all the drunks were lookin' at me. It was real excitin'!"

Kelvin added, "Yes, and Timmy's kite got caught by a train that hauled it down the tracks."

"Lord have mercy," Olympia added, shaking her head in disbelief. "Lord have mercy, ah cain't believe it."

Tammy and Kee Chin appeared on the balcony giggling and jeering in a singsong manner, "Uh-oh, Pierre's taking off his clothes."

Pierre immediately escaped Olympia's grasp and ran behind the old cistern. The girls jeered and giggled.

"How come Pierre's takin' off his clothes?"

"Pierre got dog-doo all over hiself. He got big dog-doo *all over*."

Olympia was quick to reprimand, "Timmy, that's no way to talk to those girls. You jist be careful of yo' language, ya hear, boy?"

The girls were laughing so hard that the doll Tammy was holding slipped out of her hand and fell to the patio below, splitting its head into a million pieces, causing Tammy to let out a bloodcurdling scream.

Timmy looked up. "See, Tammy, what happens when you make fun of somebody?"

Reaching over, I jerked Timmy by the arm. "*Timothy*, that's no way to talk to your sister!"

Tammy began crying violently as Kee Chin's eyes glazed with tears. The boys glanced sheepishly at Olympia, who tried to console Tammy from the patio below.

Jan appeared on the balcony trying to figure out what the ruckus was about. Sizing up the problem, she coaxed the girls back into the bedroom and comforted them. Once she quieted the girls, she reappeared to remind me that we must eat dinner soon because we had a seven o'clock French Quarter Parents Club meeting.

Pierre emerged from behind the cistern; Olympia positioned his derriere under the water spigot. He grimaced furiously at the chilly water as she lathered his behind. Rinsing him off, she wrapped him in a towel and the boys disappeared up the back stairs.

Olympia's one last reprimand was for me. "Mistah Cahr, ah swear to Gawd, you got to be more careful of those boys. They gonna get into some big trouble one o' these days."

"Yes, yes, Olympia," I said, giving her the answer she wanted.

Olympia disappeared into the kitchen to see about the dirty-rice casserole for dinner. Going about the business of cleaning up the broken doll's parts, I realized the head was irreparable. It wasn't long before Olympia stuck her head out, instructing me to wash-up for dinner.

I was still slipping into my clothes when I heard Olympia ring the dinner bell. She loved to ring that bell, "it sounds so holy, callin' y'all to one o' Gawd's meals."

We had bought the angelus bell outside the ancient cathedral in Guanajuato, Mexico, from a rather shady-looking peon who swore to us on bended knee, wildly genuflecting, that this cluster of holy bells had not been stolen from the cathedral altar but, he claimed, had been found buried near the church graveyard. We never discovered if they were antique or reproductions, but their tinkling had a magical reverberation, and we all learned to salivate at their sound. Even before Pavlov, Roman Catholic priests had trained their uneducated throngs to eat the Holy Supper after the ringing of the bells, so to what better use could they be put than to summon *our* family to dinner? I had always wanted our dinners to assume an attitude of gratitude and communion. These bells became the perfect tone-setter.

Olympia rang the bells again, more insistently, causing the kids to scamper down the stairs. The two little girls were already sitting at the table as the boys barged out from the back of the house. Scurrying across the patio, Kelvin slipped on something and took a tumble. As the boys settled down, Kelvin reached down to see what he had slipped on. He picked up the eye of the broken doll, and before I could stop him, held it up for all to see. Crying out uncontrollably, Tammy couldn't stop weeping.

Olympia sprang through the French doors. "Timmy, what you doin' yo sister?"

"Olympia, I din't do nothin', I promise, I din't do nothin', really!"

"That's all right, Olympia," Jan interjected. "Tammy'll be quiet in a minute, I'm sure."

Timmy cut in. "Daddy, why din't you pick up that doll's eyes?"

Tammy bellowed even louder.

Kee Chin put her arm around her, but Tammy was inconsolable. Olympia fetched a cool, damp washcloth and placed it gently across Tammy's face, covering her eyes. Seizing his opportunity, Kelvin slipped the doll's eye to me. I slipped it into my pocket. We sat motionless for several minutes until Tammy calmed down.

Olympia comforted Tammy. "Tammy, dahlin', now you gotta calm yourself, honey, 'cause Lympy's dirty-rice's gonna get cold if y'all don't eat it right now."

Jan spoke up. "Now who's going to say grace?"

Tammy pulled the washcloth from her face. "I want Pierre to say grace 'cause my dolly died, and his uncle's a priest and his aunt's a nun. I think he's the most religious person here, so I want him to say grace."

My choice would have been Kee Chin, to see what a Buddhist grace was like, but I was not about to cross my volatile daughter.

Pierre dutifully took on the chore of saying the blessing. He made the sign of the cross, recited the generic Catholic blessing, and ended with a special prayer for Tammy and her dolly who had died today.

Tammy whimpered.

Jan spoke forth, "That was lovely, Pierre."

"Thank you, Pierre," Tammy sniffled, "someday you'll be a nun too, like your uncle."

We all chuckled, Tammy blushed, and everybody laughed. After polishing off dinner, Olympia served some of her fresh homemade pralines. The kids oohed and aahed. Jan and I excused ourselves and told the kids to behave and mind Olympia while we were at the Parents Club meeting.

The love that radiated from Olympia never ceased to touch and amaze us. She was always generous with her affection, but her relationship with our children was exceptional and genuine, as if they were blood kin. When she referred to "her babies," it was with a devotion that transcended friendship. Of course, she knew they were our children, but we had entrusted them to her, so they were "her babies," and no one could break that trust.

We were astonished to think that thousands of white children were being raised by black women while racial turmoil raged around us. Olympia explained it away: "That's jis the way it is, Mistah an' Mizz Cahr." Her sage wisdom was not wasted on us. She was one of the family as well as a mentor.

The Parents Club was being held at the Fabrys'. They had generously offered their house as a meeting place for the fledgling club. Since purchasing and renovating the beautiful Creole townhouse, they had adorned it with outstanding pieces of international art, huge sculptures, and ancient maps. I was delighted because I knew their unusually embellished home would be an attraction to bring out members to aid our growth.

Last month I had unfortunately been elected to serve as the club's first president, a job I didn't particularly relish. Alas, there seems to be something about my aura, uncontrollable by me, which exudes an air of confidence, giving people the feeling I am well-qualified to take charge—even though, in my opinion, I am not. It's a kind of curse I have learned to live with since being elected captain of my kindergarten—an honor, I realized early on, earned not so much from my intellectual aptitude but from some intangible indefinable charisma that has nothing to do with intelligence or ability. In spite of my severe difficulty in learning to read, a burden causing tremendous internal stress, throughout school I was constantly asked, or elected, to preside over one meeting or another, ranging from hall monitor to class president. In the army I was usually chosen platoon leader; on jury duty I am always named as foreman! Whatever club I join, sooner or later I will be elected president even when others, in my opinion, are much more qualified.

The major issue on the agenda was the elevated expressway the Federal Highway Department planned to construct along the riverfront. Most of us felt it would become a bulwark forever separating the Mississippi River from the French Quarter, while looming as a twentieth-century eyesore high above Jackson Square and the French Market. The mayor and many of the city fathers were firmly in favor of its construction as a means of rapidly moving automobile and truck traffic across the Quarter from Elysian Fields to Canal Street. They cared little about the horrendous visual and environmental effect it would have on New Orleans's most hallowed ground lying at the doorstep of Saint Louis Cathedral. We were appalled at the insensitivity of considering building such a monstrosity, which would endanger the Jackson Brewery and the architecturally valuable U.S. Mint, built prior to the Civil War. Realizing the negative impact on the Quarter by such a preposterous move, our members decided to take some sort of overt action.

First, we organized a rally with a spaghetti dinner to raise operating money. Secondly, we decided we would be a protest presence in the Spring Fiesta Parade. Thirdly, we would march on City Hall with our children, complete with posters they would make. We were determined to show Mayor Victor Schiro and the City Council that Quarterites were not in favor of their outrageous plan for an elevated expressway that would have a progressively destructive effect for generations to come.

Fittingly, the spaghetti supper, held at Saint Mary's Italian School, was a rousing success, especially the bingo concession and the booth offering paintings of New Orleans artists, many of whom were anxious to donate toward the "rational preservation" of the Quarter. We were ecstatic at the realization that our efforts had netted enough money to pay the fees required to be in the Spring Fiesta Parade. We could now buy banners and posters and rent a horse whose rider would sport a placard protesting the building of the expressway.

Publicized worldwide, Spring Fiesta was one of the loveliest times in the French Quarter. It was a two-week festival presented annually since 1937 by the Spring Fiesta Association. The non-profit association consisted of a group of volunteer ladies who spent the entire year preparing a variety of "Old South" activities, commencing with a fanciful parade that invited onlookers to hearken back to the days of hoopskirts and horses, gaslights and gardenias, patios and politeness. These bustling Southern damsels also organized home and patio tours in the French Quarter and the Garden District.

Jan and I adore springtime in New Orleans and were thrilled when WDSU, as a public relations gesture, decided to sponsored a carriage—a wonderful opportunity to showcase their "First Family of New Orleans Television." The Spring Fiesta Parade, always held near Easter, culminated at Jackson Square with the crowning of the queen in front of hundreds of locals and tourists, this year including my parents, who had headed south to enjoy the pleasantries of springtime and the Fiesta.

The Parents Club rented a parade horse from Audubon Park stable, with the stipulation that we would provide a qualified equestrian. We had horses on our place in Ohio the entire time I was growing up, but it was impossible for me to ride since the TV station wanted me in the carriage with my family. My father volunteered. He had been riding horses since infancy and never let me forget he rode five miles to school through snow, sleet, and rain—uphill, *both ways!*

The wives of the Parents Club designed his costume. He cut a dashing figure in his white, raglan-sleeved antique shirt, white riding breeches, and black boots, topped off with a large-brimmed planter's hat and a black mask. He was dubbed *Pierre Deau Neaux*, the masked rider and savior of the French Quarter. He carried a placard: "I, Pierre Deau Neaux, *don't know* how long the French Quarter will survive if the 'Feds' build an elevated expressway along Jackson Square!" On the reverse side it read: "S.O.S. Save Our Square!" As Pierre, riding his high-spirited stallion with his protest sign, dad caused enough of a stir to end up on the TV news along with random camera shots of him being toasted with beer by assorted revelers and strippers along Bourbon Street. Dad relished it.

Spring Fiesta is a time when the heroines who have been fighters for historic preservation are recognized for their efforts. The carriages, festooned with garlands of fresh and artificial flowers, transport hoop-skirted ladies of many ages nestled next to their escorts clothed in the finery of the "pre-Wahr" period. The antebellum ladies, swirling their dainty parasols and dispensing rose petals and colorful Czechoslovakian beads from the carriages, are in stark contrast to the strippers and barkers along Bourbon Street.

The juxtaposition of women's comely breasts never ceases to amaze me. The uninhibited strippers, whose boobs dangle fetchingly beneath their chiffon negligees, spill out of the various joints onto the banquette to catch a glimpse of the merriment. In carriages just across the curbstone sit sedate ladies, whose breasts, firmly constricted by whalebone corsets, swell from their *décolleté* nineteenth-century necklines as they jostle merrily along behind their prancing hacks—an entrancing display.

The kids loved the cheering as our carriage approached people who recognized us from TV. "Hey look, there's Bob and Jan from channel 6!" They would applaud, holler niceties, and invariably add, "Hey, Bob and Jan, t'row me somethin'!" We had a ready supply of flowers, trinkets, and beads, which the children enjoyed tossing.

At Jackson Square, passengers disembarked to become part of the assemblage of the Spring Fiesta debutante presentation. Naval cadets escorted the maids, always in white, to the stage; a gentle applause for each couple grew more fervent as the queen reached her throne. Following the crowning ceremony there was dancing for the invited guests, while the spectators left outside the great enclosing iron fence found the streets vibrating with an array of vintage musicians and vocalists serenading from a variety of balconies.

Dad's ride through the Quarter as *Pierre Deau Neaux*, although spectacular for him, did little to change anyone's mind about the impending disaster of the elevated expressway. Consequently, on Sunday afternoon following the festivities, many of the Parents Club members gathered at Rolland Golden's art gallery to paint placards for the children to carry during our Monday march on City Hall. Our slogan, "SOS—Save Our Square," was spelled out in many forms: "Save Our Sacred *Vieux Carré*," "Swordsmen's Order to Save the French Quarter," "Seek Objective Solutions," etc. With the kids painting the posters, the group became a family, and group effort injected a spirit of camaraderie into our Club's protest. The children were piqued with enthusiasm. As concerned parents, we felt driven to protect the architectural integrity and the residential heritage of our beloved Quarter, not only for ourselves, but also for generations to come. Our plan was to have the children clustered in front of new City Hall at noon, precisely when the council chambers adjourned for lunch. We alerted the *States-Item*, the *Times-Picayune*, the radio stations, and the three TV channels to get the full blast of publicity for our cause.

Monday morning, with a couple of station wagons and a Volkswagen van, we made the rounds of the schools, picking up our children for the short trip to City Hall. Parking a block from our destination, we assembled the children, making sure their clothes were straight, hair combed, and signs properly mounted. The image we wanted to project was not one of a rag-tag bunch of hoodlums from "the Quarters" but a group of future community leaders. At approximately eleven thirty, we began our march on City Hall, chanting, "S-O-S, Save Our Square, S-O-S, Save Our Square, S-O-S, Save Our Square!" We marched in cadence past the new public library, across Duncan Plaza in front of the State Supreme Court building, and up to the front steps of City Hall.

The council session broke for lunch, spewing spectators onto the steps, followed by lawyers and, finally, the councilmen themselves. The children and their placards intrigued everyone, but the mayor was nowhere in sight. *He,* our real target, carried a great deal of influence with the highway Feds.

In frustration, we parents huddled to plan our next move. Suddenly, Mayor Schiro strode out of the Chambers and looked scornfully in our direction. He stopped, stood for a moment with hands on his hips, staring disdainfully before announcing that he could not understand how responsible parents could use their children in such an unseemly way.

The mothers approached the mayor to explain the riverfront project would affect *our* children, but also our children's children, the vitality of the French Quarter and the very future of New Orleans *forever.* As the women were trying to make their point with the Mayor, several fathers triggered the children to start chanting once again, "S-O-S, Save Our Square!" The mayor, whose slogan was "If it's good for New Orleans, I'm for it!" failed to comprehend how a hideous expressway across the historic heart of the city could be harmful. The mayor, who always hated any unpleasantness, chose a hasty exit from the chanting children as his best defense. He was heard to say, 'ere he strode out of sight, "I can't believe those misguided beatnik French Quarter parents, keeping their children out of school and exploiting them in such a shameful and boisterous manner!"

"Damn the mayor, he just doesn't get it!" one of the fathers was heard to say as one of the mothers bemoaned, "If only Jimmy Fitzmorris were the mayor or Chep Morrison were still around, we'd have a chance! Schiro lives on a landfill at the lakefront. How could he know the Quarter's the foundation of this inscrutable city?"

In the following months, as a result of our small club's effort, together with many other organizations in the city, it became abundantly clear that an expressway along the French Quarter would never be built. *Hallelujah!* Sadly, Claiborne Avenue was the Feds' final victim, destroying the longest and oldest stand of Live Oak trees in the city, along with the neighborhood.

Following Dad's triumphal ride, he and Mom stayed another week to meet up with their good friends, the rich Frank and Lucy Milburn, who were "veddy, veddy" proper but loved a hearty cocktail. We had received them in the parlor and were in the middle of our first sazeracs when we heard a commotion on Bourbon Street.

Opening the front door, I encountered one of our most famous Quarter characters, Ruthie the Duck Girl, shrieking and scrambling after her pet duck, which had escaped from its leash and was fluttering up our front steps. Stumbling to stand on her ever-present roller-skates, Ruthie hollered unmentionable expletives in her screechy voice. These were broadcast into the front parlor as her duck waddled through the door and between my legs.

Ah ha, unexpected opportunity is knocking! I can give my folks and the Milburns a cocktail party to remember by inviting Ruthie and her duck in for a drink!

Her entrance with her fowl catapulted the gathering into shock. Garbed in her ever-present tacky tutu and tights, she curtsied like a broken down ballerina, declined a sazerac but demanded "a goddamn beeah"! As I walked toward the kitchen, she roared, "When ya git *my* beeah, git one for da duck, too!"

Upon my return, the parlor was in turmoil. Our "guest" duck had pooped on our faux Oriental carpet, and Ruthie was busy wiping it up with the edge of her tutu.

"Jis pour some beeah in da ashtray for Duckie," Ruthie instructed.

I complied as my audience looked on in dismay.

Ruthie's stay was mercifully brief. She grabbed both beer bottles by their necks with one hand, and yanking Duckie by his leash, skated across our parlor and out the front door, cussing like a sailor as she stumbled down the front steps.

Our guests demanded double sazeracs!

Ruth Grace Moulon, a.k.a. Ruthie the Duck Girl, probably ten years younger than I, apparently inherited her quirkiness from her mother, who insisted on dressing Ruthie in sausage curls to make her resemble Shirley Temple. She also dressed her in thrift-shop evening dresses and mounted her on skates so that diminutive but gregarious Ruthie could roll through the Quarter like a star.

A few days after our incident, dear Duckie broke loose from his leash when scrambling for some candy corn tossed in his direction by a tiny tourist. Duckie was promptly flattened into a cutlet by an eighteen-wheeler driving illegally fast on Decatur Street. Rumor has it he was buried in a shoebox near the voodoo queen, Marie Laveau, in St. Louis Cemetery Number One.

Jan is named "Dream Girl of Pi Kappa Alpha," Bob's fraternity at Carnegie Tech, 1951 (Bob in white dinner jacket)

Jan (in the middle) on stage, 1952

Jan, outstanding 4-H member and majorette, representing Belmont County at the Ohio State Fair, 1947

Jan, Bob and his mother, Harriette Antoinette Carr and children dressed for Spring Fiesta, 1961

Timmy at City Hall with placard, 1965

Pierre, Mark, Timmy (square misspelled) and Rennie at City Hall demonstration, 1965

CHAPTER EIGHT

A Swimming Pool Baptism in "Sin Town"

It was mid-May and already "hotter than the hub of Hades," as my father used to say—one of those 90-90 days that occur so often in New Orleans summers, but a bit early, foretelling the heat and humidity that lay ahead. A swimming pool in the patio, I concluded, was what we needed to get us through the summer broil. Two major hindrances lay in my way: the patio wasn't really large enough for a full-fledged swimming pool, nor did we have enough money banked away to build one. So I decided to dig a small one myself, just big enough for all of us to wallow in—more of a wading pool.

Hacking my way down through old brick and flagstone, I was suddenly confronted with solid concrete. Historian Harnett Kane told me it had probably been put there while immigrant Italians owned the property, "because they concreted over everything in the 1930s!" What was to have been a weekend project in May dragged on until the middle of June. I had to put my diggings into shopping bags so the trash men would pick them up when they came by for the household garbage. As a tourist area, the Quarter had daily collection. There was no other way to discard the old pieces of stone, rock, and dirt from my excavation. I was now aware, first hand, how people must have suffered digging their escape under the Berlin Wall. Fortunately, I only wanted to help my family escape the *heat*. All the time I was digging and sweating, I kept wondering to myself: *How am I going to empty the pool without investing in some kind of expensive sump pump?* It occurred to me I could siphon it up and out, but the excavation was getting so deep I was afraid it wouldn't work. As I dug I kept running into the side of an old foundation. This caused me to keep readjusting the center of my pool farther and farther away from my original plan.

Feeling like some kind of nut, I kept digging, digging, and digging, obsessed with getting cool water into my pool to quench the steamy sweat trickling and tickling down my back and to quell constant badgering by the children and friends. Arriving home from the station, I would dig and dig every evening. I kept exhuming old bricks, which seemed to run in a circular pattern. Reaching my planned depth, I became obsessed: *How am I going to empty the water?* At the depth of three-and-half feet, I took my heavy pickaxe and gave the foundation a tremendous blow. Lo and behold, I knocked a brick lose; it fell downward into a great hole far below.

The hole was large enough for me to push my fist through. Timidly, I pushed my arm into the breach, any second expecting some prehistoric reptile covered with horny scales to reach up, grab my arm, and pull me kicking and screaming down into the bowels of the earth. Regaining my composure, I realized I had run into an old cistern or well. Ah ha! Providence had led me to my drain! This was my chance to empty the pool. I ran a hose into the hole, letting water run into it for an entire day to see if it would back up into my pool. It did not! All the water disappeared into some great subterranean leech-field, I assumed, eventually finding its way to the muddy Mississippi seven blocks away.

My hole dug, the next step was to apply cement to the sides of the pool and put in a spigot for a drain. I had rented a pickup truck to haul my cement, but, alas, it was too large to pull into the carriageway, so I parked on Bourbon Street. When I arrived home late Saturday afternoon, there were no parking places available in our block, so I stashed the truck about three blocks away in the tourist bar section. The children and I worked all Saturday afternoon preparing my hard-won gaping cavity for its cement coating. It was nearly 9:30 P.M. when I needed to retrieve the cement. Due to the heat I had been working all day in my bikini. Without a second thought, and since it was *my* neighborhood, I decided to take the kids' little red wagon and walk the three blocks up Bourbon to the truck. Only one fifty-pound bag of cement would fit into the wagon at a time, so I walked back and forth in my bathing suit, dragging my little red wagon and my bags of cement through the dimly-lit streets.

Numerous tourists stepped off the banquette to let me pass, probably wondering what kind of a sweaty kook I must be. I was also cruised by several fellahs from a gay bar who gave me the eye, then figured I looked a little too kinky to get involved with. Truth be known, I have always gotten a kick out of being perceived as "different," certainly out of the ordinary. Pushing these distractions aside, I kept dragging cement back to our patio. The children were so excited about getting the pool finished that Timmy kept busy with a little hoe, stirring the cement mix in a washtub. Tammy assisted by adding water, while Tom, too young to help, became disgruntled and placed his blanket under the banana trees and elephant ears, finally falling asleep about ten o'clock.

Coming out to check our progress, Jan announced, "It's getting awfully late. Aren't all y'all exhausted?"

"Dawling, you're beginning to sound like a native New Orleanian with that 'all y'all'!"

"You know I've always parroted local vernacular."

"True. Anyway, I'm going to have to work into the night to get this cement finished, otherwise it's going to dry and crack."

"An' we all're gonna help daddy."

The three of us continued into the night. Before going to bed, Jan spread some blankets and pillows down in the patio in case we got tired. She whispered to me, "Watch out for the roaches!" She tried to take Tom into the house, but he insisted, in his drowsiness, on staying put. Tired, one after another, the kids stretched out on the blankets. I worked till four in the morning finishing the skim coat. I stretched out for "a minute's rest." The next thing I knew, it was dawn!

I got up quietly and rubbed my hand gently around the side of the pool. The cement was already beginning to harden. I knew the pool should be filled with water before the cement got too hard so that it wouldn't crack. I closed the drain leading into the old hidden cistern and began filling the pool. Still sleepy, I once again stretched out on the blanket for a catnap and fell sound asleep.

When I was a kid I wet the bed. Sometimes I would wake up in the morning thinking I was floating in water. Dazed, I was having the same sensation! I stretched out my hands and realized the patio was full of water. As I awoke, so did the kids!

"What's happening…what's happening?" they screeched.

"Look, kids!" I pointed toward the pool.

The hose had filled the entire pool to overflowing, causing a flood in the patio, soaking us and our blankets and causing roaches to scramble for safety. Enthralled, the kids sprang up in the bright light of Sunday morning, tore off their damp clothes, and plunged into the pool bare "nooda"!

Our little round pond, only three-and-a-half feet deep and eight feet across, gave us the joy of an Olympic-size pool.

* * * * *

Attempting to further our relationship with God, Jan and Bill Romaine had started attending a series of prayer meetings in Lakeview. Bill Brown, a dynamic young Presbyterian minister, was leading the sessions. Jan had been raised Presbyterian in Ohio and felt very comfortable both at Bill's church services and prayer meetings. They had gotten Ann and me to go with them to the meetings, but we found the services rather like Presbyterian Punch—bland! The husband of one of the young couples who regularly attended the prayer meetings was a student at the Baptist Theological Seminary in Gentilly. Wayne and Mary Margaret had spoken of a desire to live in the French Quarter because he felt it was fruitful ground for some of his training. We mentioned an historic and picturesque maisonette just over our wall that was about to become available. After one look they signed the lease and became our neighbors.

A couple of months after moving in, they stopped by with some freshly-baked cookies as a gift of thanks. They also had a rather unusual request. Over glasses of mint iced tea, Wayne explained, "As a graduate student at the seminary I'm authorized to perform baptisms. I've been counseling a young alcoholic who has found the Lord and wants to be baptized. I'd consider it a great favor if we could use your little swimming pool for the occasion."

I was astonished. "Sure, why not? Sounds wonderful."

"Are you allowed to do it in a swimming pool?" Jan asked.

"Honey, our swimming pool is a helluva lot cleaner than the Jordan River!"

"Bob, *really!*"

Acknowledging my little joke, Wayne continued. "In looking for a small body of water that could be used for a total immersion baptism, I thought your pool would be just perfect, if you're amenable to the idea."

"I think it's a great idea."

"Can the children come?" Jan inquired.

"Absolutely, the children are invited, also any of your friends who might be interested. We'd like to have the baptism as a part of the regular prayer meeting."

"No problem with us, is there, honey?"

"No, I think it'll be exciting. We'll have plenty of tea and goodies from McKenzie's Bakery."

'Twas settled! The baptism was scheduled for early Sunday evening, two weeks hence.

Some members of our prayer group who wanted to come to the Baptism had ventured timidly into the French Quarter only a few times. One couple was particularly dubious about coming into "the Quarters" at all. I explained to them that if they drove their Volkswagen Beetle instead of their Cadillac, we could fit them into our carriageway. We'd watch for them and be ready to open the gate so they could drive right in.

I found it astounding that coming to the French Quarter was such a daring adventure for some New Orleanians. A few were probably coming to see under what conditions we lived and were rearing our children.

With help from the kids, we spent our Sunday afternoon cleaning the patio and changing the water in the pool so that all would be pristine for our religious guests. Jan brewed buckets of tea. Dusk had just begun to set in when I heard what I thought were our first guests arriving. Approaching the front door I could see a flashing light casting dancing shadows on the front parlor walls; a squad car had pulled up on our banquette. I opened the front door and stepped into the vestibule.

"Y'all get your goddamn hands up!" a man's voice ordered. "Don't move and keep your hands up!"

I stopped dead in my tracks until I realized I wasn't his target; I edged my head around the corner of the vestibule to look across the front of the house. Two policemen, with pistols drawn, had subdued a pair of suspects who were sprawled like stunned toads against the front wall of our house. Before I had a chance to even consider what the two men might have done, I heard the distinctive toot of a Beetle approaching along Bourbon Street.

I don't believe this! Here come our religious friends, scared as hell to drive into the Quarter, and now at this very moment our driveway is obstructed by the police apprehending a couple of guys. God, are you testing me?

Stepping hurriedly into the street, I intercepted their automobile, directing them to pull up on the banquette behind the squad car.

The husband rolled down his window ever so slightly, their faces cadaver gray.

"Just leave your car right here," I instructed. "Get out and come into the house."

"Leave my car right *here?*"

"Yes, just leave your car right here. I'll pull it in once the police car is gone."

"What's going on?" he asked nervously.

"Oh, some little altercation. These things happen along Bourbon Street."

"Maurice, I am *not* getting out of this car."

"Come on, Evvy, trust in the Lord," I said, being a bit obnoxious. "Get out of your car and come on into the house before any guns go off!"

Evvy balked.

"For Christ's sake, Evvy, get out of this goddamn car!" Maurice blurted. "You don't wanna be shot in the Quarters!"

Following an endless few seconds, they exploded from their bug and burst through our front door like a passel of Catholics late for a bingo game. Moments later, siren blaring, the police pulled away with the two criminals securely handcuffed in the back seat. I grasped my chance to move the Volkswagen into our carriageway. By the time I entered the house, Maurice and Evvy were feverishly telling Jan how they could not believe we exposed our children to such peril. Jan was making apologies and trying to explain.

I interrupted, "How else will the children know the *evil* that lurks in the world if they can't see it first hand?"

They looked at me as if questioning my sanity and my religious beliefs; but I was taking delight in expanding their consciousness of another side of life. However, before any of us had a chance to do much soul-searching, the baptismal candidate, along with the rest of the prayer group, arrived. As the visitors passed down our long hallway, impressed by the architectural proportions, several asked the perennial question "Golly, how high are these ceilings?"

After our pat answer, "One foot higher than a twelve-foot sheetrock," Jan and I spirited the last of our gawking guests back into the patio. The musically-inclined had already begun to sing, to the accompaniment of a guitar and flute, some good old Baptist hymns, including one of the children's favorites, "Do Lord, oh, do Lord, oh, do you remember me?"

The baptismal ceremony began. During his brief sermon, Wayne pointed out "We are all afforded here, a wonderful opportunity to be present at a holy baptism held in the very heart of a city famous for sin and degradation. Deep in the very bowels of evil, one can find joy and renewal of life; rebirth through Jesus Christ, our Lord and Savior."

Jan became teary, realizing we were raising our children in what some considered the cesspool of the world. Her tears soon subsided as we watched the young preacher remove his shoes and ease himself, fully clothed, down into the kid's pool. The young repentant alcoholic was helped down into the pool by the preacher, and the baptism took place in the name of the Father and the Son and the Holy Ghost.

As the bewildered penitent arose from the water, his now transparent white acetate trousers, sticking to his body like glue, revealed his generous manliness. The entire group cried out spontaneously, "Hallelujah! Praise the Lord!"

What, exactly, were they praising? I mused.

All began to sing, "Hallelujah, Hallelujah, Hallelujah, Hallelujah…"

The reverberation of our singing incited a cry from over the back wall, "Hey, what the hell's all that noise. What kinda shit's goin' on over there?"

"A baptism and a church service," I hollered. "We won't be much longer. Come on over and be *saved*."

The voice from over the wall was mute.

Following more good, old-fashioned spirituals and a fellowship period with Jan's tea and refreshments, the event broke up around ten o'clock. I helped the

Beetle people get themselves safely locked in their car before they ventured out onto Bourbon Street. Ere they drove out of sight, they were still mumbling, "Can't believe they're raising children in such a wretched environment!"

Jan and I were sorry we had sent the kids out for the night, for what we had speculated would be a revivalistic lark had instead been a truly exhilarating spiritual experience. Lying in bed, we discussed the impact each of us had felt from the evening. In spite of the funniness with the Volkswagen, the squad car, and the wet pants, a new spirit now pervaded our house and the patio. We felt God had in some metaphysical way focused on our little group, touching down for a brief moment to intercede in our lives and change them forever. It was time, we agreed, to make a decision on which church we wanted to settle into and how best to direct the children's religious education.

After hours of discussion, visits to many churches, and days of cogitation, we decided to go with my childhood denomination, the Episcopal Church. Our decision was solidified when our beloved friend, Bill Brown, resigned from the Canal Street Presbyterian Church to seek a new and closer relationship with his Lord. His leaving left the church adrift, whereas in the Episcopal Church, when a priest departs, the liturgy and the Eucharist hold the church and the congregation stable until another clergyman takes over. And so it was, as a family, we were Confirmed into the Episcopal Church, St. Anna's on Esplanade Avenue. Jan volunteered for altar guild, I joined the Sunday school staff, Timothy became an acolyte, and Tammy and Tom sat in the congregation and watched us perform our duties. St. Anna's was a place where we enjoyed the congregation, felt close as a family, and near God.

Many of our Parents Club friends didn't go to church, but for reasons only they or God knew, felt their children should. Consequently, each Sunday morning, I would back our little red Triumph out of the carriageway and set out to pick up church-bound youngsters. They loved riding with the top down, allowing me to pack more kids into the minuscule back seat. We became a familiar Sunday morning sight, criss-crossing the Quarter collecting a half dozen kids, singing that good old Baptist hymn *Do Lord*, or from the Episcopal hymnal, *Let There Be Peace on Earth*.

One of the children on my route was Rennie, the son of our friends Terry and Lenny Flettrich. Idolizing Timothy, two years his senior and an acolyte, Rennie loved the adventure of being taken to church and longed to become an altar boy himself. After all, he had been going to church for six or seven months with us and in the Christmas pageant had played Joseph to Tammy's Holy Mary, so becoming an acolyte seemed like moving one step closer to heaven. Rennie asked me what he would have to do to become an acolyte. I suggested he talk it over with the priest.

Father Crisler explained, "Rennie, you'll find all through life, there are things you'll want to do for which you must prepare. Being an acolyte is one of those things. Serving at God's altar is a serious job. Do you understand that?"

"Yes, Father, I do. What do I have to do to get ready, so I can be up there with Timmy Carr in those robes on Sunday?"

"Wait a minute, young man, not so fast. First, you must become a member of the church."

"But Father, sir, I've been coming here for a long time now. I thought I *was* a member!"

"You're not a member until you've been Confirmed."

"How do I do that, Father?"

"The Bishop is coming next month to perform his regular rounds of Confirmation. If you come to my catechism classes every Saturday, I think you can be ready by then."

Rennie studied diligently, cramming several months of catechism into four long sessions. On the Saturday prior to Confirmation, Rennie was asked to bring his baptismal papers and any other church information his mother could supply. Rennie arrived for his last class with no papers and the explanation that his mother was Jewish but didn't practice her religion, and his father was Catholic but hadn't been to church in twenty years and, as far as they knew, hadn't been baptized. Rennie was on the verge of tears.

Realizing it was not kosher to Confirm an unbaptized soul, the priest formulated a game plan. "Rennie, tomorrow morning, at the seven-thirty service, I'll baptize you. Then at the ten-thirty service, the Bishop will Confirm you! Please make sure your mother and father are both here. Also, I would like you to choose a godparent."

Rennie selected Timmy, his good friend.

When Rennie explained the activities for the next day to his parents, his father admonished jokingly, "Goddamn, Rennie, I don't know if I can take that much church in one day. I'm gonna feel like a religious fanatic!"

Rennie agonized as he continued to plead.

The next day, with his father, mother, and godfather at his side, Rennie became a baptized Christian at 7:30 A.M. and a confirmed Episcopalian at 10:30 A.M. And Timmy became probably the youngest godfather in the environs of the Louisiana Purchase!

* * * * *

Armed with the stuffed artichokes Olympia had prepared, we bid good-bye late one afternoon to the kids and Olympia and set off for a French Quarter Parents Club meeting at Frank and Teddy Sciacca's. We loved the Parents Club potluck dinners, with their wide array of food, everything from crawfish pie to country corn pudding.

Frank and Teddy, two genuinely sweet people, were extremely gracious hosts. Frank was taking drink orders and assisting at the bar, while Teddy, who usually reigned in the kitchen, was sitting out in the back patio reading palms. Jan and I were intrigued by the things she said as she scrutinized the lines in our hands. She told Jan there'd be another child in the future. She saw us with four. Jan's lifeline was long and healthy, and faithfulness to one man was assured.

I reached out my arm anxiously. She took my hand and massaged it, holding it with her fingers while running her thumb firmly over my palm.

"Wow!" she exclaimed.

"What do you mean, 'Wow'?"

She grasped the area of my hand at the base the thumb. "Feel that?" she said, rolling the muscle between her thumb and forefinger. "How fleshy, and full! That means you're sensuous with a strong sex drive."

All those around us giggled.

Jan affirmed, "Well, Teddy, so far you're on the right track. What do the other lines mean?"

"This is your life line. Look at that, it goes way up into your fingers. That means you have a long life. This is the really interesting line, this is your career line; see how it goes up to a certain point and then stops? But this line begins and runs parallel, then continues on alone, indicating you will have a second career outlasting your current vocation, humm?"

"What do you mean, humm?"

"Look here, your career line stops a second time, takes a turn and it looks like you have a third career."

"What kind of a career?"

"I have no idea. This first line right here must be broadcasting but it runs up here, then it fades and another career line starts before this one finishes and then, look here, it takes another turn, so there must be a third career."

Everyone was in a merry mood, having cocktails; Susie Cangelosi brought two casserole dishes meant to be appetizers, glacé of hogshead cheese and Cajun blood sausage. The native New Orleanians dove into the hogshead cheese with a vengeance; however, those still acquiring new tastes were a little slow on the uptake. Of the many times I've asked what goes into hogshead cheese, nobody ever gave me a straight answer, so I gave up asking. The name was graphic enough.

Eating blood sausage near Halloween seemed to be a witchy thing to do. Somebody suggested that eating blood was gross. Somebody else kidded, "Heck, Catholics do it all the time."

"What do you mean Catholics do it all the time?"

"Isn't it true Catholics believe wine is the blood of God?"

"I don't think it's really the blood of God!"

"Well, that's what I'm told Catholics believe."

A rather heated religious discussion ensued about transubstantiation.

"How can you really believe that wine turns into blood?"

"Because a miracle takes place on the altar at the time of consecration, and wine actually becomes the blood of Jesus Christ."

"Now that's impossible for me to believe."

"You believe what you want, and I'll believe what I want. That's what I've been taught at catechism and that's what I believe. Case closed!"

"Can't you see that wine or grape juice only represent the blood of Jesus, it isn't actually the blood? It doesn't have to be; it's still a valid symbol."

"I told you. You believe what *you* believe and I'll believe what I believe. I'm a Catholic and we believe wine turns into the blood of Jesus Christ when it's consecrated. Although we Catholics don't read the Bible too often, I know Jesus said, 'This is my body and this is my blood. Eat it and drink it!' Seems like that should be pretty clear, even to you literal-minded Protestants."

"But Jesus meant the wine and the bread was a symbol of his body and blood."

"I thought you fundamentalists believed every word in the Bible was true; if Jesus said, 'This is my body and my blood,' I don't know why you start paraphrasing when what he actually said in the scriptures was, 'Drink this, this is my blood. Eat this, this is my body.' In fact, why you substitute grape juice instead of using wine is amazing to me. After all, it says in the Bible that Jesus drank wine. He even turned water into wine at a wedding feast so everyone could celebrate!"

"We use grape juice because some people have a problem with alcoholic beverages. I must say, we use real bread instead of those flattened-down fish food wafers you use!"

"Hey, you guys," I interrupted. "Why don't you all come over to the Episcopal Church with me and then you can do whatever you damn well please?"

Frank rang the dinner bell, which acted as a referee's gong but actually announced dinner was ready. "Teddy told me to get everyone around the table for the blessing. Her spaghetti is hot and won't wait!"

We all held hands in a circle and bowed our heads.

After a dinner including sundry salads and stuffed artichokes, stuffed mirlitons, stuffed bell peppers, and stuffed manicotti, we finished by stuffing ourselves with assorted petit fours, chocolate-covered turtles, and a variety of cookies from Brocato's and McKenzie's. A heated discussion concerning our success in squelching the ill-conceived riverfront expressway followed dessert and chicory coffee. Another destructive force that seemed to be assaulting the French Quarter, was the use of drugs by beatniks strolling the streets and intimidating pedestrians.

Jan and I excused ourselves a little earlier than the rest; it had been a long day at the "broadcasting factory." We wanted to get home. When you walk through its streets in the late evening, the Quarter can take on many different attitudes, depending on the people, the lights, the traffic, or the weather. Sometimes it's peaceful and calm—the history of the buildings seems to ooze onto the banquettes. Often at this time of the year, it's slightly foggy and overcast, somewhat mysterious. Tonight there seemed to be an edge, exuding a sinister feeling as we walked through the streets. Automobiles sped down the street at a faster pace, and the clatter of pedestrian feet echoed off the plaster walls with a crisper sound. Jan grabbed my arm and held on tight as we hustled along the street to our own front door. After driving Olympia home, I checked the downstairs, then joined Jan in the bedroom. We undressed and snuggled into bed.

"I love being here."

"What do you mean?" I asked.

"I love being here in bed next to you. I feel safe and comfortable. The streets seemed kind of spooky tonight; don't you think?"

"Hmm."

"I got the feeling we were moving through the night with the Lord watching over us. I was glad we got home safely and I'm so happy we're here in bed together."

"Hmm," I remarked, sounding distant.

"What are you thinking about?"

"I was thinking about God, too."

"What about God?"

"Just thinking about the conversation this evening and how complicated people make God. Everyone wants God to fit into his or her little framework of ideas. I think God is bigger than that. People try to make him too small. When everyone was talking about religion, I got thinking how everybody seemed so anxious to sell their own beliefs that they didn't hear anybody else's thoughts. How can you learn anything if you don't listen, at least occasionally? The more people preach about what *they* believe, the less they're open to what other people believe. They won't listen to arguments about whether wine is real blood or whether it's just grape juice. Drives me nuts! Does it really make any difference?"

"No, I guess not."

"The most important thing to remember—we should all be concerned about one another, be accepting, and love each other. Who does that sound like, Jesus? The main reason we're bringing up the children in the French Quarter is that it's a hub of activity, a variety of cultures, a slice of humanity, and an opportunity to intermingle with an assortment of philosophies. There seems to be something religious in that, something about God's great composite of mankind living together peacefully and in understanding. Honey, have I put you to sleep?"

"No," she responded faintly.

"Why are you so quiet?"

"I'm quiet because what you're saying touches me so I've got tears in my eyes. When you talk that way, it makes me feel close to you."

I slipped my weary arm under her and pulled her close. A rush came over me; I felt weary and limp no longer. I held her tightly and she slipped her arms around me. How right and holy it seemed to be holding onto each other, holding onto life itself. It was the first time we really understood that making real love together between husband and wife is very much a religious experience: perhaps a sacrament, a manifestation, a physical acting-out of the marriage vows of "what God has joined together." We fell asleep entwined in a state of blissful grace.

* * * * *

The majestic old banister of our stairway climbed steadily three stories up, looking as if it were a single timber unwinding from one highly-ornamental newel in the entrance hall to a rather plain but handsome post on the third floor. Off the third floor hallway was an enormous room in the center of the house containing two large windows opening onto a small balcony clinging precariously to the side of the house. The view from that balcony was breathtaking, overlooking the Paris-like roofs of the Quarter with a glimpse of the central business district. View aside, Jan was terrified the kids might fall off, so to assuage her fear, I nailed the two huge double-hung windows solidly closed. Under the eaves on either side of the center room was an area we used for storage. Each of the storage rooms had dormer windows facing the front and the back of the house. The kids loved the big room when the weather was mild. Someday, when we had the money, we would make it into a huge family room for the kids, or perhaps a ballroom. At this point, however, it was cluttered with a lot of cardboard boxes left over from our move. When the temperature was mild the kids often ate and slept in the attic, enjoying cardboard houses fashioned from the moving boxes.

On this particular April afternoon, with the windows locked and no airflow, the room was stifling. I pushed the kid's boxes aside so I could use the area to lay out fabric for the ten-foot draperies to be used in our front parlor. Using my talent for design, I was cutting the draperies out of fabric I had obtained years before. Bob

Carrow, a college friend and our best man, and I had worked in Summer Stock—Summer Stock theatres operated over the northeast but are mostly gone now—in New England. The season had been marginally successful, so the theatre manager offered us props and fixtures as bonus for our labors. I was in a quandary: *What should I take?* Bob, who had an eye for value, suggested I take a bolt of fabric, as it was authentic India hand-blocked print and very valuable. Now, ten years later, I was slicing into it to create what would be a sensational window treatment.

For some time, l had been leaning over on my hands and knees in the overheated airless room. Feeling faint, I was glad when the kids hollered up the stairwell announcing dinner. Descending, still dizzy from the heat, I grasped the handrail; a rush of cooler air revived me.

Because we were having an epidemic of mosquitoes, Jan had decided to eat indoors. The dining room had from the beginning been one of our favorite rooms in the house. We were able to look beyond the cracked ceiling, scratched floors, and the magnificent but severely tarnished chandelier to the beautiful millwork, indoor shutters, and crown molding. I had stripped the ancient discolored paper off the walls in preparation for the paperhanger. In this condition, augmented by twilight, the room always looked slightly sinister.

Olympia had the evening off to attend to church affairs, so Tammy was helping Roxanne, the babysitter, set the table. Jan dished out the crawfish etouffee, while Timmy helped me light the candles. We always enjoyed eating by candlelight; it helped to make dinner an event, something that seemed to harken back to the Seder suppers of Israel. After all the time, money, energy, and God's good graces that go into preparing a meal, why not make it something special, rather than something just to be gobbled down?

Roxanne Robicheaux, a beautiful sixteen-year-old who loved to babysit, had the startling good looks that bring to mind the lyrics "Creole babies with flashing eyes." Actually, she was of Italian-French extraction and attended parochial school in Gentilly, where she lived. Sometimes I thought she seemed a little bit too timid or shy to control the children, especially Timothy, who was beginning to feel his oats.

Roxanne thoroughly enjoyed coming to our house, so whenever Olympia had other plans, we could always count on her. One of the greatest advantages with Roxanne was that she didn't mind staying overnight and would accept nothing extra for what appeared to be an inconvenience. In fact, she was always very enthusiastic about spending the night. If it were a school day, she would get up early in the morning to catch the Desire bus to Elysian Fields, where she transferred to the Gentilly Boulevard line.

Jan came in from the kitchen; we gathered around the table and sat down in the candlelit room.

"Who wants to say the blessing tonight?"

Tammy butted in briskly, "Mommy, you told me I could say the blessing tonight."

"Oh, that's right, honey, I forgot."

Looking the part of a mini-madonna, Tammy crossed herself ceremoniously and then reached out her arms to either side, inviting us to clasp hands in prayer.

"God is great, God is good an' we thank 'im for our food, 'specially for the French bread, cause I like it much better than that crawfish stuff we have to eat. An' a special prayer for Gamma, Granpa, and Grandaddy and Nana and Jandad and Miss Edna and Miss Landry and—"

"Tammy, just a minute," Jan interrupted politely.

"And Carrie and Sandy and—"

"Tammy, hold it," I insisted, "there's not time enough to pray for everybody right now."

"And Olympia. All-men."

"Thank you," Jan encouraged, "that was very nice."

Sometimes at dinner, the chatter would ramble on aimlessly about the day's events; however, there were also times when we would pick a specific topic to discuss so as to turn our conversation into a learning experience. I was about to ask for such a conversation topic when a mild draft fluttered across the room, causing shadows from the flickering candles to dance ominously.

Timothy, playing ghost, uttered, "Ooooh, ooooh."

Tammy and Tom's eyes widened.

"What're you tryin' to do, scare us?"

"Yah!" Timmy replied. "Daddy, I have a good idea. Let's all tell something scary that happened to us."

"What do you mean?"

"Let's tell the scariest thing that ever happen to us in our whole lives."

"Okay. Why don't you go first?"

"No, daddy, that's no fun. I want somebody else to start. Mommy, you start."

"Bob, I don't think this is such a good idea. The kids are going to get scared and they'll never get to sleep tonight."

"Come on Jan, it sounds like fun. We don't have to tell a scary story, we just tell something scary that happened to us. Then, we should tell something *good* we learned from our experience, okay?"

"I guess, if we do that."

"Come on, mommy," Timmy prodded. "Tell something really scary that happened to you once."

"Oooh, let me see, when I was a little girl about ten years old, living at my grandmother's house, we were all sitting at dinner just like this when we heard an airplane. It came closer, and closer and *closer!* It sounded so close we jumped up and ran to the window."

"Could you see it, could you see it?" Tom pleaded.

"Yes, we saw the airplane, all right. And it got lower, and lower, then *crash!*"

Tom had his head scrunched down into his shoulders.

"It dove right into our barn and *boom*, it exploded!"

Tom slid down under the tray of his highchair.

"What happened *then?*" Timmy asked.

"The barn caught fire. I was so scared I started to cry, and my sister started to wail hysterically. My daddy and grandpa ran out to see if they could save the pilot."

"What happened to the passengers?"

"The plane was small. It only had a pilot."

"Was he dead?" Tammy asked, her eyes beginning to tear.

"We watched and watched. Suddenly daddy and grandpa came out of the barn dragging the unconscious pilot."

"Does unconscious mean dead, mommy?"

"No, honey, just knocked out. Daddy drove the pilot to the hospital. When the Colerain Volunteer Fire Department arrived, they put hoses down into our cistern. Before long the fire was out."

"Did you stop crying, mommy?"

"Yes, I guess I did, but my sister, your Aunt Carole, was so frightened she refused to sleep upstairs in our bedroom for three months for fear an airplane would come through the roof."

"Gee, mommy, that wasn't a very scary story," Timmy sighed. "What was your scariest story, daddy?"

"Just a minute. Mother, what did you learn from your experience?"

"I learned it's important to help people who are in trouble."

Tom interrupted, "I wanna tell *my* scariest story next, please, oh *please*. My scariest!"

We were always amazed at Tom's ability to speak. Never speaking baby-talk, he launched into full sentences as a toddler.

"Okay, sweetie," Jan replied, "what's your most scary story?"

"It's when you locked me in the bathroom on the Natchez Steamboat and I couldn't get out and Timmy had to climb through the porthole to get me."

"Honey, we didn't lock you in. We didn't *know* you were in the bathroom. You locked *yourself in accidentally*."

"Anyway, that was the most scariest thing that ever happened to me in my whole life an' Timmy almost fell off the boat into the Mississippi. I don't never want that to happen to me anymore."

"We'll make sure it doesn't," Jan comforted.

"But, Tom, what did you learn?" I asked.

"Not to pee-pee on a boat!"

We all laughed.

"Daddy, daddy, what's your scariest story?" Tim insisted.

"Just a minute, maybe Tammy or Roxanne want to tell their scary story next."

"No, no, Mr. Carr," Roxanne beseeched. "I don't have anything to say."

"Tammy, what's your scary story?" I asked.

"The time we had a huge almost hurricane storm and the house shook and daddy wasn't home. We all crawled under the bed and Timmy called me a scaredy-cat 'cause I cried. That was my mostest scary time."

"You're right," Jan affirmed. "That was a scary time."

"So, what did you learn, honey?"

"To be brave, daddy, even if somebody calls me a scaredy-cat."

Jan gave her a hug.

"Roxanne, are you ready?"

"No, sir, I'd rather not."

"Okay, then, I'll tell *my* scary story and then we'll give you a chance to tell yours."

"Mr. Carr, I really don't have any scary story."

Jan broke in, "Bob, why don't you leave the poor girl alone?"

"Okay, all right, I'll tell my scariest story. Mine happened shortly after I joined the army and was shipped off to Camp Polk, Louisiana, for basic training, where you learn to march, peel lots of potatoes and, most importantly, how to fire a rifle!"

Timmy interrupted, "Daddy, you mean you went to the army an' you din't even know how to shoot a gun?"

"That's right, I never wanted to kill anything, so your grandfather never took me bear-hunting with him in Canada. So, I never fired a rifle."

Tom piped up, "You never killed anybody dead, did you, daddy?"

"No, I was in the army right at the end of World War II, the shooting had mostly stopped."

The boys looked disappointed.

"After the war we had to stand guard to make *sure* people stopped killing each other; but, let me get back to my story. Since the war was just over, the army was closing down many of its training grounds. Just after I arrived, Camp Polk was ordered closed. Before they ever got a chance to teach us how to fire a rifle, we were sent overseas to Italy on a troopship."

Tom interrupted again, "Did you get locked in the bathroom like me, and have to crawl through a porthole?"

"No, Tom, but I got seasick. Now, let me finish my story. We got to Italy but the colonel in Italy didn't know that most of us had never fired a weapon."

"What's a weapon?" Tammy asked.

"A gun, silly," Tim rebuked.

"Yes and no. A weapon can be any instrument used for fighting. A gun in the army refers to cannons or machine guns; but soldiers carried M-1 rifles as their weapons. *But*, the colonel, not knowing that our group had *never* fired a weapon, stationed us out on the border to guard Italy against Yugoslavia. An army truck dropped each of us separately along a dark desolate road. Some of us didn't even know how to put the ammunition clip into our rifles. I stood there alone in the December freezing cold, for about an hour and a half, lonely, shivering and homesick. The barbed wire glistened ominously in the moonlight and there were all kinds of spooky unidentifiable noises. It was really scary. Then, all of a sudden I saw *headlights!* It was a Jeep."

"Who was in it? Who was it, daddy?" Timmy screeched.

"It was the colonel and the sergeant of the guard. They drove up to me hollering, '*Don't shoot. Don't shoot'!*"

"Why did they say that? Did you shoot, daddy?"

"No! They'd found out we didn't know anything about firing our rifles."

"What'd they do?"

"They took my ammunition."

"You mean your bullets?"

"That's right, they wanted my bullets."

"Why'd they want your bullets?" Tammy whispered.

"Because they were afraid I would shoot somebody by mistake. So, they took my bullets and off they went."

"But, daddy, you were a *guard*, and you didn't have any am...am...nu... ammunition?" Tom sputtered.

"That's right."

"Daddy," Timmy asked, "what did they tell you to do if the enemy attacked?"

"As they drove away, the sergeant hollered, 'Hey, private, if anybody attacks, hit 'em with the butt of your rifle!'"

Tammy and Tom snickered at the word butt.

"You mean the 'rear-end' of your rifle?" Timmy smirked.

"That's right, hit 'em with the rear-end of your rifle."

"Did anybody attack?"

"The only thing that attacked me was the jitters." Whispering, I added, "I was so scared, I almost pooped my pants!"

They broke out in laughter.

"And that was *my* scariest time."

"I'm gonna tell my G.I. Joe *that* story," Timmy said.

"All I can say is, you better teach your G.I. Joe doll how to shoot his rifle."

"I already done that in my fort under the house."

"But, daddy, what did you learn?" Tammy questioned.

"Be prepared!"

"Okay, Roxanne," Timmy said, "time for you to tell *your* scariest story."

"I don't have any," Roxanne replied reluctantly, hoping to avoid the issue.

"Oh, come on," I insisted. "Certainly you must have had something scary happen to you. After all, you're sixteen years old."

Tears welled forth in Roxanne's eyes.

"Bob!" Jan reprimanded. "Don't force people to do things they don't want to do."

"I'm sorry."

Roxanne, covering her face with her napkin, began to weep gently. I was totally embarrassed.

Jan tried to salvage the situation. "Children, now that you're finished, why don't you pick up your plates and take them to the kitchen and we'll have desert in the family room. I'll fix praline parfaits in a few minutes."

"Why is Roxanne crying?" Tom asked.

"I don't know," I said, lifting him down from his highchair. "You three kids run off into the family room, I think *Father Knows Best* is coming on TV."

Timmy and Tammy, to escape the uneasiness, scampered out of the room; Tom, on the other hand, moved slowly across the dining room, stealthily maneuvering his little frame around the massive breakfront without once taking his steely, bright blue eyes off the scene at the table. Just as he was about to disappear into the hall, he dashed back into the room, snatched his teddy bear from beneath his highchair, and ran to the back of the house.

Jan slid her chair around close to Roxanne and tried to comfort her. "That's okay, honey, Mr. Carr didn't mean to embarrass you."

Easing her face from behind the napkin, blotting tears from her eyes, she said, "No, no, Mrs. Carr, Mr. Carr didn't embarrass me. It's just that I feel so sad."

"Why sad, honey?"

"Your family is so wonderful, I want to stay here all the time but I know I can't. I have to go home."

"You mean you have to go home *now?*"

"No, I just mean I don't want to go home, when it's time to go home."

We must have looked a bit puzzled.

Roxanne began to explain. "I don't like to go home anymore!"

"Why, what's the matter at home, honey?" Jan inquired.

"When you started talking about your most scary things, I thought about my parents and it's always scary when I'm with them."

"What do you mean?"

"Ever since my brother ran away five years ago, it seems I can't do anything right for my father. He doesn't trust me. He won't believe anything I say."

"Oh, honey, I can't believe that's true."

"Yes, Mrs. Carr, it's true, all right."

"What do you mean?"

"My father wants me to be perfect and if I'm not perfect, he spanks me."

"Roxanne, he can't spank you," I said in disbelief. "You're sixteen years old. You're about to graduate early from high school."

"He spanks me anyway. He spanked me last night when he found out I wasn't going to be valedictorian."

Jan and I were bewildered.

"I didn't get good final grades because I was so nervous when I took my exams," she began to sniffle. "I was so scared I wouldn't get all A's, that I fouled up on my final tests."

"But, honey, you always got wonderful grades," Jan comforted.

"I know, and my teachers tell me I'm a really good student, if I would just stay calm."

Jan's hug helped her regain her composure.

"But my father thinks I don't try, so he makes me repent."

"Oh, my dear, how awful," Jan said, trying to restrain herself from saying anything which would embarrass or further upset Roxanne.

"So you see, ma'am, that's why I like to stay at your house overnight because nothing like that happens to me here. I wish you were my parents."

"Do you think I could talk to your father and suggest he's being a little too severe?"

"Oh, *no*, Mr. Carr, please don't talk to him, he'd kill me. No one knows this, not anybody, except Father Lorietto, who told me I need to pray more. I just had to share it with somebody because it worries me so."

"Oh, dear, anytime you want to come and stay here overnight, please feel welcome."

"Thank you, Mrs. Carr, but it won't go on too much longer."

Jan and I glanced at each other in wonderment.

"Why not?"

"You see, sir, as soon as I graduate from high school, I'm going into a cloister to become a nun. Then I won't have to go home anymore."

Jan and I sat stunned.

As her incredible story unfolded it had briefly occurred to me: *Could this possibly be a grotesque childish whimsy?*

The three kids came barging into the dining room.

"Mommy, mommy," Timmy hollered. "We want our dessert while the break's on."

"Yah, mommy," Tom chimed in, "while the 'mmercials are on."

Tammy ensued with, "We want our parfaits *now*, 'cause it's almost time for *Gomer*

Pyle."

"Okay," Jan said, distracted from her deep concern for Roxanne.

"Oh, gosh, Jan, if it's time for *Gomer Pyle*, it means it's almost time for us to be at the Spring Fiesta meeting."

Jan got up and followed the kids into the kitchen. While the parfaits were concocted, I sat with Roxanne for a few moments to console her and test her credibility.

"Roxanne, are you sure you father's as bad as you say?"

"Oh, yes, Mr. Carr. He does even worse things to me. That's why mama wants me to go to the convent. I'll be safe there."

Convinced she was telling the truth, we encouraged her to talk to us anytime she felt troubled.

The doorbell rang; I knew it was Vivian and Stephen to walk with us over to the Spring Fiesta meeting. We hadn't seen them since the last Parents Club meeting and were anxious to hear about their new bar and restaurant, *Le Boeuf Gras.*

"Roxanne, do you think you're still up to babysitting with the kids?"

"Oh, yes, Mr. Carr, I love them; they're my friends."

"Okay," I said, involuntarily giving her a fatherly hug.

The doorbell rang again. When I opened the front door, Stephen was just lifting himself back astride his motorcycle pulled up onto the banquette.

"Hi, Stephen, we'll be right out. Jan, Stephen's here!"

"Okay, Okay, I'm coming, I'm taking off my apron." Passing the dining room, she looked in. "Roxanne, are you sure you're going to be all right?"

"Yes, ma'am, I'll be fine, thank you."

Coming toward me down the hallway, the children followed Jan like a covey of chicks. "Mommy, mommy," they all chirped simultaneously, "when are you gonna be home?"

"Don't worry, kids, we'll only be a couple of hours. We're going to Spring Fiesta headquarters at Jackson Square. We won't be too long."

They all gave her a kiss on the cheek and then came to me. I could tell by the scent and the way Tom waddled that he was carrying a load. Jan could never tell because she had lost her sense of smell, probably from all the Benzedrine inhalers used for hay fever as a child.

"Jan, you've got to change Tom's diaper before we leave."

"Oh, Mrs. Carr, you're in a hurry. I'll be glad to change his diaper. You go now."

"Roxanne, you're a very thoughtful young lady. We greatly appreciate everything you do for the children."

I added, "The children love being with you. Tammy said you're like an angel. Now, you children mind Roxanne."

As we walked out the door, Jan exclaimed, "Stephen! You brought your motorcycle tonight. Where's Vivian?"

"She's still at the bistro and told me to go on ahead."

"Why'd you bring the motorcycle?"

"I've been out for a little ride. Got a few things on my mind, a family crisis. I felt like going for a ride first."

"One thing I can say, you certainly don't look like a nuclear scientist in that outfit, black leather jacket and motorcycle."

"I guess we all lead several lives," Stephen remarked. "Jan, hop on the back."

"But, I've got a skirt on."

"That's okay, it's a full skirt, hop on here behind me. Come on. Bob, let me give Jan a buzz around the Quarter, we'll meet you in front of headquarters in six or seven minutes."

"Okay, Doc."

It was a beautiful evening with low humidity as I walked along; I paid my respects to the Douvicet sisters, who sat on their stoop every evening when the weather was decent.

"Good evening, Miss Alice, Miss Mary."

"Good evenin', Mr. Cawr. How's our sweet Miss 'Jane' and the family?"

"Everybody's mighty fine, thank you. How're *you* all doing?"

"Just fine," they responded in unison.

"We just made our groceries over at Puglia's," Miss Mary added. "They done had a special on catfish and we hada replenish our supply of red beans, you know how it is?"

"Nice quiet evening."

"'Cept for that pesky motorcycle that just went by."

Miss Alice complained, "Can't understand why people would ride on one of them noisy machines."

"Gee, I can't either." I was grateful they didn't know Miss "Jane" (as they and many others mistakenly called her) had climbed astride that pesky motorcycle! "Y'all take care now, bye-bye."

"Bye-bye, dawlin'."

Walking past Lafitte's Blacksmith Shop, a good place for gents to meet ladies, I spied the silhouette of two lovers kissing in the glow of the red votive candle on their table. Continuing along the block I passed Lafitte's in Exile, where two gentlemen lovers were holding hands between barstools. *Ain't love grand?* At the corner of St. Ann, where great jazz emanated from Pete Fountain's club, two college kids asked how to get to Pat O'Brien's for a Hurricane.

Crossing the square, I could see Stephen and Jan had already arrived and were continuing their conversation. "What'er y'all talking about?"

"Bob, I'll tell you later. I think we better get into the meeting."

"Isn't Vivian coming?"

"No, not tonight. Jan'll tell you about it."

This meeting was a briefing for the various homeowners who had consented to have their houses or patios on display during Spring Fiesta. The tours were well-organized with hostesses attired in antebellum hoop-skirted gowns, stationed in the rooms or patios of the various homes on display. The hosts and hostesses were schooled in antebellum manners. Jan and I were thrilled at being asked to open our house, though it was probably because we were TV personalities and would give the tours free on-the-air promotion. Although our house certainly wasn't in mint condition, we felt we could pizzazz things up with a little glue and candlelight. Besides, once we got the kids dressed up in their antebellum costumes, who was going to look at the house anyway?

The meeting lingered on with endless questions. As we were leaving, I overheard a retort from one "Spring Fiesta Matron" to another: "I'm so glad we snagged *that* Bob and 'Jane' of TV as an added attraction."

"Oh, yes, dahling," replied the other dilettante. "Their place will show visitors the contrasting living conditions that so often occur in the Quartah!"

Was what I'd overheard a compliment?

As we stood by the door for a few minutes talking, I could see from the corner of my eye that Stephen had made his way out of the meeting. Astride his motorcycle, he glanced back, starting to pull away. Waving good-bye, I was curious about his hasty departure.

Heading home, I quizzed Jan. "You've *got* to tell me what Stephen had to say. You were in such a deep discussion standing by the motorcycle, I know it had to be something important."

"Bob, it's unbelievable! I had a hard time concentrating on what they were saying at the meeting because I kept thinking of Stephen and Vivian."

"Are they having financial trouble?"

"No, no, it's nothing like that, but it's really odd."

"Odd? Stephen and Vivian odd? Amethyst and Joséff are odd. Malcolm and Bruce are vaguely odd! But Vivian and Stephen, odd?"

"It's weird to me. You can decide."

"So, what *is it?*"

"Well, just to start with, Stephen is going to give up his job for a year and head to Mexico on his motorcycle."

"Really?"

"Really! But, that's only the beginning. He's also going to take—remember that girl at their last party—Jackie? Well, he's taking Jackie with him."

"He's taking Jackie?"

"Yah, and they're both going on his motorcycle." Crossing the street in front of the Royal Pharmacy, Jan continued, "Just a minute. I've got to stop in here and get some Ortho cream for my diaphragm."

"Oh, *oh!* And I've got to get some shaving cream," I chuckled.

We both loved the Royal Pharmacy. First of all, they were so congenial; secondly, my dusty Coca-Cola ad still hung over the soda fountain. It was a nostalgic trip into the past.

As we made our way along Ursuline Street, I resumed the line of questioning. "Okay, so Stephen's goin' off to Mexico on the motorcycle. What about Vivian?"

"Well, that's the *big* thing."

"It sounds to me like Stephen has the big thing!"

"Oh, Bob, really! This is serious. You know the woman, Maude, who's been helping out with some of the construction work on their house and at the bistro? It seems she and Vivian are going to live together."

"Why?"

"Because they're in love." She lowered her voice. "They must be lesbians!"

"You've *got* to be kidding. Vivian's so feminine. What does she see in her? That woman has balls!"

Jan grimaced, "I don't know, but that's the story."

"You mean, Stephen's going off to Mexico with what's-her-name, and Vivian's going to stay home and live with what's-her-name?"

"Yes!"

"Now *that's* odd! What about the kids?"

"It seems the boys are going to live with their grandmother in the Mississippi delta."

"Stephen told you all this?"

"That's what took so long."

"You're right, it's odd. I'd say bizarre."

I unlocked our front door quietly. There wasn't a sound to be heard from the kids or Roxanne. So as not to awaken anyone, Jan and I tiptoed to the kitchen for something to drink. I pulled a bottle of Barq's out of the refrigerator; Jan got a glass of water.

"Honey," I said in a half-whisper, "this was a remarkable evening! First, the babysitter tells us the peculiar story about her parents, then two of our good friends decide to break up; he runs off with a girl and *she* runs off with a girl, *and* we've committed to open our house to the public with God knows who's coming through!"

"Bob, it'll be fun."

"Life's interesting in da Quarters. And, thinking back, what did we learn from Roxanne's scary story?"

"To make sure we really love our children and don't push them to the brink of despair."

I checked the French doors to the patio to make sure they were locked. Jan rinsed out our glasses in the sink, then turned to me with a look that carried the weight of the world. "On the other hand, do you think the French Quarter is the right place for us to raise our children?"

"Honey, I don't know, my mother always said sex and religion were multifarious!"

Jan looked perplexed.

"Diverse or multifaceted," I interjected in a slightly superior tone. "The only thing I can say is Roxanne's parents live in Gentilly and Vivian and Stephen are from Mississippi, so I don't know if it's the French Quarter or just the world."

Jan walked over to me and put her arms around my neck, "Oh, honey, it all scares me. Everything is so strange. Thank God we have each other."

I wrapped my arms around her waist, crunching her with a big hug. A warm stirring sprung up inside me. "Honey, I've got an idea of how we can get this stuff off our minds."

"How's that?" she asked, laying her head on my shoulder.

I pressed closer. "Feel that?"

She giggled.

"Let's sneak up the steps as quietly as we can, so we don't wake up the kids and make some mad, passionate, good ole American Midwestern normal love."

Jan giggled again as I pressed more rigidly against her. I reached over and turned off the kitchen light. We kissed. As we walked out of the kitchen, Jan reached across the counter and picked up the package from the drug store. We crept quietly up the long stairway into our darkened bedroom. Groping my way through the dark, I dropped my pants and began to unbutton my shirt; I felt myself straining at my shorts. I could hear Jan pulling off her dress. Yanking back the covers, I slipped merrily into bed, colliding with another body—*not* Jan's!

I fumbled frantically for the bed lamp. The light revealed our three angels snuggled close together. They had fallen fast asleep waiting for us to come home. My passion collapsed as Jan and I mused and chuckled.

Snow White and the Seven Dwarfs had tumbled out of Tammy's hands and fallen onto the floor. We carefully carried each child into their bedrooms and planted kisses on their cherub cheeks.

Once in the darkened warmth of our own bed, Jan and I enfolded each other, rekindling our ardor.

* * * * *

Jan and I were just about to go on the air live with the afternoon *Woolco Show* when the switchboard operator signaled us to pick up at once. Timmy was on the phone half-crying. It appeared Olympia had fallen off a kitchen chair and was lying on the floor with a broken arm and couldn't get up or reach the phone. Jan was beside herself. We couldn't both go and leave dead air, so I left her behind and ran the seven blocks home, frantic all the way, wondering what would greet me.

Olympia had picked up the children from La Petite Ecole and was on a chair putting some extra serving dishes in the top shelves in the kitchen when she toppled off and fell on her arm. Tammy was sobbing, but Timmy was a good little soldier with matters somewhat under control. Thank God, Tom was on a play date.

Olympia was positioned in an awkward way, unable to move. The bone in her right arm was protruding, causing the skin to stretch; her pain was intense. Thank God we had walked to the station, so the car was at home. Tim and I struggled to get her in the car, and Tammy stopped sniffling when I enlisted her to be Florence Nightingale and get a blanket.

I have no memory of the drive to Mercy Hospital's emergency room, but what I do remember was that the admitting nun would not accept "this woman" because she was black and probably had no insurance! I was shocked first, then furious.

"You are a nun working for God? What the hell kind of hospital is this?" I shouted.

Timmy and Tammy's eyes were filled with trepidation; Olympia moaned in quiet resignation.

I mustered up gumption from somewhere. "I'm Bob Carr from channel six and if you don't fix this lady's arm I'll report it on television! She's part of my family and I'm responsible for her bill. Get a doctor, *now!*"

My celebrity card worked!

Glaring up from the folds of her wimple, the persistent nun retaliated, "She must sign in!"

"Woman, her arm is broken!"

"But to be legal she must sign in!"

I was outraged. I took Olympia's hand and with the pen in mine we signed the admittance document.

"Oh, but you must sign as her employer, then I can matriculate her into the system; yes, you must sign also!"

The children watched aghast as I, fuming, scribbled my signature. We all kissed Olympia as she was finally whisked off to an operating room. I was exhausted and exasperated.

She wore a cast for several weeks and not once complained. I never saw the doctor at the hospital, and we never received a bill for the medical services. It was a terribly unpleasant experience, but the episode was over.

Jan and Bob in "We're a Couple of Swells," 1963

Jan and Bob in "Put on a Happy Face," 1963

Our Restored Derelict on Spring Fiesta Tour

The mothers of the Parents Club put the fathers in charge of Easter activities. The dads wanted to do something fun and unusual—but what? Jack Di Cells offered to locate some bunnies and chicks for his patio. Lenny Flettrich, whose wife, Terry, had just done a series of commercials for Bunny Bread, was certain the public relations people who dressed up like bunnies would come to their patio to play games and sing songs with the children. It dawned on me that the most famous bunnies in the world were just ten blocks up Bourbon Street at the Playboy Club. Who better to invite to my patio? The other dads applauded my idea and immediately elected me chairman of cottontail inquiry.

It was no problem to call Al Belletto, leader of the Playboy Club house-band, which had just appeared on our TV show. Al was out of town for a week so I jokingly asked the receptionist for the person in charge of loaning out Bunnies. I was put on hold for what seemed like five minutes. With an ice sharp voice, the "Bunny-mother" received my call dispassionately. When she was about to dismiss me as a crank caller, I hastened to explain that I was "The Bob Carr of WDSU-TV," a friend of Al Belletto's, and I was serious about having Playboy Bunnies as guests on our patio for the French Quarter Parents Club's children's Easter egg hunt.

"You mean you want Playboy bunnies for an Easter egg hunt at your house—for children?"

"Yes, ma'am," I replied politely, trying to bolster my credibility. "You see, we fathers are trying to do something distinctive and unusual for our children, plus it will be filmed for broadcast on our TV show."

At the mention of TV, the Bunny-mother began to sniff around. I visualized her long ears perking up with thoughts of promotional fodder. She assured me she would convince the manager to release a few Bunnies for our Easter egg hunt.

So on the Saturday before Easter, the Saturday of Glory, we gathered at Terry and Lenny's storybook home, *The House in the Bend of Bourbon Street*, now the title of a children's book written by Terry and illustrated by their daughter, Lo-Ann. The chubby Bunny Bread bunnies, costumed with enormous floppy ears and mammoth paws, all in pink terry cloth, sang songs and danced "Ring-around-the-rabbit-hutch" with the kids. Before hopping back to the bakery, they doled out miniature loaves of bread. The kids were charged with excitement; we fathers gathered the tykes

together in a military line-up along the Bourbon Street banquette and set off like pied pipers. Coached by the dads, the kids marched in cadence up Bourbon singing the "Knick Knack Paddy Wack" song at full volume. Nosey folks peeked through their shutters and appeared on their balconies to check out the commotion. Halfway along the five blocks to our house, the older girls insisted on singing, "In your Easter bonnet with all the frills upon it…"

I led the march through the side gate straight into our back patio. Three Playboy Bunnies greeted us and welcomed the kids. I was at once thrilled, albeit disappointed. Alas, the mother-hare hadn't told me her Bunnies would be clad in public relations outfits deemed, probably by Hugh Hefner, more practical or suitable for occasions outside the Playboy hutch. So, the Playboy Bunnies, instead of being in their butt-clenching panty hose, bunny tails and cleavage-crunching bodices, were attired in black sleeveless sweaters with the Playboy logo, and their white pleated skirts were tennis length—a noticeable disappointment. Nonetheless, the Bunnies turned out to be the perfect tonic for the daddies. Hot stuff for a hot day; that's New Orleans's style!

With her eyes rolling in supreme disapproval, Olympia stuck her head out the kitchen door, announcing ice-cold lemonade for the little ones.

"And something just a little bit more spirited for the daddies," I added.

The Bunnies declined any hard liquor but sipped lemonade with the captivated children. The fathers were somewhat intimidated; perhaps it was Bunny-beauty or maybe Olympia's constant gawking vigil at the kitchen window. For more than half an hour, the Bunnies' played kitty-ring-toss and hopscotch with the children. The kids thought it was fun; we dads particularly appreciated the Bunny hopscotch.

Tammy ran over to Olympia to confide that when she grew up she wanted to be a Bunny Girl, too, "Cause they're so beautiful!"

Olympia's eyes rolled back in their sockets as she sputtered, "Lawd have mercy! Mistah Cahr, you has strange ideas. Oh, an' you're wanted on da telephone."

The call was from the Mother-bunny calling her gaggle home to the club. Our TV cameraman had arrived and was catching shots of the frolic. He followed us out the gate onto Bourbon Street with the camera rolling. The Bunnies held the hands of the small children, helping escort us another four blocks to the Di Cellses'. Tourists, passers-by, and folks on the Desire bus gawked as we strode along singing, "With a nick-knack, paddy-wack, give a dog a bone…" with the Playboy Bunnies in the lead. The kids waved frantically, bidding the hutch-bound bunnies adieu.

Several of the mothers had prepared finger sandwiches, punch, and little Easter baskets filled with candies and trinkets. The children were ecstatic when they spied live bunny-rabbits and colorfully dyed baby chicks. Jack Di Cells (Betty always referred to her husband using his full name—a custom of Mississippi delta gentry) had borrowed the bunnies from a friend who ran a pet shop. He had purchased the chicks from a poultry shop with the idea of giving one to each child to take home to raise! Most of the parents had been against the idea of having little dyed chickens, but Jack thought it would give the kids an educational experience about farm animals. After all, the children lived in an urban setting with little chance to see poultry or livestock.

One three-year-old picked up a chick, thinking it was a ball of cotton, and immediately squashed it. He handed it over to his unwary father, who was aghast at the chick's popped eyes and lolling tongue. It was quickly decided that none of the chicks would leave the Di Cellses' patio. Rather, after Easter Jack Di Cells would take them out to the family plantation where they would all live long and happy lives.

* * * * *

In readiness for our Spring Fiesta house tour, I hired two Cajun painters from along Bayou La Fouche, just outside the town of Thibodaux in the Acadia region of Louisiana, some sixty miles west of New Orleans. Cajuns are not to be confused with the French Créoles who, also Roman Catholic, consider themselves much more genteel.

Marcel Boudreaux, and his helper, whom I was yet to meet, would do the exterior house painting, while Jan, Olympia, and I worked on gussying up the interior. Before settling on a price, I told Marcel the work absolutely had to be completed at least two days before the tour was scheduled. He assured me that he and his helper were the best painters along Bayou La Fouche. "Ask anybody, *mon ami!*" Which, of course, I didn't do.

Marcel had given me his card, replete with numerous misspellings, when Jan and I were appearing for the Thibodaux Volunteer Fireman's Fair. There was so much construction and remodeling going on in New Orleans that it was difficult to find anyone to do touch-up painting at the last minute—inexpensively. Marcel Boudreaux seemed to be the perfect solution.

In his mid-forties, Marcel spoke with a strong Cajun accent. I remembered he had looked as strong as an ox and about as cultured. I phoned him to set a date; he was thrilled. "Monsieur Bawb, it would do me an honor, me, to work for big TV people like you. My partner and me, we come by New Orleans and charge you very cheap price, we."

I was about to relearn the old adage, ya gets whatcha pays for!

Marcel arrived in New Orleans with his pitiful old truck, a wooden ladder—surely an antique—a series of tattered drop clothes and sundry buckets, giving his truck the appearance of an old rag picker. I showed him the window frames and shutters to be painted.

"*Pas de probléme*, Monsieur Bawb, I get t'ings outa da truck and start soon as ma partner got back from da corner grocery wit' cold drinks."

"Okay, I'm going to the hardware store to pick up paint. Be back shortly."

"Don't you worry yourself, Monsieur, I have everyt'ing ready to start, me, when you come back by, but *wooo eee!* Dis some *big* mansion, dis!"

When I returned from the store, Marcel was in the patio stacking window shutters being handed down by his partner up on the balcony. The partner, a most peculiar-looking creature even for the Quarter, had removed shutters from about ten windows. I asked Marcel if they had marked the shutters so they would know which windows they fit when it came time to re-hang them.

"Monsieur Bawb, *pas de probléme*, I know 'xactly what I'm doing, me!"

The shutters on these hundred-year-old houses were put up individually;

consequently, the spacing of each shutter-hanger varies greatly, which means each shutter fits only one position.

A groan of pain could be heard from the balcony above. Marcel's pudgy helper was leaning way over the balcony railing struggling to lower one of the shutters into Marcel's hands when he bumped the beak of his cap against the upper end of the shutter, causing his hat to fall to the ground, revealing a mass of long black ringlets.

My God, he's a woman!

"Oooh la la, ya dropped you chapeau, cher," Marcel said, looking up at his partner.

"Is that your wife?" I asked incredulously.

"Oh no, no, Monsieur Bawb, dat's my sweetheart. She does everyt'ing wit me, her!"

"I'll bet," I mumbled, hoping she wouldn't fall off the balcony, bringing down the beautiful antique wrought-iron railing with her. I instructed Marcel which color to paint the window sashes and emphasized the other color was for the shutters.

"No trouble, Monsieur Bawb, I paint da blinds and *mon cherie*, she paint da window sash, yes!"

"But that means she'll be climbing up on the ladder?"

"*Ooh la la, pas de probléme*, Monsieur Bawb, *non probléme. Mon Cherie* she grandiose but she *trés agile.*"

Agile like an elephant at the circus balancing on one of those pedestals, I fantasized.

"If you have any questions, Marcel, ask me, okay? I'll be inside."

"But of course, Monsieur *Bawb.* Cherie and me, we 'ave *non probléme*, us."

The three kids had gone to City Park for the day with a group of Club fathers to ride paddleboats. Jan, Olympia, and I had complete freedom to attack the interior of the house. Jan had spent most of the morning planting fragile begonias amongst the banana trees and elephant ears in the patio to make it look very New Orleansy. Glad to get inside away from the intensifying heat, she and Olympia were dusting off chandeliers, wiping down woodwork, and mopping floors. My job was to run the heavy but noisy floor-waxing machine rented from Katz & Bestoff.

Jan had climbed a footstool next to one of the side parlor windows and was pushing back the lace curtains to dust off the sashes. Suddenly, she turned around and started waving the dust-cloth at me wildly while moving her lips.

I turned off the roaring floor polisher. "Jan, what's wrong?"

"I don't know, but something big just went past my window!"

"What do you mean something went past your window?"

"I don't know, something came off the balcony and went past my window into the patio."

"Honey, what do you mean?"

"*I don't know, honey*, but it was something *big.*"

"For heaven sakes," I said, a bit irritated at being interrupted.

We dashed into the hall, colliding with Olympia.

The three of us rushed simultaneously to squeeze through the French door. And what to our wondering eyes did appear? *Voila! Mon Cherie*, the elephant lady of Thibodaux, sprawled flat on her back right in the middle of Jan's newly-planted begonia bed, looking ever so much like a crash-landed blimp.

Marcel came scrambling around the corner of the house covered with white paint.

"*Mon Cher, Mon Cher, comment ce va, mon petite?*"

"You son-of-da-beetch, son-of-da-beetch, you. Why you bump my ladder bottom like dat, you. It must be you da clumsiest Bougalee in Terrebonne Parish Loosianne, you. I could break my neck, me, when you knock me off da balcony like dat, you!"

"*Mon Cher, Mon Cher,* you know I don't mean to did dat, me," responded Marcel, hoping to console her.

"You still son-of-da-beetch, you. I think you want to kill me!" she said as she arose from the crushed begonias brushing an elephant ear off her brow. The imprint of her entire body was evident in the soft dirt below the crushed plants.

"*You* climb up dat goddamn ladder dis time Marcel, you! I don't go up dat ladder no more, me, while I work by you. I paint the shutters on da ground, me," she barked. "You set up dat ladder, you. An' you go up da ladder from now, you hear me?"

Oh my God, what have I done by hiring these bargain basement bunglers?

Horrified, Jan and Olympia turned around and went back into the house as Marcel and "Mon Cherie" continued to argue. I walked around the edge of the house to investigate the paint spill. Fortunately, most of the paint had fallen either on Marcel or the ragged drop cloths.

For the next several minutes Marcel and Cherie reorganized themselves. Marcel climbed quietly up the ladder with a bucket of white paint while Cherie dipped her brush in dark green and began painting the shutters. I went back inside to continue polishing floors. For the next couple of hours I didn't hear a word from the outside. In fact, I was afraid to check, not sure I wanted to find out what was going on. Late in the afternoon the hush was finally broken. I heard loud voices outside and stuck my head out to check.

"You stupid son-of-da-beetch, Marcel, you! You should have been knowing dat, you. Stupid son-of-da-beetch, you should know dat."

"*Mon Cherie,* you da stupid one. You took 'em down, you!"

"*Merd,* Marcel, you call yourself a painter, you? You t'ink you Michael Angelo and you don't even know how to do dis?"

Timidly, I continued out into the patio to investigate. Immediately it became infuriatingly evident what was wrong. She had taken down the shutters and, like I thought, neither she nor Marcel had marked the window from which they came. Putting them back had become an unsolvable puzzle. Cherie picked up a hammer to force the hinges into place.

"No, no, don't!" I screamed. But I was one *no* too late. One of the antique cast-iron hinges broke off under the pressure of the hammer's blow. Uncontrollably, I yelled, "Goddamit, what the hell are you doing?"

So startled by my outburst, Cherie dropped the hammer, which tumbled off the balcony and hit Marcel on the head. Blood began gushing from the gash on his forehead.

"*Mon Cher, Mon Cher,*" uttered Marcel as he sank to the ground.

Cherie waddled down the ladder. Grabbing one of the paint cloths, she covered Marcel's head. The red blood looked even more sinister as it oozed down over his white paint-spattered coveralls. Clutching one of their rags, I soaked it under the cold-water spigot and wrapped it around his head to help stop the bleeding.

Cher or Cherie, whatever in hell her name was, sat down next to Marcel devouring him with a French kiss on the mouth that nearly suffocated him. "*Mon amour, mon amour*, I will take you home, yes?"

"*Oui, Cherie*, I t'ink we go home, yes."

"Sounds like a good idea to me," I added hastily.

"But Monsieur Bawb, we come back tomorrow, us."

"No, no, no, you are too hurt," I insisted. "Somehow I'll get the painting finished and put the shutters back myself, *me!*"

I scurried around picking up their paint cloths and threw them in the back of their truck. Mon Cherie and I helped Marcel; he didn't want to get in the cab but rather stretched out in the back of the truck on top of the paint cloths. While Cherie wrapped him in swaddling paint clothes, I dashed back into the patio, got their ladder and hooked it onto the side of the truck. I opened the door to the cab; big Cher squeezed into the driver's seat. Just before they pulled away, I slipped twenty-five dollars through the window into Cher's pudgy hand and bid them adieu. Thanks be to God, I never saw them again—*ever*—no hospital bills, no lawsuit, no more broken hinges and no more crushed begonias!

Frustrated, I worked into the night, angrily cursing as I unraveled the shutter puzzle, indeed convinced: *Ya gets whatcha pays for, mon ami!*

* * * * *

Mother and dad had once again come from Ohio to spend Spring Fiesta with us and participate in the antebellum tours. Because mother was highly allergic to dust and had severe asthma attacks, they decided to stay at the Royal Orleans Hotel to avoid the plaster dust ever present in our house. Arriving late Friday afternoon, they stood in front of our house with Olympia to watch the annual parade. The three of them waved enthusiastically when Jan, the kids, and I, costumed to the hilt, passed by riding in our traditional horse-drawn carriage.

It would be a couple of days before our house was actually opened to tourists, so dad helped me finish off some of the projects delayed because of the fiasco with Marcel and his Mon Cherie. We also shopped the French Market for replacement begonias for Jan's flowerbed. Mother had a way with flowers and loved digging in the dirt helping Jan replant them. Back home, she always kept enormous bouquets of seasonal fresh flowers throughout the house, plucked straight from her garden.

In preparation for the parade and the house tour, a seamstress across the river in a part of New Orleans called Algiers made beautiful hoopskirt dresses for Jan, Tammy, and mother. She also fashioned little Victorian waistcoats and trousers for Tom and Timothy. For me, Jan rented a Rhett Butler outfit, and for dad, Southern gentleman's attire, both from MGM, the fashionable supplier of New Orleans's better antebellum clothes and Mardi Gras costumes. Olympia was greatly disappointed that we had not included her. Jan and I had considered the idea early on but were skittish about asking her to wear an old-fashioned maid's outfit for fear she might view it as demeaning. We had not wanted to hurt her feelings or embarrass her in any way. Actually, we had hurt her by leaving her out.

"Mistah an' Mizz Cahr, ah be proud o' my family, an' ah wants everybody that comes through this here house to know that *ah* be the one what takes charge o' my babies!"

"I'm glad you feel that way. We're really touched."

"Further mo', Mistah Cahr, if you gonna be Mistah Rhett Butler, an' Mizz Cahr is gonna be Mizz Scarlett, *ah'm* gonna be Mammy! You not gonna do this Spring Fester wid'out me. Ah'll tell you that, Mistah Cahr. Besides that, we gotta have some *eyes* watchin' all those people prowlin' 'bout this house, so as nothin' takes up feet an' walks away!"

We were delighted Olympia wanted to be included, so Jan bought her enough white cotton yard goods at "Krauss-es" (as the locals say) to fashion herself a long, full skirt to be worn over her white uniform. A bright calico bib apron with a matching do-rag completed the costume.

Olympia loved it; we couldn't keep her away from the peer mirror in the parlor. "We gonna be the bestist lookin' family in the whole Spring Fester!"

On tour day, Jan and I arrived home from the station early to be ready in plenty of time to greet our visitors. Rivet sailed in from his shop with his cache of curlers to arrange coifs. He fussed, fumed, snarled, and teased until he achieved an antebellum style with clusters of diminutive banana curls dangling from the backs of their heads, giving them the authentic 1860s look. The little curls bounced like springs as they bobbed around the bedroom getting ready. Tim, Tom, and I busily tucked ruffled bibs into our waistcoats. Tom doted on his, but Timmy kept sputtering that he looked like a fag. As for me, standing in front of the full-length mirror, I fancied myself very much resembling Mr. Butlah!

The doorbell rang, provoking a flurry of activity and excited sounds. Olympia received mother and dad. I overheard them admiring her Mammy outfit. She thought they looked just like "Miss Starlett's folk." They had arrived from the Royal Orleans fully costumed, having walked through the French Quarter attracting attention with every step, thriving on causing a stir.

Dad delighted in helping Timmy light the gas chandelier over the dining room table. I could overhear Timmy saying, "Jandad, let me do it, let me do it!"

I adjusted the electrical dimmers for the other chandeliers to give the illusion of gaslight.

The sudden ring of the doorbell induced panic. From upstairs, Jan let out a scream. "Oh my gosh, they're here. They're *here!*"

Actually, people had not arrived; it was the man with the flag. A Fiesta flag, hung at the entrance, designates each house or patio on tour. No guests were to be admitted inside until the flag was properly installed.

"Please, sir, Mistah Bawb, may ah leave the flag in the hallway for a few minutes while ah go over to Miss Madonna's grocery to git myself a cold Barq's? It's some kinda hot out there, an' y'all gonna have a big crowd at *this* house."

"Why?"

"Well, Mistah Bawb, everybody in New Orleans wants to see inside the Bawb and Jane Cawr house. Y'all a television institution in this town, but all y'all must be knowin' that!"

The flagman, who also served as the security guard, left for his Barq's before I could offer him one. I winced thinking about his comment; I hadn't really thought about people looking into our house to see the way we lived. I considered it simply as people coming to see an old house.

Jan and Tammy came floating down the stairway looking MGM technicolor fabulous as their lavish skirts swept down the stairs. With each step the little corkscrew curls danced. We all assembled in the front hall. The doorbell rang; we gasped. I swung open the door; it was the guard once again.

"Mistah Bawb, y'all ready for me to put out that flag?"

I glanced out, shocked at the long queue.

Olympia got a brief glimpse. "Oh, my Gawd, Mistah Cahr, ah can't believe you lettin' all them folks come in our house!"

"Don't worry yourself, Olympia, everything's gonna be fine, but you stay vigilant."

Beginning to panic, Jan announced, "Okay, okay, everybody, take your places."

Jan and I were posted at the front door to greet visitors as they entered. Mother stood in the archway between the double parlors, Tammy was stationed in the dining room, Timmy and Tom were in the family room, and Olympia oversaw the kitchen. Dad was located in the patio to assist sightseers as they came out through the French doors, instructing them to exit via the carriageway.

Attired in antebellum fashion, ticket-takers supplied by Spring Fiesta stood just outside our door. As the guests entered, Jan curtsied gracefully; I bowed, shook hands, greeted them, and ushered them into the front parlor, where mother began her discourse. I had instructed her to tell the folks that the crystal chandeliers were original to the house, the rosettes on the ceilings above the chandeliers were plaster, the house was built in the 1850s, the ceilings were thirteen feet high, and the mantle-pieces were original to the house. I suggested she need not elaborate on the fact we had made the drapes ourselves or that the fabric had actually come from a Summer Stock theatre. Mother was also supposed to describe the antique furniture we had acquired. The Victorian settees and chairs were embellished with a carved likeness of "Queen Victoria as Empress of India" on their backs and as the "Queen of the Nile" on the arms, etc.

All seemed to be going very smoothly, when suddenly we heard a tremendous roar of laughter coming from the front parlor. What, we wondered, could mother, who has a flair for elaborating on any story, have told them to cause such an outburst? Later Jan and I found out: when one of the ladies had asked about the somewhat damaged cabinet next to the fireplace, mother contrived a story, saying the ancient *Boulle marqueterie* cabinet had formerly been on "the plantation" and used as a safe. Yankee soldiers had pried it open. Saying "the plantation" inferred that our family must have had a plantation somewhere, sometime, which was certainly not the truth. Mother, however, was enjoying her little fantasy into the past, in spite of her northern upbringing. She had always fancied herself as a Creole lady or Scarlett O'Hara.

Another woman asked, "Ma'am, what was that cabinet used for?"

"The cabinet looks a little bit scarred because during the northern aggression, occupying troops thought it contained money. Thus, ladies, they pried it open, ruining the handsome door."

Mother thought that was the end of it until one of the ladies piped up, "Tell me, Mrs. Carr, what did they pry it open with?"

Mother, realizing that some of the ladies were taking her a little too seriously, retorted without batting an eyelash, "With *a cadillac tire iron,* of course!"

And that was when the round of laughter exploded. I dare say, half the women took her seriously and the other half realized this was all a wonderful travesty.

Holding court in the dining room, Tammy asked the visitors to notice that the gas chandelier above the dining table was original to the house, as was the mantle-piece and the coal grate in the fireplace. The knife box on the sideboard was used for storing and locking away knives. In the family room, Timothy, along with a little help from Tom, explained how we had chipped the plaster off the chimney to expose the colorful "old-reds," handmade by slaves.

Olympia, perched on a high stool that caused her skirt to billow out, loved telling how we had modernized "her" kitchen so she no longer had to pump water by hand for dishes and laundry. She seemed to be vying with mother for first place in creative story telling. After spinning her yarns, she ushered the sightseers into the patio.

Dad's fantasies told of how the original man of this house had dealt in exotic spices and treasures, delivered under sail from the West Indies via Bayou St. John, obtained in great measure from the notorious pirate and folk hero, Jean Lafitte. Also, on some nights, if you listened carefully, you could imagin voodoo sounds hovering over the wall like an ominous fog.

After the last straggler had departed, we invited the guard and ticket-sellers to have a mint julep and chat, a sort of post mortem of the event, similar to the ones we conducted on our TV programs. People were overjoyed by the friendliness of our family and the wonderful quips of history. "No boring facts," they were heard to say, "but delightful and unique stories never before heard!"

We were pleased that most of the several hundred visitors genuinely enjoyed the fanciful stories. Also high on the pleasure list was the fact that they had visited a house where a real family actually lived. Of course, inside plumbing and air conditioning had made it more livable than the first family who resided there could have imagined.

A cameraman from channel 6 had come to take pictures for a feature on our TV show. We hadn't realized the fervor that would take place after we had shown our house on television. We were besieged by organizations wanting to raise funds by sending tours through our house. Jan and I decided we could happily handle one tour a month for non-profit organizations.

The first tour raised money for the Leukemia Society. Then there was the Red Cross, the Mental Health Association, Multiple Sclerosis, and on and on.

A professional tour coordinator told us that because of our strategic location, he would be willing to pay us nicely if we would open for tour groups. At first the idea seemed repugnant, but when we realized how much money we could earn if we turned the house into a business, we reconsidered and decided to proceed; the money would help pay for upkeep and buy some new "antiques."

Jan made a schedule and tours began to tromp through once or twice a week. With the television show in the morning, our radio show in the early afternoon, plus sporadic tours, our days grew hectic. On tour days, Jan dashed home after our program while I continued with my disk jockey show. She joined Olympia at the front door in her antebellum outfit to welcome fifty or sixty tourists. If the kids were home from school, they loved joining in to show the downstairs; however, Timmy refused to don his "sissy" outfit because a chum had glimpsed his costume, spread the word at school, and made his life miserable.

We enjoyed meeting people who appreciated our house as much as we did, but our overloaded schedule was taking its toll. Nerves began to fray. When Olympia alerted Jan, and especially me, that we bought the house to live in and bring up our children, and *not* as a zoo to show off the animals, we acquiesced. There would be far fewer tours. Thank you, Olympia.

It was during a Spring Fiesta that our friend and art mentor Naomi Marshall, gallery owner and entrepreneur, told us that she had placed a low bid on the fabulous but dilapidated Madewood plantation house on Bayou Lafourche near Napoleonville, and it had been accepted for lack of other bidders. She hoped our family and my parents would join her for a long antebellum weekend at the manor house. We arrived in full dress of the period but soon learned what life was like in the 1840s. The house hadn't been updated much since "The Wahr." It proved to be a great lesson for the children on how to rough it in grand style. We had many country stays along with Naomi and her sons, Keith and Don. Her husband disliked the boondocks. Our dream was to one day own such a plantation home.

* * * * *

Mr. Homer Formby, of wood-refinishing fame, was a television guest. There occurred between us an immediate affinity when I told him we had bought a treasure of an old house that contained superb interior millwork consisting of a three-story banister, door frames, mantel-pieces, and interior shutters in need of stripping. He was willing to examine the house to advise me on the best method of removing the old varnish. Mr. Formby enjoyed walking from the station along Royal Street catching glimpses of antiques through the sun-glared display windows en route. He was delighted and flabbergasted at the sight of our beautiful woodwork. The stair rail and spindles, he said, were heart of pine, the floors of running pine, while the doors and their frames were all constructed of cypress, the chief building wood of Louisiana until the early part of the twentieth century. Since this was his first visit to Louisiana, he was intrigued by the combination of woods used, quite different from his native Carolina.

When he finished his rapturous wood-gazing visit, he whipped out a handkerchief and a flask of his famous refinishing formula and applied it to the newel post. He stood back and with great joy admired the results of his magic elixir. He promised to send us several gallons of his secret formula, if I, in turn, would promise to send him photographs after using his product.

Once the extravagant dose of refinisher arrived, Jan tackled the task of refinishing the entire stairway; it became her passion. Inch-by-inch, rung-by-rung, she toiled, working between ten and midnight, after the children had been bedded down. Before she was through she had used a bucket of Mr. Formby's solution together with masses of steel wool, reams of paper towels, and a mountain of old rags. She also invested heavily in Jergens hand lotion! Jan was determined to make the stairway her project, indeed, her *monument*.

While Jan toiled with the staircase, I had taken on the project of using the furniture refinisher to clean the old varnish off the handsome indoor shutters in the dining room. Up to my elbows in steel wool and dripping with Formby's juice, I was called to the phone to speak with a gentleman named Ben Johnson.

This has to be a joke, I thought, *probably my old college friend Bob Carrow playing a prank*. While at Carnegie Tech, he helped me get through my senior thesis on the works of Elizabethan playwright Ben Jonson.

It wasn't a joke at all; it *was* Ben Johnson, a movie director, interested in casting me in a picture he was making in New Orleans. I was flattered and astonished by his interest.

We arranged to meet the next day at the MPA studio, a motion picture producing company in a former synagogue near Lee Circle. With difficulty, I went back to cleaning the old woodwork while visions of movie contracts danced in my head.

The next day after my DJ show, I boarded the streetcar to Lee Circle. Jostling breezily along I pondered, *How lavish a movie will it be? How big a budget will it have? What kind of pay will I get? Could this be the big break that will catapult me into international Hollywood stardom? On the other hand, Jan and I are content doing our local TV and radio programs. Then again, once caught up in the world of show biz, a new challenge is always exciting.*

My Tevye-like reverie was shattered upon arriving at Lee Circle. I glanced up at General Robert E. Lee, a heroic but tragic figure standing in effigy high atop a phallic symbol representing the fatherhood of a mighty but doomed cause, now cast forever in stone to face the North in a perpetual watch.

Walking toward the studio, I deliberated, *Is my future about to be altered?*

A very cordial receptionist ushered me into Ben Johnson's office. He appeared to be rather short and stocky, though it was difficult to tell, as he was half-hidden behind a stack of film cans and manuscripts. He sprang to his feet, leaning over the desk to shake my hand. His smile was infectious. We chatted; he was aware of my theatrical background and that my wife and I did radio and television. He felt I would be a good prospect for one of the parts and asked me to take off my shirt so he could see my physique. I apprehensively glanced around the room searching for a casting couch, thinking: *Taking off my shirt is no big deal, but dropping my pants would be a whole different ball game!*

Ben deciphered my anxious expression. "Good Lord, Bob, I told you to remove your shirt, *not* your shorts! I'm not some homo who gets his kicks from looking at naked guys. The script calls for your character to have his shirt off during most of the picture."

So I removed my jacket and tie; while unbuttoning my shirt, I began to feel like a Bourbon Street stripper. I jerked off my T-shirt, which left me chilly and feeling conspicuous. A secretary walked in for a moment to deliver some papers, took one look at me, and raising her eyebrows murmured, "Hmmmm," then walked out. I felt the hair on my chest stand on end.

"Yes, yes, that will be fine; put your shirt back on, I don't want you to catch cold. However, you may want to know that this part will be performed in pajamas, or at least, pajama bottoms. We're not quite sure which."

This time I raised *my* eyebrows and went, "Hmmmm."

"Now, would you mind picking up the script for a moment and reading a few lines with me? I'll read the wife part and you read the part marked 'husband.'"

He started off with her part: "You just can't seem to make love to me anymore."

My part: "Well, there seems to be something wrong."

Her part: "Something wrong? I don't understand."

My part: "I don't understand either, dear."

We read a page and a half of what seem to be rather inane dialogue. When we finished, he said, "Yes, sir, that's fine. We're going to film over the weekend."

"You mean this weekend?"

"Yes, we're going to be filming Saturday and Sunday. If you want the part, you've got it; but we'll need you all day Saturday and Sunday. We're filming over the weekend because, as you might realize, this is a low-budget picture using many New Orleans actors who find it easier to work on the weekend."

"That'll be fine with me, our television show runs Monday through Friday."

He went on to say he would like me to be in the studio by 7:30 Saturday morning; we would sign the proper papers and releases. The part paid a flat five hundred dollars.

My thoughts quickened: *Five hundred dollars doesn't seem like much if I'm going to be propelled into international movie stardom. But, after all, it's my first opportunity in New Orleans to be in a movie, so I might as well grasp the chance. What's to lose?*

"Mr. Johnson, is there anything special I should wear or anything I should do in the meantime?"

"Just get some rest, look as good as you can, lift a few weights now and then to pump up your biceps before Saturday, and don't worry about what you're going to wear; you'll be in pajamas most of the time anyway, supplied by the costume department."

"Oh, by the way, what's the name of the picture?"

"The Frigid Wife."

"The Frigid Wife?"

"That's right," he replied matter-of-factly. "Your scenes will be the first we'll film on Saturday, so you may even be finished by late Saturday night. There may be a few retakes on Sunday morning, but that shouldn't take long. Hope you'll enjoy it. See you Saturday morning."

"It's a deal, I'll be here."

Of course, when I got home, Jan was waiting anxiously. She had already said something to the kids about my being in a movie, and they wondered if it was going to be a Disney movie or something like Tarzan. As we were talking about it, Olympia came in to tell us supper was ready. She had overheard something about my being in a movie and said, "Lawdy, Mistah Cahr, you gonna be in a pictcha show?"

"I don't know, Olympia, I'm going to be filming something on Saturday."

"Lawd have mercy, I'm gonna be workin' for a movie *stah!*"

"Olympia, don't get too excited yet, we'll see what happens."

"How'd it go?" Jan asked. "What kind of a part is it?"

"About the *part*, I don't know. I couldn't quite tell. It sounds a little on the sexy side. I'll be in pajamas for the whole picture, I think, but the reading went well."

"Pajamas! I don't want you to be in a part where you have to wear pajamas," Jan protested. "I hope it's not the kind of movie that will upset our station management.

You know, Mr. Read is very straight-laced. We don't want to do anything to jeopardize our career at channel 6."

"Oh, I don't think it'll be anything like that. I know I have to be careful. On the other hand, there might be big bucks in being king of the porno flicks!"

"That's ridiculous," she gasped, then chuckled, "besides, they don't have a wide enough screen!" We snickered together; she gave me a kiss on the cheek interrupted by Olympia, again calling us for dinner.

* * * * *

At 7:30 on Saturday morning, Jan and the kids dropped me off at the movie studio. I told them I would call later or come home on the streetcar. Armed with their red wagon, they were headed to Monkey Hill in Audubon Park and, later, the zoo.

The receptionist told me the cast was gathering with the crew in the studio. The MPA movie studio was really rather interesting. Upon entering, you came into what had once been a beautiful old synagogue with some remaining pews and balconies, a vaulted ceiling and lovely Old Testament windows—quite a sight.

The movie set was being assembled; Ben Johnson motioned me over to meet my co-star. "This is Sondra Fisher, she'll be playing the part of your wife. Sondra, this is Bob Carr."

We hadn't met before. She was a most attractive red head, a beautiful girl with a finely chiseled nose, which I assumed she had been born with. Her hair was still up in curlers; she wore a peignoir. I wasn't sure if she had just come from *her* bed or whether she was getting ready for *my* bed.

I took my eyes off Sondra to glance around the studio; one of the sets was being dressed and I realized the crew was making up a bed. Ben instructed one of the crew to get my pajamas.

"Yes, sir, Mr. Johnson, it'll just take a moment."

After checking out a couple of things about how the lights were being hung, Ben pointed me toward the dressing rooms. I was concerned as to whether or not I should leave on my boxers. I decided I would *not*. I would be bold. I stripped naked, slipped on the pajamas and my loafers, and reentered the studio. The farther I walked into the studio, the more modest I became. I slipped back and put on my undershorts.

Re-emerging from the dressing room, I was told by one of the floor crew to report to the set.

"Oh, Bob, I'm glad you're here. Come over and get into bed. Hey, Sondra! Sondra, come over and get in bed, too. We want to see how the lighting is going to look on this."

So, after having met for one brief moment, we slipped self-consciously under the covers.

"No, no, no, not *under* the covers," Ben ordered. "I want you both to sit up for a lighting check."

Actually, the bed was not a bed as in a bedroom but was an unfolded sofa couch sitting in what would be the center of the room. A couple of grips were on ladders, one practically hanging by his knees, trying to arrange klieg lights to focus on us. Behind the sofa a camera track was being set up. I had done hundreds of commercials where

I received the script early, had a chance to become familiar with it or memorize it, but I had never done anything quite like this, where we weren't handed the script before we got on the set.

I asked Sondra if she had seen the script. She had but didn't know what to make of it. She understood we would see the script in a few minutes and would have a chance to look it over and memorize it. I had a fleeting moment of horror as to how quickly I could memorize, hoping there would be plenty of time between takes.

As if on cue, a scrawny script girl appeared with pages, which seemed to have numerous alterations. She told us it was the final edit for the first scene, she hoped.

"Please take a look at this," she instructed, "and try to memorize your parts. The cameraman will be set up shortly and we'll try a couple of run-throughs, then do a take."

Sondra and I started sparring lines back and forth; the first couple of paragraphs gave us the giggles because it seemed so silly.

The director called for an on-camera rehearsal. "Now, Sondra, this is what I want you to do. The camera is going to be behind the sofa bed and when it comes on, all it is going to see is the back of the sofa with the room in the distance. Then your hand will emerge over the back, stroking the fabric sensuously; your fingers should tighten up to look tense. You will *then* sit up and say your first line. After your first line, Bob will sit up and counter with his line. Now, let's try that just to get the shots and see how the lighting looks."

We were instructed to get down in bed, out of camera sight. "Camera—Action!" Sondra's hand slipped up over the back of the bed sensuously and then suddenly her fingers clenched; she sprang up into camera view, and looking straight at the lens, she said, "What's *wrong* with you! You won't give it to me anymore, you won't give it to me anymore!"

I popped up with my line. "But I can't, darling, I *can't!*"

"I don't know what's wrong with you, aren't I desirable anymore?"

"Yes, you're desirable, but something seems to be wrong with me. I don't know what it is."

"You can't make love anymore, can you?"

"No, I'm afraid I can't, but I don't know what's wrong."

"You used to be such a wonderful lover."

"I know my dear, my love, but something seems to be stopping me."

"*Cut! Cut! Cut!*"

Ben, who had been behind the cameraman looking through the view-finder came up beside us. "Sounds pretty good. There are a couple of stilted lines we need to change but Sondra we *gotta* do something about your nighty. Bob, would you get out of bed for a minute while I have a couple of words with Sondra?"

"Of course, I'll get a coke."

When I sauntered back onto the set, Ben was still talking to Sondra. Her eyes looked fluid as if she were about to cry.

"Do you want to start shooting yet?" I asked.

"No, just stay over there for a moment." Then, directing a shout toward the crew, he said, "Take five!"

I sat down; the crew took off toward the coke machine and the johns. I heard

Sondra whisper, "I can't do it, I'm not going to do it, I can't do it. You know I can't."

What're they talking about? Am I going to be in the scene she's worried about?

Tears streamed down Sondra's face.

Ben comforted her quietly. "That's all right, dear, no one will ever know. Now let me help you."

With that she turned around slowly with her back to him, and his arms eased up under her flimsy gown and unfastened her strapless bra.

She turned to face him and began to cry. "You see, I don't have anything, I don't have anything, and everybody is going to know it."

"Don't worry about it, Sondra dear, it's going to be all right." I could overhear him saying, "We must have the bra off while your back is to the camera because it shows through your nighty. We'll put it back on again before you turn toward the camera."

The problem was obvious: poor Sondra had no boobs. Without the bra, she had no front, no cleavage. Needless to say, she was upset; however, Ben seemed to be able to console her. He slipped the bra discretely under his arm and announced to the rest of the crew, "Places again, places. Bob, hop back into bed, please."

I adjusted my pajamas, and myself, then slid down into bed as Sondra slipped down next to me.

"All right, we're going to do take-two now. Ready—Camera—Action!"

Sondra's hand eased up over the back of the sofa, sensuously caressed the upholstery, and then stiffened. She sat up, spoke her lines; I sat up and said my lines.

"*Cut! Cut! Cut!*"

Sondra and I looked at each other, perplexed. Ben was in a conversation with somebody just behind the camera; he walked over to me and whispered, "Are you wearing an athletic supporter?"

"A what?"

Quietly, he asked, "Are you wearing a jockstrap?"

"No!"

"There's some damn law in Louisiana," he moaned, "that states if two actors are in bed together, the male actor must be wearing an athletic supporter."

"I've got boxer shorts on."

"Oh shit, that's not going to do. We've got to get you a dammed jock strap. Did you bring one with you?"

"No, you didn't ask me to bring one. I don't run around wearing a jock strap, although maybe I should," I chuckled.

"Damn, we'll have to stop for a minute." Ben got up and walked over to a young black stagehand who was helping move scenery. He spoke to him briefly, then returned to the set. "Rehearse the lines," he lamented. "Elmer ran to the drug store. He'll be back in a few minutes. Go over your lines, Goddamn!"

Sondra and I began going over our lines. The more the lines unfolded, the more I realized the part I was playing was that of the *frigid husband!* We continued our lines and then stopped for a few minutes while Ben gave us *another* updated script.

"Ben, I thought this movie was called, *The Frigid Wife!*"

"It *is!* It's going to be in several episodes. We're filming the part where the *husband* is frigid!"

"And I'm playing the *frigid husband?*"

"Yes, you are!"

"Oh, ohhh. If there's one thing I consider myself, it's *not frigid.*"

"Then you'll have to act twice as hard!"

I thought to myself: *Lord, what a reputation to get. Anyway, it won't make much difference since I'm a faithful husband, whether the whole world thinks I'm frigid or not!*

Elmer came back with a package marked "athletic supporter." I slipped it on in the dressing room. Elmer, a head taller than I, and apparently longer, had bought a jock strap size *super-x.* I couldn't help but laugh; the jock strap hung practically to my knees. I pulled on my pajama bottoms and walked back onto the set.

"All tucked in?" Ben asked.

"Yeah, but did you know you sent a super-hung stud to shop? I'm not sure it's going to do much good."

"Never mind how it hangs, Bob, the law only requires you gotta be wearing one. It doesn't say whether or not it has to fit."

Sondra and I spent the rest of the morning in bed going over and over the "frigid husband" scene. We spent the afternoon filming on the set of the psychiatrist's office trying to figure out why I was frigid. Then we spent the early evening back in bed again practicing what the psychiatrist had taught us. Of course, instead of showing anything graphic, we just slid down behind the back of the sofa as the camera slowly panned to the ceiling.

By midnight, my part was finished. Charged with questions, Jan picked me up. I related all the details about the jockstrap and Sondra's boobs. We had a good laugh!

"There's one problem, Jan. It's not going to be the kind of picture our station manager, Mr. Read, ought to see, so I think we should stay low key about my being in the movie. At any rate, it was a quick $500 and that should give us enough money to put in a new bathroom for the kids."

We didn't hear anymore from the movie people for nearly six months. I was walking home late one afternoon in high spirits after pre-recording a phone interview with Patti Page, who was promoting her newly-cut disc of the title song from *Hush, Hush, Sweet Charlotte.* As I passed a Bourbon Street strip club, a poster in the window caught my eye: *The Frigid Wife* starring Sondra Fisher and Bob Carr! I gasped, deciding not to tell Jan what I'd seen. Then, alas, the next morning I spied an ad in the *Times-Picayune* with a large picture of Sondra Fisher, her breasts thrust forward. *Ah, those breasts,* I mused, *I wonder who's wearing them today!*

The Frigid Wife co-starring Sondra and *me,* was listed as a double feature with *The Facts of Life!*

Jan was unhinged. "Oh, my Lord, wait'll Mr. Read sees that *The Frigid Wife* has your name on it and the movie's showing at the Do Drive-In, the Jeff Drive-In, The Skyvue Drive-In and the Algiers Drive-In! *And* it says *adult entertainment!* Pray to God he only looks at the TV section."

We decided we'd better see the movie *immediately,* since I hadn't seen the final version. It was a balmy spring evening when we pulled up in front of the Do Drive-In screen in Old Metairie. When I hung the speaker inside the car window, the sound burst forth, filling the car as the credits began to beam onto the giant outdoor screen. Through the gnats and mosquitoes we could read: Starring Sondra Fisher, Bob Carr, with Sid Noel, etc.

On the screen came the back of the sofa with Sondra's hand stroking the upholstery; we broke into such giggles that we could hardly stand it. Jan thought it was the funniest thing she'd ever seen.

"Honey, this is supposed to be serious."

"It's so corny you should get an Oscar for Comedian of the Year!"

Suddenly, at the end of my episode, there was a break. The loud-speaker announced that attendants would be passing amongst the cars selling books for husbands and wives. This book would explain sexual problems, inadequacies, and frustrations.

"Oh, my Lord, I can't believe this!" Jan exclaimed.

"Now I get it, the money will be made from book sales!"

Following an intermission, *The Facts Of Life* beamed onto the screen. We breathed easier when we realized it was just a racy title for a long-forgotten comedy with Bob Hope and Lucille Ball. It wasn't sexy at all, just funny.

After the movie, we drove to New Orleanians' favorite Uptown hamburger place, the Camellia Grill, to get a cheese omelet and a milk shake to settle our nerves before driving to the Quarter. At home everybody was sound asleep; we crept quietly up to our bedroom.

"Now," Jan announced, "I'm going to find out if you *are* a frigid husband!"

* * * * *

The kids loved the environs of the French Market. Most every Saturday there was a need to shop at La Nasa's Hardware. Passing Brocato's ice-cream parlor, Timmy inevitably pulled the wagon up close to the long show window so Tammy and Tom could press their noses against the glass to see the *cannoli*, fig cookies and other Italian delights. The same litany was repeated week after week: "Daddy, we want some sesame seed cookies." Or, "Daddy, we want some raspberry or lemon ice." And every Saturday I'd say, "We'll get some on the way back!" (Sometimes we would!)

The delicious sugary aroma wafting along the street from the nearby praline stand would incite a new plea from the children, "Oh, daddy, we want pralines instead so we can eat 'em right now. Daddy, please, please can't we have some pralines right now!"

It was mid-October as we followed the same Saturday ritual. Approaching the French Market we could see that the produce trucks had, earlier in the day, unloaded an abundance of pumpkins.

"Daddy, daddy, daddy, we gotta get a punkun," Tammy pleaded.

"Yeah, daddy," Tim added. "We gotta get a punkun 'cause Tom's never had a chance to carve a punkun his-self. This'll be his most best Halloween ever, so we've got to get a really big one."

"Okay, okay, kids, you examine the pumpkins while I go over to La Nasa's."

I assisted the children across busy Decatur and watched as they quickly disappeared into the bowels of the produce market in search of the perfect pumpkin.

Besides looking for shutter hinges, I grabbed the chance to browse through the multitude of fascinating items on display; there was everything one needed to repair a Creole townhouse or a Victorian cottage. Replacement parts for gaslight fixtures particularly intrigued me, since they were probably available in very few places except Amish country. I fantasized about what it must have been like, in "olden nights," when the homes were lighted by the soft, mellow glow of natural gas so abundant in Louisiana. I purchased hinges, then went in search of the children busy inspecting pumpkins. Out of the hundreds of pumpkins lined up in several stalls, they seemed to have found the "perfect" one. I paused, at some distance for a few moments, just to watch them hard at work agonizing over their decision.

Spying me, Timmy dashed up, grabbed me by the hand, and dragged me toward their find. "Daddy, daddy, we found the perfect punkun; it's really big, and Tom loves it, so we gotta get it 'cause Tammy and me want him to see a really big carved punkun. It's almost big as him."

"Why do we need such a big pumpkin?"

"Because we *do*, daddy! We gotta have a really big punkun 'cause there's three of us that's gotta share it for Halloween."

Tammy, patiently holding Tom in her lap, was sitting in the red wagon pulled up next to the pumpkin of choice. Mr. Riccatto, the old Sicilian stall-keeper who had been at the market for many years, spotted me as I walked up with Timmy.

"Mistah Bub, your kids, dey find da really big apoompkin, I tink eet's da best apoompkin in da whole amarket."

"Yup, and it looks like the most expensive pumpkin, too."

"Mistah Bub, because you so nice, I tella you what, I giva you veddy gooda price on dees huge apoompkin."

"I don't know, Mr. Riccatto, that one over there looks very good to me."

Hearing my remark, the kids groaned in objection. The pumpkin I pointed to was about half the size of the one the kids had chosen. They looked at me pathetically with pleading eyes.

"Daddy, daddy, we jis' gotta have this punkun," Tammy beseeched. "It's so big we can almost put Tom inside and see if the good fairy will turn it into a Cinderella coach!"

"Yeah, daddy," Timmy added. "I know Tom wants this very punkun!"

I knew, as I approached, which pumpkin we were going to take home: the one the kids had already convinced Tom *he* wanted, the *big* one. After the appropriate good-natured haggling, Mr. Riccatto and I came to an amiable agreement about the price of the pumpkin.

"How are we going to get the pumpkin home?" I asked. "It's much too big for us to carry."

Timmy, ever the engineer, had it all figured out. Tammy would walk, much to her displeasure, so that the pumpkin and Tom could ride. It all sounded fine to me. I paid Mr. Riccatto, who helped me lift the pumpkin into the back of the wagon. Timmy and I piled Tom into the front, as counter-balance, propping him up against the pumpkin with his teddy and blankets tucked in around him. Tugging the wagon to get it started, Timmy set off down the little ramp to the street. Before I realized how much momentum the wagon had picked up, it was out of control and pushing Timmy down the ramp ahead of it. Careening, and narrowly missing Timmy, the wagon with Tom and the pumpkin bounced down off the ramp with a jolt.

There was that frightful moment of silence after the accident, before the damage was assessed. I breathed a sigh of relief; no one seemed hurt, but we watched in horror as our prized pumpkin rolled in slow-motion off the back of the wagon, tumbling into the gutter, splitting into a dozen pieces. Timothy stood horrified, Tammy let out a shriek, and Tom began to cry.

Throwing up his arms, Mr. Riccatto exclaimed, "Santa Maria, Mudder of Gawd!"

Three tourists browsing through the vegetables whirled around to see what caused the commotion. I dashed down the ramp to make sure Tom was okay; Tammy stood at the top of the ramp wailing.

When I realized Tom was okay and Tim had not been run over, I consoled Tammy. She threw her arms around me and buried her face between my legs and wailed uncontrollably. I looked over at Mr. Riccatto, who spread his arms wide apart with his palms to the sky and shrugged his shoulders in that Italian motion, which means: "So whatta we do now?"

"Mistah Bub, tella you what I'ma gonna do, I'ma gonna give you anudder apoompkin, I'ma know dere will *never* be nudder apoompkin like data one but you maka da childrens come up here and pick out anudder apoompkin. I'ma see a couple more on da truck, dey looksa real big."

Tammy's crying stopped as suddenly as it had started. Timmy jumped up from the bottom of the ramp, dusted himself off, leaving Tom and the wagon, and ran with Mr. Riccatto to the far end of the truck, where, fortunately, they found another pumpkin almost the same size.

I breathed a second sigh of relief. "Mr. Riccatto, what should we do with this broken pumpkin?"

"Mistah Bub, I'ma put dis in a bag for you, ana you taka dis homa to Mizz Jane to maka you a beeg apoompkin pie, so you have da special lagniappe. You have apoompkin pie from one apoompkin and you have a jack-o'-lantern from da udder apoompkin. Ana you have a Happy Halloween, children."

Profusely thanking Mr. Riccatto, and with Tom and the new pumpkin packed safely into the wagon, Tammy and I steadied the load as Tim pulled the five blocks home. No one even suggested that we stop at Brocato's for Italian cookies or lemon ice. All our thoughts were squarely on getting the pumpkin home. We pulled in through the side gate and drew the wagon into the patio. Jan and Olympia looked out from the kitchen to see what treasure we had brought home.

"Mommy, mommy, Lympy," Timmy hollered, "we got two punkuns for the price of one."

As Timmy and Tammy related our ordeal and the fact that Tom sped down a ramp all alone, Olympia cried out, "Mistah Cahr, what I'm gonna do wit you? You take dose' chilrin out, and you gits them in all kahnds o' trouble. Now tell me, dat baby boy o' mine all raht?"

"Olympia, your baby boy is all right. It's the *pumpkin* that's not all right."

"Bob, what's in that bag you have over your shoulder?"

"The first pumpkin, the *smashed* pumpkin."

"Yeah, mommy an' Lympy," Tammy added, "it an' Tom crashed into the gutter an' got all smashed!"

Olympia rolled her eyes as Jan rebuked me with, "Bob, I can't believe you let Tom fall out of the wagon into the gutter!"

In an endeavor to change the subject, I asked, "Olympia, do you know how to make a pumpkin pie out of real pumpkin?"

"Whachoo mean by dat, Mistah Cahr?"

"I mean, do you know how to make pie out of pumpkin that's not out of a can?"

"Ah swear to Gawd, Mistah Cahr, you think ah din't have no upbringing da way you talk to me. O' course, ah knows how to make a punkun pie out of real punkun."

"That's great, Olympia, 'cause it looks like we got enough pumpkin to make pies for the entire Parents Club."

Jan picked up Tom, realizing he obviously needed his diaper changed.

Turning into the kitchen with the bag of pumpkin pieces, Olympia glanced at Timmy, who was scratching his rear end. "Timmy, chile, ah swear to gawd, you can't be scratchin' like that in public, it's jis' not nahce."

"I'm not scratchin', Olympia."

"Chile, ah saw you scratchin'."

"Well, maybe jis' a little bit."

"Mizz Cahr, ah swear to Gawd, dat chile got those pin worms again. You better take a look at dat chile tonahght when he be sleepin', to see if he got dose pinworms. We can't have our sweet li'l Tom gittin' dose worms. Ah swear; ah don't know where you get dem worms from. Dey must be crawlin' under dis house down in that dirty fort."

Tammy piped up, "I git pin worms, too, Lympy, and the boys won't even let me go near the fort."

"Lord have mercy, chile, don't talk 'bout pin worms, young ladies not s'ppose to have pin worms."

"*All* my friends have pin worms."

"Lord have mercy, chile, must be dat school where you go to! Dey teach you to speak French an' all dat, an' you still get the pinworms."

"Let's not talk about the pin worms any more; I'll check them tonight when they're asleep," Jan said.

Children and pin worms seemed to be a way of life in New Orleans. Wherever kids played in a sandbox, on the banquette, at a playground or in school—wherever—they seemed to get pinworms. Dr. Simon told Jan pinworms were just a normal part of growing up in New Orleans. Pinworms are parasitic creatures that reside in the lower intestines and the rectal areas of humans, especially children. Checking for the little critters is a bit gross. Jan and I waited until the children were asleep so she could pull down their underpants, spread their buttocks apart and put a piece of Scotch tape across the anus, while I held a flashlight. Once removed, the Scotch tape is affixed to a glass slide and taken to the doctor. Obviously, there are two reasons for scheduling this procedure in the middle of the night: one, the children wouldn't let you do it if they're awake; secondly, the pinworms seemed to be more active around the rectum in the still of the night.

Tammy, Timmy, and I sat down at a table in the patio to carve our treasured pumpkin, soon to become a work of art. Instead of putting it in the front window, we put it up on the front balcony with a sheet around its base. According to the kids, it terrified everybody who came up or down Bourbon Street.

The kids loved to go tricking-or-treating on Halloween in the French Quarter, always a challenge because of the many sinister places. It often seemed threatening just to approach the door, much less dare to ring the bell. Over the years, we had discovered that one of the best places to get candy and treats was along tawdry Decatur Street. The barmaids in the seedy joints delighted in the surprise of seeing children in costume. Once the most dangerous section of town, where vicious murders had occurred, the area was now much less perilous, although no less shoddy. The alcoholics who frequented the bars and wandered the streets had become so mentally lethargic that they were little menace to anyone except themselves.

During the week Olympia had taken the children to "Wools-worth's" to get their Halloween costumes. Timmy was dressed as a Buccaneer like Jean Lafitte, Tammy was Snow White, and Tom looked anorexic as a skeleton. The first stop on our rounds was at what New Orleanians call the "Haunted House" on the corner of Governor Nicholls and Royal, where Madame Dauphine La Laurie had tortured her slaves in the attic a hundred and some-years prior. A slave who had been chained in the attic broke loose, fled the wrath of her mistress, and jumped from the third floor into the patio, dying in agony. According to legend, every Halloween the dead slave's screams could be heard throughout the neighborhood. The kids were terrified. *They loved it!* I don't remember ever hearing screams but I always pretended I did. However, our good friend, artist Zella Funck, who lived in the building for a short time, moved out after hearing strange wails and lamentations just prior to the mysterious dislodging of a huge dining room chandelier that came crashing down during a dinner party, scattering the guests in fright.

Our petite assemblage of goblins strolled along the street, stopping by the house where everybody said "the crazy lady" lived. Timmy bravely climbed the stoop, rang once timidly, and jumped quickly back to the banquette. Nobody came to the door, but the anticipation was scary enough. Continuing on our way, we saw numerous elderly Italian ladies with jet-black dyed hair sitting on their stoops handing out candy corn and jellybeans to children who braved the sinister evening.

On Decatur Street, the kids dashed brazenly into one bar after another, shouting, "Trick or treat, trick or treat." Either the barmaid, a longshoreman, a sailor, or a stevedore would give them a little something, mostly peanuts or pretzels. Even some of the inebriated would reach into their pockets and give them a penny or two. It seemed like an unlikely place for a family to go trick-or-treating, but the people along Decatur Street were pleased by helping the children celebrate Halloween.

One "lady," well past her prime and over her limit, clutched her bar stool and began to weep when she spied little Tom in his skeleton suit. Taking one hand from the stool, she reached out for Tom in a pathetic gesture. Tom screamed in fright, so startling the woman that she nearly toppled from the stool; to catch herself, she grabbed onto the bar and swung around, laying her head down, weeping as if in pain. Jan and I and the children stood transfixed.

"Aggie, what's da mattah?" the bartender asked.

"Dhat liddle skelton," she replied through her sobs, "is jis' the size of my precious liddle Ant'ny in a crypt at da Saint Louis Cemetery Number Two."

Her uncontrollable sobs frightened Tom into tears; Jan's eyes also began to dampen. Leaning over to console Aggie, the bartender motioned us on.

Outside the bar, Tammy wanted to know why the woman was crying. Jan did her best to explain, causing Tammy to break into tears. A slightly inebriated gentleman staggering by offered his condolences, distracting Tammy enough for her to forget her sorrow.

Our trail along Decatur took us past the Central Grocery, where the children cupped their hands around their faces as they gazed through the show window at the muffalettas and the variety of Italian foodstuffs on display. Peeking through the doors at Tujague's restaurant was fun until the sight of all the diners glaring back caused the kids to retreat without asking for treats or threatening tricks.

The ultimate treat of the evening was found at Morning Call coffee shop, where ten cents would purchase a café au lait and beignets. With powered sugar dribbled abundantly over the kids' costumes, we headed home through Jackson Square, entering shadowy Pirate's Alley. Near the house where William Faulkner wrote his first novel, we turned up the little alley that dead-ends right in front of Le Petit Salon. Timmy ran ahead to ring "Aunt Mawgie's" doorbell. In a few moments Margie leaned over the balcony and waved at us, tossing a bag of goodies. The bag burst, sending wrapped fruit-candies rolling in a circle like the wake in water when a pebble has been dropped. The kids scrambled to retrieve their treasures. We threw a kiss to Margie, who wished us happy Halloween from her cast-iron vantage point.

My mini goblins dashed merrily along toward Bourbon Street for our walk home. Saul Owens was standing in front of the club his wife, Chris Owens, was making famous. He looked as stern and intimidating as usual. The kids opted not to stop. Suddenly, Chris, bigger than life, stepped forth with a couple of her mariachi chorus girls to check out the tourists along the street. Business seemed to have slowed down along the strip on the eve of All Saints' Day. Chris recognized Jan and me from television and waved pleasantly as Timmy rather shyly declared, "Trick or treat, trick or treat, ma'am!"

Chris stooped down to Timmy's height to say hello, giving him a kiss on the cheek. Tammy wanted Tom to have a closer vantage point, so we eased the wagon up to the front door. One of the mariachi girls reached into the club and came forth with some cocktail napkins as her treat.

According to legend, Chris and Saul Owens had met and fallen in love while dancing a theatrical version of the cha-cha-cha at the Fountain Lounge in the Roosevelt Hotel. We held the fable to be true because we had seen them dancing there. Patrons had enjoyed their rhythmic antics so much on the dance floor that they opened a club of their own with Chris as the featured entertainer, backed up by some less voluptuous but very attractive "cha-cha girls." Bolstered by recorded Latin music and some bongo drums, Saul and Chris's Club was fast becoming the rage of Bourbon Street. Chris, devoutly religious and a trained nurse from Texas, had come to New Orleans to serve people through a career in medicine. It was obvious to Saul that she had other talents, which would also serve people by making them happy.

Mother Nature endowed Chris with all her attributes, but God blessed her with the gift of energy. Several times nightly, Chris bounced onto the mini stage of their nightclub with the jolt of an electric shock, her lithe, sensuous body moving energetically to the pulsating throb of the bongo drums. Pitched forward on flashing spiked heels higher than any other woman in the world could negotiate, Chris cha-cha'd, merengued, sambaed, and tangoed her way across the dance floor while the chorus girls undulated as a backdrop. The Chris Owens show became noteworthy along Bourbon Street as an oasis from the tawdry fleshpot strippers permeating the neighborhood. Chris was sensuous and appealing without shedding her clothes. Here was a place you could take grandma and grandpa from Topeka for a racy thrill without feeling raunchy. Saul and Chris, along with Al Hirt and Pete Fountain, were setting a new standard for Bourbon Street, one that Jan and I, and all the members of the Parents Club, hoped would supersede the sordid sex spots.

Continuing toward home, the kids took great pleasure in dashing up to the barkers in front of the various clubs and startling them with "Trick or treat!" The worst they received was the door closed in their faces so they couldn't see in. Club owners gave strict orders that the doors were to be closed if minors walked by.

In the use of the swinging door, the barkers are masters of the tease; tourists get only a quick glance at the strippers. Hopefully, just enough to entice them in for an expensive drink and a cheap thrill. The tourists, however, very seldom snagged a peek at the exotic headliners: Evangeline, the Oyster Girl; Jezebel, the Girl with a Thousand Movements; Ramona, the Cat Girl, etc., without paying the tariff at a tiny table. Patti White, School Teacher Turned Stripper, always intrigued Timmy, likewise his father! I always wanted to have her as a guest on our radio or TV show to talk about education (of course!), but Jan wouldn't hear of it.

At the corner of Orleans Street, two black nuns from the Sisters of the Holy Family fluttered by, paying their respects to our progeny by genuflecting slightly, then scurrying off into their convent for Vespers, the breeze off the river tugging at their wimples. I found it bizarre that their nunnery was housed in the very edifice that had been the notorious Quadroon Ballroom, the hangout for white Creole dandies who fancied "high yellah" beauties! That building needed a lot of contrition.

Crossing Dumaine Street, Timmy and Tammy announced they wanted to go into *that* place, because Ricky, who worked there as a bartender, promised he'd give them some candy on Halloween. *That* place was Lafitte's In Exile, the famous homosexual hangout.

"Jan, how in the heck do they know Ricky?"

"Ricky's that real sweet bartender who befriended your mother one day in Jackson Square when she and the kids were having a picnic."

"Leave it to mother! She makes friends with absolutely *everybody*. I'm not sure we should let the kids go in there!"

Before the words were out of my mouth, Timmy and Tammy had already run inside. We could see through the shadows of the dimly-lit bar that they were carrying on some sort of transaction. I stood on the corner with Jan, who stared in dismay. Tom was asleep in the wagon.

You could look through the door of Lafitte's and see what some might call an eternal flame burning in an open-pit fireplace. I think Tennessee Williams once referred to the flame as long and hot and licking the sky!

The kids scampered out onto the banquette; Ricky waved from behind the bar while shouting, "Happy Halloween, little dahlings!" Their loot turned out to be bar peanuts and a few swizzle sticks.

Approaching our house, we could see Uncle Lindsay, our recently-arrived West Virginia transplant, sitting on the front steps with his friend Marilyn.

"Where've you been?" he asked impatiently. "I told you I'd be over here to bring some trick-or-treat things for the kids."

Timmy pulled the wagon up next to Lindsay and Marilyn to get a closer look at the bag on the steps beside them. Since the day they were born, Lindsay had always thought of our kids as his real nieces and nephews, and whenever there was a holiday, he never failed to bring them abundant gifts. Once in the house, the children waited with thinly-controlled patience, as "Uncle" Lindsay doled out the treats in a slow and measured manner. When the goody bag fell empty on the floor, the kids quickly turned their attentions to displaying their newfound booty, to compare and divvy it up.

"Bob, you can't imagine how many people have mentioned they saw Marilyn and me on TV in the ghost story we filmed for your show."

"I had no idea so many people watched *Second Cup*," Marilyn added. "You must have millions of viewers!"

"Daddy, is that ghost story really true?" Tammy asked.

"I know it's true," Timmy stated, "'cause Nana Carr told me it was true. She said when she an' Jandad were jis' married they were drivin' to Chicago along this super highway an' they stopped for gas, and while Nana was waitin' in the car she could see this old lady sittin' on a big rock across the highway. Isn't that right, daddy?"

"That's right. The old lady wore a black dress with a black bonnet; she looked sad but had a very sweet face. When Jandad got back in the car, Nana asked him to drive over to the old lady to see if she needed help, or a ride. They pulled up by this huge rock where the lady was sitting. She told them she needed a ride to Chicago."

"Daddy," Timmy interrupted, "let *me* tell the rest. So they put 'er in the back of the car, one of those kinda cars like our Triumph, where you lean forward and the person gets in the back seat, a two-door car. Anyways, they put 'er in the back seat and talked to 'er for a little while. She was real old. When they asked her where she was goin', she told 'em she was goin' *home*. She told 'em her name was Miss Camerdale and she had the prettiest house on the block with a humongous brass door-knocker. Jandad said it wasn't too far from where they were goin', so they'd take her right to 'er house. Isn't that right, daddy?"

I nodded affirmatively.

Timmy continued. "They kept drivin' for a while an' then Nana turned around to ask her 'xactly where they oughta turn off to get to her house. When Nana looked in the back seat, the lady was *gone!* She looked on the floor, everywhere, an' she didn't see nobody. Nana was really scared so Jandad stopped the car real quick. They opened the doors an' got out an' looked everywhere, but the lady wasn't anywheres. They even opened the trunk but the lady *wasn't there!* I mean she was just gone. So they turned around an' went back a little ways but they couldn't find her. Nana remembered her number, where she lived. They finally found her falling-down old house. Jandad banged on the door, using the big old knocker she'd told 'em about. It was all blackish. Isn't that right, daddy?"

"That's right. Let me finish the story, just the way it was told to me. The place looked spooky, like an old rooming house, so Nana, afraid to stay in the car, followed Jandad to the door. When an old man wearing an undershirt answered the door, Jandad asked, 'Is this where Miss Camerdale lives?'

"The man looked at them strangely. 'You kiddin', Mister. Miss Camerdale? Good

God, Miss Camerdale sure don't live here!'

"'She moved?'

"'Good God, no! Not 'lest they moved her grave. She's been dead for some years now, killed out thar on the four-lane highway, yah, some twenty-five years ago, out thar on the new highway.'

"'Route Six?'

"'What's that, ma'am?'

"'Route Six, was she killed out on Route Six?'

"'Yah, sure was. 'Round where Six an' Thirty all comes together, all those fillin' stations, *bad* traffic, always was.'

"Astounded, Jandad asked one more question: 'How was she killed?'

"'Can't rightly 'member 'zakly, been so long now. Hmm. Do 'member she was thrown outa the car an' smashed plum against a big rock. Guess that's what really done 'er in. Why, what's it to you folks anyways?'

"'Oh, nothing,' Jandad replied. 'We just thought we met her once. We heard she was a very nice lady.'

"'Guess she was. People still talkin' bout her in this here neighborhood. They say this old dilapidated house use ta be beautiful when she owned it, 'fore it was a roomin' house. Course this neighborhood ain't what it use ta be!'"

I continued through the conclusion of the story. "Nana and Jandad went back to the car dazed as if trapped in a great grey cobweb, certain that Miss Camerdale had truly been in their car earlier in the day, even though the old man insisted she had been killed many years before, crushed against the very rock where she had appeared to be sitting."

There was dead silence for a few moments before Tammy spoke. "Daddy, that's the dumbest story I've ever heard. Nana and Jandad told you that story. Are you sure it's true?"

"Would your grandparents fib? They've told me that story ever since I was a little child like you all; they swear it's true. It's why we did that film today. Marilyn played the old Lady and Uncle Lindsay played the old man at the house; mother and I played Nana and Jandad."

"Do you believe it's true, Uncle Lindsay?" Timmy asked.

"Don't know. Don't much believe in ghosts."

"Do you believe in the Holy Ghost?" Tammy inquired.

"Well, honey, I really couldn't say."

"My teacher says the Holy Ghost is the best ghost in the whole wide world."

Jan interrupted, "Kids, you'd better get upstairs and take your baths. Remember, we have an early-morning picnic tomorrow."

"You're going on a picnic?" Marilyn asked in surprise. "But tomorrow's All Saints' Day."

"I know. That's why we're going on a picnic. Terry Flettrich suggested we all go on a picnic in Saint Roch Cemetery. She's going to take pictures for a TV photo essay. It should be interesting. You two want to join us?"

"A picnic in the Saint Roch Cemetery?" Lindsay retorted. "Are you kidding? I wouldn't be caught dead there!"

Chuckling, I showed Marilyn and Lindsay to the door as Jan took the kids upstairs.

Re-entering the front parlor to turn off the lights, I sensed I was not alone. A vague scent, akin to ether, became apparent. I switched off the lamp and was immediately conscience of an apparition standing in front of the fireplace. She was petite, dressed in a black hoopskirt and stood perfectly still. I squinted in disbelief, unable to make out her face, but I could see the back of her head reflected in the huge gold-leaf mirror above the mantelpiece. A large mother-of-pearl comb held her abundant "cow pie" hairdo in place. The comb looked like the one I had found lodged behind a drawer of the dresser we had purchased with the house. The aroma of jasmine mixed with ether invaded the room. I stood transfixed as the passing Desire bus shook the entire building. I continued to stare at the little lady, but she seemed to be fading as I squinted grotesquely, trying to lock her in my vision.

"Wait!" I beseeched. My voice sounded hollow as it bounced back across the room. The apparition was fading, but like the last burst of flame before an ember dies, her face was suddenly aglow. I couldn't make out any distinct facial characteristics, but her luminosity revealed the most beautiful smile I had ever seen. I strained to hold her in my sight but felt she was retreating to some distant place. Her image almost gone, the lips of her gentle mouth closed around her incandescent teeth, forming a farewell kiss that rushed toward me, discharging one last pungent fragrance.

Momentarily overcome, then regaining my composure, I flipped on the light. *Nothing!* I squinted my eyes, attempting to recapture my lady. There was nothing on the mantel but the dull bronze face of the clock with its back reflected in the mirror, and below, the curved black opening of the Victorian fireplace where I had seen a hoopskirt. As I reached to turn out the lamp once again, my hand brushed against the bouquet of fragrant fresh flowers Jan had placed on the table earlier in the day. *Had these ingredients conspired to form this apparition in my mind?*

With a chill tingling along my spine, I bolted up the stairs, thrilled the kids were there to meet me with a goodnight hug.

After we got the kids settled down, Jan and I fell into bed. I told her what I had experienced. Could the specter have been a friend of my great-grandmother Aupagnier, who had lived a few blocks away on Esplanade? We cuddled together whispering of ghosts, goblins, phantoms, and the Holy Spirit. When my spirit turned to things carnal, Jan defused me with a few tickles and ghostly wails. We giggled playfully before falling asleep entwined in each other's arms.

Tom in Bob's arms with Playboy Bunnies and other Parents Club kids in our patio, 1964

Bunny Bread Bunnies in Flettrich's patio, 1964

Kitty West as "Evangeline the Oyster Girl" emerging from her giant shell on Bourbon Street, 1961

Advertising poster for Bob Carr in Frigid Wife *at the drive-in movies, 1963*

Victorian settees circa 1860 with India block print drapes in restored front parlor

Louisiana four poster bed circa 1850 with Bob's added ceiling fan

Birthday Partying on the St. Charles Streetcar

T erry phoned the next morning, waking us from having overslept. She and Jan made final plans to meet at the entrance of Saint Roch Cemetery at noon for our picnic. Terry thought it would be great fun, educational for the kids, and an opportunity for her to shoot some fascinating photos for her TV essay. *Interesting and educational maybe but great fun?*

Luncheon amongst the tombs seemed a bit ghoulish; however, Terry had led us blithely into many unforgettable situations throughout our TV association, so why not give it a try? After all, we had sailed together up the Mississippi submerged in a U.S. Navy submarine, stepped through cow pies together at the grassy Franklin, Louisiana, air strip, and slept three-in-a-bed at the Plaza in New York to save money—learning experiences all—so why not one more escapade to add to our *curriculum vitae?*

Saint Roch Cemetery, begun in the 1870s and well-known for its chapel, had for many years been one of the most ardent observers of All Saints' Day festivities. Although predominately a burial ground for German-American Catholics, Roman Catholics of all ilks—Creole, Italian, Irish, Spanish, and others—descended on the cemetery on All Saints' Day, making a pilgrimage to the final resting place of their ancestors.

By the time we got to the vicinity of the cemetery, it was already hard to find a parking place; but once we did, we made our way along the ancient rampart to the front gate, adorned by two hurricane-ravaged, wingless angel statues keeping vigil atop plastered pillars, while a pair of Moorish-style gatehouses loomed as watchtowers of protection.

Clusters of people were already milling about, some socializing while others scurried in and out past the iron gates with vases of flowers. Many people had obviously risen extremely early in order to come to the cemetery so that their floral arrangements might adorn the family tomb for the entire Holy Day. During the week prior, most folks had scrubbed or whitewashed their family tombs, giving the cemetery the appearance of a sun-baked Greek island village, very Mykonosian. We spotted Terry with Rennie just inside the gate, already conducting an interview with the grave master, who chose to be referred to as the "Sexton of Saint Roch."

Tammy and Tom had spied the balloon vender and the cotton candy man, who had set up a position on the neutral ground across from the main gate. Even before they asked, I told them "yes" to the balloons and "no" to the cotton candy because we already had more than enough food in the picnic hamper. Timmy, Tammy, Tom, Rennie, and Kelvin, whom we had brought along at Timmy's insistence, all dashed across the street, dodging the mounting auto traffic to buy balloons.

Terry had arranged with the sexton for us three adults to tour the chapel so that we could view the plaster of Paris replicas of body parts placed there in gratitude for miraculous healings. It all seemed too bizarre to Jan and me, reared in the Ohio Protestant ethic of burying in the ground with nothing more than small headstones or plaques to mark the graves. The thought of seeing body parts in effigy was ominously grotesque.

The children became restless during our conversation and begged to walk around the cemetery on their own. I suggested they stake out a nice picnic spot between tombs while they wandered around. They were to use the high-flying balloons to indicate their location, enabling us to easily spot them following our tour.

The sexton motioned us toward the chapel. Jan and I felt embarrassed as he rudely nudged pilgrims out of the way so that we could move through the crowd. Terry was busy clicking away as we pushed up to the front doors of the tiny Gothic chapel, so small that it looked as if it were only part of a church yet to be built. The petite place of worship, opened almost one hundred years ago, had become a shrine to Saint Roch, who was especially beseeched by those afflicted with disease and deformities. His feast day, August 16th, and All Saints' Day on November 1st, as well as All Souls' Day on November 2nd, had become occasions attracting hundreds of people, sometimes thousands.

Edging our way to the entrance, we were bumped by ladies backing out of the chapel, genuflecting, and making the sign of the cross as they departed. Three of them were penitentially barefoot. I gawked as the sexton motioned us into the tiny structure accommodating about sixty people. The "devotees" sat or knelt facing a Gothic altar adorned with an almost life-size statue of Saint Roch. One couldn't help but be touched by the air of piety saturating this sacred place. The gathering crowd outside was so large that I wondered how long they would have to wait to enter this fraction of a church.

The sexton directed us up to the altar. He pointed back toward the stone slab we had just traversed in the miniature central aisle and said, "Look! Under there are the remains of the late Reverend Leonard Thevis, pastor of the German Roman Catholic Church of the Holy Trinity. He's the one who introduced 'supreme holy devotion' to Saint Roch at this site. He also established the cemetery and saw to the building of this renowned holy chapel."

"Who was Saint Roch?" I whispered.

"He was a popular patron saint in Europe for many centuries. In 1867, the very pious Father Thevis petitioned Saint Roch to intervene in the teeming epidemic of cholera and yellow jack ravaging New Orleans."

"What's yellow jack?" Jan asked quietly.

"Same thing as yellow fever."

It made me uncomfortable to whisper questions in front of the worshipers, although the devoutly kneeling pilgrims seemed to be unaware of our intrusion or of Terry's snapping pictures. I was surprised and shocked when the sexton pulled us through the center opening of the altar rail into the sanctum sanctorum. I was even more shocked, as were Jan and Terry, when we glanced down and saw the figure of a dead Jesus lying beneath the altar table. Jan lurched back, grabbing me by the arm; she stared at the simulated corpse much as one would view a body in a morgue. In the niche directly above the altar stood the statue of Saint Roch. We could see his staff was topped with a gourd for drinking water. Crouched at his side was his faithful dog, which, according to legend, fed him when he himself was stricken with the plague.

"I don't know if that means the dog brought him food or if he ate the dog!" I whispered to Jan.

She scowled at me with a "be quiet and be serious" look.

The left index finger of the Saint Roch statue pointed to a scar on his leg, used by his family to identify him after his death in prison.

The sexton hustled the three of us through the diminutive door to the right of the altar. For the first time in my life, I felt a sense of claustrophobia. The four of us more than filled the crypt-like chamber that was garnished with the most peculiar sights one could behold.

"These are *ex-votos*," the sexton explained, "objects left by grateful petitioners of Saint Roch to express their thanks to him for the relief of unbearable ailments. Persons who have suffered an affliction or a disease often come back to this shrine and place a replica of the afflicted part of their healed body. They come back gratefully and joyfully to let Saint Roch know that their prayers have been answered."

The sexton continued his somewhat rote explanation, but I was deaf to his words. It was as if we had all suddenly been plunged into a bargain basement of body parts: there was a liver with the word "thanks" written on it, and replicas of legs, hands, feet, a torso, and even a face hung in rather orderly but random fashion from hooks screwed into the masonry wall—all surveyed by a pair of watchful artificial eyes gazing blankly at us from their mount near the ceiling. Interspersed with these human parts were children's shoes, crutches, braces, and a set of teeth. It all seemed too bizarre, compounded by Terry's camera shutter clicking away. It was stifling; the air seemed devoid of oxygen.

The sexton pointed to a plaster leg bearing the year 1947. "That was placed here by a Navy vet wounded in the Pacific. When he thought they were gonna amputate his leg, he prayed to Saint Roch, and the gangrene went away. His leg was saved, so he put this replica here in grateful thanks."

Terry continued to snap as the sexton related his stories with great relish. I was beginning to feel breathless and queasy; Jan had taken on a color more cadaverous in hue than most of the replicas. I suggested we leave.

Reluctantly, the sexton relinquished his role as performing historian to lead us back through the tiny Gothic door into the sanctuary. We eased our way once again past the altar, down the aisle between the worshipers and out the front door into a blast of fresh air, where a now-even-larger crowd waited to enter. The sexton was needed at the front gate but suggested we cross Music Street to the other section of the cemetery and look at St. Michael's chapel with its flying buttresses. "The only flying buttresses in Louisiana, that's what they tell me."

Tammy ran up and yanked on Jan's dress, saying, "Mommy, Tom and me are tired waiting on that hard iron bench; our behinds have marks on 'em from sittin' so long, and besides, we're hungry. We wanna see what's in the picnic basket."

Terry queried the sexton, "Is it all right if we have a picnic?"

"There's a nice little grassy spot over there on the right-hand side of the cemetery next to the yellow jack mausoleum. Why don't you spread out a blanket and enjoy yourselves. It's a great day for a picnic—watch out for the *mosquitoes!*"

Tom grasped my hand. "I'm scared. I don't want to have a picnic in this dead people's park. I wanna go to City Park, where it's fun!"

"This'll be just fine," Jan consoled. "Now, let's find the boys."

Tammy took Jan's other hand, and we set out looking for the balloons the boys were to use as a signal. Wandering between the tombs was like an engraved history of the ethnic settlers of New Orleans: Podrasky, Gaczik, Tolivar, Couvillon, Michel, Boudreaux, Byrnes, Sciortino, D'Agosta, Zaehringer, Meisner, and Schwegmann. On one crypt facade was etched *Hier ruhen die familie Chardon und Healy.*

We passed beside a long row of vaults built into the outside wall of the cemetery looming high over our heads.

"Daddy, are there dead peoples in all those little places?"

"Yes, Tammy."

"What are all those little places called?"

"Many people in New Orleans call them ovens because they sort of look like old-fashioned ovens."

"Daddy, you mean like where they make bread?"

"That's right."

"Ukk," Tom asserted, "I'll never eat bread again!"

"Is this where they get the body of Jesus bread for church?"

"No, Tammy, that bread comes from a bakery. It's really bread. It's made from wheat, not from skin."

"It kinda looks like white skin when the priest gives it out."

"Ukk," Tom remarked once more.

"Daddy, daddy, mommy, mommy," Tammy interrupted. "Look up, see the balloons? Look!"

The colorful balloons danced merrily over a large tomb engraved with the family name of Anderson. We came upon the boys, already stretched out on a grassy spot in the shade of the tomb, starved and bored. Jan complained that the three boys shouldn't sit on the grass in their shorts without a blanket under them.

"Oh, mommy, it's just grass and sand. It's not like dirty dirt! It's just sand and grass we been playin' in."

"Timmy, we're going to spread out a blanket!" I emphasized. "So you boys get up and *on* the blanket. Mother and Terry are afraid you might get pin worms or bitten by red ants or something."

On hearing that, all the kids scrambled onto the blanket. Jan began doling out the food while I opened a large bottle of Barq's and filled paper cups. Terry once again began clicking away, trying to capture the scene. I was feeling self-conscious sitting in the middle of the cemetery picnicking while devout relatives walked past us mumbling prayers, making the sign of the cross, and placing vases of flowers on the stone shelves protruding from the ovens.

Two ladies with rolled stockings and jet black teased hair stopped and stared.

"Aren't ch'all...?"

"Yes," I replied.

They turned quickly and hustled behind a tomb.

Jan went about the business of distributing the sandwiches. Without warning, the two "teased" ladies reappeared around the tomb with five or six others. They stood gaping at us, as if we were on display, while we munched our lunch.

"Lord have mercy, if y'all don't look just like you do on the Tee-N-Vee," came the pronouncement from the most aggressive gawker of the group.

"We wouldn't miss y'all's program," interjected another.

"That's right. We eat our lunch watchin' y'all."

"Well, I guess turnabout's fair play. Hope it doesn't upset your stomachs," I retorted jocularly, my remark totally eluding them.

"Miss Fletcher, you look smaller than on the Tee-N-Vee!" said one of the ladies. This was probably the most common comment Terry received when seen in public by fans. It always gave me a kick: first of all, she was not Miss 'Fletcher' but Mrs. Flettrich, a well-established New Orleans name; secondly, her bearing on TV gave viewers the impression she was much taller than her five foot two. The unflappable Terry didn't stop for a minute; she kept exercising the shutter of her camera. Several other ladies pushed through the little crowd carrying jars filled with plastic flowers. One of the ladies vainly struggled to get her bouquet up and into a granite vase attached to the side of a tomb. I stood up and set the faux chrysanthemums in place for her. With a nervous giggle, she thanked me politely.

One lady who had recognized us asked, "Do you know who that is, Angelica? Do you know who that is, that's helping you?"

Angelica looked perplexed.

"That's Bawb Cawr from channel 6, and that's Miss Jane and that's Terry Fletcher, and that's all their children sittin' there!"

The whole circumstance seemed surreal: the afternoon sun shining through a bank of clouds played shadowy charades on the funerary monuments; us sitting on a plot of cemetery turf having lunch; people streaming by with memorial flowers; the subdued sound of devotions mixed with laughter and gossipy chatter. I had the strange sensation of watching the entire event on a large television screen.

Suddenly, from the other direction, two nuns approached, gliding briskly along the concrete walkway; white wimples framed their rosy angelic faces bereft of cosmetics. Terry aimed her camera in their direction; they looked away discreetly as they paused. Terry tried another shot; each nun prudently raised her hand to partially cover her face.

"You don't want your pictures taken?" Terry asked, *still clicking!*

"Portraits are for the worldly and the prideful," replied the older of the two. "They have no place in the life of one who has taken vows of piety."

Having been mildly rebuked, Terry parried with another question, "Why are you here today?"

The same nun replied quietly, "This is the day of the dead and it is well that they be remembered with an exterior manifestation of love. These flowers show remembrance and respect, and with them the people offer up their prayers." The nuns curtsied respectfully, almost simultaneously, and passed on their way, not recognizing Terry Flettrich as one of the foremost television personalities of the city.

The cemetery was beginning to turn into a veritable horticultural display. Fresh and plastic flowers were everywhere: in vases, bottles, urns, some in tin cans, others in boxes of sand. Jan and I still felt a bit self-conscious picnicking between the tombs while the reverent knelt and prayed piously within smelling distance of Terry's sardine po-boys and the kids' peanut butter and jelly sandwiches. Terry, trying to dispel our discomfort, explained that one of her elderly Catholic neighbors told her that in her day, the truly devout brought beverages and victuals so that they could observe an all-day vigil in a show of deference to their dearly departed.

The boys began to get fidgety; I gave permission to wander around a little while. Jan gave them last-minute instructions about being quiet and polite as they dashed off behind the tombs. Tammy and Tom were content to sit with their coloring books, while Terry, Jan, and I went to see the restored Chapel of Saint Michael with its flying buttresses across Music Street.

Making our way along the main avenue of the dead, we were aware of a new crowd of people who had entered the graveyard. These pilgrims were ill and afflicted: one woman with failing sight steered her course with a cane, a lame lady made her way cautiously, a crippled man in a wheelchair was pushed by what appeared to be a relative. Several persons fondled their rosaries while chanting, "Hail Mary, full of grace. Blessed art Thou amongst women, and blessed is the fruit of Thy womb, Jesus. Holy Mary, Mother of God, pray for us sinners now and at the hour of our death." There was a mother with a baby carriage and at least two ladies pushing tots in strollers.

Noticing that women significantly outnumbered men, I wondered if women possess a greater innate longing for a conciliatory relationship with their creator through love and obedience than do men. A fervent perception radiated in me that their God was near at hand, and so were the departed souls of their loved ones. Although detached, I was aware that a reverent melancholy saturated the afternoon atmosphere. This stirring scene was etched in my psyche, and for a moment I felt transported to some eastern Mediterranean village.

The incessant clicking of Terry's camera returned me to reality. The afternoon sun had become oppressively warm, so Jan and I returned to Tammy and Tom, still coloring in the shade of the Anderson tomb. I asked them to run off and find the boys while we picked up the blanket and prepared to leave.

Shortly the whole crew reappeared. The boys had stretched out on the grass for a while but had begun to feel itchy. So instead they moved over and lay down next to Jesus.

"Next to *Jesus?*"

"Yah, daddy, Jesus is right over there! They've got lots of statues of him all over the place!"

Kelvin pointed out that they were the Stations of the Cross.

"What kinda stations?" Tammy wanted to know.

"They show the stuff that happened to Jesus on his way to get nailed on the cross," Kelvin explained, while scratching at the crotch of his shorts.

Tammy and Tom insisted on taking a look. All the children were so intrigued by the artistic statuary portrayals that we visited all fourteen. At each niche, we stopped to read the words beneath the depictions. By the time we viewed the last station, the boys were complaining of itching and were tugging at their trousers with such vigor that we thought it best to get them home.

Passing through the gate, the kids spied the cotton candy vendor still plying his trade on the neutral ground. I promised to treat them all if the boys would stop their pesky scratching. Together with the cotton candy, we piled into the car and headed back to the Quarter.

By the time we got home, I noticed that Timmy and Kelvin, the only two boys who had been wearing short pants, had drawn blood from digging at their thighs.

"Boys, what's the matter? Why you are scratching so much?"

"Daddy, I don't know. I think somethin' ate us up!"

"That's right, Mr. Carr, ever since we laid down on that grass and took a little rest in the cemetery, somethin's been eatin' us up!"

"Let me take a look at it."

"Daddy, that's too embarrassin', it's all in my crotch!"

"Yah, Mr. Carr, it's too embarrassin'!"

"You want me to have Mother take a look instead?"

"*No, no, no,* not a lady! You can look!"

The boys got the giggles as I pushed up their trousers and examined the area around the tops of their thighs. Sure enough, I found some little critters that had buried themselves under their skin, little mites or maybe chiggers.

"Timmy, your mother is going to have to take a look at this."

"Daddy, it's too embarrassin'!"

"Yes, Mr. Carr," Kelvin chimed in. "Mrs. Carr can't look at me up there!"

"Good heavens, she can look at Timmy, she changed his diapers for years."

"Yah, but she didn't change *my* diapers!"

"Then she won't look at you. I'll just let her look at Timmy. Mothers always know about these things."

Timmy squirmed, giggling wildly while Jan examined the upper part of his legs and groin.

"Timmy, you've got to take your pants off."

"*Mother,* I can't take off my pants! It'll be humiliatin' in front of Kelvin."

"Well, then you better take them off in front of your father because it looks like you've got something that's worked its way down under the skin."

Timmy sheepishly pulled down his pants while Kelvin and Jan looked away. I examined his private parts; it was obvious that some little critters had embedded themselves under the skin.

Jan decided to call Dr. Simon, who from our description over the phone concluded they might be ticks or more probably sand mites. The quickest remedy, he instructed, was to paint them with nail polish so that they would suffocate under the skin. Then they could be pulled out with tweezers.

The boys grimaced at hearing the prognosis; they whooped and hollered anticipating the requisite action.

"But that's what Dr. Simon says has to be done!" Jan told the boys. "We have to paint over them with nail polish so they'll die; tomorrow, we can pull the mites out with tweezers."

"*Jan, with nail polish?* Are you sure?"

"That's what he said. The nail polish will smother them so we can pull them out."

The boys started to make a beeline out of the room; I grabbed them each by the seat of their pants and sat them down, while Jan looked for clear nail polish.

"I hate to tell you this, boys, but you're going to have to take off your pants while I dab on the nail polish."

"Daddy, that's the horriblest thing I ever heard of."

Kelvin sat quietly, his stoic face expressing disbelief.

Jan returned with an assortment of nail polish bottles, but none was clear. So we went with Fire and Ice—*tropical red*.

"Who's first?"

"Timmy's goin' first, Mr. Carr. I'm not puttin' that nail polish on my crotch. No sir, *no way!* Not on my crotch!"

"Sorry, Kelvin, but you're both going to wear this nail polish until tomorrow. Take your choice, on your crotch where it will do some good and won't show, or on your fingernails where the whole world will see it!"

"Daddy, you're cruel!"

"Okay, Mr. Carr, but *Timmy's* gotta go first!"

I started to unscrew the cap. "All right, Timmy, you're first."

Timmy backed across the room. "Mommy's gotta get outta here. I'm not gonna let you paint me with nail polish while she's in this room."

Jan left and closed the door.

I pulled off the lid with the little brush and aimed it toward Timmy. He kept backing away until he fell against his bed. Kelvin roared.

"Okay, Timmy, that's the perfect place. Now pull down your pants and lie back on the bed."

Timmy squirmed as if he were about to be molested. Kelvin suddenly became gravely serious, realizing his turn would soon follow.

"Mother *told* you boys not to play in the grass and sand in short pants. Maybe this will serve as a good lesson! Now, Timmy, pick up your thing and hold it over to the side so I can put some nail polish on top of the chiggers on this side of your ying yang."

Timmy winced as I repeatedly touched the brush to the skin of his scrotum. "Okay, now pull it over to the other side and I'll put some nail polish right here!"

He winced again.

I couldn't help but chuckle. "Timmy, you look like you've got chicken pox of the groin."

We laughed as Timmy covered himself with his hands.

"Timmy, let me take a look. Move your hands so I can see if I got 'em all." Ignoring his resistance, I continued. "I've got to see if I've covered 'em all or you'll continue to itch. You've got one almost on the end of your thing. I'm going to have to put nail polish right on the end of your ying yang."

"Daddy, that stings!" he exclaimed as I dabbed a dot of tropical red on the end of his penis. Timmy yanked up his pants and bolted across the bedroom.

"Okay, Kelvin, you're *next!*"

"No, no, no, no, no," he protested, jumping around the room, cupping his groin in both hands.

"Look, Kelvin, either *I'm* going to have to do it or I'll call in *Mrs. Carr* to do it for me!"

Resigned to his fate, Kelvin scooted up onto the bed, slid down his shorts, closed his eyes, and put his hands over his squinched face. I dabbed dollops of nail polish over the spots where the mites had burrowed.

"Okay, young man, now rest there a minute until the nail polish dries. Then you boys can go and play. Tomorrow morning, I'll get tweezers and pull those darn mites out."

The boys ran off downstairs and into their fort under the house, where they spent the rest of the day hiding.

This and other critter experiences reminded me that New Orleans is rife with mosquitoes, roaches, tics, termites, fleas, and indeed, bugs and rodents of innumerable magnitude who are also trying to eke out a living in the muck and mire of this South Louisiana ooze.

*   *   *   *   *

I walked out the back door of WDSU onto Chartres Street where Jan was waiting alone in the car with the top down.

"Where're the kids?"

"Olympia drove them up to the carbarn. I was afraid you'd be late. You drive."

Jan always hated to drive when I was in the car. I swung around and headed up St. Charles toward the carbarn on Willow. It was one of those beautiful spring days when the weather is mild, the humidity low, and the pungent scent of blooming flowers and bushes permeates the air. I looked over at Jan; her red hair sparkled in the afternoon sun and her soft white complexion appeared more translucent than usual.

"Honey, you look so serious," I said.

"I'm trying to remember all the things I'm supposed to do before we get to the carbarn."

"I thought you were preoccupied. You didn't ask me how my interviews went."

"Oh yah, how was Jayne Mansfield, all over you?"

"Hon-eee—"

"Don't give me that hon-eee stuff; I know those glamour girls are always all over you."

"Well, she wasn't all over me. Even if she had wanted to, it would have been rather difficult. She had her manager with her, her three kids, *and* there was the floor crew."

"So, how were her boobs in real life? I'm sure that's all you and the engineers had on your minds."

"Hon-eee! Do you think that's all we think about?"

"When it comes to Jayne Mansfield, I expect that's all any man thinks about. So, how *were* her boobs?"

"Pretty nifty, actually," I replied, as if describing a work of art. "She did have skinny legs from the knees down, but from there up, what a *derriére!*"

Jan's nose twitched.

"But what really surprised me was the way she treated her kids."

"What do you mean?"

"Her two little boys, Mickey and Zoltan, climbed all over her, *me*, and the sofa we were sitting on while I attempted to do the pre-taping interview. That didn't seem to bother her at all. But when her little girl, Jayne Marie, who's about the age of Tammy, asked her where she could find the bathroom, Jayne replied tersely, 'Go find it yourself! You're *always* going to the bathroom!'"

Her rude treatment of her daughter made us all feel uneasy. Margie Larson assisted by taking Jayne Marie to the ladies' room.

"Jayne's personality is her main talent. She was just plain Jayne chatting before the taping, but the minute the floor director cued us, she turned into 'Jayne Mansfield, movie star.' The transformation was shocking. But, wow, she's sure photogenic. She looked better on the monitor than she did in person. As we started taping, she suddenly asked me if we could switch chairs so that she could put her best side toward the camera. I didn't mind, but we didn't realize the tape was already rolling. When she leaned over to change chairs, her boobs thrust forward and nearly fell out of her blouse. I gasped, but the cameraman nearly coughed up his lunch; Margie ran to get him a glass of water from the studio kitchen."

"You men!" Changing the subject, Jan asked, "Did you also tape your interview with Carl Reiner?"

"He was fabulous. I wish you could have met him. He is the most ingratiating person I've ever interviewed. He wanted to talk more about being a writer and a director than he did about his on-camera persona."

"*Oh, my Lord,*" Jan screamed, causing me to slam my foot on the brake.

"What?"

"Oh, my gosh. I forgot the *Dobérge*. It's at Gambino's. I told Olympia I'd pick it up so she wouldn't have to worry about it."

"No problem. We'll turn at Louisiana Avenue and get it."

We picked up the cake at Gambino's, famous for their many-layered *Dobérge* cakes and sundry other goodies that tempt the palates of New Orleanians. As we arrived at the terminus, one of the motormen coming off duty directed us to the birthday streetcars. Timmy, Tammy, and Tom were hanging out the windows holding onto a big paper banner that read "Happy Birthday, Tammy," while Olympia stood on the outside using masking tape to attach the sign.

Having a birthday party on the streetcar in New Orleans has been a custom for as long as most people can remember. The rental is relatively inexpensive. The host provides the food and may decorate the streetcar inside and out. The best part for the mothers is that after the party is over, a transit employee cleans the streetcar and empties the trash.

Timmy and Olympia had toted the party supplies aboard the streetcar. Tammy had announced several times that it was her birthday, and she wasn't supposed to work because she didn't want to get her pretty new dress dirty. Jan and I climbed on to help with the decorations before the "little darlings" arrived. The boys started blowing up balloons using the rented balloon-blower.

"I declare, Mizz Cahr, Mizz Tammy got her ideas how she wants this all set up. She wants the punch bowl and the paper cups to sit on the beauty-seat on this side, and she wants the *Dobérge* cake and the paper plates and forks to be on the beauty-seat on the other side."

The beauty-seats at the front and back of the car ran parallel to the sidewalls.

"That's right, mommy, we're gonna have to cut the paper table cloth in half so we can put half of the table cloth on that beauty-seat and the other half over there to make it look really pretty."

"Swear to God, Mizz Cahr, that chile got some fancy ideas!"

Timmy and Tom kept blowing up balloons and tying them to the little handhold brackets on the ends of the seats. Suddenly we heard the screech of voices as Tammy's whole class arrived en masse from a couple of carpools, invading the streetcar the way a group of red ants attack a morsel of food dropped on the ground. The twenty-five or so kids had barely piled on the streetcar when I heard several balloons go pop, pop, pop.

Tom screeched, "Seymour, stop that! Seymour, stop that! I'm gonna kill you!"

Infuriated, I dashed to the back and grabbed Seymour by the scruff of the neck just as he was about to puncture another balloon. I swung him around, picked him up under the arms, and held him straight out in front of me, face to face. His actions exasperated me, so I turned red. Looking directly into his eyes, I shouted, "Seymour! Sit down and behave yourself!"

He looked straight back at me. "Mr. Carr, I'm gonna tell my mother you were mean to me."

"Seymour, why don't we go to the telephone right now so you can tell your mother that I'm being mean to you, *and why!*"

He sassed back. "My mother's not home now, ha, ha, ha!"

"We'll call your mother after we get back. You're not going to ruin this party for me or anybody. Stay right there in that seat and don't you move! *Do you hear?*"

A sulking Seymour stayed put.

Tammy was instructing her guests to put their presents on the front seat. The motorman arrived, clanged the bell several times, closed the door, and we were on our way. The streetcar swung onto Carrollton, rolled cheerfully passed Benjamin Franklin High School and the Camellia Grill, and turned onto St. Charles Avenue. Tied to the outside of the streetcar, the balloons bounced happily as we passed Dominican College and approached Audubon Park. As we rumbled past Tulane and Loyola Universities, some of the college kids read the banners and yelled, "Happy Birthday, Tammy!"

Tammy's seven-year-old girlfriends chattered about their pretty party dresses while the boys gathered around the punch bowl chug-a-lugging the Hawaiian Punch.

Above the sound of the chattering and laughing, there was suddenly a cry of pain from the rear of the streetcar.

"*Bob,* come quick!" Jan yelled.

Dashing down the aisle, I stumbled over two little girls comparing their Mary-Janes. Seymour was standing on the windowsill, holding onto the leather straps above, crying out in pain.

"What's the matter, Jan?"

"Look, the window slammed down on his toes."

"Good God!" *Should I feel a twinge of pleasure at seeing the little brat shackled?*

Somehow Seymour had dislodged the open window, and it had slammed down across the toes of his Buster Brown shoes. My first reaction was to ask the dumb question, "Seymour, why did you do that?" However, Seymour was in so much pain that he just kept howling. I tugged at the two little latches holding the window in place, but they were jammed.

"Jan, press on that side, I'll press on this side, then we'll try to lift."

Seymour was still holding onto the straps above him but was beginning to lose his strength. Olympia came running.

"Olympia, you hold him up while we try to get this window open."

Seymour's shrieking drew all the kids to the back of the streetcar. Jan and I pushed and tugged and finally got the window open. We pulled Seymour's toes free. It turned out that he was less injured than embarrassed in front of all the kids. Letting out a mournful cry, and rejecting both Jan and Olympia, he threw himself into *my* arms and began to wail as though he were really injured. For the first time, I began to feel some compassion for Seymour, whom I had held in such disdain. Jan and Olympia hustled the other kids forward, telling them they were about to light the candles on the cake. Seymour and I sat down on the beauty-seat in the back of the car.

He looked at me with his tear-dampened face. "Mr. Carr, why doesn't anybody like me, sir?"

The thought flashed through my mind—*Kid, let me count the ways!* Before I had a chance to answer, the streetcar came to a screeching halt, sliding Seymour and me forward with a lurch. After the sudden stop there was a moment of silence as the stunned kids all looked forward, trying to figure out what had happened. I slid out from under Seymour and leapt forward, running up the aisle toward the motorman. As I passed Jan, I noticed she had her arms around what was left of the *Dobérge* smushed up against the front of the streetcar; while on the other side, there was Olympia in her white uniform covered from head to toe with red Hawaiian Punch. The motorman swung around on his swivel seat to see if everybody was okay.

"What happened? Did we hit a car?"

"No, no, sir. Some little kid dropped a puppy out the window. I saw it through the rear-vision mirror so I put on the brakes to try to keep from running over it. We not s'posed ta have animals on here!"

With that, the motorman swung open the door, jumped off, and began to look under the chassis. Tom, the little kid to whom he was referring, was dead silent and white as a sheet. Suddenly, he released a blood-curdling scream. In a flash he scooted himself down the steep steps of the streetcar onto the grass, joining the motorman. There, lodged between the wheels and the track, was the puppy, the most realistic-looking stuffed cocker spaniel we had been able to find at the toy center. Tom bellowed again, startling the motorman, who, mumbling profanities, bumped his head on the bottom of the streetcar. Realizing it wasn't a real dog, he let out a few more profanities. The boys began to pile off the streetcar to see what had happened; the girls hung out the windows.

"Okay, everybody back on the streetcar," I ordered.

I lifted a sobbing Tom inside and whispered to the motorman, "You pull the streetcar forward, and I'll pull the stuffed dog out from under the wheel."

The streetcar edged forward, enabling me to retrieve the crushed cocker spaniel from the tracks. The motorman apologized profusely for stopping so abruptly.

"Really, sir, I promise ya, I sure enough thought that was a real dog." He leaned over and whispered, "That kid scared the piss out of me!"

In order to re-direct the attention of the kids, Jan and Olympia lit the candles on what was left of the *Dobérge*, and we all sang "Happy Birthday" to Tammy.

"Okay, Tammy, now let's open your presents," Jan suggested.

The streetcar rambled merrily on past Christ Church Cathedral and the Garden District as Tammy happily opened her presents. The motorman beckoned; he asked if I wanted to take the full loop down to Canal Street.

I whispered, "Let's turn around at Lee Circle and head back Uptown. That'll be more than enough!"

All the children quieted down as we headed back Uptown. I decided we'd play a little game. Any child who could identify an object I called out would win a prize. The game was called, "Who Can See?"

"First, who can see a restaurant?"

They all began to look.

Alice screamed, "There's Delmonico's restaurant!"

Alice won a prize.

"Who can see a church?"

They looked frantically. Finally, Freddy yelled, "There's a church, there's a church, Mr. Carr."

It was the old white Lutheran Church on the corner of Josephine.

"Who can see a grocery store?"

Their eyes glanced wildly from side to side.

"There it is, there it is! There's Williams grocery store!" shouted Michael, as we stopped at the corner waiting for the light to change.

"Okay, now, listen carefully. Here's a really hard one. Who can see a Corinthian column?"

"What's that?" questioned three or four kids simultaneously.

"There, there's one over there," I said, pointing to a house on the corner of First.

"Daddy, that's a really dumb question," Tammy blurted. "Don't ask questions like that anymore. Nobody knows that stuff!"

"I knew it," I said.

"Yah, but that's not fair 'cause you know everything."

"Okay, next question. Who can find a florist?"

"What's a florist?" one of the kids asked.

"A place where they sell flowers, dummy!" shrieked one of the other kids.

"There it is! There it is! There's Scheinuk's Florist, I know that place 'cause they always have lots of bunnies at Easter."

"Give that kid a candy apple," I announced.

And so we continued playing the game until the kids got tired and slumped passively into their wooden seats as we made the turn at St. Charles onto Carrollton, rumbling along under the oak trees, passing crepe myrtles and flowering azaleas.

Happily, when we finally reached the carbarn, parents were awaiting our return. They plucked their kids off the streetcar and whisked them away. By the time Jan, Olympia, and I had gotten the kids and Tammy's presents all back to our house in the Quarter, we were exhausted. The kids wanted to go for a dip in their petite swimming pool, so I stayed out in the patio and watched them while lighting the butane burner under the crawfish-boiling pot. Jan and Olympia were in the kitchen stripping husks off the sweet corn and scrubbing new potatoes. We had grown to love boiled crawfish, except for Tammy, who thought they were gross. Timmy had become proficient in pinching the meat out of the tails and slurping the brine from the heads.

Jan stuck her head out telling me she heard the front door bell. Timmy, who was always inquisitive about visitors, jumped out of the pool and ran down the side of the house hollering "Who's there, who's there?" dripping water all along the way.

"It's Uncle Lindsay. May I come in?"

"Sure, Uncle Lindsay. Let me get the gate open."

He gave Lindsay a wet handshake—the manly thing to do at his age. Dashing back toward the pool, he hollered, "Uncle Lindsay, you got here just in time. We're gonna suck heads and pinch tails!"

Lindsay raised an eyebrow.

"Lindsay, great!" I said. "You got here just in the nick of time. We're going to have boiled crawfish."

"Bob, I have to talk to you and Jan right away. It's very important."

Lindsay was always rather abrupt when he had something to say, an odd characteristic considering his public relations vocation.

"Sounds pretty urgent."

"It's important and urgent to me."

"What the heck is it?"

"I want to talk to *both* you and Jan, privately."

"Okay, I'll get Jan and we can talk inside. Let me check my pot first."

I instructed Timmy to watch the crawfish pot, and when it started boiling, to let me know. I also told him he could be the chef if he wanted to, which excited him. He loved responsibility. Jan, Lindsay, and I walked into the front parlor and sat down.

"How 'bout a drink?" Lindsay asked.

"Of course you can have a drink. What would you like? Want me to make a sazerac?"

"Oh no, they're too sweet! I'll have a dry martini."

"Okay, I'll make you a martini and we'll have a sazerac."

"How's Marilyn?" Jan inquired.

I walked into the second parlor to mix the drinks but could hear Jan and Lindsay mumbling together. I wondered: *Is Lindsay here to tell us he's getting engaged to Marilyn?*

They were sitting on the Victorian sofa looking like something from another age as I delivered their drinks.

"Hey, here's a toast," I said.

"To what?" Jan asked.

"Uhh, to...to love and friendship and marriage?"

Lindsay looked uneasy as we sipped our cocktails.

"Okay, Lindsay, if you haven't already told Jan what's so urgent, how about telling us now?"

He paused for a moment, and then blurted out self-consciously, "I've decided to come out of the closet!"

"You've decided to come out of *what?*"

"*The closet,* Jan!"

"My God, Lindsay, do I understand what you just said?" I gasped in shock. "I thought you were going to tell us you were engaged."

"Engaged? Engaged to whom?"

"To Marilyn," Jan said.

"To Marilyn? Are you kidding? She's a great friend, but that's why I'm coming out of the closet."

"I don't exactly know what coming out of the closet means," Jan whispered.

"I'm not sure I do either," I added.

"Coming out of the closet means I'm not going to play games anymore."

"What games are you playing?"

"Romantic games, letting people think I'm straight and dating girls."

Jan and I looked at him in silence, not knowing quite what to say.

"Don't you understand? I'm a homosexual."

"Oh, no you're not!" Jan censured.

"Jan, yes, I am! I'm just fooling everybody, including myself. I'm a homosexual. I'm a queer! A fruit! Can't you understand that?"

"*You are?* Are you sure?"

"I'm sure. I like girls. I have a good time with them. We have a lot of fun together, but I can't love them. They don't turn me on sexually."

"You mean men turn you on sexually?" Jan asked timidly.

"Yes, they do. I hate it, but they do. I can't get it out of my mind and I'm not going to fight it any longer. I'm just going to let it happen."

We sat silent, staring down as if studying the intricate pattern in the faux Persian carpet on the parlor floor.

"Is there someone in particular you like?" I asked.

"No, not really, it's just that I like Marilyn too much to keep leading her on, letting her think I'm romantically interested when I'm not. I know deep down in my heart I can never be with a woman. I hate it! I detest it! I always wanted to have a family. That's the way it's supposed to be. But there's something within me that keeps steering me toward men. When I look at a man in a bathing suit, or all dressed up—a handsome man—there is some thrill that comes over me that I can't control or deny. When I look at a beautiful woman, I can admire her clothes and beauty, but nothing happens, no spark. I don't feel any stimulation. I loathe it. I don't know where it comes from. I can't help myself."

"Why do you feel you've gotta make an open statement about homosexuality just now, Lindsay?" I asked.

"I don't know. It seems like it's that time in history. I've been aching and agonizing about this for so long, since before I was twelve. I don't want to suffer any longer. I know others have been suffering, too. It's time for us to finally announce to the world that we are set apart, we have a different inclination, we're dissimilar human beings. I don't want to hurt anybody by what I'm saying. Most of all, I don't want to hurt the two of you, but I feel I can't live a charade any longer. I'm tired of people asking me—straight people—when I'm going to get married, when I'm going to do this, when I'm going to do that. I want to set the record straight, so to speak," he chuckled, "and let them know what I am and who I am. If they like me, that's okay. If they don't, it may hurt, but it'll be honest. You two are the religious ones. What's that thing about truth in the Bible?"

"You mean, 'the truth will set you free'?"

"Yah, that's it. And I want to be free!"

"Lindsay, we love you," Jan responded, "no matter what you are, who you are, or what you say." She put her arm around Lindsay. "I think you're very brave."

"I'm not brave, I'm scared to death, but it's something I've got to do. What scares me the most is how your kids are going to take it."

"Do you think you have to tell the kids?"

"No, I'm not going to tell the kids now, but I mean later on, when they get a little older and start to understand these things. I love your kids, and you're my family. I don't want them to hate me because they think I'm a fruit."

"Well, *we* don't hate you because you're a fruit," I said, with a self-conscious chuckle.

Lindsay looked over and smiled.

Jan's eyes expressed astonishment, thinking I was being callous.

"Lindsay, I've suspected for a long time. I hoped it was a phase. I thought you might find the right woman and settle down."

"I thought so too, Bob, for a while, but it's not going to happen. It's just not going to happen. And it wouldn't be fair to a woman. If I loved someone that much, I'd love her too much to break her heart by having her find out I had a strong attraction to men." He paused. "I haven't come by this decision easily. My heart's pounding just talking to you two about it. For a while, when I believed in God, I even asked Him, *why?* Why this strange unnatural attraction for men? I prayed and prayed about it. I begged for relief but it never came. So, I decided I'd just have to face it and live my life as I am and *be* what I am, a thirty-year-old homosexual, a gay. You know, they call it *gay* now! I don't know why because it's anything but gay. It's miserable! I don't know who cursed me with this malady, Father God or Mother Nature. No person in his right mind would choose the gay life if he weren't made this way!"

We sat quietly for a few moments; our heads were bowed as if in prayer. I could hear our old Victorian clock ticking away on the mantel-piece.

Finally Lindsay blurted out, "Can I still come over and visit?"

I shrugged my shoulders. "I guess so, if you want to be a part of the supermarket."

Jan and Lindsay looked at me, wondering what in the devil I was talking about.

"Well, I was just thinking: Jan's a flower, the kids are like assorted vegetables, I'm a nut, and you're a fruit."

"Bob," Jan admonished, "don't you have any feelings for the seriousness of this situation?"

"Of course I do. But it's not the end of the world. We're gonna stick together. You might say, life's a supermarket and we're all different products sittin' on the shelves."

Tom scampered into the front parlor soaking wet and dripping on the carpet.

"*Tom*, you're all wet and dripping," Jan reprimanded.

"Tom, what do you want?"

Half-crying, he blurted out, "Daddy, daddy, come out and tell Timmy to stop calling me a *fruit!* He called me a fruit 'cause I wouldn't stick my head under the water without holding my nose."

Jan's eyebrows arched at Tom's words.

"Tom," I instructed, "go back out there and tell Timothy that you're not a fruit, you're a *vegetable*, and furthermore, it's not manly to call people names. If he gives you any grief I'll come out there and spank his bottom! Now scoot back outside. You're getting the carpet wet."

Tom turned abruptly and ran.

"I'm sorry about his remark, Lindsay."

"Don't worry, Jan, it's something I've learned to live with. The next time I stick my head under water I'll hold my nose."

"Huh?" both Jan and I grunted.

"So everybody will know I'm a fruit!"

"*Lindsey*, don't condemn yourself!"

"Not to worry, Jan. I'm finally coming to grips with myself. I feel like I'm no longer a shadow. I'm *me*, and I'm okay."

The three of us stood up, Jan and I put our arms around Lindsay's shoulders and gave him a hug of reassurance.

A dripping wet Tammy bounced into the parlor to announce the water was boiling. "Why are you all hugging each other?"

"Because we all think we're so great," I answered.

"I think you're great, too," Tammy replied. "Can I give you a hug, too?"

"But, honey, you're all wet."

"Gee, mommy, but I'm really clean, really."

"Come here, honey," Lindsay said, releasing himself from our embrace. He stooped down in front of her, "Here, give me a hug."

Tammy dashed across the parlor and gave Lindsay a kiss on the cheek and a wet hug.

Timmy stuck his head around the doorframe, "Daddy, you better come. The water's boiling. We won't get to suck heads and pinch tails till midnight if ya don't help me cook. Lympy said the corn and 'tatoes are ready ta eat, right now!"

The three of us laughed at Tim's remarks.

"Okay, Timmy, I'll be right out. You want to stay and suck heads, Lindsay?"

"*Bob!*" Jan reproached.

"That's okay, Jan, but I think I'll go home, take a good swim, then settle down with my newest book on self-analysis."

Jan, Lenny, Terry Flettrich and Bob at the Blue Room of the Roosevelt Hotel, 1963

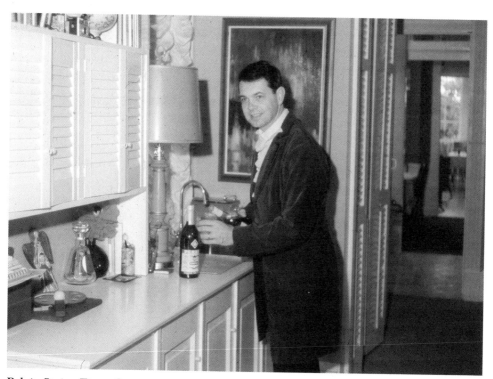

Bob in Spring Fiesta finery preparing sazeracs, 1964

CHAPTER ELEVEN

Ascending to the Highest Position in the Cathedral

Saturday morning seemed especially muggy and hot even for New Orleans. I had gotten up early to beat the heat and sweep away trash strewn along the banquette, dropped no doubt by tourists. Some say there seems to be something in the atmosphere of the Quarter inciting tourists to rowdiness. Others say it's the spirit of Bourbon Street. I submit it's the *spirits* of Bourbon, not the street, that arouse mischief in visitors who find the proliferation of twenty-four hour bars and nightclubs all too tempting. Alcohol-altered anxieties erupt in mysterious ways, which often lead to minor uproarious vandalism by most normally-righteous visitors—visitors who, if at home, would in all likelihood confine such antics to their local country club or lodge bash.

After sweeping up sundry beer cans, cigarette butts, a broken hurricane glass, and an empty package of rubbers and depositing them into the sunken sidewalk waste bin, I made my way over to La Nasa's Hardware. I needed some sheet rock nails for my Saturday project. By the time I returned home, I was hot and perspiring in spite of being dressed solely in short shorts, a T-shirt, and top-siders.

"Bob, how about an ice-cold glass of fresh satsuma orange juice and some of the cheese grits I've mixed up for the kids before you deposit Timothy at Angelo's house and pick up Marynette to play with Tammy here?"

"Jan, I want to get my sheet rock started before it gets any hotter. There's no air conditioning in the back room! If I expire of heat exhaustion, what'll you and the kids do?"

From the way she answered, I could tell she wasn't listening. "I know, but you've forgotten, I'm taking Tom uptown to see Dr. Simon because I want to check out those little red spots. The only time I could get an appointment was this morning; they said if I got there by ten they would take us."

"Okay, okay, I'll do it as soon as I finish my grits and juice."

"Tell Timmy to be good," Jan instructed routinely, going about her kitchen chores.

"What about me?"

"Oh, you be good, *also*, but you're always good," she added, tossing a kiss.

Timmy and I headed toward Angelo's house about three blocks away.

"Are you sure you wouldn't rather have Angelo come over to our house? His house seems so small to play in, do you enjoy it?"

"I like to go to Angelo's when his daddy's not home 'cause we have a good time playing all kinds of games with his mother. She tells real interesting stories about when she was a little girl in Italy; she shows us how to throw dice, how to play cards, and all kinds of nifty games."

"Why don't you like it when Angelo's father's there?"

"Well, sometimes he's okay but sometimes he gets really mean. I think maybe he drinks liquor or somethin'. He's always talking about horses and numbers and stuff like that; I don't know what it's all about but he gets really upset when he don't get no winners."

"Watch your double negatives!" I interjected before asking, "You mean, like gambling?"

"I guess so, they seem to do a lot of talking about gambling or somethin' like that."

At Angelo's, Timmy climbed up on the stoop and stretched to reach the doorbell. As usual, we could hear the creaking door open very slowly behind the closed shutters; then one shutter opened cautiously as Mrs. Scramola peeped out. "Oh, hello, Mr. Cawr," she said cordially. "We're expecting Timmy."

For a moment I thought she might ask me in out of the heat to chat briefly. However, true to her usual procedure, she kept a tight grip on the half-opened shutter, her body language indicating I should hold my ground.

"Hot day, Mr. Cawr."

I smiled and nodded affirmatively.

"How's the Misses and y'all's family?"

"Very well, thank you."

"Timmy, come on in. You're takin' too much sun out there on the banquette."

Tim slipped through the narrow crevice allowed by Mrs. Scramola, sliding past her loose-fitting cotton shift, hardly dictated by designer Rudy Gernreich, I assumed! He disappeared into the dimness of their shotgun-double-camelback. ("Camelback" refers to the second floor at the rear of the building.)

Straining to peer through the door, I could see no more than I had seen on any previous rendezvous: a snowy television screen roaring away on a plastic table sitting next to an orangey plastic upholstered chair. Both the chair and table were perched on a multicolored Congoleum carpet in what, I always assumed, was the parlor.

"Angelo and I will walk Timmy home in a couple of hours, so don't you worry yourself, Mr. Cawr."

"Fine, Mrs. Scramola, I'll see you later."

"Bye-bye," she added as she pulled the shutter tightly closed, slamming the bolt.

I headed up the street to get Tammy's friend, Marynette. Approaching the corner of Ursuline, I was nearly knocked down as Ruthie the Duck Girl, came flying around the corner on her roller skates. She was dressed from bosom to toe in a tattered and torn tulle strapless evening gown, clutching a ratty fur stole, probably purchased from a French Quarter thrift shop. She rolled past me before skidding to a halt. Swinging around, she begged, "Hey, Mistah Bawb, ya got a cigarette?"

"Ruthie, darlin', you know I don't smoke."

"Oh, yeah, Mistah Bawb," she replied, cranking up speed to resume her roll down the street.

I shouted after her. "Where's your new duck?"

Not missing a beat, she whirled around in a sort of clumsy pirouette, shouting, "Duckie's got da flu; he cain't run fast enough ta keep up wit' me when he's got da 'fluenza." Ruthie skated off into the hot sun, her flimsy gown silhouetting her scrawny legs as it fluttered languidly in the heavy air.

Continuing along, I felt the effect of the subtropical sun. Beads of sweat trickled down my back even though I was scantily clothed. I reckoned Ruthie picked that strapless evening gown with the flowing skirt so it would fan her legs, much like the action of punkahs swishing above dinner tables of elegant antebellum dining rooms.

The maid answered the door at Marynette's.

"Oh, Mistah Bah, what's you here foh?"

"I came to pick up Marynette to play with Tammy."

"Oh, Lawdy, Mistah Bah, little Marynette's gone. She done gone off with her father."

"Opaleen, are you sure she's gone?"

"Oh, yes, Mistah Bah, she *be* gone, since this mornin' first thin'. Her daddy, he come pick her up early, he did."

"Tammy'll be disappointed."

"I know, I thought she was s'posed to go over by your house an' play with Mizz Tammy. But the mistah, he come pick her up dis mornin' and said he's goin' keep her for da whole weeken'."

"How's Marynette's mother since the divorce?"

"Her mother been some upset and *so* lonely, I never seen anythin' like it. Rat now, she be upstairs tryin' to fix da fuse box."

"She's doing what?"

"She upstairs, tryin' to fix da fuse box. Da lights done gone off, da ice box gone off, da air gone off and it's hotter than da devil's fire in dis place. Dint ya notice? I cain't even Hoover da carpets. So me, I'm heading over to Puglia's to make da groceries so I can get some of their air-conditionin' to help my pressure. I swears, I be goin' lose my mind if I have dis here heat any longer. My pressure be pumpin' higher an' higher."

Opaleen pulled a large man's handkerchief from the breast pocket of her starched uniform and ferociously mopped her shiny black brow.

"Do you suppose I should help Marynette's mother fix the fuses?"

"P'haps so, Mistah Bah! *Our* mistah, he won't even talk to her. He said he hopes she burns herself to death wit' dat high voltage. He say she otta stick her fingers in da fuse socket and den roast in hell, right here in this house."

"Mr. Alexander said that?"

"Yasir, Mistah Bah. Done scared me into high pressure. Then he took little Marynette an' dey speed off in his spote car to Biloxi."

She walked over to the steps and yelled up the stairwell, "Mizz Alexander, Mistah Bah, Tammy's daddy, be down here to pick up Marynette. I be goin' out to make groceries at Puglia's. He goin' come up to help you fix da air condition. Bye." With that she stepped out onto the front stoop and closed the door.

Erica Alexander revealingly leaned over the railing. "Oh, Bob, it's you. I'm having a bitch of a time with this air-conditioning. The fuses keep blowing out, blows out everything. Would you take a look at it?"

"Sure, you bet. I'm coming."

Erica Alexander was not a pretty woman if you dissected each feature, but somehow, when all the parts were put together, she was extremely striking in a rather tenaciously, virile way, the way New England women often are. Yet behind that masculinity was a sensuous quality that oozed to the surface, manifesting itself in munificent mammaries and an incredibly engaging smile that revealed the most beautiful teeth I have ever seen.

Not knowing she had moved from the railing, I bounded up the stairs, slamming full face into Erica's ample chest. Standing two steps below her, I looked up through her cleavage and inanely muttered, "Marynette's not coming over to play with Tammy?"

There was what seemed to me an agonizingly long pause. Momentarily I felt as if I was once again exposed to the direct rays of the blazing equatorial sun.

Without moving she looked down at me, her lips rolling back to reveal her gorgeous teeth. I felt her warm breath, generously tainted with alcohol. "No, I'm sorry, that bastard came and picked up Marynette. The S. O. B. said he had the right to have her for the weekend. I couldn't think about it with the air-conditioning out. I just couldn't worry about it. At least Marynette will be cool in Pass Christian or Biloxi, wherever in the hell he's taking her this time."

Still standing in the same position at the top of the stairs, she laid her head down on my shoulder. I could feel her panting against my neck as she murmured, "I just can't cope anymore."

"Well, just a minute, let me get to the phone," I said, slipping out from under her and edging around the end of the banister. "I'm going to call Jan and tell her to take Tammy along with her to the doctor's. Then, when I leave here, I can go home and get my sheet rocking done."

I caught Jan just as she was leaving. Tammy would go along with her, a chance to get her a checkup, too. I uttered an audible smack into the mouthpiece, telling Jan I would be home shortly to start my project and see her when she got home from the doctor.

As often happens when couples have children, Jan and I had met Conrad and Erica Alexander through our kids at *La Petite Ecole*. Even when we met, it was common knowledge that their marriage had been off and on for the past five years. She had become, it seemed to me, pretty self-sufficient. Immersed in art, she was very talented with her hands. An excellent sculptor, she could also paint and was a proficient potter.

Talented as Erica was, she didn't seem particularly adept at changing a fuse. As a matter of fact, I probably saved her life. She couldn't get the fuse unscrewed, so she had broken the glass with the screwdriver and stuck it down in the center to twist out the fuse. Fortunately, the screwdriver was equipped with a plastic handle; otherwise, I think she would have gone up in a flaming jolt, just as Conrad had hoped.

"My God, Erica, I can't believe you stuck a screw driver into that hot socket and didn't get yourself jolted! Look, first of all, you've got to turn off the electricity right here." I pulled down the handle. "Look." I indicated the screwdriver. "Don't ever stick a thing like this into a hot socket again!"

"You seem to know a lot about hot sockets!"

I chuckled, pondering her wisecrack. In order to reach the fuse box straight on, I climbed astride the two stools she had been using. I removed the screwdriver, then carefully unscrewed the fuse with a pair of insulated pliers.

"Gotta another fuse?"

"I think there's one way up on top of the fuse box."

Stretching on my toes to reach up out of sight, I ran my fingers across the top of the box and bumped the fuse, which fell to the floor directly below me. Erica, standing behind me, leaned over and retrieved it.

Reaching her arm up between my legs, with the fuse balanced between her fingertips, she said, "Here it is!"

I leaned down, took it out of her hand, and stretched back up to screw it in. When I took it from her she flattened her palm against my stomach, slowly running her hand down my fly, then between my legs. A sudden rush surged through my system, almost like an electrical shock. Ignoring the event, I screwed the fuse into the socket.

"Do you have it screwed in tight?"

"Almost."

She ran one hand across my backside while reaching up the pant leg of my shorts until her other hand was full of me. Her talented fingers kneaded me as if she were shaping hardening clay.

"Hey, just a minute!" I uttered, more loudly than expected. "I'll pull the switch up here to see if the air conditioning comes on."

"You do that," she said, releasing her grip.

Pulling the switch, I could hear the rush of air come through the vent.

Her voice was low and earthy, "Sounds like it's blowing."

"Yah, that's a good sign," I replied, carefully backing down off the two stools.

I turned around slowly, not wanting to make eye contact. She had unbuttoned her blouse, pulled it off, and tossed it on the chaise lounge.

"God, it's hot in here, even this bra is wet with sweat. You guys are lucky you don't have to wear all these underpinnings."

"Uh huh."

"You don't even have undershorts on."

"Well, maybe not."

"Yah, not even a jock strap." She smirked, flashing her teeth.

Thinking: *How do you know—then realized she had already found out.*

Faster than a speeding bullet, she reached behind her back and off popped her bra. It came to rest on my top-siders.

"*You* don't have a jock on. I don't have a bra on. What are we gonna do about it?"

"What do you mean, what're we gonna do about it?"

"Just that, what are we going to do about it? We've got the air conditioning, Jan's at the doctor, my Marynette's on the Gulf Coast, and Opaleen's at Puglia's for at least a good half-hour. We're two healthy and sensual people, why waste this precious time?"

I stood transfixed as my blood raced and my mind filled with wild thoughts.

"Give me your hand," she said.

Like a robot, I held out my hand. She lifted it up and placed my palm on her breast; it felt soft and warm, moist with perspiration.

"How does *that* feel?"

"Smooth."

"How does the other one feel?"

Stupefied, I reached up and put my empty hand on her other breast.

"And how does *this* one feel?"

"Feels good."

Suddenly, I pulled my hands away. "I can't do this!" I said, shaking my head as if to jar myself into good conscience and to clear my vision.

"Why not? If you like it, why can't you do it?"

"I just can't."

Without warning, her face became contorted; in surly tones she berated me, barking, "What are you, one of those New Orleans closet queens who's married for appearance's sake but can't stand women? Would you rather have a man?"

"No," I protested. "I don't know what you're talking about."

"If you like women, what's wrong with me?"

"Nothing's wrong with *you*. The *situation's* wrong!"

She moved closer to me, lifted my T-shirt and pushed her bare breasts against my naked chest. With one arm she reached around behind me to yank me even closer. I lost my breath. Her other hand slipped down my leg and worked its way up underneath my shorts. I was motionless in anticipation. Just as she touched me, sparks began to fly. There was a loud clap and the air-conditioning system went off. I reeled around to look at the fuse box, releasing myself from her grasp.

"Just a minute, you don't need me; you need an electrician!"

"But I don't want an electrician, I want you. I've had my eyes on you ever since I met you at the kid's school. You with your flirty eyes and cocky ways, I knew I was going to get my hands on you sometime and I'm not disappointed!"

"I'm sorry, I really have to go. I'll be glad to call you an electrician or get you some more fuses but I have to get home to hang sheet rock."

"Yeah, I know you and your handy hints, I've watched you on television. You teach women how to hammer, nail, and screw!"

"I teach about hammering and nailing, I know that."

"And you can screw my fuse box anytime you'd like to."

"Look, Erica, I really have to go. You better call an electrician."

I pulled away, turned, dashed down the stairs and let myself out, running into Opaleen dragging her groceries.

"You been helpin' Mizz Alexander wid her fuse box, Mr. Bah?"

"Yah, but she didn't have much luck."

"I done got her a bigger fuse at Puglia's. We'll see if dat won't cool things off some."

"Let's hope, Opaleen. Be seeing you."

"Bye, Mr. Bah."

All the way home, I chastised myself for being some kind of a goof. *Here's a woman casting herself before me and I act like a swine. Who would have ever known? I rationalized to myself. To think I could have had an unforgettable morning and I just let it slip by. I even let her think I might be a homosexual. Here I am trudging my way home to hang sheet rock—What a dope! On the other hand, thank heaven for my built-in morality fuse.*

Although I had cut all the sheet rock the week before, I hadn't had a chance to nail any in place. Nailing was the part I enjoyed most because it's just a matter of hammering. It takes very little thought. You just do it. At the same time I was banging away at the nails, I was fretting to myself about how Erica had commented on my ability to hammer, nail, and screw. My mind was filled with giddy fantasies enlivening me to strain at my shorts just thinking about what might have been. I whacked harder and harder against the sheet rock nails as if to drive away my devilish thoughts. I began thinking: *There were many reasons why I hadn't weakened, why I shouldn't, why I must not ever, how I could get caught—that perpetual fear learned in childhood.* The phone rang, jarring me into reality, forcing me off my ladder.

The call was from a tour company wanting to schedule an historic tour through our house the following week. Would Thursday a week—as we say in New Orleans— be okay? I told them I'd have to check with Jan when she got back to make sure somebody would be home to show the visitors through the house. It would be a group of preservationists from Virginia who wanted to see a typical historic New Orleans house actually inhabited by a family.

By the time Jan got home with the kids, I had spoken on the phone a couple more times, finished hanging the sheetrock in the guest room, and had viscerally placated myself. I was beat!

Jan shouted up the back stairway, "We're home."

"Okay," I replied breathlessly.

"I stopped at Central Grocery and bought muffulettas for lunch. What would you like, Barq's or a Hot Shot?"

"Barq's, be right down." I laid down my hammer and nails and glanced over to the screwdriver that was lying on the top of my workbox. *Wow,* I thought, *it's just as well I didn't take advantage of the proffered affair. Living with the prideful purity of innocence is better than suffering the prideful guilt of clandestine conquest. Fortunately, Mother Nature has given us guys a self-gratifying device to ease our frustrations.*

"Anyone call while I was out?" Jan asked, as I emerged from the back stairwell.

"Yah, the tour company called and asked if we could have a tour a week from Thursday. Also Clay Shaw asked us to come over for a swim later this afternoon."

"Who called?" Jan asked again, finally focusing her thoughts on what I was saying.

"Clay wanted to know if we could come over to his pool and have steaks on the grill. He thought it might be fun for the kids to go swimming and we could meet his out-of-town guests."

"Okay, I guess that would be fun; I'm sure they'd enjoy it."

"Also, Frank Sciacca called to remind me to meet him at St. Louis Cathedral at

2:30. I told him a cameraman from the station would meet us there so we could go up into the belfry or the steeple or whatever Catholics call it."

"That's great! Then you'll get the film done in time to promote the *Bells of St. Louis Festival* next week."

"Yep, that's the whole idea."

"What happened at the Alexanders' house?"

I choked on my muffaletta. "Oh, nothing, what do you mean?"

"I mean, why couldn't Marynette come over and play with Tammy?"

"Oh, because her father took her to the Gulf Coast for the weekend."

"How's Erica doing? Is she making out okay by herself? Maybe you should go over from time to time to help her out."

"I don't think so. She's making out. She's making out just fine." Hoping to change the subject, I added, "More important, what did Dr. Simon say about Tom? What's that rash, the chicken pox or what?"

"No, daddy," Tammy piped up. "Tom doesn't have the pox, he's got the rosy-ola."

Jan added, "Yes, the roseola. He has roseola. Henry said we should be careful with him; we should keep him quiet but it's not a severe case, so it's not much to worry about and he's no longer contagious. Once you break out with the rash you can't give it to anyone."

The doorbell rang. "Oh, Bob, would you get that while I get these ice cubes out of the trays? Tammy, honey, you can put the ice cubes in the glasses. Tom, you can help, too. Maybe that's Timmy home from Angelo's."

Jan continued chattering. I opened the front door; there stood a wide-eyed, plainly dressed but attractive young lady about twenty-two years old.

"Have you been saved?" she questioned.

"Saved from what?"

"Saved from the sins of Satan!"

"Oh, that kind of saved."

"The Lord loves you! Even though you're a sinner," she replied sinisterly.

My thoughts darted back to my morning encounter. "Honey, I'm a sinner but not as much of a sinner as you might think. I've had a few golden opportunities to seriously sin, but the good Lord slapped a bridle on me and with a bit in my teeth, reined me back. What's your church?"

"Jehovah's Witnesses, I study at Kingdom Hall."

"Hallelujah, sister," I replied. "Hallelujah."

"The Lord loves you, brother."

"And the Lord loves you, sister."

"The Lord died on the Cross for you."

I parried with, "The Lord died on the Cross to rectify our sins and to give us salvation that we may confess our sins and be redeemed by his Holy Blood. Once we give ourselves up to him we are born again." I paused and looked her straight in the eye, "Sister, are *you* saved?"

She stood for a few moments quite befuddled. "Brother, I would like to give you this *Watch Tower* magazine."

"Thank you, Sister, my donation to you will be my Episcopalian *Book of Common Prayer*, if you would like to take it along, we'll call it even."

She appeared dumbstruck by my remark, but I secretly admired her tenacity and courage.

Timmy walked up with Angelo and his mother.

"Sister, this is my son, Timmy, his friend Angelo, and this is Angelo's mother, Mrs. Scramola."

She turned to Mrs. Scramola and in almost robotic style asked, "Have you been saved?"

Without batting an eyelash, Mrs. Scramola replied, "No, no dear, I haven't been saved, I'm a Catholic. We don't believe in all that nonsense."

The confused young lady backed away and disappeared down Bourbon Street.

"Daddy, I wonder, can Angelo come over and play for a little while this afternoon? We wanna play down in the fort."

"Okay with me if it's okay with Angelo's mother."

"Mr. Cawr, I don't want to take advantage of your hospitality. Angelo spends a lot of time over here."

"Oh, no, no, that's fine. As a matter of fact, we're going to take the kids swimming over at Clay Shaw's pool later this afternoon. Maybe Angelo would like to go swimming, too."

"Ta whose pool?"

"Clay Shaw's. You know, he lives over on Burgundy. He remodeled that series of Creole cottages. His has a beautiful swimming pool."

"I'm not sure I'd like Angelo to go over there."

"Oh, it won't be any bother."

"No, Mr. Cawr." Lowering her voice, she said, "I mean, Mr. Shaw has a—has a reputation."

"Oh, what kind?"

"Well," she said, glancing around and couching her voice in a half-whisper, "You know, he's a...a homo...sexual."

"Oh, that's right," I said, as offhandedly as possible, realizing her insinuation. "Yes, he is a homosexual but he doesn't mind the children coming over. He has many married friends and even some who are divorced."

"Sir, I think it might be better if Angelo came home with me."

"Oh, daddy, daddy, can't he stay and play in the fort?"

"Mama, can't I please stay and play with Timmy?" Angelo begged.

"Mrs. Scramola, why don't we do this. If Angelo can stay and play in the fort for the afternoon, I'll drop him home before we go swimming."

Angelo tugged at her skirt as she hesitated a few moments before giving in. "All right, all right, if you be sure to bring him home *first*, that'll be fine. Thank you very much, sir."

I closed the door and followed the boys back into the family room to finish my muffaletta.

"Mommy, yippee, you're home from the doctor," Timmy yelled as he ran over to give her a peck on the cheek.

"Thanks, honey," Jan said in response to the kiss. "I'll get you and Angelo a sandwich and a Barq's. You can take it down to the fort if you want to."

"Thanks, mommy." Timmy hollered across the room, "Daddy, what's a homosexual?"

"What?" Jan exclaimed. "Why do you want to know that?"

"Mrs. Scramola was whispering to daddy that Angelo couldn't go over to Mr. Shaw's house because he's a homosexual. So what is a homosexual?"

"Well, err," I hesitated. "A homosexual is a man who likes men better than he does women."

"Then I guess I'm a homosexual!"

"What do you mean, you're a homosexual?"

Jan piped in fast, "No, you are *not* a homosexual."

"Just a minute, Jan, let's see what he means; maybe he is?"

Jan gasped, "What do you mean, Timmy?"

"Well, I like boys better than I like girls, I mean I like Angelo and I like Kelvin and I like Pierre, and I think girls are kinda dumb. So if I like boys better than I like girls, I guess I must be a homosexual. Is that supposed to be bad?"

"No, that's not bad, Timmy," I answered. "Being a homosexual is not bad. It just means something a little different than you think it does. It means, errr—" I was at a loss for words. *Here was my opportunity to set him straight, as it were, on the road to not being a bigot, but what do I say?* I glanced over at Jan, who was looking a bit horrified by the whole subject.

Regaining my composure, I said, "Well, Timmy, you are probably not a homosexual. Homosexuals are people who don't like to get married because they want to stay single so they can stay friends with—"

Timmy cut in, "Gee, daddy, I guess I'm not a homosexual 'cause someday, I'm gonna want to get married to a girl, even if they are sort of dumb now. I know they get smarter 'cause mommy's smart."

Thank heavens he interrupted! I thought. *How do I finish this conversation?* "Homosexuals are people who, when they grow up, the men like men better than they like women and the women like women better than they like men. Is that clear?"

"I guess, it all sounds kinda dumb to me. Anyway, I like Mr. Shaw 'cause he's got a swimming pool and that's fine with me."

"Good, Timmy, and that's fine with me, too."

The discussion had ended; Jan breathed a sigh of relief.

"Now can me and Angelo take our muffalettas down to my fort?"

About the time we finished our sandwiches, Timothy came back upstairs and returned the basket and the empty pop bottles.

"Daddy, can I go out on Bourbon Street for just a minute. I gotta go out there an' fix somethin'."

"What do you have to fix?"

"Somethin'. I'll tell you about it in a minute."

"Honey, careful of the cars."

"Oh, I'll be careful, mommy, I'll just be out there for a couple of minutes. But I've got to go up to my room first to get something."

"Just be careful, like mommy told you."

Timmy scampered up the back stairs. We could hear his footsteps march across the floor through the ceiling above, stop for a minute in his room, come down the front stairs, then slip out the front door.

"What's he doing?" Tammy asked. "What's Timmy doing?"

"Yah, daddy, what's Timmy doin'?"

"I don't know, kids, but we'll ask him when he comes back."

In three or four minutes Timmy emerged through the front door, closed it gently, and came down the hall wearing a rather satisfied, smug look.

"What the heck were you doing out there?"

"A s'prise! I'm goin' down in the fort with Angelo now and in about two minutes, y'all go out and stand on the banquette."

"Why?"

"Jis do it, *please!* You just go out there and stand in front, okay?"

Tom slithered down from his booster chair at the same time, saying, "Let's go, mommy, daddy, and Tammy, let's go!"

"Hold on, he told us to wait about two minutes and then go out on the sidewalk."

"Daddy, you mean the banquette," Tom corrected.

"Yes, the banquette and the sidewalk are the same thing."

"How come there's two words to mean the same thing, daddy?"

"Because they're simonims!" Tammy announced proudly.

"What's a cinnamon?"

"That's two words that have the same meaning," Tammy replied. "Isn't that right, daddy?"

"Yes, that's correct."

"Sounds silly to me. Don't see why we got so many extra words for the same thing, it jis gets ever' body 'fused."

"When you get older you'll see that synonyms make for a richer language."

"Daddy, maybe you're right, but it jis sounds like a lot of extra spellin' to me!"

Jan butted in. "I think it's time for us to go out in front."

The four of us walked down the front steps and stopped.

"Wonder why we're doing this?"

"I don't know, honey, I guess because he asked us to."

Suddenly Tammy clutched her skirt against her legs while at the same time letting out a shriek that so surprised Tom that he, too, cried out.

"What's the matter?"

"Daddy, daddy, it's a snake, it's a snake!"

"Uhh, daddy, it's huge and wiggly!" Tom chimed in.

"Oh, my God," Jan said, jumping up onto the front step.

Tom dashed between my legs, bunting me in the crotch with his head. Tammy joined Jan on the step, continuing to shriek, "It's a snake, it's a snake!"

Sure enough, a little snake was slithering across the sidewalk directly toward the house.

"Should I stomp on him?"

"No, daddy, no, daddy, you'll get killed."

"He'll bite you," Jan warned.

"I don't think so. See that thread?"

Tammy, Tom, and Jan slowly eased toward the snake's route to cautiously scrutinize the situation. Was this the surprise? The boys were in their fort under the house.

Timmy had planted the little rubber snake down in the gutter with a black thread that ran from the gutter across the sidewalk into the cast-iron air ventilator under the house. I could see the boys' eyes peering out from the ventilator as they slowly pulled the thread, dragging the snake across the sidewalk.

"That's a terrible thing to do," Jan reprimanded.

"Oooh, that's scary."

"Personally, I think it's kinda fun," I said. "Wish I'd thought of it."

"Daddy, yuk!"

We could hear the boys laughing under the house as the snake disappeared up and into the air ventilator, out of sight.

Tom picked up a stick from the gutter and poked it through the ventilator.

"Tom, don't do that," Jan reproached. "You might poke out one of the boys' eyes!"

"They oughta get poked or somethin' for that dumb trick," Tammy admonished.

"They're just having fun."

"Fun for them, daddy, but that snake scared me so, I almost wet my panties!"

"And I almost did a poo!"

"Tom, I think you're kidding us!"

Jan gathered them like a mother hen. "Children, let's go back inside."

We got to the kitchen as the boys came running up from the fort.

"Whatcha you think, whatcha you think?" they implored.

"That's a terrible thing to do, Timothy."

"Oh, mommy, it was fun!"

"Frankly, I think it was fun, too," I added. "Just be careful you don't scare somebody too much."

"We won't do it too many times or people'll catch on. But can't we do it sometimes?"

"You can do it a few times."

"Bob, that's terrible. Think of your mother walking by, she'd be frightened to death."

"Jan, they can do it a couple of times. It's not going to hurt anybody."

"Yah, daddy, we just want to do it till we scare that mean old Mrs. Jeanville who lives down in the next block. She's the one that's always hollering at us, the one who never gives us any candy on Halloween. She's a mean bitch!"

"*Timmy!*" Jan gasped. "What did you say?"

"Mrs. Jeanville is a mean b…"

"Timmy, don't say that again!"

"But mommy, Uncle Lindsay calls people that all the time."

"Timmy, that's enough."

"But daddy—"

"That's enough, Timmy. Don't bug your mother. Uncle Lindsay's a grown up and you're not!"

Several weeks later we heard Miss Jeanville was hospitalized with a dislocated shoulder. After quizzing the "string snake terrorist," I was relieved to learn that Miss Jeanville had toppled off her commode in the middle of the night after falling asleep. Not a pretty sight, but at least my guys had nothing to do with it.

I glanced at the clock. "Oh Lord, Jan, I've got to change my clothes and dash over to Saint Louis Cathedral to take some promotional shots for their festival."

"Fine, but I think you better put on long pants to go into the cathedral. I know you have beautiful legs, but I think shorts are undignified."

I did as Jan suggested, and within ten minutes met Frank Sciacca, 1963 festival chairman, at the front entrance. Teddy, his wife, had written a theme song, *The Bells of St. Louis.*

"Bob, this is Father Nick, pastor of the cathedral." He had strong Mediterranean features and a firm hand shake. Frank continued, "Father is very pleased you're going to do some publicity for the festival on *Second Cup.*"

"Gee, thank you, Father, we're glad to do it."

Mike Lala, our cameraman, arrived. "What're we gonna shoot, Bob?" he asked, shaking everyone's hand.

"Don't know. Father, what'll it be?"

"Something only a very few people have been privileged to see."

"What's that?"

"If you think you can film inside, Mike, we can climb to the very top of the old bell-tower."

"Great, Father, I love a challenge."

"Okay with you, Frank?"

"Fabulous, Father. I've never been up there myself, and I've lived here all my life."

"Give me a couple of minutes to get a few shots of the cathedral from Jackson Square, Father Nick. I'll meet you inside so you guys can get out of this scorching sun."

While we waited, Father Nick gave us a little history of the first Catholic Church in the Louisiana Territory, constructed in 1718 on this very spot, chosen by J. Baptiste Le Moyne De Bienville, founder of New Orleans.

Presently, Mike appeared, interrupting our history lesson. We processed to the nave, where Father brandished a huge antique key to unlock a creaking wooden panel door, revealing a dusty spiral staircase.

"Father," I said, "I've heard there are wrought-iron steeples inside the shingled roofs of the towers. Is that true?"

"There certainly are. Those three wrought-iron towers were built before the roofs were put on the steeples. Many years ago it was thought the steeples would be more attractive if they were covered. Also, I'm told, there was a great amount of water leakage coming through the roof below the wrought iron."

"That's a shame, the wrought iron must have been very stylish and so in keeping with the rest of the Quarter."

"That's probably true. If this building could talk, I'm certain it would have some interesting stories to tell about the facelifts it has experienced from each generation. First there were the French, then Spanish, Americans, and the most recent influence, Sicilian immigrants who settled in the Quarter in the early 1900s."

"Hey, that's my people you're talkin' about, Father Nick," Mike injected. "I'm a Lala."

"You're a lollapalooza, Mike. Now, how do you want to shoot this?" I asked.

"You go first, I'll shoot behind you as we climb. Then I'll swing the camera back around as Father Nick and Frank follow us up the steps."

"Is this sound film?"

"No, Father, it's silent. We'll put appropriate background music to it, then Bob will do a narration when it's shown on *Second Cup*."

"Sounds wonderful. When it's broadcast, I'll gather the priests and nuns in the Parish House so we can all watch. Most of them have never been up here," he smiled. "They might be jealous."

"Is that one of the Seven Deadly Sins?" I asked.

Father Nick chuckled.

The stairs creaked under our weight as we circled upward. The spotlight attached to Mike's camera cast eerie moving shadows on the ancient walls encasing the stairwell; the air felt heavy with history. My trendy double-knit polyester pants flexed easily as I climbed each steep tread. My mind wondered: *How difficult it must have been for priests and nuns, a hundred or so years ago, to scale these steps in their heavy habits or cumbersome clericals!*

We pushed steadily upward as Mike manipulated his camera. I shattered the silence with a muted cry when my hand came in contact with something bristly and furry. What I thought for an instant was a bat or dead rat turned out to be a great hemp rope hanging from the belfry. Relieved and continuing to mush ahead, we reached the point where the masonry tower stopped and the steeple began; sure enough, there it was, as shown in some history books, the old wrought-iron steeple, its intricate filigree pattern perfectly preserved under the slate roof but invisible to tourists in Jackson Square seventy-five feet below. At that point we crossed to the center of the cathedral behind the massive clock whose antique works have chimed the time to the surrounding inhabitants for two centuries. Then, up another little winding stairway into the main spire, we were afforded an amazing view of the square through the ventilator slots.

I shouted down, "Hey, fellahs, I feel like Quasimodo from *The Hunchback of Notre Dame*."

"You mean the Humpback of Saint Louis!" chuckled Father Nick. "Frank, maybe Teddy should write a song or a story, *The Humpback of Saint Louis!*"

I could see the stairway stopped abruptly just before it reached the top of the spire.

"Keep on going up to the very top," Mike urged, continuing to shoot film. I did as he instructed, venturing to the very top. I held onto the rusty wrought iron to steady myself and catch a breath. It was dark and very hot.

"I can't go farther," I announced, wiping my sleeve across my forehead. Brushing away cobwebs, I activated several spiders that scampered across the underside of the roof rafters. "This is the top of the tower!"

"Hey, Bob," Frank hollered up to me, "you've risen to the very top of the Catholic church and you aren't even a Catholic!"

"Yah! Father Nick, does that make me a Pope or an Archbishop or something?"

"Something. I'd say a saint for promoting our *Bells of St. Louis Festival*."

"You guys might all feel like saints," Mike hollered, "but I feel like the devil. It's hotter than hell up here. It makes me feel like I'm in purgatory."

"That's for sure," replied Father Nick. "We better climb down before we have a heat stroke."

Once on the ground floor, the priest shook my hand; as our hands separated, his arm raised, making the sign of the cross, while pronouncing a small blessing. "On behalf of the church and the clergy, I thank you for coming out on this hot Saturday to film a promotion for the Cathedral." He grinned. "Especially when you're not Catholic!"

"Father, that's not totally true, I'm an Episcopalian, an Anglican Catholic, which is really part of the Holy Catholic Church."

"Ah yes, my son, you're quite right, the Catholic Church Universal."

"Yah, Father, the same blessed sacraments with half the quilt!"

Smiling, Father Nick excused himself, saying he had to prepare for a wedding. Genuflecting at the altar, he disappeared behind a screen. Mike stayed on for more shots but assured me the film would be ready to edit Monday morning.

Frank crossed himself with holy water. "Let me treat you to beignets and coffee at Café du Monde before we go home."

Pigeons scurried airborne from the hot pavement as we strode across the square.

"It just occurred to me. Ronnie Kole is going to be a featured guest on our show Thursday. Why don't we have him play an instrumental version of Teddy's *The Bells of St. Louis* as background to the film we just shot? Then next week we'll have Anita Sonfield sing the lyrics as the camera grabs live shots of the cathedral towers from the roof of the Royal Orleans. It'll be a great promotion for the festival."

"Gosh, do you think that could be done?"

"Don't know why not, I'll give Ronnie a call. I'm sure if we can get the music to him ahead of time he'll be happy to do it, he's very obliging."

"Teddy will be thrilled to death to hear her song played by Ronnie."

Finishing our café au lait, we did the necessary—brushing the spilled powered sugar off our clothes. Wandering back toward home under the French Market colonnade, we enjoyed the wonderful fragrances of fresh fruit and flowers, punctuated occasionally by the strong acrid smell of fish. The nosey intrusion of an occasional diesel delivery truck spewing its foul exhaust into the air jarred our senses. Passing Brocato's, we could see Angelo was hand-packing fresh raspberry ice. I bought two quarts for Clay Shaw's party as a "thank you" for our swim and also picked up Tammy's favorite, Italian hard-shell date nut cookies adorned with colored candy sprinkles.

By the time I got home, the kids were chomping at the bit in their bathing suits, ready to head over to Clay's. We traipsed out with a straw bag full of towels and raspberry ice, pausing to take Angelo home so his mother wouldn't agonize about his sexual safety.

Clay Shaw, Executive Director of the International Trade Mart, a successful and respected businessman, was a great advocate of rescuing architecturally-significant deteriorated buildings in the Quarter. He had restored several cottages on Burgundy and Barracks Streets, one of them said to be the home of naturalist painter John J. Audubon during the 1820s. Presently, Clay was in the process of renovating the Old Spanish Stables on Governor Nicholls between Bourbon and Royal; however, we were on our way to his most recently completed project, one of two early Creole cottages he used as his residence. He was particularly proud of the manner in which he had integrated the swimming pool into the patio. Clay seemed able to easily move in both the heterosexual and homosexual worlds. In sexual matters, New Orleanians are very progressive, though they discuss the topic endlessly.

He was a large man with an imposing demeanor that belied any effeminate traits. His Looziana drawl, dispensed in a deep, well-modulated voice with genuine politeness, let you know immediately that he was a proper "Southern Gentleman." Clay welcomed us cordially, telling the kids to pass through the living room and dive into the pool. Obviously he was clueless about children.

"Listen to me, children," Jan instructed, in a tone requiring obedience. "You may go out by the pool, but *sit* on the edge until daddy and I come out."

Timmy raised his hand but Jan anticipated his question. "Children, you *may* put your feet in the pool to check the water temperature but *do not* go in until daddy and I come out. It won't be long."

Clay introduced us to his other guests. We met Mario Bermudas, who lived in a St. Charles Avenue mansion with his wife and family. Mario was stag. He, also, was enthusiastic about restoring old buildings in the Quarter and spent a good bit of his time combing the area for "finds." He was able to invest in numerous pieces of Quarter property, having acquired considerable money in his native Colombia while employed at the *International House* trade organization.

Another of the several guests was an older man who turned out to be a prince from northern Italy near Venice, or *Venezia*, as he chose to note. He and I struck it off at once, discussing the years I had spent in Gorizia, a city in the Venezia-Giulia region during my years in the army of occupation along the Morgan Line. The prince was traveling with a younger fellow sporting the physique of a Roman statue with a personality as apathetic as a piece of freshly-mined Carrara marble. The "statue" apparently spoke no English, which may have contributed to his apathy, but he also uttered very little in Italian.

Across the room, obscured in a cloud of smoke, were two hearty and hefty middle-aged women perched on a pair of spindly Louis XV chairs. They chose to remain by themselves in a seclusive corner talking and gesticulating incessantly to each other in carefully tempered tones.

Everybody was sipping dry martinis on the rocks or sazeracs. I opted for my favorite, a sazerac, as did Jan.

Clay announced, "Please, make yourselves at home, enjoy the pool and the drinks. Jeremi will be putting out a light supper for us shortly; he and I thought *hors d'oeuvres* and beef tartare, *but* for those of you who don't like your meat raw, Jeremi will grill it over the barbecue, just let him know of y'all's desire."

Jeremi, a sinewy young man with muscles that rippled with each movement under his silky jet-black skin, was Clay Shaw's houseboy. In what sounded like a Haitian accent, Jeremi instructed the gentlemen guests to remove their clothes in one bedroom and the ladies to change in the other. I pulled off my trousers, revealing the boxer swim trunks I had put on at home, as a safety precaution. Jan emerged from the other bedroom in her swimsuit and we joined the children at the pool.

"Daddy, daddy, hurry," the kids entreated. "Daddy, hurry. We gotta get in the pool, we jis' gotta!"

"Okay, okay." I ran out onto the deck, jumped over their heads, and landed in the pool with a great splash that sprayed the three of them. The water was refreshingly cool and the tingling sensation of the air bubbles invigorated my skin as they rushed past in my downward plunge. Opening my eyes as I bounced back to the surface, I could see Timmy and Tammy joyfully slipping from the deck and sliding into the water. Tom, who didn't know how to swim, remained on the edge.

"Daddy, you splashed me, you splashed me. I'm freezing, I'm freezing," he screamed, clutching his towel around him like a shroud.

I could see he was both afraid and embarrassed as he agonized on the edge. I picked him up and eased him into the water as Jan slipped in close by. For a few minutes it seemed it would only be the Carr family in the pool. Then the prince and his young companion emerged through the French doors in their scanty Italian bikinis. The prince's bikini was so skimpy that one testicle was protruding, giving new meaning to "one hung low."

Jan stared and then glanced away in horror as she caught my eye. I whispered, "And now my dear, you have witnessed a royal ball!" She chuckled discreetly, even though she was shocked. She wasn't looking when the prince's young charge noticed what had happened; he reached over and readjusted the prince's bathing suit. Both men giggled as they jumped into the water.

The young man swam with the speed of an eel, back and forth, back and forth, the length of the pool. Finally, up out of the water, he stretched out on the diving board and lay there in the diminishing sun like a horizontal Adonis.

The prince paddled to our side of the pool to tell us how much he admired our beautiful children, which, of course, immediately rendered him a friend. He was particularly taken with Tom. "Ow old ees thees *bambino?*"

"He's three years old."

"Ee ees like a golden God, wit' the eentelligent blue eyes of an ahngel."

Jan was thrilled by his remark, but Tom reached down in the water and splashed the prince in the face.

"Ah, you see, signora, ee has fire. Ee's like my own *bambini* back in Eetaly."

"*You* have children?" I asked, nonplused.

"Oh, but si, I 'ave two boys. One eez ten, ee's veddy dark and veddy Eetalian, and dee odder eez seven, ee's veddy blownde, as ees his Swedish modder."

"Are they here in New Orleans?" Jan asked.

"Oh, no, dey are not. Dey are wit' der modder. We've two lives. She lives eidder in *Firenze* or een Stockholm; I live een da *Palazzo* outside from *Venezia*, when I am not een my flat een New York Ceety or visiting friends, as I am now een New Orleens."

Jan, who has little ear for foreign accents, strained to understand the prince and was a bit relieved when the splashing of the kids overwhelmed their chat. Timmy, 10, and Tammy, 8, had received some swimming lessons but were doing the doggie paddle back and forth across the pool.

The prince took note of their rather barbaric approach to swimming and summoned his young charge. "Antonio, don't lie dere like some fallen *statua di Roma*, come over 'ere and eenstruct dees cheeldren on 'ow to sweem da European style."

Antonio took his orders obediently; rolling off the side of the diving board, he plunged into the pool and swam to the kids.

"*Signor* and *signora*, I 'ope you will not be upset but eet would be interesting for Antonio to show your bambini 'ow to sweem een European style."

"Oh, that's fine, that's really great, they'd love to learn."

Without saying a word, Antonio motioned Tammy and Timmy over to the other side of the pool and began instructing them on the proper arm and leg movements.

"Der ees nothing more thrilling to me," said the Prince, "than a sweemmer wit' a lithe bowdy and a firm stroke."

"Quite right."

"Yah, that's sure true," Jan replied, in her most Midwestern fashion.

Having made his statement, the Prince turned, plunged into the water, and glided across the pool like a sensuous sea creature.

I looked at Jan in amazement. "I'm not 'sweemming' a stroke in this pool in front of 'heem,' if it's the last thing I do!"

"Me, too," Jan replied, easing up onto the deck.

I reached for Tom, who had been occupying himself on the steps in waist-deep water. I held him horizontally in the water as he paddled. Tom was my defense for not having to swim in front of the two Olympians.

The descending sun left behind a mild breeze, causing a welcomed chill as we emerged from the pool. With much coaxing, the kids reluctantly came out of the water looking like shriveled andouille sausages. Jeremi fetched their terry cloth wrappers from the house and offered to cook beef tartare into little hamburgers. Jan made sure the children didn't know their burgers were made of "that tartare stuff." Jeremi also served them each a Barq's and champagne to the adults. Following the raspberry ice, we excused ourselves with apologies that the children were getting tired. As we shook hands and gave the usual good-byes, I noticed the two hefty ladies in the corner, who had been conversing all evening, never looked up or broke eye contact with each other to acknowledge our leaving. Through the billow of their Turkish cigarette smoke, I could see the older one had her hand on the knee of the other. "Hummm!"

As Clay ushered us out, the prince beckoned, "Now eef you are ever een *Venezia*, *per favore*, look up me! And bring doze *belli bambini* to da *palazzo* to sweem. Zey are like miniature adoolts. *Fantasico* behavior! *Ciao*."

I wanted to ask his *canal* address but didn't have the guts, certain his invitation was rhetorical.

We slipped sleepy Tom into his stroller and started our three-block trek home. On the corner, a couple of tourists seemed to be lost.

"Where's Bourbon Street at?"

"We're heading that way, we'll show you."

"But you have children with you!"

"Yes, we're taking them home."

"You mean youse *live* in one a these houses?"

"You bet; we live on Bourbon Street."

"Gees, we didn't know real people lived in these crummy places!"

"Behind these shutter doors are many nice homes with families," Jan interjected.

"Where are you from?" I asked.

"Iowa. Gees, this place is like bein' in a foreign country for us."

They were rendered speechless as they walked along, peering into all the patio gates and looking through as many shutters as they could. We turned onto Bourbon Street.

"We'll stop here. You just keep walking up Bourbon toward Canal and you'll find all the strip places."

Tom rallied in his stroller. "Yah, there'll be lots of frippers up there. Go see the frippers like I do."

Bewildered, they trudged on their way.

I hollered after them, "Check out the Old Absinthe Bar for *Nobody Likes a Smart Ass!* with local actors Sam Adams and Billy Holiday. You'll love it!"

"Bob, maybe we should have asked them in for a few minutes to show them we have a nice home."

"I thought of that, too, honey, but I think we're all too tired to 'public-relate' to a pair of small-town hicks tonight. Besides, this way they'll have more to talk about when they get back to Idaho."

"Iowa."

"Yah, honey, whatever."

We read the children a couple of goodnight stories and said their prayers.

"Gosh, I feel itchy in this damp bathing suit. I should have taken it off at Clay's house," I said, as we walked into our bedroom.

"Bob, can I ask you a question?"

"Honey, of course you can ask me a question. Why do you always ask me if you can ask me a question? You know you can ask me a question. What's the question?"

"Well, something's been bothering me ever since we were at the pool."

I struggled, pulling off my damp bathing suit while walking into the bathroom to hang it over the shower spigot. "I can't hear you," I shouted back toward the bedroom.

Jan whispered the question.

"Honey, I can't hear you. Why are you whispering?"

"I don't want the kids to hear."

"The kids are asleep."

"I don't want the kids to hear anyway."

"Huh? For God's sake, what's the *question?*"

"Well, it's sort of a funny question."

"So it's a funny question. Maybe I'll give you a funny answer. But, what the hell's the question?"

"If you had one of your testicles hanging outside your bathing suit, wouldn't you know it?"

"Now, *that's* a funny question."

"Well, would you?"

"Yah, I think I would. If you had one of your boobs hanging outside your bra, would you know it?"

"Bob, of course!"

"So why did you ask?"

"Well, I mean, if the prince knew it was out, do you think he did it just to see what our reaction would be?"

"I don't know," I hunched. "But, it *was* sorta funny."

"Maybe. One thing about living in the Quarter, there's never a dull moment."

"Speaking of bras—here, let me help you, whoever creates these bra hooks has got to be some sort of a maniac." I struggled with the bra and it finally dropped away. I reached around Jan and cupped her breasts in the palms of my hands.

"*Honey!*"

"Something wrong?" I murmured, nuzzling my nose along the back of her neck.

"No, but your freezing hands surprised me."

"You should be used to my surprises by now." I pressed against her, nudging her toward our four-poster. "Let's get under the covers."

"Why?" she asked teasingly.

"Because, Miss Scarlett, ah've got ideas."

"Ashley, dahling, ah've got ideas, too."

"What do you mean, *Ashley?* I thought I was Rhett."

"*You* think like Rhett if you want too, but I've got *Ashley* ideas about you, honeychile!"

Man-made snow blown into the Brulitour courtyard for Christmas show that killed all the plants, 1964

CHAPTER TWELVE

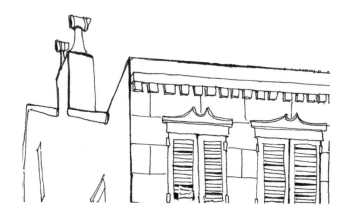

The Wild Maus, Paddleboats and the "Discovery"

It was another beautiful Saturday morning in New Orleans. My to-do list was different from Jan's, the kids', or the TV station's. My wish was to paint our bedroom walls, but the kids wanted me to take them to Pontchartrain Beach. Jan had other ideas for my Saturday chores but conceded getting the kids out of her hair would be great. However, first I had to report to the station to pre-record an interview with some hotshot woman who had written a sizzling new sex book.

The author, Helen Gurley Brown, was a rather sharp-featured, brittle, banty-hen sort of woman, possessing charm and magnetism beyond her wizened looks and petite stature. To my delight she was fascinating, with a life-story to match. Drawing on her own vivid memories, she published *Sex and the Single Girl*, contrary to the nation's prim and proper '50s mentality. Previous books, she felt, "All treated the single girl like a scarlet-letter victim, a misfit." But *her* book fiercely defended the "single girl" as "the newest glamour girl of the 60s." She called it a strategic guide to dating, work, beauty, and finance. *Sex and the Single Girl* had sold 150,000 hardcover copies. The book opens with her firm reassurance: "The rich, full life of dating doesn't require great beauty, money, or flamboyance. Rather, you work with the raw material you have, namely you, and never let up."

Her next challenge, she confided to me, was to become editor of *Cosmopolitan Magazine*. Time didn't permit, but on her next trip to New Orleans, she wanted to meet Jan and see our home in the Quarter. She deemed, from my answers to her questions, we must be a very special family. As we parted she gave me a very warm, moist kiss on the lips and reminded me to have my wife read her book. I wiped her ample lipstick from my mouth, inadvertently trailing it down the side of my white duck pants.

Those hard narrow lips delivered quite a punch! I was convinced Helen would achieve her goals.

Now it was the kids' turn to have a piece of me while Jan and Tom attended the birthday party of a three-year-old. Timmy had invited Kelvin, Pierre, and Mark to go to the amusement park. Tammy had invited two little girls from school whom I had not met before. Fortunately for me, Timmy and Tammy had arranged the whole deal, so the children would meet in front of *La Petite Ecole*—good planning, I assured them. This way I didn't have to drive the station wagon all over town to pick them up. As we drove toward the beach, the kids were enjoying reading the advertising billboards and street signs. I noticed Timmy didn't seem to be joining in.

Suddenly, one of the boys yelled, "Hey, Timmy, you can read *that* sign 'cause it's got a picture with it."

Timmy's eyes lit up as he said, "Yah, that's for Camel cigarettes."

Through the rear vision mirror I glanced at the boys in the back seat. "What do you mean, Timmy can't read the signs unless there's a picture?"

The boys clammed up and sat quietly but Tammy spoke up, "It's true, daddy! Timmy can't read 'less there's a picture!"

"What do you mean, a picture?"

"Daddy, I mean Timmy can't read 'less there's a picture with it. He can read *that* sign 'cause it's got a picture of a camel; so he knows that's Camel cigarettes."

"Is that true, Timmy?"

"Maybe it is and maybe it isn't!" Changing the subject, he promptly asked, "Daddy, when are we gonna get there? We're all gettin' anxious."

We stopped for a traffic light. "Can you read that street sign?"

"Robert E. Lee, Robert E. Lee Bull-vard," the girls yelped, before Timmy had a chance to answer.

"I meant that question for *Timmy!*"

"But daddy, he couldn't read that sign, it doesn't have any pictures."

"Tammy, let me ask the questions I please, to the person I please!" Glancing again into the mirror, I said, "Now, Timmy, what does that sign over there say?"

"Pontchartrain Beach," he said proudly.

Tammy spoke up, "Daddy, he knows what the sign says 'cause it's got a picture of the Zephyr roller coaster on it."

We continued to the end of Elysian Fields, where the boulevard flowed into a large circle in front of Pontchartrain Beach. Several groups of children and parents were emerging from NOPSI buses onto the large, sheltered waiting-area supported by pillars that looked as if inspired by ruins from Crete. Halfway around the circle I turned into the huge parking lot. I was lucky to find a space near the front entrance. There was a sign directly in front of us.

"Timmy, what's that say?"

He thought for a moment. "Bali Ha'i Restaurant!"

"You're right. Tammy, see, he *can* read."

"Daddy, he fools you. That sign's right by the restaurant. He knows that's the Bali Ha'i Restaurant 'cause we been here other times."

Everybody scrambled out of the car and dashed toward the main entrance.

"Don't run so fast; do you want to get hurt?" I shouted rhetorically, letting them go because I knew they couldn't get in until I bought the tickets. They stood fidgeting around me as I fumbled with money. The boys grabbed their tickets and clamored through the turnstile to the consternation of the attendant. On the other hand, the girls flocked around me, struggling through the turnstile.

Pontchartrain Beach was the entertainment paradise for New Orleans's white kids. Although federally-ordered integration had become law in 1959, black families still went to the inferior Lincoln Beach, a couple of miles to the east. Tradition dictated blacks and whites could not swim together. There was also thinking by the white-governed Levee Board that the Lincoln Beach waters, being closer to the Gulf, would be more readily cleansed by the tides. The Pontchartrain Beach management, plus the Levee Board, which governed all beaches, agonized over action to be taken the first time a black child attempted to buy a ticket. Because of that concern by the white public and the possibility of trouble at the gate, the park was less crowded than usual.

The amusement park was a good mixture of sun, sand, and thrilling rides; above all, it was clean and safe. Besides the upscale Bali Ha'i restaurant, offering south seas-style food, there were the usual hot dog stands, ice cream booths, and cotton candy vendors. Every Saturday around noon, and then again in the evening, the Beach offered live entertainment on the imposing moderne-style stage, looming some twenty feet above the sand. I doled out the tickets for each of the rides as the kids jumped up and down with excitement and meticulously compared their tickets to make sure each one of them had the same amount.

"Daddy, daddy," Tammy begged, tugging at my trousers, "can we go on the Zephyr first, 'cause the Zephyr is the most scariest and I wanna go on it lots of times. Please, please, *please*, can we go on that first?"

"Whatever you want, *but* listen, girls, you stay by me: if the boys get lost that's one thing, but you girls stay by me. *Do you hear?*"

"But Mr. Carr," Pierre said, "*We* want to go on the Wild Maus first, the Wild Maus is absolutely the scariest of all the rides and that's the newest one!"

"We've never been on it before, daddy," Timmy chimed in.

"Yeah," Mark added, "the Wild Maus is s'posed to be the scariest of any ride in the whole world! We wanna go on that first."

"But, before we go on anything, I hafta go to the bathroom," Timmy exclaimed, dancing around clutching his crotch.

"Timmy, you always hafta go to the bathroom," Tammy complained.

"That's embarrassing!" Timmy bounced back. "I can't help it if girls never hafta go to the bathroom, *so* you just be quiet."

"Kids, don't bicker! We're going to have a good day if it's the last thing we do! Timmy, listen to this closely: we'll wait here, *you* run over to the bathrooms. Anybody else?"

They all signaled negatively by nodding their heads.

"Okay, Timmy, you hurry to the john. Kids, let's wait in the shade."

We moved under one of many shade trees along the midway that created an oasis from our sub-tropical sun. From where we stood, there was the sound of clanking chains and gears above our heads. We glanced up in unison at the Wild Maus ominously looming above. The *clank, clank, clank, clank* sounded menacing as the steel mechanism of the gears pulled the little mouse-shaped cars toward the top. For a moment there was total silence. Then the cars plunged forward and down the steep incline. Wild screams broke the silence. The mouse cars could be seen whirling around and around in a whipping action, inciting further screams, then back up to the top again for a second, a third, and a fourth death-defying dive.

"Golly gee, looks like fun!" the boys bellowed.

"Yah, daddy," Tammy screamed through the racket. "That looks like fun! Me and you can go together, and Beth and Sandy can go together and there's four boys so they can divide up in two cars."

"Honey, I didn't think I'd be going on the rides."

At that moment it occurred to me we should have invited one more girl to make an even number. Carnival rides always make me sick to my stomach and give me a headache. Even as a child during the Depression, when my father traveled to county and state fairs selling ploughs and was given free tickets to the amusements, I would throw-up.

"Mister Carr, where's Timmy at? We gotta get goin'!"

"I don't know, maybe you better run over and see if you can find him."

"Yeah," the other kids chimed in, "tell Timmy to hurry up, he's wastin' our whole day. We'll never get any rides in."

Kelvin took off like a shot.

"Daddy, can we have some cotton candy or one of those red candy apples?"

"Not yet, honey, let's go on a few rides first. Then you can have something to eat."

Timmy and Kelvin finally came back across the midway through the increasing crowd. Kelvin was laughing but Timmy looked sheepish.

"What took you so long?"

"He went in the ladies' room." Kelvin snickered in a singsong manner, "Yah, Timmy went in the ladies' john."

The girls put their hands over their faces and giggled wildly.

"How did you happen to go into the ladies' john?"

"Because they had them marked wrong, daddy," he huffed indignantly.

"They had them marked wrong? You mean they had 'Ladies" on the Men's and 'Men's' on the Ladies'?"

"Daddy, they had the wrong names on them."

"I don't know what you mean."

"Oh, they had their right names on them, Mister Carr."

"What did they say, Kelvin?"

"One said 'Ladies' and the other said 'Gentlemen.'"

"So, how did you get in the wrong one, Timmy?"

"Daddy, they're dumb here. Usually they say Men and Women."

"Yah, but you know that women and ladies are the same thing."

"But, I go by which is the shortest word."

"What do you mean the shortest word?"

"I look on the door; if it has a short word, I know it's for the men to go in because a long word means it's for the ladies to go in."

I was perplexed, but began to figure it out. *Men is a shorter word than women and ladies is a shorter word than gentlemen.*

"Timmy, you mean you don't read the letters in the words, you just look for the shortest one?"

"Yah, I just look for the shortest one."

"No wonder you got in the wrong john, 'ladies' is a shorter word than 'gentlemen.'"

"I told you, when it's the shortest word I go in."

"See, daddy, I told you he can't read," Tammy chirped. "He has to have pictures."

The screams of the passengers above us on the Wild Maus interrupted our conversation. The commotion directed the kids' attention to their primary objective, so they scrambled to the entrance gate. I stood for a moment looking up, a lump developing in my throat. *I'm going to ride on that. I'm going to vomit!*

Tammy grabbed my hand and pulled me along, "Come on, daddy, we're going on the Wild Maus first." As, indeed, we did.

The experience left me reeling. I sat down on one of the shady benches along the midway while the kids went on the bumper cars. I sat with my head in one hand and my stomach cupped in the other, exacerbated by the knowledge that Timmy is unable to read.

John and Harry Batt, the owners and operators of the amusement park, passed by, inspecting the cleanliness of the midway. "Hi, Bob, we heard you were here," John said cheerfully.

"Gosh, how did you know that?" I asked, hoping not to regurgitate in their presence.

"The ticket-takers let us know when celebrities come in."

"How do they know?"

"*They know!* How long do you expect to be here?"

"Donno, couple of hours at least, probably three hours." I felt vomit in my esophagus and swallowed hard to keep on talking. "The kids are on the bumper cars right now; we've just gotten started. They've dictated their demands, at least three rides each on the Zephyr."

"Are you feeling okay? You look pale."

"That Wild Maus you've just installed may be designed to scare the hell out of the kids, but it makes me want to throw up! Have either of you ever ridden on it?"

Both deferred with a chuckle. "Would you like to go to the dispensary?"

"No, no, I'll be okay by the time the kids are off the bumper cars."

Harry reached into his pocket. "Here are a few more ride tickets for the kids."

"Thanks, Harry. I'm going to tell the kids these can only be used by children!"

"If you start feeling better and are going to be here a few more hours, maybe we can ask a favor of you."

"Sure, what is it?"

"We're having a bathing suit contest on the beach stage at one o'clock, and our M.C. called saying he won't be able to make it. Realizing you were here, we thought maybe you might stand in. We know the crowd would be delighted with the appearance of channel 6's Bob Carr."

Harry butted in. "We'd have asked you to M.C. these stage shows before but we figured you and Jan had such a husband-and-wife-team image, the station probably wouldn't want you to M.C. a contest with a bunch of busty bathing beauties."

"Good Lord, I don't think the station would care, if Jan doesn't mind. Sounds like fun for me, and I'm sure the kids will get a kick out of it, too."

John added, "We don't expect you to do it for free. We'll make it right with you, of course."

"Sounds great."

"If it's all right with you, report to the office about twelve-thirty so we can zero you in on the procedure, give you a chance to meet the girls and go over the format."

John intervened once again, "Bring the kids along; we'll have a table for them over in the Bali Ha'i. While you're getting set up for the contest they can have a bite to eat and then come out and watch the show."

"Sounds fabulous, thanks a lot. Should be fun. Besides, anything that'll keep me from riding the Caterpillar or the Zephyr will be great. It'll be a good excuse to tell the kids I can't get too disheveled since I have to be onstage."

The kids loved their day at Pontchartrain Beach and I had a wonderful time being the M.C. for the beauty contest. Standing on that high stage above the crowd in the middle of the Beach was a heady experience as my voice exploded forth from the enormous speakers. I glanced down at the kids, who waved at me proudly but timidly. It was the kind of day Mother Nature doles out sparingly so that we mortals will be appreciative. The iridescent sky was the perfect natural backdrop for the cumulus clouds majestically riding high above the beautiful blue water of Lake Pontchartrain. The white sand sparkled brilliantly, reflecting the bright sun. Hundreds of colorful little flags strung from the guy wires flapped ferociously, almost to the beat of the music throbbing forth from the sophisticated maxi-amp sound system. The scene was festive and charged with excitement as the twenty luscious contestants marched onto the high stage platform to be judged. Each young lady stretched her *de rigueur* spandex bathing suit to the fullest. Supposedly, a "mother-superior of breast scrutiny" was backstage checking for falsies. New Orleans girls are a beautiful mixture of French-Spanish "Creole babies with flashing eyes," combined with a plentiful smattering of Italian and Anglo-Saxon heritage.

Following much stiletto-heel strutting, mammary maneuvering, and derriere dancing, and with the overwhelming approval of the rowdy sun-soaked and half-naked crowd, Barbara Bollinger, a busty beauty, was selected by the judges as Miss Pontchartrain Beach of the week. She would enter the finals later in the summer. I, too, had hopes of being asked back!

Walking toward the parking lot after the show, Tammy, holding my hand, giggled and chided, "Daddy, mommy's gonna be jealous o' you!"

The other girls snickered.

"Why?" I asked, feigning ignorance.

"Cause you were up on that big stage with all those pretty girls in their bathing suits."

"Better than *without* their bathing suits!"

The girls all tittered.

Just before we passed through the turnstile exit, the boys announced they had to go to the john.

"Okay, but get into the right one this time, y'all hear?"

"Yah, daddy, we will."

On the way home, I dropped the boys at their own homes before taking the two girls back to school, where Tammy had prearranged for them to be picked up. When we got to *La Petite Ecole*, the girls' parents had not yet arrived, so I had the kids get out of the hot car and sit in the shade on the front stoop. Finding the door ajar, we pushed our way in to get relief from the heat. I hollered to see who was there. Timmy's teacher, Miss Bacchish, was in her classroom correcting papers. I seized the opportunity to chat with her for a few moments, telling the kids to wait in the vestibule so that they could keep an eye out for the girls' parents.

I told Miss Bacchish I was very concerned about Timmy's lack of reading ability.

"Mr. Carr, I'm aware of the problem. This school is small; with its liberal attitude and open classrooms, it may not be the best environment for children who are easily distracted or have a reading problem."

When I asked her advice, she hesitated but admitted it might be well to transfer him to a school that puts more emphasis on reading.

Jan and I were thrown into an educational quandary.

*   *   *   *   *

The alarm went off at 8:30 A.M. My head was buried in one of the expensive super-soft down pillows grandma had sent us for Christmas. I glanced at the alarm clock with one eye as I pulled an arm loose and reached over to push down the lever. I lingered in that foggy state of euphoria just before one becomes wide-awake. The bed was warm and inviting beneath me as I lay on my stomach stretching my legs to the very tips of my toes. I arched my back to exercise my muscles and pressed my throbbing early morning stiffness firmly against the mattress. *Gees, I've got to go to the john.* I became aware of Jan lying asleep next to me and smiled, remembering our delicious lovemaking the night before.

"Daddy, are we going to church today?" came a voice from our bedroom door.

I relaxed and sank back into my pillow, replying halfheartedly, "Do you want to go to church, kids?"

"No!" they chimed in together. "We want to go to City Park to ride the paddle boats."

"That settles it," I mumbled.

Jan stirred from her half-sleep before I was able to finish my sentence. "Settles what?"

"Are we gonna go to church, mommy?"

"Uh-huh."

"*That* settles it. Get ready for church."

"Oh, daddy, do we have to?"

"Yes."

"Who said so?" Tammy asked.

"Your mommy said so."

"I did?" Jan whispered from her pillow.

"She didn't do no such thing," Timmy admonished.

"Yes, she did," I countered. "Remember, I have to teach Sunday school and besides, Santa Clause says we have to go to church."

"Daddy, that's silly," Tammy chortled.

"Not so silly. Remember, he sees you when you're sleeping, he knows when you're awake, he knows if you've been bad or good, so you'd better be good for goodness sake and go to church, or you won't get any toys for Christmas."

"Daddy, that's really silly, Christmas isn't for a long time."

"Santa Clause didn't say you should be good just near Christmas time, you gotta be good all the time."

Tom had been taking in all the Santa Clause chatter; his eyes were as big as balloons when he spoke. "I'm not taken no chances, Holy Mary Mother of God, Saint Anna's, here I come!" With that, he dashed out, reluctantly followed by Tammy and Timmy.

"I can't believe it, Tom sounds more like a Catholic everyday. It must be the neighborhood."

"What?" Jan asked, pulling herself up in bed.

The three kids peeked around the door and solemnly asked through their spokesman, Timothy, "Are we goin' to City Park after St. Anna's?"

I replied teasingly, "I guess we *will!*"

"Yippee, yippee, yippee," they shouted, jumping up and down. Then, like a flock of attacking hornets, they dashed over and hopped into bed with us.

"Ooh, not on top of me," I groaned. "I have to go to the bathroom."

With that, Timmy sat on my back.

"Ohhh, I went!" I exclaimed.

Timmy started to laugh, "Daddy, you didn't pee in the bed!"

"*Timothy!*" Jan rebuked.

"Yes, I did!"

"*Bob!* Stop leading them on."

Tom stuck his head down into the pillow next to me. "Daddy, you didn't wet the bed. I don't even wet the bed!"

"Well, maybe I did and maybe I didn't, but you all look the other way while I jump out and run to the bathroom."

"Ohhhh, I saw daddy's hiny," Tom screamed, as I dashed into the bathroom cupping my hands over my extended ying yang, as the kids say.

I heard Jan say, "Okay, kids, hop out of our bed. Go to your rooms and pick out your clothes for church."

Jan and I had grown to truly enjoy St. Anna's. Father Hal Crisler, an ingratiating priest, was intelligent, down-to-earth, and ecumenically and racially progressive. But most of all, we felt the presence of the Holy Spirit hovering over the Eucharistic table during Communion, something we hadn't found at other mainline Protestant churches, in spite of their erudite sermons and outstanding Sunday school presentations. Instead, at St. Anna's there was an intrinsic draw, inviting one to sample more and more each week of that which was truly sacred.

As I left to pick up Rennie and Billy Bob, the kids and Jan were still trying to figure out which outfits to wear to church. Now dressed, they were standing in front of the house when I circled back. A couple of early morning Midwestern tourists were shyly snapping pictures of the quartet as I pulled up.

"We hope youse don't mind if we take a few Polaroids of yuns," they croaked. "We didn't know real people lived in these places!"

They looked so gullible and silly in their double-knit stretch made-to-match leisure suits that I was obliged to remark, "Oh, we have to live here so 'my woman' can be near her work; she's a stripper at night. Maybe you saw her on a billboard down thataway on Bourbon, 'School Teacher Turned Stripper'?" Then I whispered, "She's the *teacher!*"

Their jaws dropped.

Tammy, taking care not to rumple her organdy dress or shift her chapeau, squeezed into the mini back seat with Timmy and the boys. Slipping into the front seat, Jan fastened her seat belt, put Tom on her lap, and off we sped, leaving the tourists with their mouths open and their drying Polaroid photo flopping from the camera.

In my Sunday school class of six- to ten-year-olds, I tried to explain that God had given several great gifts to man.

Little Jennifer spoke up. "But, Mr. Carr, did God give any gifts to girls?"

"Yes, Jennifer, he gave gifts to girls and boys and men and women. Can any of you tell me what those gifts might be?"

A hand popped up.

"Yes, Rennie, what do you think that might be?"

"Gifts at Christmas, Christmas presents."

"Yes, that's something, but usually those aren't from God, those are usually from—"

"From Santa Clause!" Tammy broke in.

"That's true, from Santa Clause and, maybe, daddy and mommy and friends. I'm talking about different kinds of gifts. All of us in this Sunday school have special gifts, one really important gift. What do we all have?"

They sat silent.

"Gee, Mr. Carr, can't you give us a hint?"

"Maybe, let's see, how can I explain this? When we were all born, what did we have?"

"Wet diapers!" Timmy blurted.

Everybody giggled, including me. "That's right, maybe we had wet diapers, but what did we all have the very minute we were born?"

"Breath, 'cause we were cryin'."

"Very good, Tammy. We all had breathed; breath brings life. We all had *life*, that's one of God's main gifts, life."

"Animals have life, too."

"Good, Rennie, animals have life, too. That's a gift from God to the animals. But boys and girls and men and women have something animals don't have. They have another gift from God. Does anybody know what that might be?"

"People have houses and animals don't."

"That's right, Jennifer, and something else?"

"They got schools, too," Timmy added begrudgingly.

"Yes, people have schools, and why do people have schools and animals don't?"

"Because people are smarter than animals."

"Uh huh, that's another gift. People have intelligence, people can make plans and animals can't. What's important about that?"

"We can invent stuff," Timmy answered.

"And we can paint pictures, like my daddy," Rennie added.

"We can build things," Mary chimed in.

"That's right, we can do all sorts of wonderful things, so it's important for us to remember God gave us the wonderful gift of life, then he gave us our smart minds, so we should use them to do wonderful things. We have an opportunity to do great things: to teach ourselves, to help other people, to invent machines, to be kind to animals and do good things for others, because God wants us to have a useful life."

A hand shot up.

"Yes, Billy Bob?"

"God borned Jesus in 'swallowing' clothes!"

"Yes." I chose not to correct him. "Jesus was born, but *why* was He born?"

"To teach people stuff."

"You're absolutely right, Rennie. God sent his Son, Jesus, into the world to teach us how to be good and kind and generous to each other. Jesus is our older brother. He was born to teach us about love."

The bell rang, announcing the end of class and startling the kids.

"Oops, just a minute, before you leave. Next week, when you come to class, we're going to talk about someone we love and why. Now, fold your hands. May the Lord Jesus bless us and keep us and make His face to shine upon us, and be gracious unto us, and give us peace. Amen." The minute I said "Amen," the children scampered out as though trained by Pavlov.

It's a wonder I had remained religious at all, considering my third grade Sunday school teacher had ridiculed me unmercifully when he made our class read from the King James Version of the Old Testament. Being highly dyslexic, I could never see the difference between "thou," "though," "through," "thorough," "thee," "the," etc. It caused me great pain and embarrassment.

I had made arrangements for Rennie and Billy Bob to be taken home so that Jan and I, and the kids, could go directly to City Park.

Driving down Esplanade Avenue, its oak and camphor trees in full foliage lining the neutral ground, is an enchanting sight. Fluttering stippled tones of green shaded the center of the boulevard from the high-noon southern sun playing shadowy patterns on the pillars, pillars, pillars—Greek classic orders, Italianate, Gothic Revival. An amazing archive of architectural styles adorned the once-gracious mansions of the wealthy and titled Créole families of *La Belle Nouvelle Orléans* who had reigned over *L'Avenue d'Esplanade*.

It's even more enjoyable driving along with the top down. As we passed the various corners, we shouted out the musical-sounding street names like a Creole history lesson—Villere, Dorgenois, Prieur, Galvez, Miro, Bayou, and Tonti.

At a triangular intersection where Esplanade, Tonti, and Bayou Road intersect, a Roman goddess holding a laurel leaf surmounts an impressive deep red terra cotta monument. "She's a beautiful queen," Tammy would say, overlooking the missing arm. There's no date on it and no name; gossip says it was originally ornamentation at the 1884 Cotton Exposition in Audubon Park.

Crossing Broad Street toward City Park, the architecture suddenly switches to 1920s and 30s adaptations of Classic and Spanish architecture, mixed with an ample smattering of Eastlake and a variety of other late-Victorian styles. But the street names still conjure up the history of Louisiana—de Soto, Dupry, Gayoso, Lopez,

Maurepas, Mystery, Verna, and Leda.

To the right on Verna Street is the remnant of a viciously defaced Italianate villa, at one time a private home, eventually becoming the exclusive Jockey Club for the Fairgrounds racetrack nearby. Across from what used to be the mansion's front lawn is the Church of Our Lady of the Rosary and Cabrini High School with a shrine to the Virgin Mary.

Tammy insisted we stop and take a quick look at the Virgin and say a couple of prayers, "'Cause it's Sunday."

Esplanade Avenue ends abruptly at the Bayou St. John bridge, where one is confronted by a huge equestrian bronze statue of General Pierre Gustave Toutant Beauregard of the Confederate States of America; famous for ordering the first shot fired against Fort Sumpter in Charleston's harbor, Beauregard is credited with starting the "Wahr b'tween the States"!

"That's Pierre's uncle," Timmy remarked respectfully, proud to be associated in some remote way with the great Southern hero.

Classic white columns on either side of the entrance welcome visitors to City Park; the impressive Delgado Museum of Art, now the New Orleans Museum of Art, can be seen at the far end of the grassy mall. To the right, the kids glimpsed the lagoon with the white swans and became more and more excited as they talked about the paddleboats we would soon be peddling. I circled around in front of the museum so that the kids and Jan could giggle as we passed the naked male figure of an archer who displayed, vividly, his genitalia while preparing to shoot an arrow high into the sky. An exceedingly masculine Cupid, he was later removed to a more private place.

Asking the kids where they wanted to go first was my biggest mistake because each child came up with a different answer. Ultimately, though, it didn't seem to make much difference as long as there was a plan to see most of the things along the way.

Storyland, built in 1956, is a children's favorite. The kids charged through Puss *and* Boots and the big blue whale with Pinocchio. They paused briefly in the shoe-house of "The little old lady who had so many children she didn't know what to do." They paid homage to King Cole's Castle, the Magic Dragon, Cinderella's Pumpkin Coach, and Snow White. They scampered through Storyland so fast that I thought they would be pooped before they ever got on the merry-go-round, but no such luck. The brightly-colored antique merry-go-round, handmade in 1906, was one of the oldest carousels still operating in the country.

"Hurry up, daddy, it's going to stop," they nagged, pulling on my trousers as I stood at the kiosk purchasing tickets. Tammy and Tom took Jan's hands, and Timmy pulled me by the arm, scrambling us up to the gate just as the carousel was slowing down. Tom jumped up and down like a banshee wanting to get through the ticket gate. The carousel came to a complete stop and the riders exited. As soon as the ticket-taker released the turnstile, Tom shot through, frantically screaming, "I want a camel! I want to get on the camel!"

Timmy was right behind him, explaining, "Tom, Tom, you don't want a camel 'cause the camels don't go up an' down."

"Then I wanna get on this black horse."

"The black horse doesn't go up and down neither."

"Then I want the lion. I want the lion." Tom was beside himself watching his choices narrow as other kids climbed astride their steeds.

"Lions don't go up and down."

Tom swung around, put his hands on his hips and shrieked, "Well, what the poo *does* go up and down, Timmy?"

"These horses right here go up and down. See, you have to look up at the top, and you can tell by the way they're hooked up there if they go up and down or not."

"Mommy and I are going to sit right here in this sleigh seat. These three horses right in front of us go up and down so you and Tammy and Tim get on these horses, we'll watch you. Hey, you can all go up and down right in front of us."

The calliope tooted a familiar Italian jig as the three children scaled up the sides of their horses and the carousel began to turn. Tom's blue eyes grew as big as saucers when the up-and-down motion began. The beveled mirrors in the top of the center drum made the action seem even faster. Around and around and around and around we went. The horses in front of us went up and down, up and down, and up and down and around and around. The faster we moved, the longer we rode, the sicker I became. My propensity toward motion sickness was once again in control.

"Jan, I've gotta get off this damn thing before I throw up!"

"But Bob, that sign plainly says don't get off while the carousel is in motion."

"Honey, there are two alternatives: break the rule or vomit!"

I swung myself off on the farthest side of the carousel away from the attendant so I wouldn't be seen breaking the rules. I leaned against the guardrail with my eyes closed until the damn thing came to a halt.

"Daddy, daddy, we want to go around again."

"*Absolutely no!* There're other things to ride." Still feeling uneasy, I walked with them out of the carousel rotunda.

The kids dashed toward the Ferris wheel. "Come on daddy, come on daddy, it's loading."

"Thanks, kids, but mom wants to take you on the Ferris wheel."

I stretched out on the grass to avoid watching them. I felt a bit better as we wandered over to the station for the train ride around City Park. At the boat stop we rented one paddleboat for Timmy and Tammy and another for Jan, Tom, and me. When Jan finally conceded it was safe, I pulled Tom's shoes off and sat him on the bow so that he could dangle his feet in the water.

The bayous and lagoons of City Park are mystical with the flora and fauna of Louisiana: palmetto palms, live oaks draped with moss, cypress trees, crepe myrtles, dozens of little islands—one with a pigeonaire, all with an abundance of ducks, swans and geese—with fishermen on the banks. The gracefully arched bridges are reminiscent of Venice or Kyoto. Finding the sun a little too hot in the center of the lagoon, we sought shelter near the shore. We took refuge under an oak tree, where we unpacked our lunch. The kids enjoyed feeding a few of the sandwich scraps to the ducks, which fluttered feverishly around our picnic enclave. An hour of pumping the paddleboats in the sun was sufficient. Once on shore, we made a potty stop at the refreshment casino before crossing the park to the car. Tammy's organdy dress was now wrinkled beyond belief but, thank God, she didn't seem to notice.

Her rumpled dress looks like I feel!

We left City Park with the children entreating for yet one more thing. They loved to drive across the old Bayou St. John bridge. Looking as if it had been built with Timmy's erector set, the bridge was just the right width to accommodate our Triumph.

"Hey, kids, let's go get some ice cream!"

"Yippee! Ice cream, ice cream," they all screamed. "Where're we gonna get it from?"

Jan, who had set up an appointment for us, told them, "We're going to a friend of daddy's and mine. She's a real nice lady who lives in Old Metairie. When we get there, we're going to play a few games."

"What kind of games, mommy?" asked Tammy, who loved to play games, only if she could win.

"It's sort of a surprise; she'll tell you about it when we get there."

"What kind of ice cream is she going to have, mommy?"

"I don't know. We'll just have to wait and see. It'll be a surprise."

"Why does she like to play games?" Tammy asked again.

"Well, she likes to stay young, I guess, and she likes kids."

"What is she?"

"What do you mean, Timmy, what is she?" Jan inquired.

"I mean if she likes kids, is she some kinda school teacher?"

"Well, sometimes she teaches school."

"Yuk! I *knew it!* A schoolteacher! I don't wanna visit any schoolteacher, not on a Sunday! That really *stinks!*"

"*Timothy!*"

Despite our concerns that Timothy's reading ability was below standard for his grade, Miss Edna, the principal, felt there was "really no problem." And yet he seemed to be falling further and further behind in subjects dependent on reading skill, such as geography, history, and English. Narrative problems in math were particularly difficult.

Marty Lindly had appeared on one of our television programs discussing the advantages of teaching children phonetics. After the program, Jan had told her of our concern; she suggested we bring *all* the children to her house so she could test their reading skills.

Marty welcomed us graciously into her home. The children were immediately captivated by her manner of speech and her interest in them. She further won them over with heaping dishes of ice cream in five different flavors. She had five places laid out on a long table, a spot for each one of us.

"We're going to play a few games," she announced.

"What kinda games?" Tammy asked eagerly.

"This is going to be a game about eye-hand perception and coordination."

"Oh," Tammy remarked, not really comprehending.

"You see—" She spoke to all of us as equals. "Some people see things one way and some people see things another. Some people pick up things one way and some people pick up things another. Some people write with their right hand and some people write with their left."

"I know *that*," Tammy said, "'cause I write with my left hand and Timmy writes with his right hand, and Tom kinda writes with both hands when he draws stuff."

"You're a very smart little girl."

Tammy tittered and cringed with embarrassment, not knowing quite how to handle the compliment.

"Some people write slowly and some people write fast. Some people read fast and some people read slowly. Some people talk fast and some people talk slowly."

"My teachers read fast all the time," Timmy complained.

"All your teachers read fast?"

"Yes, ma'am, most of the time when they read, they read really fast, a lot faster than me."

"That's very interesting. Maybe we'll find out something about that in the game."

Nearly an hour passed. Marty had us writing things, picking things up, putting them down on the floor, picking them again, putting them on the table, writing more things down, then taking turns reading them back. She gave us some sheets of paper from which we each had to read. Then she showed us flash cards; we had to go along one by one telling her what letter was flashing by. Some of the flash cards had consonants, some vowels, some diphthongs, and some short words: was and saw, hit and hut, bit and but, pin and pine. After an hour of activity, she announced, "That's it, y'all, game's over."

"Already?" Tom asked.

"Already," she replied with a smile, obviously pleased with his alertness.

Tammy was quick to query, "Who won, who won?"

Marty announced that everybody won, causing Tammy to look a trifle disappointed.

Timmy inquired, "What do you mean, Miss Marty, everybody won?"

She responded gently, "The reason I said everybody won is that you *all* learned something from the game, didn't you?"

We all nodded affirmatively without really knowing just what we had learned.

"You all learned some new words and new sounds, you learned we all do things a little differently from one another, we have different speeds and we each have a different approach."

"What's an approach?"

"Good question, Timmy. An approach is the way you look at something. *You* look at something a little differently than Tammy looks at it or Tom looks at it, or your mom or dad. We don't all see things exactly the same way. And that's fine, 'cause if we did, it would be sort of a boring world, wouldn't it, Timmy?"

"Uh-huh," he said, looking as if he didn't quite follow.

"And now if you children don't mind, I'd like to talk to your mom and dad for a few minutes. Would you carry this pitcher of lemonade out to the backyard, and I'll bring you some freshly baked brownies, if it's all right with your parents. You can sit out there and have your snack while you check out my dogs and cats and the several neighborhood squirrels. We'll just be a few minutes."

The kids glanced over at us for approval. We nodded affirmatively, their cue to spring for the door.

"So, Marty, what do you think?"

"I wasn't kidding the children when I said everyone has a different approach, and it's quite obvious you each do. It may come as a surprise to you, Bob, but you and Timothy seem to have the greatest difficulty in perceiving the letters and some of the words on the flash cards."

"Gosh, I hoped you wouldn't notice."

"Hey, I noticed, all right. Did you have trouble reading in school?"

"Gee, since I'm a radio announcer and a TV personality, it's a little embarrassing to say. Yes, I've always had trouble reading. I really hate to admit it because it's always been an embarrassment. Frankly, I can't remember reading a whole book all the way through until well after I'd graduated from college. I just couldn't keep up. I read so slowly. I guess one of the remarkable things, so far as I was concerned, was that I got through college with really rather good grades."

"Did you ever feel like there were times when you were getting by more on your personality than on your scholastic skills?"

"For sure. God, Marty, you've found out my secret! There were lots of times when I *did* get by on my personality. Sight-reading has always been an enormous problem. Until this day, as the engineers and the continuity writers at the station know, if I don't get a chance to read over the minute spots or the commercials at least once before I have to tape them or broadcast them live, I'm in real trouble. Sight-reading has been a great big problem since the first grade."

"It's wonderful how you've been able to surmount your affliction in a positive way. The tragedy of a reading dysfunction is that it often adversely affects a person's personality, sometimes resulting in negative behavioral patterns. The basic problem seems to stem from a genetic deficiency that's handed down from parent to child or grandparent to grandchild. We don't know exactly how it travels through the genes, but it's passed on to the children in many cases, and apparently, Timothy has inherited that tendency from you."

"Dammit! How can you tell?"

"I'm no great wizard, but my training enables me to recognize clues. It was evident by the way Timothy perceived the flash cards; his hand usage when he was picking up the various blocks and setting them into place; the manner in which he was writing things down; these were all tell-tale signs, showing me he was having great difficulty comprehending the various letters and words as they were transmitted to his brain. Even when he could perceive the letters, he had a great deal of difficulty in knowing how to arrange them to create a word. It's quite obvious to me his problems in school don't stem from a lack of intelligence, but a lack of perception of the written word, which I picked up in many ways; one of them is his eye-hand coordination; another when I showed him 'hit' and 'hut'; he really couldn't tell the difference. When I showed him 'was,' he said 'saw' and vice versa. Reversal is also a part of the overall problem.

"What about Tammy and Tom?"

"Fortunately, there seems to be no problem there. As a matter of fact, what I picked up was, they're probably a little above average in their perception of the letters and words. This diabolical problem doesn't usually hit every member of the family."

Jan, normally grim-faced when anyone talked about problems with the children, very hesitantly asked, "What can we do about Timmy's reading?"

"You see, one of the great problems schools present today is they try to teach children to read the whole word instead of laying the groundwork with phonetics and teaching them how to sound out the word, create the word and, finally, recognize the word. Of course, English, a non-phonetic language, magnifies this tremendously. People with Timothy's difficulty must have a background in phonetics; otherwise they're just going to drift through school doing mediocre work because they will never have a foundation in reading: the basis of education. I hate to belabor the point, but I feel this is one of the greatest tragedies in our school system today."

"You know, Marty, I agonized over reading all through school. When I got into high school and finally took Spanish, I was amazed to find out I could read Spanish more easily than I could read English because it was a phonetic language."

"I'm not surprised. This problem doesn't exist as severely in languages which are phonetic, like Spanish or Italian."

"In fact, when I was a kid, I used to lie awake at night and cry because I couldn't read and would pray that someday they would make a language that I could understand. As I got a little older and realized there was such a thing as a phonetic language like Spanish, I hoped that someday the President of the United States would make English into a phonetic language. Then, by the time I got into college, I was really amazed to learn there was such a thing as an International Phonetic Alphabet. In fact, I used to take all my college notes in the phonetic alphabet, which I found easier to comprehend than the English language. Besides, my spelling has always been abysmally poor!"

"Sadly, that's another problem with children who have this disability. Their spelling comprehension is always very minimal."

"Gosh, this is depressing news," Jan declared, still rather long-faced. "Now I can understand why Timmy's teachers say he's lazy in class and doesn't try to learn."

"Good Lord, Jan, sometimes teachers are oblivious to students' problems. Obviously, Timothy is having a problem with reading. It's not because he's lazy or stupid, it's because he can't comprehend what he sees."

On the verge of tears, Jan asked, "What can we do about it?"

"Dear, now calm down, don't get upset," Marty said, putting her arm around Jan. "We'll figure something. I'll do a little investigating. Maybe we can get a tutor or we might find a different school for him. We'll do something. He's a very bright boy and not beyond repair. There are teachers who teach remedial reading."

"Good God, and we're paying for a private school!"

"Now look, you two, don't be so troubled, we'll figure out something. I didn't ask you here to upset you, but to find out if there's a problem. Okay?" Marty reached out and squeezed our hands.

The screen door slammed. Tom announced a dog had eaten one of the brownies and a big black cat had chased a squirrel up the tree.

"Oh, dear, that's one of the neighbor's dogs. We'd better go scoot him away."

Jan broke down in tears. "Oh, Bob, what can we do?"

"Honey, Marty told us it's going to be all right. She'll help us out. I think we'd better get the kids packed up now and head on home. It's getting late."

We gathered up the kids, strapped them down in the back seat, and set out for home. We were still waving goodbye when a flash of lightning filled the sky.

"Yikes!" came the cry from the back seat.

"Oh, kids, that's just heat lightening, summer lightening." A clap of thunder interrupted my words.

"Maybe you're right, Bob, but that thunder tells me we'd better put the top up."

Jan and I jumped out, pulled up the top, snapped it into place and drove off. The kids were chattering away when the back seat babbling intensified.

Suddenly we heard Tammy say, "You did, *too!*"

Timmy responded vehemently with, "I did *not!*"

Followed by a round of: "You did too. I did *not*…did *too*…did *not*. You did *too*—"

"Now y'all stop that *right now!*" I reprimanded.

Tom, who was nestled down between the two of them, tattled, "Tammy said Timmy gave the wrong answers for that game at Miss Marty's house."

"He did give the wrong answers, daddy, really he did. He read some of those words backwards, 'cause I could see 'um."

Timmy raised his voice, saying, "I did not, I did *not!* My words weren't none of your business anyways."

"You read 'um backwards."

Timmy reached across Tom and gave Tammy a swat on the chest, repeating, "None of your business, *none of your business, dummy!*"

At that moment a fierce New Orleans squall skittered across the road, hitting our car. The raindrops on the roof sounded like a hundred bass drums beating away.

"Daddy, Tammy thinks she's so smart just 'cause she's a girl."

"Children, stop fighting," Jan pleaded, trying to quiet the kids down.

The rain pelted the roof fiercely. I slammed my foot on the brake throwing the kids forward tightly against their seat belts—dealer-installed at Jan's insistence—not only getting their attention but stopping their aggravating chatter instantly.

I swung around in my seat as best I could and with an intense glare. "I told you to stop arguing, so stop it *now!* You hear?"

There wasn't another peep until we reached home.

The rain had nearly stopped by the time we got to the Quarter. The glow of the antique lamps twinkled in reflection along the streets, radiating a pleasant shimmer that created that occasional enchanted atmosphere that artists try to capture on canvas.

Under the strain of the day's activities, and having been reprimanded, the kids had nodded off from exhaustion. I lifted Tom out of the back seat and handed him to Jan, who carried him in. I eased Tammy over my shoulder, then took Tim by the hand and pulled him along in a sleepy daze up the stairs. We pulled off their clothes, covered them, and kissed them goodnight. While Jan and I were undressing for bed, Jan kept repeating her concern about Timothy and his reading ability.

"Honey," I said, "we can't worry about that right now. We can't problem-solve tonight. Let's go to bed and get a good night's sleep. Fiddle-lee-dee, we'll worry about that tomorrow!"

"I don't think you're taking this problem seriously."

"Yes, I am, honey, I promise. *I've* had that problem all my life but I'm too tired to worry about it tonight. Now, how about taking this seriously?" I asked, as I rolled over against her.

"What?"

"This," I said, as I put my arms around her, kissing her passionately, while visions of sugarplums and sexual pleasures danced through my head.

Her latent lips expressed fatigue.

Anon, I loosened my grip, fell back on my pillow and sleep overtook us.

* * * * *

After our visit with Marty, there was no doubt that we should find Timothy a different school in the fall. We agonized over where to send him. Since Jan and I were both products of public schools, that was our first choice. McDonogh No. 15, named for John McDonogh, the founder of the New Orleans Free Public School System, was only a few blocks away on St. Philip Street. With great hope we checked it out. The principal spent considerable time discussing the virtues of public education but gave us little hope his school would be well-suited for a child with any kind of learning disability. Like many of the schools in the city, Mc Donogh 15 was in a crisis mode due to the violence and discontent associated with the racial integration of the entire system. He was sure we were aware of the continuing problems of the schools on nearby St. Claude Avenue.

"Unfortunately, I can't tell you folks from one minute till the next whether we'll have our doors open in the fall or not, way things are goin' in the South. Breaks my heart to see our schools on the news every night with Negroes and whites glarin' at one another. It's a catastrophe in the makin'. I know you TV and radio people are well educated and want the best for your children so they'll get into Tulane or some good Yankee college. My honest suggestion, at this moment in history, is for y'all to place them in a private school until this integration thing blows over."

Jan and I felt more and more disheartened as he continued.

"O'course, we got this 'white flight' thing goin' on to all the private schools for students whose parents can afford it. I understand you can't even get your child into an accredited private school this fall."

We were devastated as we walked the several blocks home.

"Maybe it's time to leave the Quarter!" Jan sighed.

"Honey, it's not the Quarter that's the problem, it's the city, it's the state, it's the South, dammit!"

"Well, then maybe it's time to leave the stupid South!" she barked, tears flooding her eyes.

"Now, honey, that's silly." I put my arm around her, knowing I had to take charge of this dilemma. "We can't be stupid just because everyone else is. The *place* isn't stupid, it's the people, but not *all* the people; we know that! We've got to be rational while the world catches up. I know in my heart there will be a place for Timmy this fall."

Olympia met us in the hall as we walked through the front door. "Mizz Lindly wants that you should call her *at once!* She gots some good news."

Jan flew so nervously to the phone that she misdialed three times. She didn't say much, mostly listened to whatever Marty was telling her. She smiled happily for a spell, then looked puzzled or wary as if there was some problem. She thanked Marty profusely, telling her she would have to check with Bob.

"What did she say? What was so important? Was there some problem?"

"It's about Timmy, *and* Tammy, *and you!* You know Marty has connections at all the private schools and she's found a school with a marvelous phonetic reading program, *and* they have space for both Timmy *and* Tammy to start in September."

"That sounds great. So, what the problem?"

"*You!*"

"*Me?*"

"She's afraid you won't like the school."

"Why?"

"Because it's Baptist, Mid-City Baptist. She knows you have a thing about their proselytizing and literal interpretation of the Bible."

"I do? Well, *I do!* Yes, I do, but if they can teach the children to read, I can overlook that. Besides, I'll teach them the Bible better at home and at St. Anna's. Call her back right now and tell her we agree."

Tuesday morning after Labor Day, we all got up extra early to get ready for the first day of school. Jan and Olympia hustled around getting the children dressed while I battled with the boiling water to try something new on the market, "instant" grits. Apparently, I didn't follow the directions properly because I cooked up something the color of grits but was loose and lumpy in consistency. Tom, climbing up into his booster chair, said it looked like pigeon poo. I wasn't surprised when Timmy and Tammy turned their noses up at it and the shriveled bacon strips. Jan, however, forced them to down their vitamins with a slug of newfangled frozen orange juice, which I had partially thawed in a pitcher of water. With breakfast finished, they ran up to the balcony and watched for the school bus.

What we thought was going to be a large yellow school bus turned out to be a Volkswagen van painted bright blue with "Mid-City Baptist School" stenciled boldly on the side. Tammy was the first to spy the church vehicle soberly lumbering along Bourbon Street, narrowly missing a couple of leftover revelers who were staggering home at 7:45 A.M. As the van approached the house, the driver pressed the horn, emitting the distinctive sound only a Volkswagen van coughs forth. The kids had already scampered down the front steps and were out the door when the van came to a halt in front of the house. They boarded the van with such enthusiasm that Jan and I were overwhelmed. Although changing schools, they were doing it with a great deal of joy and excitement. We stood on the banquette watching as the van rumbled clumsily down Bourbon until it turned the corner and disappeared. Touched by the new chapter in our lives, Jan and Olympia wiped their eyes. Our moment of reflection was disrupted by Tom's tugging on the hem of Olympia's uniform to demand his usual stroller ride to Wools-worth's and the Whitney Bank.

Both kids were eager to relate their stories about school over dinner. Surprisingly, they were also anxious to do their homework. During the summer, I had built both of the kids a special desk where they could work. I hoped to advance their study habits and instill a feeling of pride in their homework. I decorated the desks in Pennsylvania Dutch primitive style and painted each name on the top. I'm great at "setting the scene," but Jan was the one who actually helped the kids with their studies. Timmy's homework consisted of dissecting words phonetically, while

Tammy's emphasized memorizing Bible passages.

Our dining room had one corner designated as the unofficial stage for after-dinner performances by any member of the family or friends who wished to exhibit a talent: singing, dancing, reciting, whatever. Olympia had cleared the table and was serving dessert when Tammy got up from the table and proudly announced that she had just memorized her Bible verse for the day.

"John, three sixteen: For God so loved the world, that he gave his only begotten Son, that whosoever believeth in Him should not perish, but have everlasting life. Amen!"

She curtsied, sat down with a self-satisfied air, and dug into her bread pudding, meticulously pushing each raisin aside. As our conversation unfolded, Tammy announced there was an assembly the evening after next; both parents were expected to attend. Timmy pulled a note from his pocket that gave the information.

"Bob, I can't go that night, I have to do a special fashion rehearsal for the Woolco account, but I'm sure it will be fine if you take the kids."

"Can I go, too?" Tom asked.

"Fine with me, you can go and pretend you're mommy," I remarked jovially.

"Daddy, that's ridiculous!" Tammy said with great consternation.

"Yes, daddy, that's 'diculous! How can I be mommy?"

Timmy chimed in. "Daddy, my teacher said both your mommies and daddies are s'posed to come."

"I'm sure if your mother can't come for a good reason, it will be perfectly all right to have one parent there. I'll get the station to write her an excuse."

"Daddy, that's silly," Tammy interjected.

"What kind of assembly do you think it is?"

"I don't know, daddy, it's just an assembly."

So, two evenings later, we dropped Jan at the station, then proceeded to the Mid-City Baptist assembly hall. I could see that most children were accompanied by both parents. We were greeted pleasantly at the door and asked to sit toward the front. By the time the meeting began, every seat was filled. The program opened with a fervent prayer by the minister of Mid-City Baptist Church, which owned and operated the school. He followed the prayer with a bloodcurdling sermon of "hell, fire and damnation," leaving my kids wide-eyed and pinned to the back of the pew. A moment of silence was penetrated by the bulky elderly lady sitting next to Tammy. The lady broke wind with an explosion that seemed to originate low, then rumble up and out through her tightly-laced Krauss corselette. Scattered muted titters erupted as heads turned, seeking the guilty source. The stone-faced woman sat rigidly, her secret revealed by the telltale crimson hue of her face. Her expression remained stoic as if she committed this offence often but didn't want to claim it. Tammy squirmed, then nestled under the edge of my sport coat.

The principal, who was eventually introduced, related the objectives of the school and the fund-raising that would take place during the year. Finally, the honored guest, a missionary just returning from many years in Central Africa, was presented. Following a long and graphic talk on how the Baptists were making God-fearing Christians out of black Africans, the preacher again mounted the podium.

I'd had a long, hard day, and my attention span began to wane when the minister asked us to close our eyes in prayer, a seemingly interminable prayer. As he rambled on and on about sin and salvation, I became drowsier and drowsier. The kids on either side of me began to twitch and turn as he talked of burning in eternal hell. Tammy searched out my hand and held it tightly; Tom nestled his little frame up against me as if he were trying to climb inside. Timmy, beyond Tom, could be heard humming some rock n' roll melody under his breath while tapping his feet in rhythm on the floor. We remained in this mode with eyes closed and heads bowed in prayer for six or eight minutes—or was it an hour?

Through the dim vale of consciousness between slumber and alertness, I heard the preacher utter the words "*stand up!*" Without opening my eyes, I rose up and felt the children rising up also. There I stood with my eyes closed, still in prayer and in partial slumber. The voice of the preacher stopped. I continued to stand there with my head bowed and my eyes closed. Suddenly, feeling uneasy in the silence, I suspiciously opened my eyes, lifted my head and looked around only to realize that *we* were among the very few aloft in the large congregation. Befuddled, I glanced around. Walking rapidly toward the end of our pew, an usher leaned across the elderly transgressor sitting on the aisle and reached out to hand me a little card; in a stage whisper he hissed, "Brother, God loves you, I'll see you at the Lord's Table for a banquet of thanksgiving, following the service."

"See me at the Lord's Table?"

"Yes, brother, God bless you. You *will* be saved. But now, y'all may jis sit down. Hallelujah, brother!"

I looked at the card embossed with a golden dove of peace and the words "Jesus loves *you.*" Still stunned, I eased slowly back into the pew. I racked my brain, endeavoring to recall what I might have heard the preacher say causing me to stand. I closed my eyes to think, to get a better track on his words. Surprisingly, there they were in my memory bank: *All of you sinners who have not been saved by the blood of Jesus Christ, please stand up.* In my weary inattention to his words, only the phrase "please stand up" had registered!

A hand from behind patted me on the shoulder; the warm breath of a lady whispering "God bless you brother, God bless you" tickled my ear.

Tom was once again huddled up against me as tight as could be. On my other side, Tammy looked up at me smiling, asking timidly, "Daddy, when do we go up front to God's Table, for our blanket?"

"I don't know, Tammy. It's not blanket, it's banquette, I mean banquet. Oh, God, whatever!"

Timmy's constant fidgeting caused me more anxiety. *Oh my Lord, what do I do now, how do I get us out of here before we're dragged up front, kicking and screaming, to be saved?*

I leaned over and whispered, "Kids, when this service is over, you follow me as fast as you can—I mean *make tracks!*"

"Are we goin' up front, daddy?"

"No, we're goin' out the back door, and y'all hold hands and follow me as fast as you can."

There was yet another prayer before the minister finally raised his arms and pronounced the benediction. The congregation responded with a loud "Amen, Brother, Amen, Amen and again, Amen."

I jumped up with such a start that the kids popped up beside me like a trio of marionettes. We started toward the aisle but were hampered by the elderly couple sitting next to us; the flatulent wife flashed a coquettish glance as they eased themselves out of the pew.

I prayed softly to myself: *If I can only get us out of here before that usher gets a hold of us, we'll be saved from being saved!* We pushed ourselves out into the aisle, totally exposed.

The usher fought his way toward us feverishly. "Brother, brother, God bless you, how wonderful you want to come up front and be *saved!*"

I was at a momentary loss for words, then blurted out, "God Bless you, too, brother, but there's been a terrible mistake, we're already saved. Yes, we're already saved, but thank you anyway." I turned and bolted toward the exit, dragging my little flock behind me. Not once looking back, I headed straight out the door, across the parking lot and into the car. I sat behind the wheel scrambling for the ignition key. "Hallelujah, we've been saved!" I hollered.

"Hallelujah!" the kids mimicked.

I took a moment to compose myself.

Tammy spoke, "Daddy, you made us miss God's banquet and me and Tom are hungry!"

"Honey, you can have ice cream, candy, cake, and a Coke when we get home before you go to bed! Just put on your seatbelts so we can get the hell outa here."

"Daddy, you said a bad word!"

"Just don't tell your mother!"

Jan was still at the studio when we arrived home, so I fed the kids their treats, gave them their baths, tucked them into bed, and said their prayers. I was exhausted, as was Jan when she finally arrived. We slipped out of our clothes and crawled into bed discussing our day. When she finished telling me how her rehearsal went, she asked me for a blow-by-blow description of the assembly.

The more I related the happenings, the more she giggled until she broke into a full laugh.

"Honey, it's not funny, I was mortified. I'll tell you this, the next time there's an assembly at that school, you're gonna take the kids."

"Sweetie, don't be so upset. After all, you gave the usher the right answer."

"What do you mean?"

"You *are* saved."

"I know I'm saved, but how do you explain *that* to a Baptist in thirty seconds?"

"Well, the next time somebody asks you if you're saved, just say yes, thank you, I am, and go about your business."

"I guess you're right, honey, I shouldn't worry about the long form."

We giggled and giggled until we were exhausted. We lay quietly for a time, then rolled over and embraced, ultimately indulging ourselves with one of God's greatest gifts to man and woman, one I would not discuss at my Sunday school!

Another Lunatic Stalking Fan—the FBI to the Rescue

Over the years I had numerous strange encounters with admirers but by far my most bizarre fan letter experience commenced during our days at WWL radio and continued over a period of several years. I began receiving letters from a writer who was passionately affected by me. She had never seen me but had fallen prey to the mellifluous sound of my voice; and in spite of everything she did to keep from hearing me, my voice would come through to her even when I was not broadcasting. Concerned about the problem, she had gone to her parish priest to discuss it. He directed her to stop listening to the radio, to forget the name of Bob Carr, and to pray assiduously. She followed his instructions but found no peace.

Her weekly letters arrived for several years and became increasingly sensual and graphic. These letters were always unsigned with no return address. On Valentine's Day I received an oversized envelope containing a ten-page epistle rambling on in the large grotesque handwriting of an obviously tortured soul. This tome vividly outlined the various ways I was inflecting pain on my pitiful victim. She claimed my voice was piercing into the very depths of her private parts; every word I uttered on the radio caused her uterus to quiver.

This bewitched fan began to call the radio station regularly to inform the switchboard operator that she had been listening to Bob Carr's program and as a result, her uterus was quivering! Needless to say, receptionist Mrs. Stark was appalled by the whole incident and dreaded answering the phones. Occasionally one of the fellows would walk past the switchboard as a call was coming in from "her," and Mrs. Stark would invite him to listen in on the inane verbal maundering. Some of the guys found it to be a bit of a turn-on.

The calls suddenly ceased after she was told her number was being traced by the New Orleans Police Department; however, the letters continued with weekly regularity. One letter stated that she had gone to church and prayed all day on her knees, severely aggravating her phlebitis. In hopes of quelling her uterine quivers, she had made several ejaculations in front of the statue of the Blessed Virgin!

Being unschooled in Roman Catholic terminology, I jumped to the conclusion that an ejaculation was some sort of a female climax. I was shocked yet intrigued by the thought of this poor wretched woman reaching her sexual peak at the rail of an out-of-the-way altar in some godforsaken church in Gentilly.

When I let one of my Catholic friends read her sensual ramblings, he chuckled as he explained that in Roman Catholic jargon, an "ejaculation" refers to the utterance of a short or quick prayer. Obviously this miserable woman was vehemently trying to rid herself of the torment of hearing my voice through her uterus by prayers and supplications short and long. This was becoming too wacky.

Over a period of six months, I began receiving even longer scribbled ramblings. One, mailed from Dallas, stated that she had gone to visit her sister to get away from my voice; however, I was still penetrating her uterus. Then several weeks—no letters. Perhaps, I hoped, the vibrations had stopped.

A twenty-five-page dispatch from California lamented, "Even here in San Francisco I can find *no* relief from the torture of the resonant utterances emitted deep into my uterus by your tongue. The 50,000 watts transmitted by WWL continues to deliver your voice into the very depths of my being, so I have no recourse but to come back to New Orleans and do something serious about halting your torture of me. You must be stopped!"

Until this time, these correspondences seemed like crazy pranks, but Jan was becoming anxious. What did she mean about coming back to New Orleans and doing something about it? This was getting really gross and extremely scary.

Strangely, the letters suddenly stopped! Perhaps Jan's and my switching from WWL to WDSU had cleared the airwaves of my "evil spell." A call from the Federal Communications Commission office in New Orleans informed me that the commission had received a complaint against me for lewd conduct. The written report related the whole scenario of how I was sending radio waves that were causing audio sexual harassment!

"Look, guys, you must be kidding!" I said into the phone. "How could I be causing sexual harassment to anybody with radio waves?"

The humorless voice on the other end explained they were obliged to investigate every written complaint to the fullest. They wanted to talk to me first. Then they would consult with station management. In the typical tardiness of government agencies, before the F.C.C. got back to me, several instances occurred.

Somehow, Lady X had gotten our unlisted home phone number and related to Olympia how Mr. Carr was sexually harassing her, causing her inflamed uterus to throb. On several occasions she got the children on the phone but simply told them their father was harassing her; fortunately they didn't know what harassment meant and turned the phone over to Olympia, saying it was the "kooky lady." Horrified, Olympia discontinued having them answer the phone.

One day, a neighbor stopped me on the street. "Bob, I hate to tell you this 'cause it's too ridiculous and kinda embarrassing, but we got a call yesterday from this weirdo who asked us to look over your wall to see where your radio transmitter is located. She said you were harassing her with your radio waves, *and* you were causing her uterus to swell and throb. Yuck!"

I explained it away with a laugh. "Well, you know how it is when you're a matinee idol!"

"You must have quite an antenna!" he chuckled.

Very concerned, Jan and I feared what the woman might do next. She had our phone number and that of our neighbors, so she undoubtedly knew our address. Was she lurking on Bourbon Street keeping a vigil on the house? Was she stalking the comings and goings of Olympia and the children *and* us? Should we contact the police?

A major incident occurred that brought things to a head. Our radio manager at WDSU, Harold Wheelahan, affectionately known as Wheel, often ate lunch at his desk, located just off Royal Street. If the receptionist was away, anyone could walk into the offices, and that is exactly what happened.

Wheel, I was told, was sitting at his desk having an oyster po-boy—his usual when not entertaining a client at Brennan's down the block. His feet, always encased in shiny cordovan penny-loafers, were crossed and propped up on the edge of his desk. He was leaning back in his chair relaxing to the music of the *Bob and Jan Noontime Radio Show*, when into his office paraded the lady who had been writing me loony letters. She was bedecked in ill-fitting clothes, high top sneakers with stockings rolled to the knees, sporting white gloves and a crushed felt hat.

Striking a firm stance in front of his desk, she boldly asked, "Are you the manager of this radio station?"

Taken aback, he reached for the napkin tucked neatly into his shirt and wiped the oozing mayonnaise from the corner of his mouth. "Yes, yes, ma'am, I am. I'm the manager of WDSU AM and FM."

With her question confirmed, she announced, "I want to show you what Bob Carr is doing to me!"

Having said that, she took hold of the hem of her skirt and lifted it straight up over her head, revealing her problem! Shocked by what he saw, Wheel hurled his feet into the air, causing him to flip over backwards out of his chair. Rallying from the floor behind his desk, he pulled himself up, peering timidly over the blotter.

Dropping her skirt, the woman continued. "And if you don't do something about Bob Carr, I'm going straight to the police. Somebody must get Bob Carr to stop sending his vibrations into my uterus!" She turned and briskly stomped out.

Wheel was so shocked by the episode that he stared blankly into space as he obliviously tossed the rest of his po-boy into the trash basket.

Terry, Wheel's secretary, who had just returned from lunch, poked her head around the corner and asked, "Who was that outlandish creature leaving your office? If it was one of our listeners, so much for our latest demographic survey! Hey, are you okay?"

"You will never, never believe! No, you will never believe what that lady just showed me while I was eating my po-boy."

"Maybe I will. Try me."

He explained.

"Mr. Wheelahan, that must have to do with the F.C.C. complaint I've been trying to get you to read all week!"

"Terry, you know how busy I've been with the ratings challenge! What are you talking about?"

"I'm talking about the F.C.C. complaint saying Bob has been molesting some woman sexually."

"Good God, get me that report and get Bob on the intercom and have him in my office the minute he's off the air!"

Jan and I both appeared in Wheel's office to shed light on the F.C.C. grievance. We explained that this mess had been going on for nearly four years, and it was getting scarier by the moment.

"She's gotten our home phone number," Jan cut in. "Also our neighbor's number. She's been calling people all over the Quarter. I'm frightened!"

"People stop me on the street. 'Hey, Bob, this strange woman told me you're driving her nuts with your guttural vibrations!' Wheel, we've *never* ever laid eyes on her!"

"Well, *my* eyes have! This noon I practically threw up my po-boy all over my blotter. She's something to behold, believe you me!"

Sensing Jan's discomfort, Wheel tried to be jocular. "Ugly thighs but great ankles!" He and I chuckled. Jan scowled.

"You men are cruel and it's *not* funny. This poor lady is in agony and mentally ill. Something has to be done. She needs help and we need protection."

Our session with Wheel left nothing resolved.

Three days later I received a lengthy, rambling, tormented treatise threatening drastic action, and for the first time, *she signed her name*.

The next evening Jan and I were at the studio taping a public service announcement for the F.B.I. about missing children. During a break in our session, the floor director signaled an urgent call for me in our office. It was 9:00 P.M., so I was concerned about the children. I was astounded to hear my mother on the line calling from Ohio.

"Mother, we're taping. Is something wrong?"

"Bob, honey, I just got a phone call from New Orleans *collect*. I took it 'cause I thought it might be you or Jan. It was from a woman sobbing into the receiver telling me you had just raped her with radio waves on the neutral ground at Napoleon and St. Charles Avenues. She was at a pay phone in front of Katz & Besthoff's drug store! She rambled on and on, saying she couldn't take your abuse any longer."

"Mother—"

"I have no idea how she got *my* phone number. Now is this true or not? Did you do anything to that woman? Did you—"

"*Mother!*" I interrupted. "How can you even believe anything like that! Remember I've told you about a weird woman who sends me strange letters?"

"I know, dear, but it makes me very nervous. I still can't believe I accepted her collect call and paid to listen to that obnoxious drivel. What the hell's the world coming to?"

"Mother, don't worry, I'll take care of it, okay? If she calls again, try to get her phone number. Tell her you want to call her back with some information about my long antenna!"

"Huh?"

"Never mind, mother, I have to go."

Back in the studio, I explained to Jan and the F.B.I. public relations man why I was delayed.

"Bob, Jan, maybe our agency can help if this is harassment. Have you had any interstate letters or other calls?"

"Yes!" we replied eagerly.

"Which?"

"Both," Jan was quick to answer. "Bob's had letters postmarked Texas and California and phone calls…"

"In that case, we really might be of assistance."

"This must be providence or astrology or something that brought us together. We really need help. This unfortunate episode has been going on far too long. Jan is a wreck over it."

We resumed our taping about missing children, which I considered a far worse problem.

The next day an FBI agent visited our home to obtain statements from us and Olympia. He also perused my stack of rambling letters. As pieces fell together, the case was eventually turned over to the New Orleans Police Department. From her scrawled signature and the city directory, a relative was located who revealed the address of their "poor, crazy aunt."

"That old broad," as the police detective referred to her on the phone, "is crafty and elusive. We've almost nabbed her twice but she cuts out the back door. I think she knows her numbers comin' up. I'll keep you posted, sir. We'll get 'er n' put 'er in the nuthouse."

I walked into the front parlor as Jan, in tears, hung up the extension phone.

"Honey, what's the matter," I asked. "It's almost over!"

"That poor, distressed, miserable woman, being hunted down like a criminal. It's horrible. Somehow I feel we're partly responsible."

"*Partly responsible?* I can't believe you're saying that. What do you mean?"

"I don't mean we're responsible for her mental illness but we all took delight in her predicament. You have to admit you and the guys got a lot of lewd laughs at her expense."

"I'm sorry, honey, but you'll have to concede this has all been pretty bizarre and a bit scary."

Jan wiped away a tear. "Bob, I hope this kind of thing never happens to your mother or *me* someday. Mental illness is cruel and can strike anyone!"

"Honey, I'm sure this long charade is almost over and she'll get the psychiatric help she needs at De Paul. She'll be so much better off and she'll be safe there."

"I hope so. It's so sad."

The next day Detective Boudreaux phoned to let us know they had successfully delivered Lady-X to De Paul mental hospital.

"Was there any sort of struggle, detective?"

"Let me say this, Mr. Cawr, she sure wasn't anxious to go along with us but once the hospital matron and me got her into the straightjacket then there wasn't nothin' she could do. I tell ya this, Mr. Cawr, I think you're clear of 'er now, 'cause as she sat incarcerated with me in the backseat of the squad cawr, she got fixated on me. In fact, looked me straight in the eyes and said, 'No, no, it wasn't Bob Cawr, it was *you*. All the time it was you tormentin' me with those radio waves!' So, ya see, Mr. Cawr, I don't think she's gonna be botherin' ya no more."

I hung up the phone in relief, my mind scanning back over those tormented letters. Musing in sadness, I decided not to tell Jan about the straightjacket. Like Jan's fan incident some years earlier, Lady-X dropped out of our lives.

* * * * *

As if my fan episode weren't enough, we had become distressed about Bill Romaine's increasingly peculiar behavior. *God, was it something in the Mississippi water we were all drinking?*

Ann had confided to Jan that living with Bill had become a nightmare. He seemed obsessed with the teachings of the Old Testament and demanded they eat nothing that wasn't referred to in the Bible. The girls were forbidden to play in pants or jeans as they were regarded as men's clothes—unfeminine. Bill had taken down all pictures and photographs, even a prized oil of grandpa: he considered them graven images!

Ann paid us a visit, and the poised and elegant Ann we knew was shattered and despairing. She had rented an apartment Uptown for herself and the three girls to escape Bill's harassment. She confessed that until her parents were dead and buried, divorce had not been an option. They would have heartbrokenly viewed her marriage as a failure, but now she could, and must, make her own decisions. The children's well-being was paramount.

Bill reacted vindictively by keeping most of the fine furniture handed down from his grandparent's mansion in Bennington, Vermont. On weekday afternoons Bill was the beloved King Cotton Kid on TV; however, on weekends he would sit on the neutral ground across from Ann's apartment and chant, taunt, and cat-call to entice the girls to come out on the porch so that he could read excerpts from a children's Bible.

Bill had been our program director and my best friend in New Orleans. Ann beseeched me to visit him at his house to try to reason with him. He greeted me warmly and offered me a beverage made from some kind of grain. It tasted thick and nasty, but I pretended to enjoy it. The minute our conversation turned to Ann and the girls, his conciliatory mood changed dramatically. He became irrational. His thought process seemed to meander, his eyes darted from left to right. He was restless and irritable. I noticed he had meticulously scraped each human figure from the French toile wallpaper in the dining room and chiseled off the Victorian faces on his grandparents' priceless dining chairs.

Trying to reason with him, I became so frustrated and angry that I flung one of the antique chairs in his direction. He stood stoically murmuring for me to kill him if I must. It would be God's will! A chair leg broke and splintered. I cursed what I had done. It broke my heart that our deep friendship had disintegrated and that Bill's mental stability had become so fragile.

In a session with Bill's psychiatrist, I was advised to keep my distance. It saddened me to be unable to help, yet I hated that I was being sucked in and emotionally affected by his mental illness. His doctor said there were new drugs that promised to be effective for paranoia and schizophrenia.

I fell into melancholy for a time, agonizing over how a warped sense of religion manifests in the psyche of some minds. I felt a chemical reaction in his brain was altering his thought and behavioral processes and killing our friendship. This period gave a poignantly different meaning to the 1960s Neil Sedaka hit I occasionally played on my radio show, *Breaking Up Is Hard To Do.* Jan and I both mourned the loss of his companionship.

After Ann filed for divorce, Bill was allowed to have the girls visit him twice a month. At his insistence, they each had to be dressed in a primary color, each child different from the other, and they must have matching accessories, crayons, drawing paper, hair ribbons, etc. Yes, it was bizarre, but Ann complied to keep peace.

Ann, who never lost her elegant flair, remained close to us, but Bill, dropped by King Cotton, left New Orleans, sadly fading from our lives.

* * * * *

"But, Bob, the children *will* take piano lessons," Jan insisted. "After all, we live in the Quarter and we're trying to offer them culture and appreciation of good things in life! I *want* them to take piano lessons."

"Okay, okay, fine," I conceded, being well acquainted with that determined tone of voice. "*But,* darling, there's that little problem of not having a piano!"

Jan had already investigated a solution. Werlein's, famous in New Orleans for music and pianos since 1842 (almost twenty years before The Wahr), was conveniently located nearby on Canal Street. Jan had ordered a piano on trial. The children would take lessons; the cost of the lessons would be discounted from cost of the piano, or something like that. Anyway, Jan got her wish and we got the piano. We went through a bevy of piano teachers. By now, Timmy was ten, Tammy eight, and Tom four. All three were eager to take lessons, they thought!

The first Werlein's teacher was an effete young man who would fly in, teach them very rapidly, and then fly out again as if dancing on musical notes. He lacked rapport with the children, giving the impression he had never been a child himself. Timmy said he walked like his shoes were made of feathers. His erratic attendance was cause for dismissal.

Jan talked to a much older man on the telephone. He assured her he had great patience with youngsters, just loved young children, and had been teaching for over sixty years. She scheduled him to come to the house. Since he lived in the furthest reaches of Gentilly *and* had to come by public transportation, he arrived a little bit late via the Desire bus. It was a hot day, and he was perspiring profusely when he sat down on the piano bench.

Timmy was his first victim. This older gentlemen was certainly much more patient than the young flighty fella, but Timothy found it hard to concentrate. When Timmy finished, Tammy sat down to take her half-hour of lessons. Tom went last and required a lot of understanding and patience.

One of the prerequisites of this old gentlemen was that he be paid one month in advance so that he could be assured the children were going to take a month of lessons, two sessions a week. The lessons finished, Jan settled up and sent him on his way.

Following their lessons, the children dashed out into the patio. Jan went out to inquire if they were happy with the lessons.

They were all moaning, "Oh, oh, we've gotta get air. We've gotta get air, yuk, yuk, yuk!"

"Children, what do you mean you gotta get air?"

"He's a pee-yoo man," Tom whined, "a pee-yoo man."

"Oooh, I can't stand him," Tammy chimed in. "I can't take lessons from that pee-yoo old man."

"We're not gonna take lessons from stinko again," Timmy asserted.

"He couldn't have been nicer. I just paid him $50. You've got to take lessons. What's wrong with him?"

"Mommy, you got a bad smeller, like daddy says, if you can't smell *that* man; he's the pee-yooyist man I *ever* smelled."

"What do you mean, the pee-yooyist?"

Tammy groaned. "Mommy, that man has feet that smell worse than the fish market on Friday. I can't sit on that piano bench next to him, I can't breath. You want me to suffocate?"

Timmy followed with, "I betcha that man hasn't had his shoes off for six months."

"He has already been paid and he is going to teach you for a month. He'll be back in three days. It was a hot day today. He's an older man and he probably perspired. I'm sure he'll be all right the next time."

"Mommy," Tammy pleaded, "I can't do it next time. If he comes again and I have to sit there, I'm gonna throw up. I know I'm gonna throw up!"

Tom echoed, "Yes, mommy, I know I'm gonna fro up, too. I'll fro up all over the keys an' wreck the piano!"

"Children, stop complaining this minute! I have paid him and you are taking the lessons when he comes again on Thursday. You understand that?"

"*Mommy!*"

"You *are* going to take those lessons I paid for. Fifty dollars is a lot of money!"

Thursday came, and the children sat down at the keyboard with the pee-yoo man and they went through the routine of their lessons. Jan was at the TV station and didn't get home until after the lessons had been completed. Entering the house, she was met by Olympia.

"Olympia, where are the children?"

"Mizz Cahr, they all out in the back patio tryin' to get some air. Those poor chilrins say they can't stand to take those pie-anah lessons no longer 'cause that man's feets smells bad. When ah came in here to see how they was doing at the pie-anah, ah tell you Mizz Cahr, ah smelt that man's feets, too. An' they smells *some* strong. They smells lahk sperled Limburgh's cheese!"

"What am I going to do? I already paid the man for a whole month of lessons."

"Simple, Mizz Cahr, you jis tells that man his feets smells bad an' he's gotta wash 'em 'fore those chilrins take their next lesson."

"Olympia, I can't tell him that, I'd be too embarrassed."

"You can't tell him that, Mizz Cahr? Then *ah* gonna tell him that, the next time he sets his feets in dis house."

True to her word, the next time he came, Olympia told him he had bad-smelling feet, and he had better wash those feet or he wasn't going to have any pie-anah students left. He confided to Olympia that he had wondered why he was always losing his students.

She told him, "Sir, you gots feets that smell *real* bad. You gotta buy them things called Odor-eaters an' put 'em in yo' shoes. Man, how you 'pect those little chilrins to concentrate on that pie-anah when you have feets that smell *so bad!*"

After Olympia's talk, he apparently tried to do something about his feet, but the children never ceased to complain. They took a united stand, insisting they were absolutely *not* going to take further lessons from "stinky feet."

We hoped the third time would be the charmer, a woman piano teacher. When Jan spoke with her on the phone, she sounded absolutely delightful. Upon arrival, a new problem was apparent. Mrs. D'Angostoni was so large that she and the children could hardly fit on the piano bench at the same time. On top of that problem, she enjoyed playing the piano herself more than she enjoyed teaching the children how to play. She lasted for about five lessons; we switched teachers again.

Jan assured Olympia this new teacher would be just fine. He was only 36 years old, but on the phone he sounded very mature, although a bit disorganized and vague about street addresses. He told her he lived in Metairie but thought he would be able to find Bourbon Street.

"I don't know too much about the French Quarters, Miss Cawr, but I'll be driving 'round 'till I find it."

Jan tried to explain that sometimes it was difficult to park on Bourbon Street.

"Don't you worry, Miss Cawr, I've been around. Drove my mamma to Birmingham once."

Jan was guardedly heartened.

We were on a remote broadcast in Hammond, Louisiana, when the fourth teacher appeared. On lesson day, Olympia greeted him at the door, showed him to the piano, and summoned Timothy. The lesson had barely commenced when the children complained about automobile horns honking in front of the house. The sound was drowning out the piano music, such as it was. Louder and louder it became, to the point that Timothy was finding it difficult to concentrate.

Hearing the commotion from the kitchen, Olympia, Tom, and Tammy scurried to the front of the house to see what was happening. Unconcerned, the piano teacher was blithely giving Timmy his lesson as they passed by toward the front door.

The Desire bus, with a whole line of traffic behind it, was stopped because a car was parked along the curb on our side of the street. No cars were *ever* permitted to park on our side because the street is too narrow for traffic to pass with cars parked on both sides. The bus, being wider than an automobile, absolutely could not proceed. By this time the driver was out of his bus looking up and down the street, trying to find the owner of the car. Automobiles were backed up practically to Canal Street, ten blocks away. The various drivers were venting their frustrations by laying on their horns or getting out of their cars and ferociously hollering all manner of indignities.

It dawned on Olympia that the car in question might be the piano teacher's. "Excuse me, sir," she asked, "but do you got a blue Oldsmobile cahr?"

He nodded affirmatively, still fingering the piano keys.

"Is it parked in front of dis here house?"

"Yes."

"Mistah, you *be* in trouble! Ah swear to Gawd, Mistah. Ah swear to Gawd! Don't you know you can't park there? You be stopping all the traffic!"

He majestically arose from the piano, strode outside, and approached his car.

The driver in the automobile behind the bus yelled, "You stupid son-of-a-bitch, don't you have any sense?"

The piano teacher slammed the car door and whirled around. "Who's callin' me a son-of-a-bitch?"

"I'm callin' you a son-of-a-bitch," the driver bellowed as he approached the teacher. "A *stupid* son-of-a-bitch!"

"There's no way you can call me a son-of-a-bitch!" With that, the piano teacher unexpectedly threw a punch, hitting the guy in the face and knocking him flat.

The bus driver had just returned from Mrs. Madonna's grocery, where he had used the pay phone to call a tow truck to haul away the vehicle.

Curious to see what was going on, the kids flocked around Olympia's skirt like a covey of quail. She pressed them back against the front of the house as a mounted policeman galloped up to investigate. The moment the policemen rode up, the flattened driver sprang up screaming, "I'm gonna sue you, you son-of-a-bitch, I'm gonna sue your dumb ass off, but *first*, I'm gonna put you in jail."

The policeman dismounted, tied his horse to the hitching post in front of our house, and strode over to find out what was going on. The bus driver started to explain that the car had been blocking traffic for at least the last ten or fifteen minutes. Interrupting the bus driver and shaking his fist at the policeman, the irate driver shrieked, "That son-of-a-bitch has gotta go to jail. That son-of-a-bitch assaulted and struck me and he's gotta go to jail *right now!*"

The siren of a squad car could be heard coming along Ursuline; it stopped abruptly, and two policemen came running around the corner. The mounted policemen told them the piano teacher was obstructing traffic, had disturbed the peace, committed assault and battery, and should be taken off in the squad car.

Immediately, one of the officers slapped handcuffs on the piano teacher, took him around the corner to the squad car, locked him in, and then sped in reverse up Ursuline Street against traffic toward the police station.

Lo and behold, the police had taken away the piano teacher with the keys to his car in his pocket, leaving the car still in the street. The policeman mounted his horse, reined him toward Ursuline in galloping pursuit of the squad car, but *alas*, he was too late. He circled back around in front of our house mumbling, "Oh, shit!" and jumped off his horse.

Olympia clutched the three children close to her.

The policeman and the bus driver put the offending vehicle in neutral and shoved it onto the banquette. At last, the bus and the fifty or so blocked vehicles were able to pass. Sometime later that afternoon, the police tow truck arrived to picked up the errant car. We never saw the irate piano teacher or his car again; nor did he get paid for the portion of the piano lesson he taught Timothy.

After this episode, we seriously discussed whether guitar lessons would be better. However, when Jan spoke to Werlein's about returning the piano, they diligently searched for another teacher. That's when we finally found the delightful and talented Mr. Milton Scheurmann; the children loved *him* and loved learning.

The whole piano incident was of such interest to Werlein's that we were asked to do their Christmas promotions for television using our whole family. They were enthralled with the idea that Tom, only four years old and having only a few piano lessons, could play one of the basic tunes surprisingly well. One evening in November, getting ready for the rush of Christmas commercials, we gathered the three kids together at the station to videotape Werlein's Christmas spot. They were promoting their new line of electric organs and wanted one of the children to play an organ instead of a piano. They preferred Tom, thinking it would be delightful to have a four-year-old demonstrating their instrument. Tim and Tammy pouted a bit when they realized they were not going to be featured players. Tom, a *bambino prima donna*, decided he would play for the rehearsal and one "take," as he put it. He rehearsed several times, followed by numerous "re-takes" caused by technical failures. As often happens when a crew is shooting a commercial, any number of things can go wrong: bad camera angle, wrong mike placement, poor music pick up, camera malfunction. The list is endless. Things kept going haywire.

Our TV director, the very pleasant John Domec, announced over the studio intercom, "Okay, just *one* more take and that ought to do it."

"Star" Tom was getting tired and exasperated having to do so many "just one more" takes that he hollered at the loud speaker: "That's all I'm going to do, *one more take*. Then I'm quitting and mommy and daddy will take me home and that's *it!*"

"Tape's rolling," came the sound from the loud speaker.

The camera tally-lights came on. Reggie Hendry pointed his finger, and Tom began to play.

"Cut, cut, cut!" came the voice over the loud speaker. "We had a breakup in the picture."

Tom shouted toward the intercom, "I told you 'one more take' and that one was *it!*" He slipped off the organ stool and walked off camera to the news set, sat down in one of the chairs normally reserved for interviewing guests, folded his hands, and locked his feet around the bottom of the chair legs. He wouldn't budge.

Jan and I approached him pleading, "Just one more time. It wasn't their fault, they couldn't help it, the camera picture broke up. Just one more time? Please, sweetie?"

"I told 'em I've done enough. I'm not going to do even one more; that was my *last* 'take' and I mean it!"

Reggie came over and pleaded with Tom, but to no avail. Buddy, the cameramen, came over and pleaded with Tom; he would not be appeased. Finally, the director came out of his booth and pleaded with Tom—not a budge!

Then Timmy approached and said, "Tom, if you don't play the organ one more time, I'm gonna play it and *I'll* be the star."

Tom quietly unfolded his hands, unlocked his legs from the chair, marched to the organ, mounted the bench, and announced in an authoritative voice, "I'll do one more 'take,' but that's it!"

Hallelujah, Tom played, the cameras worked, and the commercial became a holiday success for Werlein's. "One take Tom" became a Christmas star.

Timothy liked piano lessons all right, but acoustical guitars were becoming so popular that he really wanted to go in that direction. Rennie Flettrich was also interested in guitars. His mother, Terry, was doing a television special on the music of New Orleans. She had run across Danny Barker, a well-known and highly respected jazz musician, guitarist, and banjo player. She talked him into taking on these two boys as his protégés. They responded immediately to the gentle black rhythms that fell easily from Danny's guitar as his learned fingers manipulated the strings. He strummed his guitar and banjo as if he were caressing a sensuous woman. This man had the patience of a mother bird feeding her young; the boys devoured every scrap of information they could get. Danny seemed to thoroughly enjoy being able to give a bit of his heritage over to white boys who were so obviously appreciative.

After several months of lessons and practice, the boys became amusingly good. The television station had asked us to do a remote broadcast and personal appearance in Houma, Louisiana, to help increase our small town and rural audience. Among other things, we were asked to appear at the Thibodaux Country Club, along with Terry, to narrate a fashion show sponsored by Arthur Copeland's stores in Houma and Thibodaux.

Jan and Terry created a fashion show format. Terry would recite a treatise on the history of fashion, and Jan and I would describe the fashions being worn by the club members as models, quite simple and straightforward. However, Terry and Jan concocted an idea using all our kids *and* Danny Barker that I was afraid might cause complications or embarrassment to either the small town country club crowd or us. I lost the argument, so during the intermission, Danny Barker, Tim, and Rennie played guitars and banjo accompanied by Tammy on the washboard with Tom on the maracas. They were an enormous hit. For 1964, it was a unique picture to see a black man surrounded by four young white kids playing on the same stage in a Louisiana country club. We were invited to join the members for dinner, provided Danny would eat with the help-staff in the kitchen. We declined the dinner offer, opting instead to stop at a Cajun diner in Blue Bayou, Louisiana, for gumbo and praline ice cream. The buzz that Bob and "Jane" and Terry "Fletcher" from channel 6 were in the restaurant gave the Cajun staff and diners little chance to be concerned about the black man "minding" the children.

* * * * *

Knowing the kids loved double features, I asked them to invite some friends to the movies one Saturday afternoon. Tammy invited Sandy and Carrie, Tom chose to go alone with me since he would have to sit on my lap in order to see the screen, and Timmy invited Pierre, Mark, Mike, Rennie, Oscar, Danny, Joseph, Jamie, and Kelvin. I had an ulterior motive for selecting that particular Saturday. Ann-Margret was playing in *Bye Bye Birdie*. I had never seen the movie but was looking forward to interviewing her on our TV show. She was gorgeous, yet her fragility and timidity seemed unusually unique for a blossoming movie star. She had sung and danced like dynamite on the Academy Awards Spectacular. Here was a chance to kill two birds with one stone: see Ann-Margret and let the kids have a Saturday outing in cool, quiet, air-conditioned comfort.

Hoping not to be noticed by the police, I packed the more-than-a-dozen kids and myself into Jan's station wagon and traveled out Elysian Fields to the Famous Theater. At the confection counter we bought fifteen popcorns, ten Barq's, four cokes, and one orange. Then we added one additional popcorn to replace the one bumped out of Tom's hand.

The Famous Theater had a curious configuration. You entered in the front of the movie house under the screen and moved up a slight grade toward the seats in the center of the theater. The rest rooms were located up the grade in the back of the theater. The kids insisted on sitting 15 abreast. Through some Cecil B. DeMille-caliber miracle, we were able to find such a row almost mid-house. I recollected that most kids liked to either sit up front where their pupils dilated or in the back rows where they could neck. My little battalion chose wiser than most.

The newsreel was just ending to unanimous applause from the puerile assembly. An inane and vivid color cartoon was followed by *The Wolfman Meets Frankenstein*, a flick that kept the little darlings so glued to their seats in terror that not one stirred for ninety minutes. The instant *Bye Bye Birdie* credits came on screen, the entire assembly erupted from their seats and headed toward the rather inadequate johns at the rear. Since I had seated myself at the end of the row, I had the feeling the whole world was passing back and forth in front of me while I was trying to get a glimpse of the movie I had come to see. Sooner or later, things calmed down, the film progressed, and Ann-Margret was just about to launch into her final big dance number.

"Daddy, daddy." I felt a tug at my shoulder from the aisle side of my seat. I shrugged it off in an effort to concentrate on Ann-Margret. "Daddy, daddy." Another tug followed.

"Timmy, I'm watching the best part of the movie."

"Daddy, daddy, ya gotta come with me, Kelvin's caught!"

"Tell him to wait a minute," I replied, trying to focus on the screen.

"He can't wait. He's startin' ta cry."

"Oh, hell, where is he?"

"In the john," Timmy whispered. "Come with me, quick!"

Timmy led me up the aisle, tugging my hand all the way. The half-broken sign above the door spelled "Me" instead of "Men." Timmy pulled open the door, disclosing a long, narrow stairway leading to the men's room far below. I could see Kelvin jumping or dancing around in front of one of the urinals. *He's caught?* I thought to myself, turning to grab another squint at Ann-Margret shaking her derriere in Panavision at the other end of the theater.

"Daddy, go down, I'm goin' back to my seat."

Emitting a deep, regretful sigh, I descended the stair. "Kelvin, what's wrong this time?"

"Look, Mister Carr, it's caught. Ouch, it's caught!" he yelped, dancing around so erratically I couldn't decipher what he was alluding to.

"My dingus, my dingus!" he howled. "It's caught in the zipper."

"Oh, Lord." I knew just how he felt because the same thing had happened to me once when I was quicker to zip then to flip, dashing from the studio to the john and back during a station break.

"Kelvin, just stand still!" I instructed, kneeling on both knees to gain a more advantageous *modus operandi*.

I fiddled with his zipper, trying to be as gentle as possible. Suddenly, I heard the door at the top of the stairs fling open, revealing the last strains of Ann-Margret's song and the outlined image of a man.

"What ya doin' ta that boy?" the figure shouted.

Oh, my God, what must this look like? How will I ever explain this from jail? "This is my son," I shouted back, not really cognizant of my remark.

"Oh!" replied the theater manager. He then closed the door.

In an instant the door flew open again, and down the stairs, livelier than Santa descending a chimney, came a uniformed policeman.

"What the hell you doin' widat kid!" he yelled as he bounced to a landing on the urine-wet slippery tile floor. "Git yer God damn hands up! Son, is this your father?"

Kelvin's eyes welled with tears, but he replied by shaking his head, *no!*

"Get against that wall, you filthy bastard!"

Stumbling back, nearly falling into one of the graffiti-ridden toilet stalls, I tried to explain. "I'm just trying—"

"I know whachoo tryin', Mistah!"

Kelvin began to whimper audibly.

"That's okay, son, it's all over now," said the cop, thinking he was comforting Kelvin.

Kelvin cried louder.

"What's da mattah, son?"

Kelvin couldn't speak, so I blurted out, "His Goddamn penis is caught in his zipper!"

"What?" the cop asked, irritated I had spoken.

"The kid's dick is caught in his fly!"

"Oh, my Gawd! Well, don't just stand there wit chur hands in the air. Help him!"

"That's what I was doing, dammit," I cursed, as I got back down on my knees, already stinging from the wet urine on my pants.

"Oh, my Gawd," the cop said one more time. Then he put his gun in his holster, and rather like Santa again, up the stairs he flew like a flash!

"There, Kelvin, it's loose."

"Thanks, Mister Carr," Kelvin declared, giving his zipper such a quick and ferocious yank that I thought he could have sliced his peter in half if it hadn't been tucked back in his shorts. Unabashed, Kelvin dashed up the steps. When he pushed the john door open, I could hear the final musical notes of the sound track over the closing credits of *Bye Bye Birdie*. Shucks!

* * * * *

Following our TV show, I passed through the newsroom to return a script left behind by news anchor Alec Gifford. I was still chatting with Reggie about the next day's program, but we quieted down quickly once we noticed newsman Bill Slatter doing an off-the-cuff interview at his desk with a rather scruffy-looking young fellow who had attracted the interest of the entire room. The wild-eyed guy, referred to as Lee Oswald, was raving about Castro and the social benefits of communism. He had been parading around town passing out leaflets praising Cuban achievements. No one was taking him very seriously, but he held the newsmen spellbound. He jabbered at length about being born in New Orleans, claiming Soviet citizenship, and the decay of the free market system *ad nauseam*.

The Oswald fellow was mesmerizing, but knowing Jan was waiting to go over tomorrow's show, I retreated to our office. We loved our view overlooking the famous Brulitour Courtyard, a tourist favorite. Birda, an elderly maid with the station for many years, took great delight in leaning over the third-floor balcony railing when tour guides brought groups into the patio. The guides would explain these were "the Quarters" where slaves lived and worked. Birda would bend over the rail and cry out, "An' dey still does!"

A look of bewilderment usually followed on the tourist's faces, and sometimes a round of applause.

Several weeks later, November 22, 1963, in my chair at the radio control board doing the *Bob Carr Show*, I was in the middle of a live one-minute commercial for A&P touting frying chickens for only 29 cents a pound when Alec Gifford slammed into the studio roaring, "Give me the mike, give me the guest mike *right now!*"

Glaring at him while stumbling through my spot, I made it obvious I was appalled at his rude interruption.

Looking as if he were about to have apoplexy, he hissed in a stage whisper, "When you finish with A&P, give me the guest mike!"

I finished the ad and switched on the guest microphone.

"This is a *bulletin* from the WDSU-Newsroom. The President of the United States, riding in a motorcade in Dallas, Texas, with Mrs. Kennedy, has been *shot!* He has been taken to the hospital. His condition at this time is unknown! I repeat..." Alec continued, filling in more details. Then he was gone.

Attempting to continue my show, I spun a record of Jerry Vale's version of *Who Can I Turn To?* Alec was back in a few minutes with an update, followed by *NBC News on the Hour*. Network radio and television fed news of the shooting to a shocked world.

Vice President Johnson raced to the hospital and remained until Kennedy was officially pronounced dead. Then he went to the airport where the presidential plane waited. Mrs. Kennedy and the coffin holding her husband's body arrived later. At 2:39 P.M., aboard the plane, Lyndon Baines Johnson was sworn in as the 36th president of the United States, flanked by his wife and by Mrs. Kennedy.

Johnson was the first Southerner to become president since Andrew Johnson, who succeeded Lincoln following his assassination in 1865, almost one hundred years before.

Coming into the studio, a shaken Bruce Miller relieved me at what would have been the normal beginning of his radio show, so I was free to go home. I was emotionally exhausted. Except for station breaks, there was no more local programming for three days.

Jan and Terry Flettrich had spent the day on the Mississippi gulf coast pre-taping a series of interviews. Arriving home, we found Olympia glued to the television. She had sent the children upstairs, away from the TV set, to do their homework. It was Friday afternoon so we had no shows until Monday morning. We were glued to the TV for the entire weekend, watching in horror as our country was irrevocably changed.

After four days of intensely watching the TV screen, we were relieved to switch off the set.

Gregory Peck being interviewed by Jan, 1961

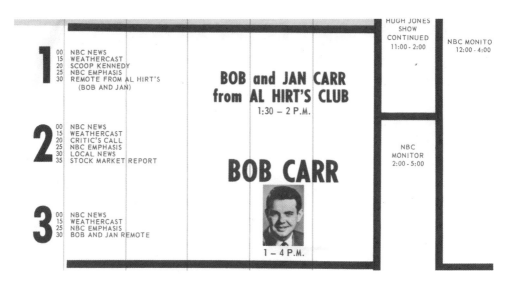

A section of the WDSU-AM radio schedule, 1964

Timmy, Jan, Tom and Tammy at the Wurlitzer organ for Werlein's TV commercial, 1964

Tammy, Rennie, Danny Barker, Tom and Timmy during a country club performance, 1965

Bob and Jan with other people's kids at a fund raiser event in Houma, Louisiana, 1964

CHAPTER FOURTEEN

Sex, Erogenous Zones and Foreplay—Red Cross Lady

Opening my eyes, I was conscious of the built-in alarm system we all seem to have. There was enough early morning light creeping through the shutters and playing on the clock to let me spy the real time. Rolling over on my back, I pushed the covers away toward the center of the bed against Jan, still sound asleep. The ceiling fan I had hung in the center of the canopy of our four-poster played cool breezes over the hills and valleys of my pajama-less body; I could see I had to go to the john. I gazed briefly at the fan and sat up with a start, shaking the bed.

Jan, deep in slumber, quietly moaned, "What's the matter?"

"Good God, it's five minutes after five. Remember, I have to sign on the AM radio station this morning at 5:30 with the *New Bob Carr Show!*"

Having scrambled out of bed, Jan stood sleepily at attention in her old-fashioned calico nighty, awaiting instructions.

"Get my T-shirt, shorts and socks. I'll jump in the shower for two minutes. After radio, I'll shave during the newsbreak before our TV show. I won't have to worry about clothes because D.H. Holmes is supplying my outfit today."

Bumbling around, I stumbled out the front door at 5:15.

The station, only twelve blocks away, gave me the choice of taking the bus or walking. I dashed over to Royal Street to see if the Desire bus was coming, but with none in sight, I began to jog.

A bus overtook me near the Cathedral garden. The driver slowed down and opened his window. "Hey Bob, whatcha runnin' for? Ya need a ride?"

As he hollered it dawned on me I hadn't brought my wallet or any money. "I gotta be on the air in 12 minutes, but I don't have any money. Lord, I'm running late!"

"Hop on, for Gawd's sakes. I'll take ya the next five blocks, on the house. Jis say somethin' nice about the NOPSI bus drivers on your program."

"It's a deal."

There were only three other people on the bus, all women in starched white uniforms. I assumed they were going as far as Canal Street to connect with the streetcar uptown to the St. Charles Avenue mansions. The driver sped up and dropped me off right in front of the station. I dashed up the carriageway through the Brulatour Courtyard, unlocked the door, got my records, and sat down at exactly 5:30. I played the sign-on, the national anthem, and then got to work. "Good

morning, ladies and gentlemen. Welcome to the *New Bob Carr Show*."

Due to low ratings in the morning, the station management decided to switch my popular afternoon show to the morning slot, hoping to give the numbers a lift. At 6:00 A.M., I joined the NBC network for a 15-minute version of *World News Roundup*, affording me the chance to dart to the men's room, shave, and collect my thoughts. Most listeners probably think the announcer sits patiently at his desk in front of the console during network breaks, but this was certainly not the case with WDSU announcers. We always looked forward to the NBC newsbreak on the hour, *NBC-Emphasis* on the half-hour, and any other NBC breaks that came along. They gave us a chance to get a cup of coffee, go to the john, or whatever.

During the 7:00 A.M. NBC newsbreak, my special guests arrived: Bob and Ray, the comedians. Between records, commercials, station breaks, and weather reports, we bantered back and forth. Their inane humor eluded me but was nationally popular. They were in town promoting a couple of products and their new radio inserts. After kidding around with me and trying to set fire to the minute spot I was reading for the ever-present A&P—again advertising whole chicken fryers for 29-cents a pound—they left for their next guest shot at WSMB with Nutt and Jeff, my arch-competitors. I spun *I Left My Heart in San Francisco*, the hit record by Tony Bennett, programmed as a promotion for his guest appearance the next morning. Following the weather forecast, I hit the network at 8:30 sharp.

Already exhausted, I sprang out of the announcer hot seat, making room for Lynn Cole to take over with his DJ show, then raced next door to the roof of the Royal Orleans Hotel. It was always a transitional jolt to jump from an unpretentious radio studio to the bedlam of a television set. Radio is a solo flight. A D.J. is totally in command. His hands are on all the controls, the records, the mikes. The job is very tactile. A TV show is altogether different; it's a scattered chaotic development of action fighting toward unity. It looks as though everybody is at odds—indeed, sometimes they are—but when the floor director shouts, "One minute till air time," everything falls together.

The weather was perfect on the Riviera roof of the Royal O. The panorama of the Mississippi River, the business district skyscrapers, the city's lush green trees, and even Lake Pontchartrain in the distance seemed more spectacular than usual.

I was on the roof by 8:35 A.M. Mika Brenner, the swimming coach, was sitting on the edge of the pool instructing some of her young charges in the swimming configuration they would form for the opening of the show. Windy McCall, our weather girl, emerged from the dressing rooms in a tennis dress. She carried a copy of the latest weather forecast. Jan was going over a Tetley Tea commercial while the cameraman was testing a zoom shot on the glass of iced tea she was holding. Louellen, Donna-Kay, Lidja, and Lady were busy gussying up for the modeling segment. Floor director Reggie was on the intercom instructing the director to "send up the sound" so that Anita Sonfield, our show's vocalist, could rehearse the lip-sync she was going to be singing as she walked along the observation deck. Suddenly, the music burst forth, and we could hear Anita's voice loud and clear. "Fly me to the moon and let me drift among the stars…"

Producer Al Shea grabbed my hand. "Come on, Bob, get in the dressing room. You've gotta get into that outfit from Holmes. As soon as you get your clothes on, go stand in front of the palm tree where you usually do the Holmes commercial, because today it's *your* outfit they're promoting. You're going to have to stand very still because they're going to zoom in on your crotch."

"Zoom in on my crotch?"

"Hey, look, after all these years of zippers, the new thing is a button-fly!"

"Well, if that's what they *want!* Isn't today the day we're going to have Ann-Margret?"

"That's right, and *that's* what I've gotta talk to you about. She's here promoting her newest picture."

"What's the name again?"

"It's a preview of *The Pleasure Seekers*."

"From *Bye Bye Birdie* to *The Pleasure Seekers*. Wow! She can pleasure me by unbuttoning my fly anytime!"

"Bob, cool it right now! That's exactly what I want to talk to you about. Her manager spoke to me yesterday about her guest appearance. They want her to mention the movie, but they don't want you to talk about the fact that it's sexy."

"Al, would I do *that?*"

"Indeed you would, but *don't!* They're afraid they might get an 'X' rating."

"Well then, I'll just talk about *Bye Bye Birdie* and what happened to Kelvin in the men's room at the Famous Theater!"

"*Bob*, please be serious, time's running out! Your other guest, whom you and Jan will interview together, is a lady from the Red Cross; she'll be talking about teenage sexual abstinence. You can get your kicks talking to *her*."

After slipping into the informal denim jacket, I finished buttoning the fly of the denim trousers. "Al, maybe I ought to stuff a sock in here for the TV commercial?"

Al glanced around on his way out of the dressing room. "Bet you've got quite enough there for the little ladies at home sipping on their second cup of coffee. You don't want 'em to choke."

The cameraman pushed his camera toward me as I emerged from the dressing room. "Don't you look cute—just like a little blue fruit!"

"Buddy, obviously you have no sense of fashion," I chided back, chuckling.

"Yeah, you wear that outfit out on Royal Street and see how long before some guy grabs you by the ass!"

Jan stepped from behind the camera. "Bob, we'd better get to the upper level for the opening shot." She stopped for a second, looking me over. "Honey, you look so cute."

"Buddy thinks I look cute, too."

"Really?"

"Yah, says I look like a cute fruit."

"*Really!*"

Suddenly we heard the director's voice over the loud speaker. "Five minutes till airtime." Jan and I climbed the steps to the observation level and sat down at the umbrella table where there was the usual coffee service setup for the opening. During a moment of quiet I looked over my scripts for D.H. Holmes, Whirlpool, Walker-Roemer milk, the questions I was supposed to ask Ann-Margret, and a couple of lead-in questions I was supposed to direct to the Red Cross lady.

Jan interrupted my thoughts. "By the way, Marty called this morning."

"Who?"

"Marty. She called about Timmy and his reading problem. She has a great idea, if we can get it okayed. She thought maybe we could do a public service television show. If channel 6 would go along, we could do the program first thing in the mornings using Timmy and Tammy as students. It would be a TV school on phonetics. Timmy could learn his phonetics along with thousands of other kids in the area."

"Gee, honey, that sounds like an interesting idea."

"Everybody, we're in the station break!"

Glancing over the edge of the observation rail, I could see that Mika Brenner had the kids all lined up along the pool ready to dive in on cue. How clean-cut they all looked in their white bathing suits! Windy eased up onto the edge of the railing, her position for the opening shot; Anita climbed over the railing and walked out onto the roof where she would lip-sync her song. A lady in a Red Cross uniform emerged from the elevator, as Reggie raised his hand and shouted, "15 seconds."

"Where's Ann-Margret?" I asked.

Reggie shrugged. "I guess she's on her way—five, four, three, two, one. Pour the coffee!"

At that moment the Royal O waiter poured our coffee, the theme began, and camera one zoomed in on the steaming cup inscribed with the *Second Cup* logo. Reggie cued camera two on the lower level and the coach motioned the swimmers to dive into the pool, forming an intricate star design. The camera on the coffee cup swung around to pan the city's skyline. Then, while the camera on the lower level grabbed one more shot of the swimmers, the camera on our level focused on a two-shot of Jan and me. Reggie cued us.

"Good morning."

"And welcome to *Second Cup*."

"I'm Bob."

"And I'm Jan."

Together, "We're the Carrs."

The booth announcer broke in, "New Orleans's First Family of Television. Your summertime fun from the roof of the Royal Orleans starts now at 9 o'clock, right here on *Second Cup*."

I continued. "And our special features today are the Mika Brenner swimmers you glimpsed during the opening."

Jan followed with "We'll have a guest from the Red Cross talking about sex education and young people."

"Anita Sonfield, our *Second Cup* songstress, will entertain us with the currently popular song *Fly Me to the Moon*."

"And Bob has a very special guest today he'll interview."

"That's right, Jan, directly from Hollywood, Miss Ann-Margret—ta dah!"

"That's enough, Mister Carr! We'll be back with all this and more right after the news break with Ed Plainer in the channel 6 newsroom."

The instant the news ended, camera one cut to Jan, who delivered her Tetley Tea commercial. Then camera two caught me introducing Windy, who presented the weather forecast, while camera one cut back to Jan's introducing Anita. Once her prerecorded song was playing, I leaned over the railing and shouted to Reggie, who was getting the Red Cross lady into a chair. "Where's Ann-Margret?"

"I don't know. She's supposed to be here any minute. All I know is we gotta get her on and off as soon as she gets here. They're running her all over town, but we're first! You and Jan better come down here to get set up for this next interview."

I bounced down the stairs ahead of Jan. As I emerged from the archway that leads to the main patio, Ann-Margret appeared on the other side of the patio. Anita's song had just hit the line "In other words, darling, kiss me." I looked across the patio and smiled; Ann-Margret smiled back. A gentleman, probably her manager, shadowed her. Al dashed up and intercepted them both. Reggie told director John, over the intercom system, that Ann-Margret was here. Suddenly, over the loud speaker, we heard, "Get the Red Cross lady out of that chair and get Ann-Margret in!" Reggie got the befuddled Red Cross lady out of the chair and ushered Ann-Margret over to the same spot. I sat down next to her. Reggie declared, "No, no, Bob, you have to do the D.H. Holmes commercial first. *Then* you walk over and sit down next to Ann-Margret."

"Oh, okay, I remember." I walked over to the palm tree. Anita's song came to a climatic end with the camera focused on the waving palm tree. The camera pulled back to reveal me standing below in my baby blue denim outfit. The camera zoomed in to show the stitching on the collar, then pulled back a bit as I turned around and showed the back cut of the jacket. I turned full front; the camera zoomed in on my fly. I reached down and ran my fingers across the buttons. I could see the cameramen chortling behind their viewfinders. The director cut to a D.H. Holmes logo slide. As I continued imparting information about the men's fashion department, I walked over and slipped into the seat next to Ann-Margret.

"Hi," she said seductively, as was her style. "That's a cute outfit."

"Really think so?"

"Uh huh, it looks very California," she said in an alluring tone.

"Gosh, you're even more beautiful than I expected."

She grinned shyly.

"And you're smaller, too."

"That's what everybody says. I guess the big screen makes people think I'm larger than I am."

"Maybe so. I'm on the small screen everyday, so I guess people think I'm smaller than I am." I blushed at my inane remark.

She winked. "I wouldn't know."

I cleared my throat.

As we discussed her career, her Scandinavian past, and her new film, I began speaking more and more quietly. I was amazed by her shyness and her incredibly diminutive voice; I was entranced by her sweet smile and auburn hair, which framed her petite, perfectly-placed features.

The interview seemed to last forever, yet at the same time appeared to speed by instantaneously. She was swept away by her manager-guy as soon as the cameras pulled back from our set. Then she was gone. I don't really remember everything said in the interview; all I recalled after she left was a warm, pleasant feeling, shared also by the cameramen, who had enjoyed caressing her face with their lenses.

Making my way over to the swimmers for an introduction, I edged past camera one. "Buddy, how about that, she liked my blue outfit."

"I saw the sneak preview of her movie last night at the Saenger! Maybe she likes what's so well packed behind those buttons on the fly of your fruit suit!"

While the swimmers were performing, the grey-haired Red Cross lady was ushered back into the spot she had been swept from earlier. I eased into a chair beside her as Jan settled down on the other side. Reggie threw our cue. Jan did a brief introduction, then looked at me with eyes that said, "You ask the first question."

Over the years working together, Jan and I had devised an incredible set of signals with our eyes and body language; I knew what the look she had given me meant. I glanced down at the table to see my questions and realized I had left them on the table upstairs. *No problem,* I thought, *we've had other members of the Red Cross on our program a number of times. I'll just start off with an easy question.*

"Well, ma'am, which of the wonderful Red Cross services are we going to discuss today?"

"Sex, its *erogenous zones* and its *foreplay,*" she responded brightly, readjusting her wire-rimmed spectacles.

"Huh?" I said, reeling in my chair. *What's that got to do with teenage sexual abstinence?*

"Sex, dahlin'," she responded brightly, "it's probably one of the most misunderstood pleasures of mankind. *And,* since the State of Louisiana seems hell-bent on keeping the entire population ignorant as to sex and sexual practices through it's lack of education in the schools, I find the responsibility for sex education must be picked up by some other sector."

"Oh!"

More than ever Jan gave me the "you ask the question" stare, but I was speechless.

"How long have you two darlings been married?"

Still befuddled, I answered, "Twelve years, ma'am."

"Honeykins, it's thirteen!"

"All right, you two have been married thirteen years give or take, you have three children, which means you have had sexual relations together at least *three* times." She chuckled suggestively. Looking straight at me with penetrating eyes, she asked, "Can you identify your wife's erogenous zones?"

"Huh?"

Before I had a chance to collect my thoughts, she swung around to Jan and asked a similar question. "You know there is only *one* erogenous zone most wives are aware their husbands respond to, but indeed there are a myriad of pleasure zones for both men and women, as this extremely well-written, intelligent book relates. The clitoris is one of the best kept secrets of mankind or perhaps womankind." She chuckled again. "And you know, man's nipples were not put on his chest just to look like a pair of bachelor buttons. The amount of pleasure derived from gently touching the hand or the tongue against a man's chest can evoke immeasurable pleasure and sexual stimulus."

Jan and I exchanged startled glances.

"There's a wonderful chapter in this book about foreplay, which should indicate to the woman, even more so than to the man, the old idea of 'wham-bam, thank you ma'am' is no pleasure at all. Next to eating and relieving ourselves, relieving ourselves of sensual and sexual tensions is probably the most thought of desire in man's mind. I find it absolutely intolerable to think the educational system of this state, nay the entire nation, does not address itself to the sexual needs and pleasures of the entire population. Our children are growing up completely ignorant of sex. You may ask why a gray-haired old lady like myself is so interested in sex education? The answer is easy: I feel as though I have been denied my sexual pleasures through the years. I feel *cheated!*"

Looking straight into the camera, grasping a visual stranglehold on the lens, she pleaded, "Women of the Sixties, our time has come, your time is now, when you must discover the smorgasbord of sexual pleasures available to you. If you have been secreting or starving yourself from sexual pleasures, now is the time to come out into the open. Men have no corner on the sexual enjoyment of the species. Examine, investigate, and enjoy sex; yes, and your man will be happier for it. Men, don't allow your woman to be sexually ignorant and sexually shy. She craves the same fulfillment and enjoyment you do. Don't be duped by mid-Victorian mores."

The two cameramen had swung their heads around to the sides of their cameras and were staring at us with naked, bulging eyes. Al was paralyzed in his stance and Reggie was on his knees holding up a bent finger meaning half-a-minute.

Grabbing her cue like a pro, the lady continued, "We have only thirty seconds; I want to remind you ladies and gentlemen, sex plays one of the most important roles in your life, so don't be ignorant about it. Go to your library or your nearest bookstore and buy a good book on sex. A good book will give you the knowledge you need to be educated about one of the most important aspects of life." Relaxing back into her chair, she released the lens from her gaze. Acknowledging both of us, she said, "Bob, Jan, thank you so much for allowing me to be a guest on your delightful program. I hope you will take this book as a gift of love, and put it to good use tonight!"

Wildly giving us the wrap-up, Reggie held up a cue card promoting tomorrow's guests. We could hear the closing theme begin to play.

Jan announced, "Tomorrow's special guests will be Danny Thomas of the *Make Room for Daddy Show*."

I countered, "And the swim team from Jesuit High School."

Jan parried, "Plus the new Executive Director of the United Fund."

I closed with, "And Bob Harrington, Chaplain of Bourbon Street. This is Bob—"

"And this is Jan for channel 6."

The closing credits began rolling slowly over the three-shot the camera still held of Jan and me and the Red Cross lady.

Jan and I knew our mikes had been cut because we could hear the theme music in full. The Red Cross lady turned to me, and making an up-and-down motion with her clenched fist, declared, "You know, Bob, there is more to sex than occasional masturbation."

My eyes raced to the monitor to see if her gesture had been telecast. Thanks be to God, the director had already faded to black. The camera lights were hardly off before the stage crew swarmed around the Red Cross lady to look at the book.

"Are there any pictures?"

"Absolutely," she responded, picking up the book and flipping it open, landing on a page depicting an erect penis. The floor crew all leaned in closer to get a better look.

She chuckled once again. "There, you see how interested you are? Do you know the number one question I'm asked?"

They shrugged.

"The number one question I'm asked is, what is the average size of the penis? And of course, my immediate retort is that the size of the penis is of minor consequence, it's the manner in which it's used that's of utmost importance. If the owner has been educated so it is used with intelligence, kindness, and loving care, it can be extremely useful and desirable. If it's used as a weapon, it can be mean and cruel. The myth that a large penis is more sexy than a small penis is not necessarily true; however, I must say, when a woman grasps a penis in her hand, a large penis would probably give her a more sensual thrill, unless, of course, she has a kind and loving relationship with one somewhat smaller."

Jan, looking as though she was going to break out in a rash, interrupted. "Bob, I've got to take off this dress and hang it back on the Holmes rack. Remember, we have to meet with Al Shea about tomorrow's show, and you better change your clothes, too, so they don't get sweaty."

"Okay, okay, I'll be right there." I kept an eye on the book so that it wouldn't, as we say in New Orleans, take up feet and walk away.

Known affectionately to the crew as the sex lady, she answered a few more questions. She closed by beseeching, "Men, men, do not deny your wife her sexual gratification by staying ignorant of her desires and vital pleasure zones. *Her* enjoyment will only add to *your* satisfaction."

She pushed her chair away from the table, got up, brushed off her uniform, and firmly announced, "Golly, I must be on my way. Ta-ta, y'all." With that, she strode primly off the set.

Jan and Anita came out of the dressing room.

"*Bob,* I can't believe you haven't changed your clothes yet!" Jan commented harshly. "Come on!"

At the conclusion of our meeting, we reported to the radio-recording studio to tape our series of weekly radio commercials for Woolco. Now it was time for our noontime radio show with special guest Al Hirt, promoting a new recording of *Java* as well as his newly remodeled club on Bourbon Street. Al was also high on the Billboard Pop charts with his albums *Honey in the Horn* and *Cotton Candy*. Hard to believe he had time to father *eight* kids!

After an exhausting morning, we made our way to the Tallyho luncheonette on Charters and Conti run by another husband-and-wife team, Burt and Tilly, who, as usual, were bickering over their hot griddle; they turned and smiled, inquiring if we wanted the usual.

"Yep, same as usual."

"Okay, two cheese omelets," Tilly replied, as Burt ordered the bus-girl to bring us one chicory-coffee and one iced tea.

While we sat waiting for our omelets, Jan told me she had talked briefly with Mr. Read about a phonetics program as a public service. He seemed to like the concept but wanted to talk to us that afternoon about costs and what it would involve production-wise.

Al Shea walked in and sat down. He had just come from a meeting with the sales department; he had some distressing news.

"Oh?" we responded. "About what?"

"About our program, *Second Cup.*"

Tilly delivered the omelets in person, giving me a kiss on the cheek and a big smile for Jan and Al.

"Thanks, Tilly. As usual I'll need some ketchup."

"Yes, sir, comin' right up."

"So, what's the bad news?" we asked almost simultaneously.

Clearing his throat, "Well, it seems as though NBC is demanding the nine o'clock slot for the *Dinah Shore Show*, and all affiliate stations have to comply."

Jan gasped. "So what would happen with *Second Cup?*"

"Well, uh, this won't happen for another month yet," Al said, trying to soften the blow. "But if it does happen, and the station can't keep that time slot, it means *Second Cup* would have to go off the air."

Jan's eyes filled with tears.

"But, just a minute, Jan, honey, don't worry," Al hastened to say. "It means the 'Bob & Jan; team would become a part of the *Midday* program, which would be extended from a half hour to an hour. *Midday* will have a cast of thousands, airing from 12-noon until one o'clock. An integral part of that program will be Terry Flettrich, Wayne Mack, the news, Nash Roberts with the weather, and Bob and Jan. What a cast!"

"But we won't have our *own* show!" Jan sighed, a tear rolling down her cheek.

"That's true. However, you'll still have your own identity, and you will be a part of the *Midday* extravaganza."

"What are the chances of this happening?"

"I don't know. The sales department thinks it's a done deal. Some of the stations around the country have rather poor nine to nine-thirty programs. They feel Dinah Shore would bolster their morning time slots."

"But Al, our show has the best nine o'clock rating in the whole city," Jan exclaimed, tears now rolling down both cheeks. "Doesn't that dumb sales department have any idea how much the audience likes our program?"

"Jan, darling, it's not the sales department's fault. It's the network demanding the time; since we're an NBC affiliate, we have to go along with network demands."

"That's just dumb!" Jan protested, wiping her cheeks with the flimsy paper napkin.

"Honey, don't get so upset."

"Bob, you never get upset with anything, you make me so damn mad!"

"Honey, there are just some things you can't get upset about. I mean, some things you just have to accept."

"Maybe, but I don't have to like it. It's dumb, just dumb!"

"I don't say I like it, but I know that if we have to do it, we have to do it! You've got another idea?"

"Yah, quit and go to channel 4 or channel 8."

"God," Al blurted. "Come on. Be reasonable. You have a good rating, a good audience, the station loves you, and they're anxious to put you into another time slot if they can't keep you in the one you have. Got it?"

"Okay, but it makes me mad. Doesn't the dumb network realize that New Orleans is different?"

"Honey, the NBC network is run out of the RCA Building in New York City, how would they know New Orleans is special? They've probably never been south of the Hudson River."

"Maybe we should call them. Sarnoff or Weaver or somebody."

"I'm sure Mr. Read is handling things as best he can. He knows all the people up at NBC and doesn't want to do this any more than anyone else. After all, you're his 'kids.'"

Jan picked up the crumpled paper napkin again and blotted her cheeks.

"Now, honey, shut up and eat your omelet." Smiling, I leaned over and kissed her damp cheek, tasting her salty tears.

"Oh, by the way," Al added. "I saw Irma in the hall; she said Mr. Read was clear to see you at three o'clock this afternoon. He wants to talk to you about *Second Cup*, and also another project you had suggested."

"Don't you wanna have something to eat?"

"No, no, I gotta run over to *Le Petit*. They're gonna have tryouts tonight and I wanna pick up a copy of the script. See ya later."

Jan quit eating her omelet and looked over at me with her big moon-eyes. "It just isn't fair, it just isn't fair."

"I know it, honey, but that's the way it is. I mean, it's show biz after all."

"It just isn't fair. We've worked so hard for this program. We've done such a good job, we've gotten really good ratings. Our audience likes us; why does the network have to destroy it?"

"I don't know, honey, but let's go over and meet with Mr. Read, so he can explain how things are going to work out."

Being invited to Mr. Read's office was akin to bring invited into the *sanctum sanctorum*. It was accessed from the Brulitour Courtyard via an antique two-passenger, European-style lift that ascended to the third floor of the Francois Seignouret mansion. Built in 1816, the mansion was beautifully appointed with expensive antiques, tapestries, thick carpet, and a row of French doors facing a balcony. The enormous anteroom contained a dazzling ages-old built-in Aeolian pipe organ that gave the place a *Sunset Boulevard*-like appearance, the perfect sinister setting for a serious meeting with the top brass!

We arrived at the office about five minutes of three; Mr. Read was talking to New York. Although his door was closed, we could hear his muffled voice in what seemed to be a heated conversation. Fortunately, Irma Stiegler, his secretary, belied her surroundings by greeting us warmly. "Mr. Read is expecting you kids." Pointing toward an antique sofa, she asked us to have a seat for a few moments. *Long, torturous moments.*

Finally, Irma's intercom buzzed. "Are my kids there?"

"Yes, Mr. Read, they're waiting for you."

Mr. Read invited us to sit down in two large wing chairs facing his desk.

"Bob and Jan, you know how much I think of you. After all, I'm the one who hired you. I know how much you've given to the station, and I feel the station has favorably given back."

Something was coming, but I wasn't sure what to expect. It sounded a little bit like this was going to be a grand *farewell*. I got a lump in my throat. *Maybe he's kissing us off.*

"I've been on the phone for several days, and just now for an hour and a half, with the high-muckity-mucks at NBC who handle the affiliates, but I'm afraid I'm fighting a losing battle."

My throat was dry. I tried to swallow but couldn't, nor could I look at Jan.

"NBC wants to take away our nine o'clock slot, which, as you both know, has been set aside for local programming for some time. They want us to pick up The Dinosaur Show—excuse me, *The Dinah Shore Show.*"

His nervousness caused a chill to slither up my spine; I shook but tried to appear that I was readjusting to a more casual position in my Chippendale chair.

"In return, we'll get an extra half-hour of network-free time at twelve-thirty P.M."

My mind clogged. *Is that noon or midnight? He's gonna bury us at night!* For a moment, I was so nervous that I couldn't think straight.

He continued. "Which means we'll have an hour of local time at noon."

I exhaled audibly. In my peripheral vision, I could see Jan relax slightly. He went on to explain what Al had already outlined at breakfast, but we listened attentively, trying to maintain our composure. I was glad Jan had already shed her tears, giving her the strength to listen and respond to Mr. Read's remarks.

"So, the bottom line is, we'll do four more weeks of *Second Cup*, meanwhile telling viewers the *Midday* program is going to become an hour show, and 'Bob & Jan, The First Family of Television' are going to be an integral part of the *Midday* cast. I advised advertising to run promotional spots on AM, FM, and TV. We'll also buy billboards to promote the whole new concept. Don't worry, kids, you are still important members of the channel 6 family—so much so, I want you two, and whichever of your children you choose, to join Marty Lindley with her reading program. Let me know what you need and how I can help. Giving our Louisiana children an education is our hope for the future. You can tape it at your convenience. It will play early in the morning right before *Bill Stanley's Breakfast Show.*"

When the meeting was over, we felt like two rung-out dishrags. Collecting ourselves, we descended the long winding stairway leading to the channel 6 main reception lobby.

Marie Mathews, the switchboard operator, smiled. "Hi, kids, I just got a call from one of your fans."

"What did they say?"

"They said they watch your *Second Cup* every day and wanted to ask a question."

"What's the question?"

"They wanted to know if 'Bob & Jan' were as sweet in real life as they appear on television."

We chuckled. "What did you say?"

"I told them you are even sweeter in real life than y'are on television. They said that was nice to hear but Bob sometimes gives Jan grief."

"What do you mean, grief?" I asked.

Marie laughed. "Sometimes you treat her like you think she's not as smart as you are."

"I *do not!*"

They both raised their eyebrows.

"I do? Do I do that, Jan?"

"Well, honey, sometimes you do act like you're Mister Perfect."

"Yeah, that's it," Marie came back. "Of course, Bob, I don't fault you for that; I guess it's just the way men treat women."

"Ummmm, Marie, have you gotten calls from other fans who felt the same way?"

"Oh, sometimes, but most of the time they just want to know if you're as sweet in real life as y'are on television."

"I guess I can fool some of the people some of the time."

Jan retorted, "Yes, and it's obvious, you can't fool all of them all of the time."

The girls guffawed at my expense.

"Marie, we're running a little late, so if Olympia calls from home, tell her we're on the way, would you please?"

"Yes, ma'am. You know you can count on me."

We walked through the carriageway onto Royal Street and into the bright sun, heading home toward our end of the Quarter.

I was still hanging onto the thought Marie had planted in my head. *Did I actually treat Jan as if she weren't as bright as I am? I tried to dismiss it with the thought that if, indeed I did, I did it for the drama and tension it brought to the program. But then it worried me; maybe I did it to make myself look better because I was insecure?*

A turning carriage interrupted my thoughts.

"Bob, watch out! Take my arm, honey. I don't want you run down by an old mule in the middle of the Quarter, even though sometimes you treat me like a horse's patooty."

"Honey, I don't."

"Just kiddin'!"

"Hi, Bawb and 'Jane', how's da family?" asked Inez Perrelli in her best Irish Channel accent as she stuck her head out of her trinket shop.

"Everybody's fine, thank you, Mrs. Perrelli," Jan replied, pulling my arm. "Honey, we've gotta cross over to the A&P for a minute. I promised Olympia I'd bring home some filé for the gumbo she's making and told the kids I'd bring them some popsicles or ice cream."

The French Quarter's A&P Supermarket is a treasure trove of edible delights and is rife with paper products and other humanoid necessities jam-packed into a space defying the conventional navigation skills of a shopping cart.

"Hi, Mistah Bawb and Miss 'Jane,'" came a greeting from the checkout girl. "Saw y'alls *Second Cup* program this mornin'. Ya got that *book* witcha?"

"What book?" Jan asked, fumbling in her purse for money.

"Yah, which book do you mean?"

"Oh, Mistah Bob, you gotta be puttin' me on. The book that Red Cross lady was talkin' about this mornin'."

"Oh, *that* book!"

"Y'all ain't got that book widya?" she asked in a hushed tone, giggling and putting her hand over her mouth.

"Gosh, I'm sorry, we don't. We had so many things on our mind when we left the station, we left the book behind."

She leaned over and whispered, nearly covering her face, "If you get any new pointers, let me know, hee hee hee!"

"Monalee, I'll show you personally."

Jan glared at me.

The cashier giggled once more, jiggling her nearly two hundred pounds. "Ah'll be a waitin', Mistah Bawb! Bye, bye."

"Jan, let's cross over here a minute. I want to walk up Pirate's Alley."

"But Bob, we've got to get home, remember we've got popsicles."

"I know. This will only take a few minutes."

"Where are we going?"

"Have faith, follow me."

We walked to the side door of the Cathedral.

"We're going in here?"

"Honey, I think with all the things we've got on our minds, it would be nice to stop and say a few prayers before we head home to the kids."

I reached down and took her hand and pulled her up the steps. She leaned down and kissed the back of my hand, and we walked through the door. We genuflected, knelt in a pew, made the sign of the cross, and both retreated into silent prayer.

A nearly lifelike figure of Jesus hung from an old rugged cross at the far right of the high altar. Through the years, I had stopped by the St. Louis Cathedral numerous times to make a visitation before that cross of Jesus in agony. It had given me faith, hope, peace, *and* strength, gazing into the face of God. Of course I know that the statue was *not* God, but the plaster face and eyes and the tortured body became real when I closed my eyes and reflected on the countenance of Jesus. *God, give me the strength to face the minor problems I have, compared to the enormous burdens of other members of the human race. Give me the strength to be a leader and proper example to my family, to be an understanding and compassionate father and husband.*

My prayer continued: *Help me to overcome my weakness, that I don't deride the weaknesses of others, especially my wife and children. Give Jan and me and Timmy's teachers the understanding and compassion we need in helping him overcome his reading disability. And I ask for special prayers for the strength and understanding of Marty and channel 6 in helping us reach thousands of children and families throughout the area; there is a great need for an improved educational and reading system in the city and state. Help us, too, Lord, through the transitional period of our occupations. Lead us, if you will, in your peace. And, thank you Lord for the gift of three healthy and wonderful children who, in our absence, are patiently and lovingly cared for by Olympia. I pray, Lord, that we will be quiet enough to hear your response to our pleas. Thank you, Lord, for allowing us to come into your House. May we always be grateful for the blessings you have bestowed upon us. Lord, make me aware of your graces, and give me the strength and courage to use the blessings and talents you have given me to comfort others, and by so doing, help me overcome my own adversities. Thank you, Lord, for listening, but I'm cutting this short 'cause I gotta get the popsicles home to the kids! Amen.*

I made the sign of the cross and sat back in the pew glancing over at Jan, who was still in intense prayer. A tear trickled down her cheek; she finished her prayers momentarily. We walked home silently, arm in arm.

Coming around the corner onto Bourbon Street, we could see there was a rather large crowd standing in front of our house.

"What are all those people doing?" I asked, not really expecting a response.

"Oh, my gosh! I don't know," Jan, replied, jumping to the conclusion, as most mothers do, that something was wrong with the kids.

As we got closer, we noticed the kids on the front balcony waving to the people below. It was obvious, drawing closer, that a group of tourists were taking great delight in the kids waving at them. We could also see Olympia in her white uniform standing at the front door. Spotting us over the heads of the visitors, she announced graciously, "Oh, an' here's my madam and the mistah of our house, Mistah and Mizz Cahr."

The crowd turned and looked at us; the lady right next to me said, "Oh, I love your house, and you have the sweetest children."

"Thank you."

"I just love that ceiling fan hanging in the your canopy bed!" she tittered.

"You were in my bedroom?"

"Oh yes, those darling children of yours took us all through your lovely home."

Yee gods, I thought, *we never take tours upstairs; somebody might fall down and sue us. Besides, my dirty socks and shorts were probably lying on the floor!*

The lady next to her in a frilly pink dress said, "I still can't believe people really live in these quaint old houses."

"Guess you can believe it now!" I remarked cavalierishly.

"Bye, bye, y'all," Olympia announced with a cordial gesture of farewell. The crowd moved across Bourbon Street, still smiling up and waving at the kids, some snapping photos before disappearing around the corner.

"What was that all about, Olympia?"

"Mizz Cahr, you know you scheduled that group, but they came this week instead o' next week. You just gonna have to get yo'self better organized."

"Oh, my God, you mean I wrote it down in the wrong place in the book?"

"No, Mizz Cahr, you din't write it down in the book no ways. Ah were lookin' for it in the book, but it weren't there."

"Oh, Lord, I guess I wrote it on the telephone directory and forgot to put it in the date book. And, *they came!* I had told them I would be here in a hoop skirt!"

"Mizz Cahr, somehow I jis gonna have ta git you organized! You women today tries to do too many things!"

"Bob, I don't know whether it's worth having these paid tours through the house. Between the television program, the radio shows, taping commercials, *and* trying to show people through the house, I don't know if there're enough hours in the day."

"If it means a tax write-off, it's probably worth the trouble."

"Olympia, what'd you do when they came to the door?"

"Lord have mercy, Mizz Cahr, the chilrins jis got back from school, told 'em to go upstairs and do their schoolworks. Then, that doorbell rang, and this tour guide said he had a vouch o' vouchah, o' *somethin'*. Ah looks out the door, and all those people was standin' there in the bright sun lookin' real hot. And that guide-man, he showed me his 'vouch' that they all could come in the house. Ah tol' him, ah din't know nothin' bout it, but he were the same guide-man been here 'bout three weeks ago, so ah figured it would be all right, so ah tol' him to jis wait a couple of minutes; then ah closed the door, to git my composure, so ah wouldn't git my pressure up." Olympia took a long, deep breath.

"Then ah called up the stairs an' told Tammy to git into her hoop skirt real fass an' the boys to git into their Spring Fester uniforms fass as they could move. The boys gave me some grief but they 'bliged, an' came a flyin' down the stairs an' helped me show those tourist peoples through the house. Our chilrin are *real* smart. They know more about this here house and these Quarters and New Orleans than any book you could ever look at. Ah'll tell you what. Those tourist peoples *loved* our chilrins. That's why they stayed so long, they jis kept askin' em questions and questions and more questions—couldn't get rid of those people, they had such a good time. But ah chuckled when they done spied Mistah Cahr's *underdrawers!*"

"Olympia, you make me blush. I hope they were clean."

Putting her hands on her hips, feigning an indignant stance, she began to laugh. "Ah swear to Gawd, Mistah Cahr, ah weren't about to leave your underdrawers out there fo' the whole world ta see. Ah done picked 'em up first thing this mornin'. They done been *cloxed!*"

"Then they didn't spy my drawers?"

She retorted, smiling, "Yes sir, they *din't!* But those women, they mighta lahked to! Hee hee hee!"

"Olympia, you're some kinda tease!"

"So you, Mistah Cahr."

Jan leaned over and gave her a big hug. "Olympia, you're so wonderful. What would we ever do without you?"

Olympia's beautiful white smile shone brightly against her deep brown lips. She knew we loved her, but reassurance is a good tonic.

"Mommy, daddy, mommy, daddy," the kids screamed as they came racing down the stairs with Tammy lifting her hoop skirt, revealing ruffled pantaloons. They encircled us shouting, "How much do we get, how much do we get?"

"What do you mean, how much do you get?"

"We mean, we did the tour, you gotta pay us."

"But you live here. That's pay enough."

"Daddy, that's not fair," Tammy rebuked.

"Honey, I figured *you'd* say that. You're the biggest miser I've ever known."

"I am not. What's a miser, daddy?"

"It's somebody who keeps all their money."

"I don't keep all my money, you and mommy always borrow it from me."

Tammy was right. Somehow she was always able to save every cent she ever had; whenever we needed streetcar fare, or small change to get ice cream or go to the store, Tammy always had some money hidden away.

"Daddy, you already owe me fifteen dollars."

"Okay, okay, we'll pay you for the tour."

"How much do we get?"

"One dollar for each of you and two for Lympy, 'cause she's the boss."

They jumped with joy, so I dropped the subject.

"Mizz Cahr, did you pick up that filé at the A&P fo' mah gumbo?"

"Yes, Olympia, and here's some popsicles, a little melted. Better put 'em in the freezer for later."

"Yippee, Popsicles."

The kids dashed back upstairs to change their clothes.

"Mizz Cahr, let me take these things back by the kitchen."

"Were there any phone messages?"

"Yes, ma'am, two people called. Mizz Lindley called sayin' she had some good ideas about a television program; then that man called that you talked to one time befo', an' said if Timmy still wants to be in the Soap Box Derby contest, they got him a sponsor for his car."

"Thanks, Olympia." Seeing me rifle through the mail, Jan asked, "Anything interesting other than bills?"

"This one's from my sister."

"What does she say?"

"The whole family, all six, want to come down, and for us to let them know when would be the most convenient time. The rest of these are just bills, I guess. Oh here, this one must be from *your* sister."

"From Carole?"

"Looks like it."

Jan opened the letter, read through it, and chuckled. "Carole and Jess want to come down for a visit with their four kids."

"When?"

"It doesn't make any difference, whenever it's convenient! There's one thing for sure. We've never been at a loss for guests since we moved to New Orleans, have we?"

"That's for sure. Why don't I mix us a Sazarac. We'll go out in the patio and relax for a few minutes?"

"Sounds wonderful," Jan replied, kicking off her shoes.

We walked outside with our drinks. It was still warm and muggy in the late afternoon sun, so I kicked off my shoes, pulled off my socks, and started slipping my pants down.

"Bob, what are you doing?"

"I'm going to sit down by the pool and dangle my tired feet in the water."

"But you're taking your pants off."

"I know I'm taking my pants off; I don't want 'em to get wet."

"But, everybody is going to see you."

"Everybody is going to see *me*? Honey, nobody's looking."

"Well, they might."

"Then, that's their problem, or perhaps their delight!"

"Olympia can see you out the kitchen window."

"Honey, Olympia has seen me in less than my undershorts."

"She *has*?"

"Yes, in my bikini. Besides, I don't think she's going to pay much attention if I sit here in my dress shirt with my feet dangling in the pool, unless she pulls off my shorts to *Clorox* 'em!"

"Guess you're right."

"This water is soothing, why don't you roll down your nylons and stick your feet in, too?"

We contentedly splashed the water with our feet.

"Are you upset *Second Cup* is going off?" Jan asked.

"I knew that's what you were thinking about, honey."

"Well, are you?"

"Yah, I'm upset."

"Do you think we can get used to working with Terry Flettrich and Wayne Mack?"

"I expect we can; I expect we'd *better!*"

"I hate changes."

"Everybody hates changes, Jan, but that's what living is all about; we're changing all the time. The ones who resist change are the ones who don't survive."

"Guess you're right. After all, we've made some big changes in our life, in just the few years we've been married. I'm sure we can stand a few more."

I put my arm around her. "Yep, honey, I'm sure we can."

We heard giggling from the balcony above. Leaning over, Tammy hollered, "Daddy, shame on you. You haven't got any pants on!"

"I don't?"

"No, daddy, you don't have any pants on."

"Nobody can see me."

"*Daddy*, I can see you, and I'm somebody."

"Yah, and I can see you, too," Tom yelled.

"Then don't look."

"But we gotta look!"

"Why ya gotta look?"

"'Cause you don't have your pants on."

"That's your problem, sweetie."

"Daddy, you're so silly."

Timmy interrupted. "Can we go for a swim before dinner?"

"Okay, gang, but a real quick swim."

They dashed into the house to emerge shortly in their bathing suits. By the time they had gotten down, I had slipped off my shirt, T-shirt, and wristwatch so that I could be ready to jump in with them. As we frolicked and swam around and around in the little pool, it occurred to me: *This was one of the best holes I've ever dug myself into!*

Olympia came out to announce dinner on the table in five minutes, so we had better get ourselves dried off.

"Olympia, maybe we can eat out here?"

"Mistah Cahr, ah've done set up the table in the dinin' room. Ya gotta let those chilrins eat like respectable peoples do sometimes. *Me*, Olympia, says y'all gonna eat in the dining room tonight!"

"Yes, ma'am. We'll get the hell outa this water!"

"Mistah Cahr, you don't talk like that front the chilrin, hear?"

"Yes, ma'am. We'll be there in a minute." I saluted her; she turned toward the kitchen, but not before flashing a grin.

"Who's saying grace tonight?" I asked, sitting down at the table.

"I am, I am," Tammy pleaded.

We crossed ourselves, then held hands. Tammy came forth with, "God is great, God is good, and we thank him for our food, by His hands, we all are fed. Thank You, Lord, for our daily bread. *And,* especially bless mommy and daddy and Timmy and Tom and Lympy and grandma and grandpa and granddaddy and Nana and Jandad and Aunt—"

"Tammy, that's enough, the food's going to get cold."

"And all our friends. Amen!"

Turning to Timmy, Jan said, "I talked to the man about the Soap Box Derby; they've got you a sponsor, but I'm not sure if it's the kind of sponsor we want."

"What do you mean?" I inquired. "Who's the sponsor?"

"Hmm, that's the thing. The man in charge said it was difficult to get sponsors, but he thinks he has just the right sponsor 'for a kid who lives in the Quarters'!"

"So, who *is it?*"

"Joe's Jungle Bar on Canal Street."

"Joe's Jungle Bar?"

Timmy piped up. "Joe's Jungle Bar? I'm gonna write Joe's Jungle Bar on the side of my Soap Box Derby car, daddy?"

"That's it! I can see it now, on both sides of your racer, *Joe's Jungle Bar."*

"What's that he sayin' 'bout Joe's Jungle Bahr, Mizz Cahr?" Olympia inquired, as she brought in the French bread.

"Joe's Jungle Bar is going to be the sponsor for my Soap Box Derby car," Timmy proudly announced.

"You gonna let that boy be sponsored by some bahr? That jis don't sound raht to me."

"Oh, Olympia, you're an old prude."

"Maybe so, but that's the way ah am. Mistah Cahr, drinkin' dun caused enough problems in the world, not to have some po' little boy promotin' some jungle bahr."

"Well, we'll see."

"It doesn't mean that Timmy has to go to the bar," Jan interjected. "It just means they'll pay the money for the car to race in the Derby."

"Y'all do what you want, Mistah Cahr, an' ah knows you will, but seems to me like he could find some nice gas station or funeral parlor to sponsor his cahr." She returned to the kitchen mumbling, "Jis don't seem raht to have that chile takin' up for some kinda jungle bahr."

"Also, Bob, I talked to Marty. She has a catchy name for our reading program."

"What?"

"Fun with phonetics. When the credits come up on the screen, Fun is going to be spelled P-H-U-N, and Phonetics is going to be spelled with an F instead of a P-H. *Phun With Fonetics.*"

"Isn't that a little cutsie?"

"I don't think so, it gets the message across."

"What's this fun program you're talking about, daddy?" Tim asked.

"This is a good time to talk to you children about it, over dinner. We have an idea about helping you learn how to read better, while at the same time, you can help thousands of children in the New Orleans area read better, too."

"How can we do that?"

"You see, Timmy," Jan answered, "Mrs. Lindley has worked out a program called *Phun With Fonetics*. We'll all go to the station to record it. It will play early in the morning on channel 6 so that many children can watch. You three are going to be on the program with us and Mrs. Lindley. She's going to teach us how to read with phonetics and learn how to spell. Won't that be fun?"

"Yuk," Timmy exclaimed. "You mean I have to go to real school, *then* I have to go to school on television, too?"

"That sounds hideous," Tammy interjected.

"Wouldn't you like to help children all over the city learn how to read better?"

"Not if I have to go to school *extra!*"

"You won't really have to go to school extra. This will be the same as doing homework, only it will be on television."

"Well, maybe that's okay."

Tammy spoke up. "How can Tom be on the program if it's about reading? He doesn't know how to read at all!"

"I do so," Tom bellowed.

"You do not!"

"Okay, kids, just one minute. The program is for everybody to learn to read or read better, and it's going to be a lot of fun." *If it kills us!*

The doorbell rang.

"Mistah Cahr, ah'll get that doh. Y'all finish y'all's coffee."

"Thanks, Olympia."

"Daddy," Tammy asked, "if we're going to do a television program, are we going to get some money for it?"

"Yeah," the boys said, "are we gonna get some money?"

"*No*, none of us is going to get paid for the program. It's called a 'Public Service Program.'"

"Public what program?"

"Public service. That means you're giving a service to the public."

"What's the public, daddy?"

"The public means all of the people."

Jan broke in. "We're going to do a program all the public can see, and it's going to help them learn."

I added, "We live in New Orleans, and New Orleans has been very good to us. Now it's time for us to give something back."

"Don't you and mommy get paid for being on television?"

"Yes, but that's different. We're on to entertain and sell products. But we want to do a program to *help* people in our city; this program will help them with their education."

"I still don't know why we can't get paid!"

"Tammy, it's important to give something free to people. You give away your love and you get more love, so if you give away your knowledge to other people, everyone can be smarter and we'll have a better world. So we're going to give away our knowledge free on a television program for all the people."

"What're we getting back for it?" Tammy asked.

"We're going to get back satisfaction, the satisfaction we've helped somebody."

"That's right. You know when we go to Sunday school and learn about helping other people? This is just another way we can help other people."

"Well, I hope it works," Tammy persisted, "but I'd still like to get some money."

We could hear voices in the front hall; Olympia came into the dining room. "Mistah Cahr, Mizz Cahr, ah think you'd better come to the front parlor. There's a lady here says she wants ta see y'all." Olympia hushed her voice. "She looks like some kinda white-trash, if ah must say, ah din't know whether ah ought to be lettin' her in."

"Okay, Olympia, thanks. We'll go right in. Kids, you'd better go up and start your homework."

"Yes," Jan added, "and I'll be up to help you in just a few minutes."

As usual, Jan handled homework.

"Mistah Cahr," Olympia said with some urgency, "you better get yo'self in that front parlor an' talk to that lady-person, before she snatches somethin'."

Walking into the front parlor, I looked at the woman sitting on the sofa and was struck by the bizarre combination: a young woman shod in platform spike heels, mesh hose, tight leopard-skin dress, sporting a henna dyed bee-hive coif, planted in the center of our antique sofa surrounded by gilded carved images of prim Queen Victoria as Empress of India and Queen of the Nile.

"Oh, Mistur Bahb, Mistur Bahb, please excuse my intrusion, but I don't know where else I can go."

As she uncrossed her extraordinarily long legs and arose sensuously, it occurred to me that someone was playing a joke. Surely this person was in drag—a female impersonator one of our friends had sent to play a trick on us.

"Do we know each other?"

"Not rilly, I jis know you from your TV stardom, but I know your choldern, 'cause my patio backs up to your patio wall."

"Oh, you're one of the *strippers*—er, uh—I mean you're one of the *ladies* who lives behind us."

"Yeah, yeah, Mistur Bahb, I'm an exotic dancer. Miss Starr, you know Blaze Starr?"

"Sure, she's Governor Earl Long's girl friend!"

"And our headliner. I'm one of the backup girls."

"Oh!" I acknowledged. "Y'all are right next door to the 'Teacher Turned Stripper,' aren't you?"

"Yeah. I mean, yes, sir, that's us. I don't rilly think she was ever a schoolteacher, least she don't talk like one. That's my oh-pinion."

"Maybe the school of hard knocks!"

She looked at me quizzically. "Mistur Bahb, your choldern are divinely sweet, and you and Miss Jan look so nice on the TV, I jis *knew* you could help me."

She's about to put the touch on me for money. "Help you with what?"

"Mistur Bahb, sir, I don't know how to git into this, but you see, my manager, I mean—he's rilly kinda like a manager and my boyfriend. Well, he's rilly upset with me, cause he's rilly jealous and all, and he thinks I've been makin' eyes at these guys, but I rilly haven't. Anyway, he won't give me any of my money."

Ah ha! My fears are confirmed. "You need some money?"

"*Oh, no*, no, Mistur Bahb. I don't need any money, rilly. I know how to save my money whin I git it. It's jis that he rilly gets so mean and rambunctious sometimes, he scares me half to my death."

Jan walked in; I made a rather bungling attempt at introducing her.

"What—um, what's your name?"

"Sir, my stage name is Joy Hour. Well, that's not my name rilly. My name is rilly Eunice Elizabeth Singlehoffer, but rilly, I mean *rilly*, who could use that on the stage? Grandpa says it used to have a Von, like Von Singlehoffer er something, but *rilly!*"

"Von Singlehoffer doesn't sound particularly exotic," I quipped.

"Oh, Miss Jan, you and Mistur Bahb are so wonderful, rilly. You're the 'Ozzie and Harriet' of New Orleans, I come over here 'cause you're so nice."

"Jan, Miss Singlehoffer, Joy, told me she's having a problem with her boyfriend. He's also her manager, I think."

"Yeah rilly, you see, he treats me kinda like I'm an ass." She put her hand over her mouth, "*Excuse me*, Miss Jan, but you know, I'm not as smart as him."

"Gee, that's terrible," I remarked sympathetically.

Jan cocked her head and glanced at me. "Yes, I can certainly understand *that!*"

"Yeah, and he gets rilly mad, and sometimes he beats me up."

"He beats you up?"

"Yeah, he beats me up 'cause he says I'm rilly stupid."

"Are you?"

"*Bob!*" Jan rebuked.

"Yeah, I guess I'm pretty dumb. My daddy told me I was dumb, my stepfather told me I was dumb, my manager tells me I'm dumb, so I guess I'm dumb, rilly *dumb*. Fact, I must be dumb to get myself in a scrape like this."

"Where're you from?"

"Nebraska."

"Why did you come to New Orleans?" Jan inquired.

"You see, this boy I met in community college came down to New Orleans to work on a boat. He's a kinda *hunk*, if you know what I mean, but a rilly nice guy. He treated me rilly respectful and everything. Anyways, he went out to sea, like to Guatemala or one of them places on a banana boat; then he came back up for a visit to Nebraska. It was the same time my mother got killed in a car wreck. My stepfather, he was kinda comin' on to me after the funeral. Anyways, my grandparents are rilly old, and live way off in Wichita, and since I haven't seen my ril daddy, rilly sober for five years, I was rilly lost and lonely. Like my spirit had fled my body or somethin', rilly low. So, when this boy said he'd take me down to New Orleens, I thought, I might as well. Wasn't anythin' happenin' good for me at home; fact, I didn't rilly have a home no more."

"So, what happened to the boy you came down to New Orleans with?"

"Oh, he got rilly hurt when they were loadin' bananas down in Honduras, and he's still down in Honduras in a hospital, cripple like a freak, all bent up. Can't have kids nor nothin' like that, crushed his crotch. You know what I mean, Mistur Bahb? His pelvic, rilly sad!"

Concerned, Jan asked, "How did you get to be a…er…performer on Bourbon

Street?"

"You mean a stripper? 'Cause I guess that's what I rilly am even though my manager says to say 'exotic dancer.'"

"Well, yes, I guess so."

"You see, I tried waitin' tables for a while, but I rilly wanted to send some money back to my grandparents 'cause they're rilly old. Ya-know, ya make no kinda money workin' tables at a place like the Pearl Oyster House. Anyways, I was complaining to one of the other waitresses one night. She says, 'Honey, you got a rilly good figure. You oughta go into show business on Bourbon Street.' Ya see, she was ril friendly like, not romance, er sex, er anything like that, an' rilly friendly with this guy who said he'd be my manager, 'cause he was always lookin' for fresh talent."

I couldn't resist asking, "What was it like the first time you went on stage?"

"Gahd in heaven, I was scared ta death, 'cause I was afraid I'd fall down in them spike heels we gotta wear to lift our butt, but hey, I din't. And I was so blinded from that spot light, I couldn't see the customers, but I could feel 'em."

"What do you mean? You could feel they were out there?"

"Oh yeah, I knew they were out there 'cause I could hear 'em breathin', but I could feel 'em cause they run their rough old hands over my ankles."

"*They did?*" Jan exclaimed.

"Uh huh, but, thanks Gahd, that's as far as they could reach across the bar."

"Can I ask you one more question? What was it like to pull off your bra the first time?"

"*Bob!*"

"I was so spooked I closed my eyes, an' jis yanked it off. When all them customers clapped and carried on, I felt good, like I did somethun right at last, so I wasn't scared no more. Now I've been doing it fer 'bout six months, and that's how long Louie's been my manager, 'cept now he sorta thinks he's my boyfriend. But, I rilly don't like him all that much 'cause he don't treat me respectful. I s'pose it's 'cause I'm so stupid. So I guess, he rilly has every right."

"You're *not* stupid," Jan interjected forcefully. "You just let people make you think you are. You've got to stop hiding behind the feeling you're stupid. Obviously, if you went to a community college, you must be pretty smart. You mustn't let any man tell you you're stupid when you're not. *You're not stupid.*"

Jan was surprising me. She was speaking up as if she were getting her strength from another source. In a convoluted way, I felt she was also speaking to me.

"You've got to stop living a masquerade and pretending you're stupid when you know you're not. Pretending consumes your energy, keeps you tense and apprehensive all the time. You must start being yourself and *believing* in yourself. You have intelligence, you know what's right; you've made it on your own. If you don't use that strength and intelligence, it'll dry up. Put your intelligence to work. *You* know you're smart. You've got to let this manager or boyfriend, whatever he is, know you're intelligent, and don't let him verbally abuse you. And, *do not* let him lay a hand on you. Don't play dumb for him. You've got to be yourself, be authentic. He's never going to respect you unless you stand up for yourself. That's probably why he beats you up, just wants to see how far he can go."

I couldn't believe Jan was so wound up. I lamented to think how I had underestimated her qualities. She had naively survived the crazies of New York City, and along with the likes of Arlene Francis, Lucy, Dinah, and, locally, Terry, Jan was, indeed a pioneer woman in television, and she didn't even know it! But now I knew it and would be changed.

"Oh, Miss Jan, you're so strong. I knew if I came over here, something wonderful would happen to me."

The kids came clattering downstairs, popping into the front parlor to say they had finished their homework. Upon seeing her, they ran over. "Miss Joy, Miss Joy. What are you doing here?"

Joy lit up. It pleased me to see the children treat her with kindness.

"I come here to see your mommy and daddy," she said, as she began to weep.

Looking up at her with his big blue eyes, Tom asked, "What are you cryin' for, Miss Joy?"

"Because you're all so wonderful."

"How come that makes you cry, then?"

"Don't know."

"Sometimes people cry when they're overcome with emotion."

"What's that mean, daddy?"

"That means Miss Joy is really happy to see all of us."

"Oh, I see, daddy, she's got happy tears."

Olympia walked into the parlor. "Miss Jan, you want I should take our chilrin upstairs? Ah think it's *way past* time for their baths." Olympia's eyes rolled around and her face squinched up in disapproval. She folded her arms across her chest and looked like a first sergeant waiting to reprimand the troops.

Timmy butted in. "Where's Miss Snowball? I haven't seen her for a long time."

"Oh, she moved up to St. Louis."

"Oh, heck."

"Why did you say 'oh heck'?" I asked.

"'Cause she had some big cotton snowballs she was gonna give me and she never did. If you see her, Miss Joy, you tell her I'm still waitin' for those snowballs!"

"Okay, Timmy, honey. I've got some balloons I'll give you tomorrow over the wall."

"Can I have some, too?" Tammy and Tom asked simultaneously.

"Sure, I've got some rilly big ones."

I choked at that remark.

"I'll give y'all some tomorrow. And they've got my name on 'em, too, rilly! They've got a great big 'Joy' printed on both sides. And just like I say on stage, Mistur Bahb, the bigger they are, the more joy they bring!"

Was she talking about balloons? I added, "Yah and the bigger the pop!"

Jan gulped. "Children, I think it's time to go upstairs. I'll be up shortly to tell you a story."

"Mizz Cahr, they gonna git baths first!" Olympia informed us.

"Yes, children, you go up and get your baths with Olympia, I'll be up shortly."

Before leaving, one by one, they came over to give Miss Joy a hug and a kiss on the cheek, then gaggled up the stairs behind Olympia, who looked over the railing with her eyes still rolling and her face still squinched.

"I can't rilly tell ya how much you've helped me git my spirit back. You rilly are nice people. I'm so glad I came over here. You've been more help than you'll ever know, *rilly*."

We each gave her a hug as we walked her to the door and bid her good night. The rattle of a horse-drawn carriage drew near, and, as a group of tourists passed by, we could hear the driver say, "Yes, and real families live in these old houses along Bourbon Street. They been here for hundreds o' years!"

Jan and I looked at each other and I mused, "Honey, I feel like we've been here a hundred years just today."

"Me too."

"Mommy, daddy, where are you? Come tuck us in," came a cry from the top of the stairs.

"Okay, okay. Mommy will be right up; I'll be up as soon as I take out the garbage."

The garbage cans of the French Quarter are like no others in the world. They're sunk down into the banquette or sidewalk. It cost us a hundred dollars to get two garbage cans sunk down in the cement. When the garbage men come along to empty the containers, they lift the cover, pull the garbage can up out of the ground, empty it, and then plop it back down into its hole again. They are aesthetically designed so tourists don't have to gaze on our garbage and trash along the street—great idea—until someone drives a car up onto the banquette and crunches the top of the cover down into the garbage can. We'd replaced two covers, so we finally had to do what many Quarterites did: install hitching posts in front of them so that cars couldn't drive up on the curb.

Putting out the garbage was also a social event of sorts. There was always someone stoop-sittin' or walking along wanting to pass the time of day, morning or midnight. The company was, and is, part of the joy of living in the Quarter.

By the time I got upstairs, Jan had just finished the bedtime story and said prayers with the kids; they kissed us good night with clenching hugs.

As we walked into our bedroom, I remarked to Jan that those dime-store storybooks were getting a little old and tiring for me. "We must ask Mother for her set of Robert Louis Stevenson's *Books of Stories and Rhymes*, the ones I heard when I was a kid. She's certainly not using them."

"Great idea."

"Next time my parents come down, they can stick the books in the trunk of their ever-present Cadillac, packed around dad's precious golf clubs."

Jan sighed heavily. "I'm really tired."

"Me too, honey. Let's shed some clothes and sit out on the balcony."

"Sounds relaxing, I'm gonna slip into my nighty."

On a balmy evening we found nothing more pleasant than sitting on our balcony listening to the myriad sounds passing below. Gazing at the ancient buildings and roofs of the neighborhood as caressing shadows dance across their facades and the damp evening breeze stimulates the senses with the fragrance of honeysuckle and a whiff of freshly ground coffee and chicory from the nearby roasting ovens, one feels an awareness of history, a part of all that has gone before,

There are two places that enthrall my spirit and beckon my soul home: one is the French Quarter and the other is Manhattan. As a contemplative youngster, I would at times wander far out to the vast side-lawn of my parents' home, gaze to the East and daydream. I fantasized: *Someday, I will live in a New York skyscraper and become famous.* Unbelievably, some of it came to pass—an eighteenth-floor Stuyvesant Town apartment, a Conover Modeling stint, and marriage to a beautiful, talented, and understanding wife who truly loved (and loves) me.

"Bob, what are you thinking?"

"Just daydreaming, honey."

"Oh, by the way, look at this memo I received earlier today from Bill McHugh. With so much going on in our lives I almost forgot to tell you."

"Just tell me what it says, I'm too tired to read it."

"Through his Kottwitz Agency connections in New York, Bill learned the *Today Show* is looking for a new girl-Friday to replace Maureen O'Sullivan. Bill sent one of our Woolco spots, plus an excerpt from my interview with Anthony Perkins and my résumé to the producer of the *Today Show*. I'm sure nothing will come of it but Bill thinks there might be a chance."

"My god! And you forgot to tell me?"

"Bob, I'm sure it could never happen. I'd be terrified. And, you know, I'd never go on TV without you anyway."

"I can't believe you didn't tell me. My God, New York!"

"Don't get your hopes up. Remember, 'I'm Just A Little Girl From Little Rock!', or in my case, from Colerain."

I kicked off my shoes, pulled off my socks, stripped down to my T-shirt and boxer shorts, and walked out onto the balcony. I settled into one of the two wicker easy chairs we had splurged on during the weekend flea market at the old U.S. Mint. Jan sat down facing me on the narrow balcony.

"Look how bright the stars are tonight, zero pollution."

"Yep, and look at the American Bank Building and the Hibernia Tower; see how bright they look in the night sky? Soon it could be the Chrysler Building and the Empire State!"

"Bob, don't get your hopes up. I'm sure there's not much chance."

"Ya never know. Don't underestimate yourself. Isn't that what you told Miss Joy?"

"I don't even want to think about it. Let's just relax."

"Honey, I was so proud of the way you spoke to Joy, I didn't realize you had such strong convictions. You spoke to her like a friend and a parent. I think it really helped. She certainly seems to have a good heart. It's hard to believe what strained but intriguing lives are going on right around the corner from us, isn't it?"

"I know, we're so lucky to have each other." With her bare feet she started playing tootsies with me. She rubbed her soft toes up and down my calves, arousing a tingling sensation.

"Honey, are you ready to play for keeps?"

"Maybe I am, and maybe I'm not," she teased, grinning back at me as she pulled her feet away.

I returned the gesture, stretching my leg until my toes reached under her nighty and caressed the insides of her thighs. She felt soft and warm, and she was sighing softly. The sound of happy voices passed below us, and a bright white moon popped out from behind one of the few clouds, bouncing trembling moonbeams off our balcony.

"You want it?"

"Want what?"

"This." My glance dropping to my gaping boxers.

"Bob, put that away, the moonlight will singe it!"

"Then let's go inside before it ignites!"

"*Bob!*"

She rose quietly. I got up cautiously, taking care not to expose myself in the moonlight to the pedestrians below. I closed the massive shutters, adjusting the louvers to obstruct the view from the street but allow the night air to enter. We met under the covers of our massive bed.

Extraordinary things happen when two people drown themselves in the joys and pleasures *and* responses of one another, perfecting the art of unselfish lovemaking and sustaining a rapturous spell until, with the final burst of joy, the two lovers behold a brief glimpse of heaven's treasures. We knew something miraculous had happened. A new life was being formed. It was as if the whole cosmos had focused, for one brief instant, on the loving actions that took place in the confines of our four-poster haven.

I lay numb for a few moments watching the ceiling fan dangling from the canopy. Adjusting the pillow, my entire body collapsed in exhaustion from my journey through the universe. The fan rotated rhythmically, spewing its gentle gust over our weary bodies. *I hope to God it doesn't fall down and grind us to a pulp,* I mused.

I nudged Jan with my elbow. "Honey, I just happened to think. We did pretty well, even without the Red Cross lady's book!"

Producer, Al Shea; floor director, Reggie Hendry; Jan; director, John Domec and Bob toasting the last day on the Second Cup set, 1963

MIDDAY
THE LOCAL LIVE WOMEN'S SHOW . . . WITH THE RATINGS!

Bob and Jan during a telecast of their public service program "Phun With Fonetiks," 1965

TREME • TCHOUPITOULAS • CABILDO • GODCHAUX'S • GUMBO • VOODOO • ZYDECO • LAFITTE • KREEGER'S • OYSTERS

CHAPTER FIFTEEN

ALLIGATOR PEAR • STEAMBOAT • NEUTRAL GROUND • FLAMBEAUX • BROCATO'S • PO-BOY • PRALINE • FRENCH MARKET

Hurricane Betsy and Baby Tiffany Descend

Second Cup died and evaporated into electronic heaven. Our mourning morning fans began to write and call channel 6 protesting the change. The station's promotion department was trumpeted into full battle using all advertising and promotional tools at their disposal to let the channel 6 viewing public know that their "First Family of Television," Bob and Jan Carr, were not gone but just being moved to "a more convenient time," whatever that agency spin meant! It wasn't the first time Jan and I had been preempted and probably wouldn't be the last. But, it was the second time a show of ours had been preempted by a star we particularly admired. Dinah Shore had become one of our favorites when she started throwing kisses for Chevrolet in the early 60s. We loved *her* but hated the idea she would be a rousing success in *our* 9 o'clock slot. Dinah was apple pie. A little slow to react to outside influence, it might take the New Orleans audience time to be totally captivated by her, but we knew she would succeed.

Years before, when we were doing a program on WTRF channel 7 in Wheeling, our program was preempted by Kate Smith, another great lady of both radio and television. Our long-time admiration for Miss Smith was forever altered when we attended a broadcast of her show in New York. She treated her stage crew so wretchedly that we had little stomach to meet her. When an NBC public relations peon introduced us, she extended her chubby hand limply, greeted us curtly and made a hasty exit to Ted Collins, her announcer and "front" man, leaving Jan and me and a host of other NBC affiliate "stars" with the impression that we were little better than chopped liver!

There is a plethora of "failure-rationalization" aphorisms in the New Orleans vocabulary. Sometimes God is blamed for the lack of success: "It was Gawd's will!" Sometimes it's man's fault: "He just didn't have enough filé in his gumbo!" And sometimes it's more philosophical: "One doh shuts, an' another doh opens up!"

That last adage was used by many of our friends and associates to console us over the loss of *Second Cup*. We appreciated their consolation, but after all, one could close a door in a nice warm and cozy house, and walk out into a raging blizzard! On the other hand, as in New Orleans, one could be on the street on a hot sunny day, open the door and walk into a nice, air-cooled room. As it turned out, we walked through a door from one pleasant TV studio to another.

Terry Flettrich, the granddame of channel 6 and of New Orleans television, welcomed us into the newly expanded *Midday* with open arms, an attitude that led to an even deeper friendship over the years. Mo Trahan, a station account executive, and Bill McHugh, the prominent advertising executive, recognized our talents and sold them to a variety of accounts on both radio and TV. What we had feared might be a descending star became the beginning of a prosperous and more active career for both of us.

Our new schedule was extremely strenuous because it included daily shows on WDSU-AM radio, various radio and TV prerecorded commercials, the *Midday* program, *plus* the prerecorded *Phun With Fonetics* show with Marty Lindley and our children. And oh, yes, there was the *Bob & Jan Radio Show* live from the Al Hirt Club on Bourbon Street! Al had totally remodeled the interior of his club at Bourbon and St. Louis, directly across from the 500 Club, where Kitty West starred as the "Oyster Girl."

Al's club now featured a revolving stage large enough to accommodate his entire band for two shows nightly, but weekdays it was transformed into a luncheon Mecca for gloved and be-hatted local ladies. From 1:00 to 1:30 P.M. Jan narrated an upscale fashion show with professional models accompanied by rising star Ronnie Kole at the grand piano. Promptly at 1:30 we hit the air live with the *Bob & Jan Radio Show*, featuring interviews with guest headliners such as Lionel Hampton, Roberta Sherwood, and many others. Plus, there were competitive games with the audience, who competed fiercely for loaves of Bunny Bread as if they were the $64 prizes. It was great fun but exhausting. Al Hirt, who was wrestling with his demons of incredible fame, financial complications and marriage difficulties, only occasionally dropped by. He loved Jan and always met her with a hearty hug and "How ya, darlin'? You guys are a class act!"

Our new tightly-packed routine amazingly afforded us more time with the children. We loved being a team at home akin to what we were on the air, especially since Jan was expecting, *again*—was it the water or the Catholic culture? Nay, the Red Cross lady, methinks!

Jan and I arrived at the station about 10:30 A.M. As we walked into our new office off the catwalk above the studio, Al Shea noticed us from the studio floor below and hollered up, "Hey, just a minute. I've got to come up and see you, so don't go away."

We continued to the *Midday* office suite. Ellen Hardemann, the ever-vigilant assistant producer to the show, advised Jan that Rivet would put her wig on as soon as he finished fiddling with Terry; finally, a lady from Prompt Succor was waiting in our office. I talked to the church-lady, telling her we'd be happy to make a guest appearance and M.C. their event. I explained we were not Roman Catholic, but we would do it *pro bono*. She seemed a little distressed about the wrong religion, but the price was right. As it turned out, the Succor nuns treated us with about the same gratitude as the talent fee we charged!

Al bounced into the office. "Bob, Bob! We've got a special deal for you today."

"What kinda special deal?"

"You're going to be hypnotized, right on the program! Is that great or what?"

"Hypnotized! Why me?"

"Because nobody else will do it."

"Thanks a lot."

"Only kidding! The hypnotist really wants *you!* He's watched you on television, and he says you're the perfect type."

"What's the perfect type, someone who's weak-minded?"

"No. Somebody who's open and susceptible to the hypnotist."

"How do you think up all these things, Al, and why me?"

"Because I've got such a creative mind, and this is show biz, *or,* because you're so willing and so handsome," he cajoled. "This will be even more fun than that boa constrictor I got you to wrap around your neck last week! You're really putting *Midday* on the charts. Now excuse me, I've got to run over and see Jan while she's getting her wig combed to give her a little background information about Barbara Stanwyck traveling the circuit promoting her *Big Valley* series."

"Al, do you ever take a breath?"

"Only at night in bed; then I breathe hard! Wanna know more?"

My phone rang; it was Mo Trahan reminding me we had some new Bunny Bread commercials in our Al Hirt Club radio show that afternoon. He also told me that he had talked to Bill McHugh at the advertising agency. McHugh reminded us that the New York clients would be in town from Woolco listening to our *Woolco Vignettes.*

Ellen returned holding an armful of clothes. "Bob, can you help me with these darn things? They're all falling down. I need to hang them up on the rack over there."

"Sure, honeybunch, what are these?"

"Jan's new clothes for the month. They're all from Maternity and Baby Lane."

"Oh, that's right, I forgot that starts today, doesn't it?"

Ellen nodded and dashed out to answer her phone. Irwin Poché, the director, came by a little early to go over the format. Jan and Terry came out from under Rivet's hot hair-teasing tool. We all gathered briefly in the reception area to run down the agenda for the program. Ken Mueller, the technical director, reminded us it was a tight show: stay on time, take our cues and *get off!*

Al, always interested in the visual portion of the show, reminded us to smile, look happy, be cheerful, and keep moving. "Okay, y'all get dressed, see you down on the set in a few minutes."

Jan and I went back into our office and closed the door. I helped her carefully slip the maternity dress over her head without mussing her wig. I pulled off my khaki trousers and slipped into the trendy double-knit suit provided by D. H. Holmes.

"Do I look like a house in this dress?"

"Honey, you look terrific, it's great seeing you in maternity wear again."

"Lord, I feel like I'll be in a maternity dress forever. If Mo Trahan hadn't been so quick to sell Maternity and Baby Lane, I wouldn't be in these clothes for another couple of months."

"We've got to take the sponsors when we can get them."

"I just hope the viewers won't get tired of seeing me in baggy clothes, *but* just think, this is our fourth baby and it'll have a program all its own."

"What's that?" I asked, not paying complete attention as I zipped up my trousers and straightened my tie in the mirror.

"Honeey, Tim was born on *Calling All Carrs* in Wheeling, Tammy was born on our *Current* program in Huntington, and Tom on *Second Cup*—practically on the air—and now, this baby is going to be born on *Midday*. So every time we get a new program, we get a new baby; or maybe every time we have a new baby, we'll have a new program."

"Jan, what *are* you babbling about?"

"Don't know, just rambling on. We better get down to the set."

Ellen rapped on the door. "Ten minutes 'till air time!"

We walked on the set just as Barbara Stanwyck arrived with a P.R. person. We introduced ourselves and Jan mentioned she would be interviewing her.

Miss Stanwyck reached out graciously to shake hands with both of us. "My dear, what beautiful red hair you have. And how wonderful to be in your fabulous New Orleans."

Jan, sometimes apprehensive in the presence of movie stars, was immediately put at ease.

Al introduced himself as the producer of the show. He showed Miss Stanwyck where to sit until airtime, also pointing to the portion of the set where she and Jan would be holding their interview. Grabbing me by the arm, he said, "Come over here, you have to meet Mr. Delesseps, the hypnotist."

"Oh, my Gawd!"

"Bob, don't worry, he's a very nice man."

Indeed he was. He explained to me that there's no magic associated with hypnotism. It's a matter of deep, complete, and well-directed concentration. He showed me a small crystal hanging from a chain, which he would use in directing my concentration to induce me into a hypnotic trance. While under his spell, I would be assigned a post-hypnotic activity. I would respond only on *his* cue. He assured me that in no way would I do anything immoral or obscene.

"Five minutes 'till air time," came the announcement over the loudspeaker from Ken Mueller.

"Thanks, Mr. Delesseps; I'll be back in just a moment."

I dashed out of the studio to go to the rest room, which was always my final accommodation before airtime. The closest facility was just inside a reception room where the twenty-five or so daily lady guests were retained before being ushered onto the set to view the *Midday* program live. They perched on folding chairs, all facing toward me as I approached. The ladies were watching *Days Of Our Lives* on the television monitor, which happened to be adjacent to the door leading to the lavatory. As I entered the reception room, I could hear several of them say, "Oh look! There he is. There's Bob."

I smiled, waved quickly, and using my derriere to push the door, backed into the tiny rest room, containing only a sink and an exposed toilet. The door opened in, so I pushed it shut and bolted it. Not having to use the john, I stood at the sink to wash and dry my hands quickly, then began combing my hair. Suddenly, I felt I was *not* alone. Looking deeper into the mirror, I could see a lady's hat reflected over my shoulder and heard the sound of tinkling water. In a flash, I realized there was a woman sitting on the commode right behind me. She had forgotten to lock the door. Without looking back, I yanked on the doorknob, which came off in my hand. Still not glancing behind me, I carefully stooped down and reassembled the doorknob onto the shaft, unbolted the door, and eased it open. Slipping into the hall, this time I felt as though there were twenty-five pairs of eyes staring at me, knowing that I, and *that* lady from their group, had been in the powder room together! A feeling of panic overtook me as I dashed back into the studio, almost knocking over Mayor Schiro, an on-air guest. I crossed over to the back of the set and sat down, trying to regain my composure. In just moments, those twenty-five ladies would be brought into the studio, where the yellow daisies tied with green ribbon and planted on a white straw hat would reveal the secret of my cohabitator in the john!

The musical tic-toc-clock theme for *Midday* filled the entire studio, indicating the show was beginning. Gay Batson's *basso profundo* voice pedantically announced the agenda for the day. Camera one panned the entire set, while the other focused on Terry. Cued by the tally lights, Terry made her usual brisk walk directly toward the camera, ending at a podium from which she confidently read her opening remarks. When finished, she spun around toward Alec Gifford, announcing he would report the noon news. At this point, all the cast and crewmembers hastened to their appointed positions on the set. The next hour would be fast-paced; it was essential we all be ready when signaled.

Several commercials followed the newscast. Jan and I were poised and ready with our homespun segment. On cue, we discussed ways "mama" should advise siblings when a new baby would be joining the family. Terry followed with her photo essay of the day, "Life in the Desire Housing Project."

More commercials ensued, as off-camera, Barbara Stanwyck was ushered into a chair next to Jan. Movie icon Stanwyck, for all her big-screen savvy and all the stars she'd known, was strangely intrigued by Jan's "unusually mellifluous voice." She was so overtly attracted to Jan that she nearly neglected to promote her forthcoming TV series placed in the Old West and tentatively titled *Big Valley*. However, her P.R. lackey signaled the two of them from the wings, so all was not for naught.

Odd woman, I thought.

Across the studio, Mr. Delesseps and I were ready; I was stretched out on a sofa when the camera opened on us. I queried Mr. Delesseps about the fundamentals of hypnosis. He explained, and further reassured me, I would do nothing in conflict with my moral code. He dangled the crystal pendant in front of me as I lay on the sofa. All the while he encouraged me to go into a state of compete concentration. He found me to be a willing instrument; the experience of being hypnotized was very calming. I was surprised that I could focus my attention so directly on Mr. Delesseps while at the same time be aware of activities taking place in the periphery of my sight and hearing. He asked me to do a couple of silly things like take off my shoes and put them on the opposite feet and sing *Ave Maria* in soprano. These acts brought giggles from the crew, cast, and the visiting Club ladies; however, Mr. Delesseps did not want to leave the audience with the impression that hypnosis is a deception or voodoo. He then regressed me to the age of ten.

"What's your name?" he asked.

"Bobby."

"How old are you?"

"Ten."

"You seem upset, Bobby. Why?"

"I'm mad at my sister!"

"Why are you mad at your sister?"

Tears tumbled down my cheeks.

"Bobby, why are you crying?"

"Because she tells all the kids I still wet the bed, and I'm just a big baby!"

"What makes her do that?"

"Because my mother hangs my sheets on the clothesline to dry every morning before washing them later; they're wet with big yellow spots." I sniffled and wiped my tears away. "The kids all pass our house on the way to school and my sister tells them those are not *her* sheets on the line. 'They're Bobby's, he wets the bed, you know!'"

Terry and Jan were so touched that they tried to console me. Mr. Delesseps asked them to stand back while he brought me out of my trance. However, before bringing me completely out, he whispered a post-hypnotic suggestion that would be triggered later during the program.

Emerging from my trance, I was shocked to find my cheeks wet. I wiped them dry as the studio throng looked on in amazement and Mr. Delesseps offered some closing remarks. Somehow, I had the presence of mind to cue the next commercial.

Out of the commercials, Terry became embroiled in an interview with the mayor about the sit-ins that were taking place at Woolworth's and Katz & Bestoff's lunch counters on Canal Street. The Federal law required lunch counters, schools, etc., to be integrated, but there was great pressure on the mayor to keep the status quo: two lunch counters, one for whites and one for blacks. Terry was outraged that the mayor was not taking a stronger stand by implementing the law. She became especially distraught when the mayor explained New Orleans traditionally had two major shopping areas, Canal Street for whites and Dryades Street for blacks, and it would take time for citizens to get used to the changes. Making little progress, Terry ended the interview, but not before emphasizing to Mr. Schiro he was the mayor of *all* the people, and it was time for all of us to learn to live together and *shop* together! The mayor was livid.

Before the mayor could get out of his chair, and before the director cut to a commercial, Mr. Delesseps spoke the command words, triggering my post-hypnotic suggestion. Compelled, and without hesitation, I sprang to my feet, crossed the studio, and planted a kiss on the mayor's forehead. All were astonished, including the Mayor, but none more so than me. This is something I would *not* normally have done, particularly after such a serious interview as Terry and Schiro had just had. It more or less defused a tense situation, and for that we were all thankful. Mr. Delesseps used the opportunity to explain the power of post-hypnotic suggestion in practical ways, such as dieting or pain control.

Jan was still flustered when she got up to do her modeling commentary for Maternity and Baby Lane. Two recorded spots followed. Now it was my time to interview the visiting Club ladies. Wayne Mack, who usually did this stint, was away on a sports assignment. I questioned the ladies one by one about their philanthropic fund-raising activities. Suddenly, I spied the white hat with the yellow daisies tied with a green ribbon; I faltered and choked up. The lady sat primly with her white-gloved hands folded on the luncheon table. She responded with her name, but we never made eye contact. The woman sitting next to her extolled Miss Yellow Daisy Hat as their number-one fundraiser. She had contributed more to their pot than anyone else. I maintained my decorum with great difficulty as the closing theme played and we all waved good-bye.

I fled toward our office, passing through the studio kitchen. Our friend Betty Guillaud, a.k.a. "Nancy Nation," the voice of the national food chain known as "the meat people" was preparing for a commercial shoot. She was beating a large round steak with a tenderizer mallet.

"Bob, dahlin', I *loved* your hypnosis segment. I'll bet Dr. Delesseps could cure all kinds of wonderful problems I have. Maybe he can help me cope with my unrealized fantasies! Whatcha think, dahlin'?"

"Maybe so, darling, but until then, just keep sprinklin' tenderizer on that piece of meat you're about to flash!"

"Bob, dahlin', you're a tease! And, ah may add, a lech and—"

Before she could finish her retort I was out of there and in our office, my feet propped up, my eyes on our window. I was still chuckling about Betty, who was destined for bigger things. She was about to join the *Times-Picayune* and, as "the mouth of the South," would become the newspaper's most popular and prolific gossip correspondent with her daily *Lagniappe* column with the familiar tag "But you knew that!" According to legend, she coined the expression "New Orleans—The Big Easy!"

Exhausted, I stared at a stack of new mail that had been placed on our desk. An envelope from NBC caught my eye.

Recalling when Jan and I had been despondent about losing *Second Cup*, Bill McHugh had written the *Today Show* on Jan's behalf. We knew it was a long shot. I sliced open the envelope; a rush of adrenaline hit me as I scanned the opening text.

"With great interest we viewed your video and biographical background. We anticipate some major changes in our on-air staff in the coming months, especially with regards to Maureen O'Sullivan, who has notified us she wishes to pursue other ventures. At this time we have no programming plans that would call for a couple, but we are looking for a *Today* Girl who would appeal to our Mid-America audience. Therefore, we would be interested in flying Jan Carr to New York for an on-camera audition as soon as possible. If interested, we will forward various scripts to be used in your on-camera work. We were impressed by your informal ease on-camera, an extreme plus, although most of our work is done with cue-cards because timing is crucial on the *Today Show*."

There was a bit more to the letter, like "Please inform us by return mail of your interest," but I was so excited that I had to find Jan.

She, too, was excited by the letter but immediately said, "No! Not if it doesn't include you!"

"But, honey—"

"We'll talk about it tonight. I've got to get the kids from school. Remember, Olympia went to a special function at her church today."

Lying in bed with the children safely asleep, we decided Jan would at least go to New York for the audition. I guiltily felt I was pushing her beyond her desire, the same way I had in 1952, when she was reluctant to go through with an audition for the Radio City Rockettes. She never wanted to be a Rockette because the grueling schedule kept her away from me. Now this *Today* deal might mean the same thing, even though I insisted it would not.

"But, honey, I'm nothing without you. We're a team. I don't want to work alone but I'll go through the audition to please you. Anyway, I probably won't get selected. I'm sure there are lots of women out there much more talented than I."

Two weeks later, Jan flew to New York. We didn't want the station management to know our intent, in case it might hinder our careers on *Midday*. So far as anyone knew, Jan was going to Ohio to visit her grandmother.

Jan made a very favorable impression on the NBC brass. They told her that she was in the final running to be the *Today* Girl. They also told her about the delicious salary and the rigorous schedule she would be facing. A limousine would drive her to the RCA Building by 4:45 A.M. for make-up and rehearsal. For her convenience and the sake of her family, she would probably want to live in Manhattan or Queens, always *my* dream!

She arrived home exhausted, but I was thrilled and exploding with questions. From her evasive demeanor, I could tell she had already made up her mind.

"New York was great when we were young and just starting out. It was fun then, but now we have children, a new baby on the way, a house, and a life, *and* a career together. I don't want to leave what we have here, *together*. I was nervous and frightened up there but I was really good. They all said so, even though I was scared to death without you. I don't want a career without you. I would be miserable and eventually you would be too. I told them, *no!* So I never had to tell them I'm pregnant."

"But, honey, I thought it was something we'd always wanted, a career in New York."

"Honeykins, it's something *you* always wanted. I love our life here in New Orleans. We have so many blessings. New York was exhilarating for a couple of days, but the pressures are, and would be, enormous on all of us—me, you, and the children—*and*, what about Olympia?"

She could see from my expression that I was devastated.

"I know you're disappointed. I'm really sorry. I love you, Bob Carr!"

"I know." I rolled over away from her so that she couldn't see I was quietly gasping for breath. The nerve endings in my entire body seemed to be short-circuiting. One of my fondest dreams was crushed; I couldn't move or speak. Jan knew I was in pain, but, painfully, I knew she was right.

Jan snuggled up against my back. She reached over and held me firmly in her hand—it didn't help. We lay motionless for some time until we fell asleep.

*   *   *   *   *

As long as there has been a city of New Orleans, there has been a danger of hurricanes. This fabulous city, established in an improbable place by a group of naive Frenchmen, has prospered through storm, famine, heat, and pestilence. Tenacity and *joie de vivre* still run through the veins of the inhabitants. There's a thrill and excitement, an adrenaline rush that begins to attack New Orleanians when there's a hurricane on the horizon. The threat of impending disaster produces an inordinate amount of camaraderie not normally present between residents. People begin gathering at the supermarket to buy canned goods, candles, flashlights, and batteries; cars queue at filling stations to gas up; discussion revolves around our common peril. The frenzy of activity is exhilarating. The *threat* of a hurricane is exciting; the *reality* of a hurricane is frightening and can be disastrous.

During our nearly six years in New Orleans, Jan and I had lived through numerous hurricane warnings, but none had made its way into the city. Then suddenly, September 9, 1965, Betsy loomed on the radar, its eye sinisterly moving toward the city. Betsy was the second storm of the season. She seemed to be heading straight up the mouth of the Mississippi River with 110 m.p.h. wind gusts. According to the natives, Betsy was the worst possible scenario. Due to the seriousness of the situation, all announcers were asked to stay at WDSU, ready to broadcast until the hurricane had dissipated, changed course, or, God forbid, struck the city.

Station personnel, sent out to buy hurricane food for the stay-over, arrived back from various restaurants with sundry sandwiches, cookies, and the ever-present sickeningly sweet *petit fours*, enough to feed an army for several weeks, it seemed to me.

I was flabbergasted at how rapidly "hurricane fever" grew. The excitement of banding together to ward off a common enemy became evident. The day was sunny, balmy, and devoid of any threat of an ominous force heading toward the city. Stories of the destruction by previous hurricanes began circulating. Some of the engineering personnel who had been in New Orleans most of their lives began calling wives and families advising them to come into the city and stay in hotels overnight for fear of flooding in Metairie, Gentilly, Chalmette, and along the lakefront. Mayor Schiro announced that he was readying a hurricane headquarters near the lakefront marina. If it did not change course, Betsy would arrive in New Orleans within the next six to eight hours.

Since our house was so close to the station, I had ample time to walk Jan home before reporting for duty. Striding along Royal Street, we felt the hubbub of increased activity. A heavy, moist breeze spilling out of a still-clear sky wafted across the ancient rooftops. People's pace had quickened as they hustled up and down the street. Jan and I stopped at the A&P to pick up batteries. The furor within the store gave us the first real inkling that something critical was about to take place. Native Quarterites who had been through storms before were busily stripping the shelves of canned goods, bread, and batteries. When we spied a customer with a dozen candles, we were swept into the buying delirium, although we knew Olympia always kept our pantry well-stocked.

Olympia had picked up the children from school early. We felt an intense seriousness when Olympia asked if she could please leave to be with her own people when the storm came. Before departing, she insisted I go around the house and close all the blinds or shutters to protect the house and the windows against any flying objects. She made Jan, in her expectant state, promise to stay on the second floor, in Tammy's bedroom, which she felt was the safest because it had the least number of windows. She was adamant about them being on the second floor in case of a flood. In New Orleans, we live with the fear that if a hurricane comes straight up the Mississippi River, it will bring tidal waters, which will flow over the levees into the major parts of the city, already below sea level. Olympia left, catching an already overcrowded Desire bus toward the Lower 9th Ward. I finished battening down the house, kissed Jan and the kids good-bye, and dashed back to the station.

When I arrived, the staff and crew were in frenzy. Nash Roberts, WDSU's pride and joy and the pre-eminent weatherman of the region, was calmly doling out reams of information on the weather. On television, we were breaking into the network every 15 minutes. On radio, the breaks occurred after every commercial and the upbeat records I had selected. By the time I took charge of the radio control board, the storm was not more than three hours away and moving rapidly toward New Orleans, although it was still uncertain whether it would hit the Gulf Coast of Mississippi or come up the mouth of the Mississippi River.

I was trying to run a normal-sounding radio disk jockey show, but each time a newsman broke in with an update, he sounded frantic, especially Alec Gifford. Our station manager beseeched us to please sound urgent, businesslike, *but calm.*

In order to fill time with hurricane information, one of the newsmen came in and gave a five-minute talk about hurricane side effects. The main brunt of the story was that more babies are born during and right after hurricanes than at any other time. Apparently, it has to do with low pressure when the eye of the hurricane passes over.

Hearing *that*, during the next break I immediately called home to find out how Jan and her pregnant tummy were doing. She said so far, so good. The baby was jumping around more than usual, but the scary part was the wind's whir and the constant rattle of shutters frightening the children. The door from the kitchen into the patio had flung open, breaking the latch, but she managed to tie it shut with a jumping rope.

Hurricane Betsy slammed into New Orleans late in the evening. 110 m.p.h. winds and power failures were reported in the city. The eye of the storm passed to the southwest of New Orleans on a northwesterly track. The northern and western eyewalls covered southeast Louisiana and the New Orleans area from 8 P.M. until 4 A.M. the next morning. In Thibodaux, some 50 miles west, winds of 130 to 140 m.p.h were reported. By 1 A.M. the worst was over.

Levees failed along the Lower 9th Ward and on both sides of the Industrial Canal. The floodwater reached the eaves of some houses and over some one-story roofs in the Lower 9th. Some residents drowned in their attics trying to escape the rising waters.

The levee breaches flooded parts of Gentilly, the Upper 9th Ward, as well as Arabi and Chalmette in neighboring St. Bernard Parish. President Lyndon Johnson eventually visited the city, promising federal aid.

Hundreds of people, most of them black, scurried from their houses onto their roofs, terrified, not knowing how high the water might finally rise in the darkness. Communications with various parts of the city began to fail, and since there was no flooding in the French Quarter and the floor of the station was dry except for rainwater driven through the roof by the winds, we had little idea how much damage was taking place in other parts of the city.

Every hurricane has an eye, some of which measure many miles across. We kept informing the public to be aware that while the eye passes, there will be calm winds. Once the eye has passed, south winds from the hurricane will produce new gales, and people should stay inside for protection.

While the hurricane raged, I called Jan several times before the phone lines went dead. As Olympia had insisted, they were huddling in Tammy's room on the second floor, but the battering winds continued to shake the house ominously, terrifying the kids. Without electricity they were using the A&P candles, trying to read and tell stories. Tom had finally fallen asleep. Jan was beginning to feel more and more discomfort in her abdomen. I told her I would try to run home during the eye. Since I had been serving on the air for the past ten hours, there were plenty of people to back me up. She pleaded with me not to go outside. I assured her that during the eye of the hurricane, there would be a great calm and plenty of opportunity for me to get home. After all, it would take only about six or eight minutes to dash between the station and the house. It was about this time that our illustrious Mayor, Victor Schiro, announced in his most memorable simulcast, "Don't believe any false rumors, *unless they come from me!*"

When Nash Roberts announced that the eye was beginning to pass over the city, I rushed out onto Royal Street and began my dash toward home. Dawn had come; the sky was an ominous magenta; there was almost no wind. The street was deserted, but tiles, shingles, and shop signs were strewn everywhere. I made my way, staying as close as possible to the buildings, ducking under galleries and balconies. Intermittent spurts of driving rain showers and unexpected wind gusts gave me the unsettling feeling that I was running through a war zone. At the corner of Ursuline, I heard that awful noise, like a freight train. I snuggled back into the outer vestibule of a house. The roar was explosive; the wind whipped furiously in front of me, raising aloft the roof of a balcony across the street, then slamming it down onto the pavement. It was terrifying, especially considering the roof dropped where I would have been running, had I kept going.

Then dead silence—no wind. The eye was passing over. I used these precious moments to sprint the two more blocks to the house. Squeezing into the entryway, unlocking the door, and pushing it closed behind me, I darted breathlessly up the stairs to find my family huddled together. Jan was wide awake; the three kids were sound asleep. She began to cry uncontrollably as we embraced, relating the frightening night and how active the baby had been in her tummy. I assured her I would remain with them for the rest of the storm.

The eye passed; the wrath of the south side of the storm descended on the city. Again the house shook, the shutters banged, and the windows rattled. For the first time, I was terrified. Buried deep inside the studio, I had not experienced this fear.

When our transistor radio announced it was safe to go outside, shutters, doors, and windows began to open. People flooded into the street to survey the damage.

We were very fortunate. It seemed those old French Quarter buildings had survived so many years, through so many storms and hurricanes, that they were pretty well set in their ways. However, around the city there were hundreds of thousands of dollars in wind damage. The major disaster, though, was the tremendous flooding that took place in the lower parts of the city. People had been drowned, some had been sucked into the sewers as water rushed to be drained out of the city by the overworked pumping stations. Hundreds of drowned animals—dogs, cats and rodents—were floating in the water, their bodies bloated almost beyond recognition. The city was declared a disaster area.

The next morning, I struggled, wading through hip-deep water, down to Olympia's neighborhood. It had become hot and muggy with an overpowering stench in the air, the smell of sewage and dead animals. Olympia, her relatives and neighbors had spent the night sitting on top of their houses after hacking through their roofs from the attics. They were still terrified. She refused to leave her neighborhood until she was able to offer help. She made her way to her badly-damaged church to utter an offering of thanksgiving for having been spared. It brought tears to my eyes. It was an emotional experience to see how much damage had occurred and how grateful the people were that they still had their lives and could rebuild. As I stood surveying their neighborhood, my pent up emotions unraveled. I broke down and cried like a child. Incredibly, Olympia consoled *me!*

After hours of assisting Olympia and her relatives, I returned home, soaked and smelly. Jan said there must be something about the tradition that hurricanes cause babies to be born. She was beginning to feel uneasy. Though the phone lines were still out, I was able to wend my way Uptown by car, through broken trees and fallen signs, to Dr. Goldman's obstetrics office. As hard as Jan had been working the last few months, plus the trauma of the hurricane, he felt it would be advisable for her to go into the hospital for a rest and the possibility the baby would come early. Unlike the mad dash to the hospital when Tom was born, Jan had the luxury of peace and quiet awaiting this baby.

I had asked Dr. Goldman and the hospital staff to let me be in the delivery room with Jan while the baby was born; they all rejected that as a ridiculous idea. They informed me Touro Infirmary had a perfectly good waiting room; fathers would only get in the way and probably pass out at the sight of their newborn child emerging.

Finally, I heard the wonderful words: "It's a girl, it's a healthy girl!"

For years I had the fantasy I would have two boys and two girls. A big brother, a sister, another big brother, and a sister. My fantasy was fulfilled. Of course, she was the most beautiful baby we had ever seen: a wisp of silky dark brown hair, twinkling eyes, and a broad mouth that was capable of bellowing forth to the housetops. The nurses loved her, calling her their "little star."

One said, "She's going to be a singer, I can tell by that tremendous voice."

Another said, "No!" as she cuddled her close. "She's going to be an actress; I can tell by her changing moods, and the wide variety of expressions she has on her little face."

Tiffany Louise Carr, named after Jan's mother, came home to our house on Bourbon Street to join her siblings: Thomas Robert Tiffin, the artistic one; Tamson

Antoinette, the parsimonious "little mother," and Timothy Fitzsimmons, the builder/engineer. But Tiffany became the new apple of Olympia's eye, "My youngin'ist baby!" she'd articulate merrily.

* * * * *

Our lives were ideal, but sometimes when life is good and stable, and you know things are going well, there is a nagging fear it can't last. I prayed and thanked God for His blessings. We had a wonderful new baby, three other healthy kids, a prospering career with channel 6, great friends, and a unique place to live. As Olympia would say, "Thanks be to Gawd!"

It was 1965, a warm and aromatic November night, the kind New Orleanians treasure. Jan and I eased down into our wicker chairs on the front balcony. Evening dusk in the French Quarter can be magical. Pink twilight shadows turning into lavender began stroking the buildings across the Quarter like a great painter's brush; the antique streetlights flickered on and twinkled along Bourbon Street, leading away endlessly through the Quarter in diminishing perspective. I scooted closer to Jan, kicking off my loafers so that I could stroke her feet with mine.

"We done good, dahlin'," I said in New Orleansese. "We done made ourselves a good place to stay. We're home!"

"Whatcha thinkin' about?"

"About the $500 we had when we arrived in New Orleans; how $500 was all we had in the world. Now, six years later, we have a house that's a *home*, a growing family and more love for each other than we ever dreamed possible."

We sat quietly cherishing the moment. A blazing star shot across the sky, then staggered out of sight like a bit of falling ash in a fading fireworks display.

"Grandma always said a falling star was good luck."

"Your grandma was right."

For a few treasured minutes we sat quietly, save for the street sounds below.

Our reverie was shattered as Tammy called, "Mommy, daddy, where are you?"

"On our balcony, honey."

She stuck her head through the lace curtains. "Mommy, daddy, baby Tiffany's awake. She's lonesome. I looked at her; she's crying. I think she wants to come outside with y'all."

Jan went in to attend to our newest angel. I sat alone on the balcony, reflecting on the wonderful things that had happened to us since we had moved to New Orleans. We had grown and stretched in our outlook about the world. The friends we had made had helped us grow and blossom, while our wonderful jobs had given us the opportunity to share in other people's lives.

Closing my eyes to meditate and pray, I was grazed by a gentle breeze sweeping across the balcony. A divine feeling cradled my entire being, causing me to shiver: Was I being touched or nudged by God? At first, it was a vague and obscure feeling that grew more intense. I sensed a mystical union with something heavenly. It was as if Jesus were there, saying, "You've been given all these good things, now take care of them. It's up to you, my beloved and trusted child! Cherish them, mister!"

"Thy will be done," I murmured.

Tammy broke through the curtains, "Mommy, mommy, come out here. You and baby Tiffany come out and sit right here next to daddy."

Tom and Tim had heard the commotion and followed. Tammy eased up onto my lap.

"What y'all doing out here, anyway?" Timmy asked.

"We're enjoying the view, communing with nature and talking to God."

"Oh!"

"Can we sit out here, too?" the boys asked simultaneously.

"Sure, then we'll have the whole family together."

"'Cept for Lympy!"

"She's at her church tonight, singin' an' prayin' an' thankin' God," Timmy added.

"Yah, 'cause she loves God a lot," Tammy remarked.

Tim and Tom sat on the floor, slithering their legs under the bottom railing, allowing their feet to dangle over the edge. Tom kicked his feet wildly.

Timmy quickly reprimanded him. "Tom, don't knock your shoes off or they'll drop down in the street like they've done before."

"Timmy, don't boss me around, only daddy and mommy and Lympy can do that."

"I'm tellin' ya, if you drop your shoes, *you're* gonna have to go get 'em this time, not me, ya hear?"

"Hey, boys, calm down, let's just sit here quietly and enjoy the peaceful evening."

For the next three or four minutes, not a word was spoken, not even a car passed on Bourbon Street. Eventually, we could hear the hoofbeats of a horse-drawn carriage, its lanterns casting fanciful images on the pavement as it rattled to a stop below.

We overheard the driver say, "And real peoples live in dat house, dey on da television all da week long."

The tourists glanced up and spied us.

Tammy waved demurely while the boys kicked their feet enthusiastically. Not surprisingly, Tom dropped one of his shoes.

The gentleman passenger got out of the carriage. With the heave of a left fielder, he tossed the shoe back. Tim caught it and thanked him for the embarrassed Tom. To a chorus of "thank-you," the carriage trundled on its way.

"Okay, gang, its time for bed."

"But daddy!"

"No buts, *anybody!*"

Tammy swiggled down off my lap as the boys carefully pulled in their feet. Jan carried Tiffany into the girl's room; the kids said their prayers, we tucked them in and kissed them goodnight.

Closing the door to our bedroom, Jan walked over and encircled me with her arms. She looked up, "Bob Carr, I love you so much."

"And I love you so much, too, Fitzy Fitzsimmons!"—a love name I hadn't used since college.

She kissed me. "We're so lucky. We have each other and four healthy, wonderful children."

I kissed her. "And I'm the same age as Jack Benny."

"What do you mean? He's a lot older."

"I'm 39. He always says he's 39, the best age to be, 'cause everything still works!"

"That's for sure, 'Mr. Bawb,'" she parried with a sensuous giggle.

We kissed again.

"We still have our whole life ahead. I know the best is yet to come." I backed away from our embrace but held Jan's hands in mine. "You may think I'm crazy, honey, but when I was sitting out on the balcony by myself, while you were inside getting Tiffany, I felt touched by God. He reminded me to always take care of my family; I promised Him I would."

"Bob, God has played a important part in our lives. Why don't we get down on our knees and pray? We can thank Him for all the wonderful things we have."

"I don't know if I can do that, I feel rather self-conscious, especially when we're half undressed."

"You don't feel self-conscious when you're kneeling down in church. Come on, kneel down next to me, right here by our bed. I'll hold your hand."

A variety of thoughts trudged across my mind: *Though I'm the one purported to be the religious and sanctimonious head of our family, Jan is steadfastly leading us in prayer and thanksgiving.* I felt inadequate. Reaching over, grasping my hand, she began to thank God for our marriage, our children, Olympia, our families, friends, our work, our wonderful home, this incredible city—

"Honey, stop already, you sound like Tammy saying Grace. I surrender!"

Uncontrollable tears began to flood my cheeks; I capitulated. Reaching out I pulled her close, and there at the foot of our bed kneeling on the floor, we held one another in a long embrace. Miraculously, I experienced change.

"It's hard for me to say 'I love you,'" I said. "I guess it's hard for *men* to say 'I love you' unless we're wrapped in love-making! Then we'll say anything that keeps things goin'. But it's hard for me to just say it. I feel it's beyond words, it's beyond passion. When I say 'I love you and need you, and you're everything to me,' it's got to be coming from my heart and soul. Everyone thinks I'm gregarious, but it's hard for me to really articulate the romantic stuff."

We both began to sniffle, holding tightly to each other for many minutes. Slowly we rose to our feet still embracing. I began to tremble; passionate desire interceded. Jan felt the same gnawing. We backed away from each other, disrobed and slipped quietly under the covers of our "ancestral" four-poster bed.

"Before this goes any further," I whispered, "truly, I love you!"

"Me too! I mean, *I love you*, Bob Carr."

The sharp clip-clop of shod horses' hoofs echoing in the distance, shafts of sensuous moonlight slicing through the louvered shutters, and the balmy air, laden with the intoxicatingly sweet scent of night-blooming jasmine gently stirred by the punkah-like fan dangling from our canopy, combined to inspire the thought: *How little has changed in New Orleans since the days of great-grandmother and great-grandfather Aupagnier.*

A FINAL WRAP

The Carr children today: it can't always have been easy being a child of "Bob & Jan." There were many times when you had to stand around waiting and listening when a fan encountered your parents in public and ogled over them endlessly or lashed out over some TV news story we had nothing to do with. And there were those holidays when you were dragged along with mom and dad to "look cute" at some commercial event or fundraiser. Of course, there were some wonderful perks of which you were probably not even aware. But through it all there was always the love and devotion that sprang from a happy marriage filled with humor and discipline. Most of all there was the assurance that there was always someone at home who loved you—someone to confide in.

Timothy Fitzsimmons Carr, with a Ph.D. in computer science, married Christine Setser in 1986. They have one son, Shane, a senor at Whitfield School in St. Louis and live in St. Charles, Missouri. In 1988 the Carrs established their own company, Hypersoft, Inc., Avionics systems engineering specialists. With his New Orleans roots, he started the Krewe of Misfit Artists and serves as its Captain. He and Christine are actively involved in historic preservation and community action.

Tamson (Tammy) Antoinette Carr Richardson married Thomas Richardson of Rome, Georgia, in 1979 where they settled after her graduation from Emory University. Thomas, an attorney, is active along with Tammy in cultural and social activities. She has been a staunch supporter of the Junior Service League and the feeding of the homeless. They have two sons: William, a second-year student at Mercer University School of Law, and Taylor, a sophomore at the University of Georgia.

Thomas (Tom) Robert Tiffin Carr graduated from Princeton University. In 1993 he married Sabina Howell in New York City. They live in Atlanta, Georgia, with their twin girls, Margot and Camilla, who are in kindergarten at Trinity School in Buckhead. Tom, who travels often in his role as Senior Vice President of the Discovery Networks, followed his parents into the television industry. With Sabina, who serves as Director of Marketing and Communications for the Atlanta Botanical Gardens, he is active in cultural functions.

After three years at LSU, Tiffany Louise Carr Rieveschl graduated from the Neighborhood Playhouse in N.Y.C. and followed an acting career. In 1995 she married David Rieveschl, a lawyer. She continued further studies and graduated from Loyola University of the South. She is a tutor and children's yoga instructor. Daughter Carlisle is a seventh-grader at Country Day, and daughter Haley a fifth-grader at St. George's School. They reside in New Orleans and stay active in sports, theatrical, and cultural events.

Olympia, after years of serving as a guiding force, a helping and a spiritual leader to our family and to her beloved church, was called home to her heavenly Father. She is remembered lovingly and missed greatly.

You may be interested in what our adult children have to say about us today:

Timothy: "I would say that your long marriage has blossomed over the years because of your mutual devotion to one another."

Tammy: "You have never assigned specific 'his or her' roles or duties to your marriage but have let each other's talents unfold in a natural manner without conflict."

Tom: "You two focus on the spirituality of your marriage and compliment each other's strengths and weaknesses: i.e. Dad catches every flu. Mom never gets sick. Mom interprets things literally. Dad interprets things subjectively."

Tiffany: "Though no couple can ever have a life that is always blessed and without trouble, Mom and Dad have a remarkable ability to find what is good in any situation and make the most of it."

In addition, our grown children seem to be unanimous in some variation of the following remark: "Mom and Dad, you both love the crazy culture of New Orleans—it's in your blood—you love the French Quarter characters as friends and don't realize that you yourselves have become beloved French Quarter characters as well!"

The Carr family, 1965

The Carr family, 2010:
Tom, Tammy, Jan, Bob,
Tiffany and Timothy